Max Frisch

NOVELS, PLAYS, ESSAYS

The German Library: Volume 90
Volkmar Sander, General Editor

Max Frisch

NOVELS, PLAYS, ESSAYS

Edited by Rolf Kieser
Foreword by Peter Demetz

CONTINUUM · NEW YORK

1989
The Continuum Publishing Company
370 Lexington Avenue, New York, NY 10017

The German Library
is published in cooperation with Deutsches Haus,
New York University.
This volume has been supported by a grant from
Pro Helvetia.

Printed in the United States of America

Library of Congress Cataloging-in-Publication Data
Frisch, Max, 1911–
Novels, plays, essays.

(The German library ; v. 90)
I. Kieser, Rolf, 1936–   . II. Title.
III. Series.
PT2611.R814A25 1989   838'.91209   88-35195
ISBN 0-8264-0321-2
ISBN 0-8264-0322-0 (pbk.)

Acknowledgments will be found on page 351
which constitutes an extension of the copyright page.

Contents

Foreword

Most of Max Frisch's compatriots like to see themselves as a nation of upright peasants, craftmen, and burghers, intent upon sharing their concerns with order, law, and cleanliness. They want us to believe that theirs is a literature sober, didactic, morally uplifting, stark as a woodcut, and not particularily driven to analyse the psychological *chiaroscuro* of dubious people outside their communities. In Switzerland, the traditions of the historical chronicle, and of narratives offering useful religious and civic examples are certainly strong but, as younger critics have suggested recently, the stuff of disorder, irritation, frustration, and revolt has never been missing, not even in the minds of the great nineteenth-century Swiss writers respected as *Classics* (including thorny Gottfried Keller and melancholy Conrad Ferdinand Meyer) or in the lives and achievements of talented outsiders, mad loners (like Robert Walser, much admired by Kafka and Walter Benjamin), and gifted authors who prefered to roam through the Thai jungles rather than to conform at home. The younger among Max Frisch's contemporaries, especially if they write literary German, are not certain any more whether they want to belong to a *Swiss* literature; and though they certainly feel at home in their villages and in their local dialects they rightly suspect that too many demands would be made upon them by the Establishment who likes to see Swiss writers ossify in provincial sets of attitudes as predictable as the qualities of *Emmental* cheese or *Sprüngli* milk chocolate.

It is helpful to know something about Czech or Italian history if we want to understand the novels of Milan Kundera's Prague or

Giorgio Bassani's Ferrara fully, and it may be of equal importance to be aware of Max Frisch's origins, his native city of Zurich, and his ambivalent and often highly critical views of his fellow citizens. What is even more important, I believe, is to observe what he does with his heritage, how he handles the challenge of a narrow world, and how he transforms his opposition to provincialism into a distinct criticism of modern consciousness at large. Frisch's Württemberg and Austrian ancestors settling in Zurich (haven to Georg Büchner and Lenin, the Dadaists, and James Joyce) provide a cosmopolitan strain to his family myth, and he often recalls that his mother worked as governess in Old Russia before returning home. The rhythm of Frisch's life is one of lovingly dwelling and trying to escape somewhere else, of reaching out and returning home again, and the story of his life reads, for considerable stretches, as a report about recurrent and restless journeys to romantic and fictive islands as well as to the more grim realities of New York, Mexico City, Rome, Washington, Prague, and Berlin. As a writer, he has been always happiest where he was not.

Frisch has never been afraid to move, geographically or intellectually, and the paradoxical continuity of his writing is one of impatient breaks, creative dislocations, and new beginnings. He may seize on a genre or literary form but he easily discards it again in order to try something else; and while he remains attentive to a few substantial questions of social and private experience he does not feel bound at all to rehearse literary procedures, once they have served their purpose, again and again, and he would rather risk another astonishing failure than to repeat himself. His impatience with convention distinctly emerges from his many plays which, at least in the fifties and early sixties, obfuscated to many critics, especially in Europe, his rapid and marvelous development as a writer of prose. He may have taken his early theatrical cues from the late Strindberg, Thornton Wilder, and Brecht, and yet it would be far more difficult to determine the shape and interest of his plays in a few well-defined terms, as we are able to do when we speak about his contemporaries in the French or British theater.

Frisch began with lyrical poetry dramatized (even in his *Chinese Wall,* in which his pet figure of the contemporary intellectual makes first its appearance), and then alternated between "public" plays about the meaning of history (none, really) and explorations of the private self as it tries to reassert itself against the preconceptions of others. Later he wrote sparse parable plays about anti-Semitism and violence, and went on to a more radical effort to construct a theater of "variants," of what could have been but unfortunately did not happen, and a serene dramaturgy affirming the substance of life that is glorious and unchangeable. Ultimately, Frisch felt irritated by the material immobility of the theater and the predictable expectations of the public; he came to love the theater as an "erotic institution," and yet he ultimately discarded it, without much remorse.

As one of the great prose writers of our century, Max Frisch worked hard and long to emancipate himself from the masters of the past. He is not a novelist who discovered what he really wanted to do when he started writing immediately before and during World War Two. There was a good deal of Gottfried Keller, the *Zurich* classic of the 19th century, and of the *fin-de-siècle* Thomas Mann in his early stories about art, sensibility, and death among the aesthetically priviliged middle classes, and his brief encounter with Albin Zollinger, a shy Zurich novelist (largely unknown to American critics) may have done much to strengthen his courage to break away from the precious narrative and to face the more exhilarating necessity of inventing new ways of dealing with experience in our time. What he discovered, above all in the novels from *Stiller* to *Gantenbein* (one of the most important novels of our time), was the fatal danger of making images. People wanted to be independent and authentic selves, and yet they were incapable of realizing their own lives because they were unable to strike through the mirror systems built by others around them, disfiguring and falsifying everything. In these novels, the elaborate style gives way to a more irritated writing that is almost "spoken," and increasingly relies on individual stories, collages, changes of narrative perspectives, and unreliable narrators—never content with experimenting without a distinct commitment to human emotion. Even when Frisch seems most distant and sparse, as in some of his late prose pieces, he does not silence his urgent shout of compassion for vulnerable human beings.

Max Frisch admirably manages the astonishing feat of being a sceptic and a Romantic at the same time. The modern intellectual, sober and analytical in the habits of his mind, and the man of feelings, obsessed with the absolute, even in the most unstable of relationships, are recurrent figures in his plays and novels. At times they begin to melt into each other; at others they are simply one. In Frisch's world, Heidi of the Mountains is definitely absent, and we move in a contemporary, professional, and middle-class sphere of lawyers, publishers, editors (as the young American woman in *Montauk*), doctors, actresses, and professors who easily travel back and forth between Zurich and Manhattan, in an almost fashionable mobility reminiscent of some of the great American novels of the later nineteenth century. Frisch has been always proud of being a critic of false convention and petrifying society but, rather than arguing himself out of the living context of political experience into a self-willed ideological isolation (as did some of his younger German contemporaries of 1968) he never ceased to look critically at himself when he criticized, and he presents his case, often deeply disturbing, to his fellow citizens, ironically and fully conscious of the dangers of dogmatic ideas, including his liberal ones. Later readers may one day discover that Frisch, by his close attention to women and men enmeshed in the struggle for the authenticity of living, has become the father of a new generation of writers who (after being intoxicated by the social collective and the impersonal forces of history) have discovered human intimacy again, fragile, irresistible, and tremendously enduring.

PETER DEMETZ

Introduction

Max Frisch is the writer who has brought twentieth-century Swiss German literature into its own. Born in Zurich on May 15, 1911, he is, together with Friedrich Dürrenmatt, the most important Swiss contributor to contemporary German literature.

In introducing Max Frisch's work one is bound to talk about the heritage of the Enlightenment that America shares with Europe. This tradition is presently under fire, and threatenes to be replaced by the facile literary clichés of the worldwide corporate "global village." We need to understand that Frisch's writing is ultimately based on his hope that the Kantian belief in the emancipation of mankind from its self-inflicted dependence has not been entirely abandoned in our time.

Frisch is a maverick among contemporary authors writing in German. His stubborn defense of the right of the individual to fall out of step, and to resist attempts by self-proclaimed authorities to manipulate man's mind in the direction of irrational "explanations" or "solutions" for rational problems, has always made him suspicious of political parties and social clubs, but also of literary groups. Standing as he does independent, tall, and straight, he is one of the most impressive figures of contemporary German literature, and a classic as well.

This volume, consisting of excerpts of some of Frisch's most important novels, literary diaries, plays, speeches, and other prose texts, presents a survey and offers an introduction to a much larger literary oeuvre. Some of the texts have been made accessible in this country through the effort of his publisher, Helen Wolff. Others have been translated into English for the first time by Alice Carey, Lore Segal, and myself.

One thing about this collection is unique: Max Frisch himself selected the texts. Frisch's participation in preparing our volume displays his great interest in this country, where he lived and traveled for many years and where he received two honorary doctorates, an honorary fellowship of the Modern Language Association of America, a Commonwealth Award for Distinguished Service in Literature and, most recently, the Neustadt Prize of the University of Oklahoma. His selection of his own texts can also be considered a literary calling card for an American reading audience less familiar with his works than his European public. It is a self-introduction to Frisch's literary pursuit of ideas and concepts from the end of World War Two to the present. The reader will recognize the interrelation of topics and ongoing discussions that extend over several decades.

Sketchbook 1946–1949 represents in many respects the key to Frisch's art. The basic concept of the literary diary, as it appears in this work, is more than a literary exercise; it also reflects Frisch's political, intellectual and aesthetic credo, a restless and energetic striving to change the individual as well as society. The biblical commandment "Thou shalt not make any graven image" is translated by Frisch into the fundamental humane principle of decency and tolerance.

The traces of this ongoing exploration into the mind of the individual and into the consciousness of a fast-changing society can be found in three great novels of the fifties and sixties, *I'm Not Stiller* (1954), *Homo Faber* (1957), and *Gantenbein* (1964). The basic situation that unites the three books is the problem of identity, characterized by a self which, trying to analyze its own biography, comes to the immutable conclusion expressed in *I'm Not Stiller:* "You can put anything into words, except your own life."

The time during which these three very successful novels were published was also the period of Frisch's triumphs as a playwright, beginning with *Now They Are Singing Again* (1945), his first stage success, a requiem for war-torn Europe full of musical components that not only appear in the title, but also permeate the language and structure of the play.

Frisch's most accomplished drama is his bitter comedy version of the classic Don Juan legend, *Don Juan, or the Love of Geometry*

(1967). His variation of the legend changes Tirso de Molina's and Molière's seducer into a modern intellectual who falls victim to his own reputation as a romantic lover. *Andorra* is a sharply analytical drama of prejudice, the nucleus of which was already administered in one of the early *Sketchbook* texts. The anti-ideological political satire *The Fire Raisers* (1958), a play which Peter Demetz refers to as "the darling of American college theaters," is also Frisch's proof that a parable can be interpreted in any direction; in this respect it is his answer to Brecht's *Lehrtheater*.

Frisch spent much of the seventies and early eighties traveling widely and working in New York, Berlin, and Switzerland. The late sixties brought a change of mood and style to Frisch's writings. *Biography* (1967) is an example of a play in which an intellectual broods about the helplessness he feels toward a life that has been imposed on him by his own psychological disposition, world events, and private catastrophes.

Frisch's bittersweet satire *Wilhelm Tell: A School Text* (1970) is a sharp attack on an "establishment, complete with flag, masquerading as *Heimat*—and owning the military to boot" as Frisch defines official Switzerland (and for that reason any "establishment" in a world that confuses patriotism with flag waving). He deals with his growing alienation from his country in the address "Switzerland as *Heimat*" (1974), where he develops his own concept of *Heimat,* and in *Military Service Record* (1974), his corrective sequel, thirty years later, to a "naïve soldier's diary."

The ripple effects of the Vietnam War on American society, which Frisch observed in this country, and a series of marital disasters, changed the boyish and at times almost frivolous optimism of the early writer into the more skeptical mood of the older man coming to terms with his fear of death. This discussion starts in his *Sketchbook 1966–1971* and projects into the death images of his play *Triptych* (1981), which is a modern version of the Orpheus myth.

In the story *Montauk* (1975), which unravels before the backdrop of New York and Long Island, a narrator who calls himself Max Frisch probes into his past, comparing fragments of memory and experience with the ongoing journal of a brief encounter between a sixty-year-old man and a thirty-year-old woman. In *Man in the Holocene* (1979), a story that I would call Frisch's masterwork, the lonely individual, an aging man, confronts the timeless powers of nature, recognizing that his own decline parallels the ongoing self-extinction of *Homo sapiens,* a species that turns out to have been one of nature's unsuccessful whims. Unsuccessful, since all the accumulation of human knowledge has not changed the fact that "the human spirit we have trained is programmed for self-destruction," as Frisch puts it in one of the grueling questions of "Questionnaire 1987."

Yet this master of modern German letters does not give up his quest for the advancement of enlightenment (as in his statement "Foreignization 1" [1965], for example, which deals with international xenophobia as a counter-enlightenment mode). In his speeches and his "questionnaires" (in *Sketchbook 1966–1971* and in his most recent text, "Questionnaire 1987"), he associates himself with the tradition of European emigration, which he pits against the concepts of a narrow political and intellectual parochialism. His addresses and statements that cover the period of his most accomplished writing, associate him with his great literary models Georg Büchner and Bertolt Brecht (*Emigrants, 1958*), and clarify his road as a thinker from utopia to eschatology. "Perhaps there is not much time left for our species," says Frisch in a recent address, "not another worldwide millennium: without any breakthrough to ethical reason, which can only come about through resistance, there will be no next century, I'm afraid. Nowadays an appeal to hope is also an appeal to resistance."

Reading through this selection of Frisch's texts, we can acknowledge them as the writer's own appeal to resistance against anything that threatens human dignity and humiliates the human spirit. As Peter Demetz points out, "as a compassionate observer of the sensitive self and its painful consciousness of social pressures of both the intimate and the public kind, he has no equal among his fellow writers in German."

On this high level Max Frisch has taken his place in world literature.

R.K.

PART I

NOVELS AND OTHER NARRATIVES

From
SKETCHBOOK
1946–1949

*T**hou shalt not make unto thee any graven image*

It is remarkable that the persons we love most are those we can least describe. We simply love them. And that is exactly what love is, and what is so wonderful about it: that it keeps us in a state of suspense, prepared to follow a person in all his possible manifestations. We know that every person who is ʼ ʍed feels transformed, unfolded, and he unfolds everything, the most intimate as well as the most familiar, to the one who loves him as well as to himself. Much he seems to see as if for the first time, because love has freed it from its imagery. That is the exciting, the unpredictable, the truly gripping thing about love: that we never come to the end of the person we love: because we love them; and as long as we love them. Just think of poets when they are in love: they look for comparisons as if they were drunk, they seize on everything in the universe, on flowers and animals, on clouds, stars, and oceans. Why? Because the person one loves is as ungraspable as the universe, as God's infinite space, he is boundless, full of possibilities, full of secrets—
Only when one loves can one bear it.

Why do we travel?
This too because it brings us into contact with people who do not

claim to know us through and through; so that once again we can sense the possibilities life has to offer us—

They are few enough in any case.

Once we feel we know the other, love is at an end every time, but the cause of that, and the consequence of it, are perhaps not quite as we have always imagined. It is not because we know the other that we cease to love, but vice versa: because our love has come to an end, because its power is expended, that person is finished for us. He must be. We can do no more. We withdraw from him our willingness to participate in further manifestations. We refuse him the right that belongs to all living things to remain ungraspable, and then we are both surprised and disappointed that the relationship has ceased to exist.

"You are not," says he or she who has been disappointed, "what I took you for."

And what was that?

For a mystery—which after all is what a human being is—for an exciting puzzle of which one has become tired. And so one creates for oneself an image. That is the loveless act, the betrayal.

It has been argued that the miracle of prophecy can to some extent be explained by the fact that the future happening is presented by the prophet in words that create an image, and it is this image that finally causes, induces, makes possible, or at least facilitates the happening.

The nonsense of telling fortunes by cards.

Judgments based on handwriting.

The oracles of the ancient Greeks.

Regarded thus, do we really divest prophecy of its miraculous quality? There still remains that miracle of the word, which made history:

"In the beginning was the Word."

Cassandra, with her premonitions, her plausible, her disregarded warnings—was she always entirely innocent of the catastrophes she foretold?

Whose images she created?

Some fixed idea in the minds of our friends, our parents, our teachers—that too can prey on one like the oracle of old. Half a lifetime is spent with the unspoken question: will it happen or will it not? The question at least is branded on our foreheads, and one does not dispose of an oracle except by bringing it to fulfillment. The fulfillment does not, however, have to be direct; its influence can still be seen when one does the opposite, when one decides *not* to be what others think one is. One becomes the opposite, but becomes so because of others.

A teacher once told my mother that she would never learn to knit. My mother told us time and again of that declaration, which she had never forgotten and never pardoned. She became a dedicated and very accomplished knitter, and the many socks and caps, the gloves, the pullovers that eventually came my way I owe ultimately to that one exasperating oracle! . . .

To a certain degree we are really the person that others have seen in us, friends as well as foes. And it works both ways: we ourselves are the author of others; in some mysterious and inescapable way we are responsible for the face they show us, responsible not for the disposition itself, but for the development of that disposition. It is we ourselves who stand in the way of a friend whose settled habits cause us concern, for the reason that our opinion that he is settled in his habits is a further link in the chain that binds and is slowly strangling him. We would like him to change—oh yes, we wish the same of whole nations! But all the same we are by no means prepared to give up our preconceived ideas about them. We ourselves are the last to change those. We think of ourselves as mirrors, and only very seldom do we realize to what extent the other person is himself the reflection of our own set image, our creation, our victim—

The Andorran Jew

In Andorra there lived a young man who was believed to be a Jew. It will be necessary to describe his presumed background, his daily contacts with the Andorrans, who see the Jewishness in him: the fixed image that meets him everywhere. Their distrust, for instance, of his depth of feeling—something that, as even an Andorran knows, no Jew can possibly have. A Jew has to rely on the sharpness of his wits, which get all the sharper because of it. Or his attitude toward money, an important matter in Andorra as elsewhere: he knew, he could feel what they were all silently thinking; he examined himself to see whether it was true that he was always thinking of money, examined himself until he discovered that it was so, he really was always thinking of money. He admitted it; he stood by it; and the Andorrans exchanged meaning glances, not speaking, hardly even drawing in the corners of their lips. As regards national loyalties, he knew exactly what they were thinking: whenever he spoke of his "native land" they turned their eyes away, as from a coin lying in the dirt. For Andorrans knew that a Jew either adopted or paid for his native land—he was not born to it as they were. However good his intentions, it was like speaking into a mask of cotton wool when he talked of Andorran affairs. Eventually he realized that he was lacking in tact, indeed he was told so quite openly when once, upset by their attitude, he lost his temper with them. Once and for all, patriotism was their business, not his. He was not expected to love his native country; on the contrary, his obstinate efforts and overtures only served to increase their suspicions: he was trying to curry favor, seeking an advantage for his own purposes, they thought, even when they themselves could not see what those purposes could be. And so it went on, until one day he realized, with the acuteness of his restless, analytical mind, that he really did not love his native country, and least of all the epithet itself, which always caused embarrassment whenever he used it. Obviously they were right. Obviously he could never love anything, not as Andorrans understood the word: the heat of passion, which he certainly had, was modified by the coldness of his intellect, and this they saw as the secret, ever-ready weapon of his revengeful feelings; he lacked sensitivity, solidarity, he lacked—undeniably—the warmth of trust. His company was stimulating, certainly, but not agreeable, not reassuring. He could not become like all the others, and so, having tried in vain not to make himself conspicuous, he began to wear his otherness with a certain air of defiance, of pride, concealing a watchful hostility which he—since he himself did not find it congenial—tended to sweeten with a busy show of courtesy; even when he bowed, it was a kind of reproach—as though his environment were to blame for the fact that he was a Jew—

Most of the Andorrans did him no harm.

And so no good either.

However, there were some Andorrans of a more liberal and more progressive spirit, as they called it. They acknowledged humanitarian principles: they respected Jews, they pointed out, precisely because of their Jewish qualities, their acute minds and so on. They stood by him right up to his death, which was cruel, so cruel and revolting that even these Andorrans, who had not come to realize that the whole of life is cruel, were horrified. That is to say, they did not actually grieve for him or, to be quite frank, even miss him—they were simply angry with the people who had killed him and the way in which it was done—that in particular.

It was talked about for a long time afterward.

Until one day something came to light that the dead man himself could not have known: he had been a foundling, whose parents were later discovered, as much as Andorran as any of us—

The case is no longer talked about.

But the Andorrans, each time they looked in a mirror, were horrified to see that they themselves had the features of Judas, every one of them.

Thou shalt not, it is said, make unto thee any graven image of God. The same commandment should apply when God is taken to mean the living part of every human being, the part that cannot be grasped. It is a sin that, however much it is committed against us, we almost continually commit ourselves—

Except when we love.

On writing

What is important is what cannot be said, the white space between the words. The words themselves always express the incidentals, which is not what we really mean. What we are really concerned with can only, at best, be written about, and that means, quite literally, we write around it. We encompass it. We make statements which never contain the whole true experience: that cannot be described. All the statements can do is to encircle it, as tightly and closely as possible: the true, the inexpressible experience emerges at best as the tension between these statements.

What we are presumably striving to do is to state everything that is capable of expression; language is like a chisel, which pares away all that is not a mystery, and everything said implies a taking away. We should not be deterred by the fact that everything, once it is put into words, has an element of blankness in it. What one says is not life itself; yet we say it in the interests of life. Like the sculptor plying his chisel, language works by bringing the area of blankness in the things that can be said as close as possible to the central mystery, the living element. There is always the danger that in doing so one might destroy the mystery, just as there is the danger that one might leave off too soon, might leave it as an unshaped block, might not locate the mystery, grasp it, and free it from all the things that could still be said; in other words, that one might not get through to its final surface.

This surface at which all that it is possible to express becomes one with the mystery itself has no substance, it exists only in the mind and not in Nature, where there is also no dividing line between mountain and sky. Is it perhaps what one means by form?

A kind of sounding barrier—

Translated by Geoffrey Skelton

From
I'M NOT STILLER

I shall tell her the little story of Isidore. A true story. Isidore was a dispensing chemist, that's to say a conscientious fellow who made a pretty good living, the father of several children and a man in the prime of life, and there is no need to emphasize that Isidore was a faithful husband. Nevertheless, he couldn't stand his wife's perpetual inquiries as to where he had been. They made him furious—inwardly furious, he didn't show a sign on the outside. It wasn't worth quarrelling about, for at bottom, as I have said, theirs was a happy marriage. One fine summer, as was the fashion just then, they made a trip to Mallorca, and apart from her never-ending questions, which annoyed him on the quiet, everything went well. Isidore could be extremely affectionate when he was on holiday. They were both delighted with the beauty of Avignon, and walked along arm in arm. Isidore and his wife, whom we must imagine as a very amiable woman, had been married just nine years when they arrived in Marseille. The Mediterranean sparkled as it does on posters. To the silent annoyance of his wife, who was already on board the steamer for Mallorca, Isidore had to go back at the last moment to buy a paper. It may be that he did it partly out of pure spite because she asked him where he was going. God knows, he didn't mean to; it was simply that, as their steamer wasn't going yet, he went for a bit of a stroll. Out of pure spite, as I have said, he plunged into his French newspaper, and while his wife was actually sailing to picturesque Mallorca, Isidore, when the wail of a siren at last made him look up with a start from his paper, found himself not at the side of his wife, but on a rather dirty tramp steamer filled to overflowing with men in yellow uniforms and also under steam. The great hawsers had just been cast off. Isidore watched the quay recede into the distance. Whether it was the devilish heat or the uppercut from a French sergeant that shortly afterwards rendered him unconscious, I cannot say; on the other hand, I venture to assert with complete confidence that Isidore the chemist had a harder life in the Foreign Legion than before. Flight was out of the question. The yellow fort, where they made a man of Isidore, stood alone in the desert, whose sunsets he learnt to appreciate. No doubt he sometimes thought of his wife, when he was not simply too tired, and he would probably have written to her; but writing was not allowed. France was still fighting against the loss of her colonies, so that Isidore had soon seen more of the world than he would ever have allowed himself to dream. He forgot his chemist's shop, of course, as others forgot their criminal past. In time Isidore even lost his homesickness for the country that claimed in writing to be his home, and it was pure decency on Isidore's part when—many years later—he came through the garden gate one fine morning, bearded, lean as he now was, his sola topi under his arm, so that the neighbours—who had long ago assumed the chemist to be dead—should not be distressed by his somewhat unusual attire; naturally he also wore a belt with a revolver. It was a Sunday morning, his wife's birthday, as I've said, he loved her, even though he had not written her a postcard in all those years. He paused for an instant, looking at his unaltered home, his hand on the garden gate, which had not been oiled and creaked as it always used to. Five children, all bearing a certain resemblance to himself, but all seven years older, so that their appearance took him by surprise, were already shouting "Daddy" from a distance. There was no turning back.

So Isidore strode on with the determination of a man who had seen hard fighting, and in the hope that his dear wife, if at home, would not ask for an explanation. He strolled across the lawn as though he was coming back as usual from his shop, and not from Africa and Indo-China. His wife sat speechless under a new sunshade. Isidore had never seen the expensive dressing gown she was wearing before either. A maid—another innovation—immediately fetched a second cup for the bearded gentleman, whom without doubt, but also without disapproval, she took for the new "friend of the family". "It's cool here," said Isidore, pulling down his rolled-up shirtsleeves. The children were delighted at being allowed to play with the sola topi, which naturally led to some quarrelling, and when the fresh coffee arrived it was a perfect idyll, Sunday morning with bells ringing and birthday cake. What more could Isidore want? Without a thought for the new maid, who was just laying the cutlery, Isidore grabbed his wife. "Isidore," she cried and was unable to pour out the coffee, so that the bearded guest had to do it himself. "What is it?" he asked affectionately, filling her cup up at the same time. "Isidore," she cried, close to tears. He put his arms around her. "Isidore," she asked, "where have you been all this time?" The man, as though momentarily stunned, put down his cup; he was simply not used to being married, and stood in front of a rose tree with his hands in his pockets. "Why didn't you write me so much as a postcard?" she asked. Thereupon he took his topi away from the dumbfounded children without a word, set it with military precision on his own head, which is supposed to have left an indelible impression on the children for the rest of their lives—Daddy with a sola topi and revolver holster that were not only genuine, but showed visible signs of use—and when his wife said, "You know, Isidore, you really shouldn't have done it," it was all over with Isidore's cosy homecoming. He drew (once more, I expect, with military precision) his revolver from his belt and fired three shots into the still untouched cake decorated with sugar icing, which, as may readily be imagined, caused a pretty frightful mess. "Isidore," screamed his wife, for her dressing gown was spattered all over with whipped cream—if the innocent children had not been there as witness she would have thought the whole visit, which cannot have lasted more than ten minutes, a hallucination. Surrounded by her five children like a Niobe, she watched Isidore the irresponsible walk coolly out through the garden gate, the impossible topi on his head.

After this shock the poor woman could never look at birthday cake without thinking of Isidore, a pitiable state of affairs. Her friends advised her confidentially to get a divorce, but the brave woman still hoped. Her husband's guilt was obvious. But she still hoped he would relent, lived entirely for the five children she had by Isidore, and like a Penelope put off for another year the young lawyer who paid her a visit and urged her, not without reasons of his own, to divorce her husband. And sure enough a year later—again on her birthday—Isidore returned, sat down after the usual greeting, rolled down his sleeves and once more let the children play with his topi; but this time their delight at having a daddy lasted less than three minutes. "Isidore," said his wife, "where have you been this time?" He stood up, without shooting, thank goodness, and without taking his topi away from the innocent children, rolled up his sleeves again, and went out through the garden gate never to return. His poor wife wept as she signed the divorce petition, but it had to be, especially as Isidore did not put in an appearance within the legally specified period; his chemist's shop was sold; the second marriage proceeded without ostentation and after the legally specified period had elapsed was also sanctioned by the registry office; in short, everything followed an orderly pattern, as was so important for the growing children. There was never any answer to the question of where Daddy had got to. Not even a picture postcard. Mummy didn't want the children to ask where he was; she ought never to have asked Daddy herself. . . .

* * *

You can put anything into words, except your own life. It is this impossibility that condemns us to remain as our companions see and mirror us, those who claim to know me, those who call themselves my friends, and never allow me to change, and discredit every miracle (which I cannot put into words, the inexpressible, which I cannot prove)—simply so that they can say:

"I know you."

* * *

My counsel was beside himself, as was found to happen sooner or later; he did not lose his self-control, but self-control had made him white in the face. Without saying good morning, he looked into my sleepy eyes, silent, his brief-case on his knees, waiting till he felt I had sufficiently recovered my senses and was sufficiently curious to know the reason for his indignation.

"You're lying," he said.

Probably he expected me to blush; he still hasn't grasped the situation.

"How can I believe anything you say?" he complained. "Every

word you utter begins to seem dubious to me, extremely dubious, now that this album has come into my possession. Look," he said, "just look at these photographs for yourself."

Admittedly they were photographs, and I won't deny that there was a certain outward likeness between the missing Stiller and myself; nevertheless, I see myself very differently.

"Why do you lie?" he kept asking me. "How can I defend you, if you don't even tell me the whole and complete truth?"

He can't understand.

"Where did you get this album from?" I asked.

No reply.

"And you dare to tell me you have never lived in this country, that you couldn't even imagine living in our town!"

"Not without whisky," I said.

"Just look at this," he said.

Sometimes I try to help him.

"Herr Doktor," I said, "it all depends what you mean by living. A real life, a life that leaves a deposit in the shape of something alive, not merely a photograph album yellow with age—God knows, it need not be magnificent, it need not be historic and unforgettable— you know what I mean, Herr Doktor, a real life may be the life of a very simple mother, or the life of a great thinker, someone whose life leaves a deposit that is preserved in world history—but it doesn't have to be, I mean, it doesn't depend on our importance. It's difficult to say what makes a life a real life. I call it reality, but what does that mean? You could say it depends on a person being identical with himself. That's what I mean, Herr Doktor, a person has lived and his life has formed a deposit, however wretched it may be—it may be no more than a crime, it's bitter when all our life amounts to is a crime, a murder for example, that happens, and there's no need for vultures to circle overhead—you're quite right, Herr Doktor, those are just circumlocutions. You understand what I mean? I express myself very unclearly, when I don't just lie for all I'm worth for the sake of an outlet; deposit is only a word, I know, and perhaps we are talking all the time about things that elude us, things we can't grasp. God is a deposit! He is the sum of real life, or at least that's how it sometimes seems to me. Are words a deposit? Perhaps life, real life, is simply mute—and it doesn't leave photographs behind, Herr Doktor, it doesn't leave anything dead. . . ."

But dead things are enough for my counsel.

"Look," he said, "just look at this photograph of you feeding swans. It's definitely you and in the background, you can see for yourself, is the Great Minster of Zürich. Just look."

There was no denying it. In the background (not very clear) you could see a kind of small cathedral, a Great Minster, as my counsel called it.

"It really all depends," I said once more, "what we mean by living—"

"Look at this," said my counsel, continuing to turn the pages of the album. "Just look: Anatol in his first studio, Anatol on the Piz Palu, Anatol as a recruit with cropped hair, Anatol outside the Louvre, Anatol talking to a town councillor on the occasion of a prize-giving—"

"So what?" I asked.

We understand each other less and less. If it were not for the cigar he had brought, in spite of his annoyance, I shouldn't have spoken to my counsel at all any more, and it would have been better, I think. I tried in vain to explain to him that I didn't know the whole and complete truth myself, and on the other hand was not disposed to let swans or town councillors prove to me who I really was, and that I should tear up on the spot any further albums he brought into my cell. It was no use. My counsel would not get it out of his head that I must be Stiller, simply so that he could defend me, and he called it silly make-believe, when I contradicted him and swore I was no one but myself. Once more it ended in our bawling one another out.

"I'm not Stiller," I shouted.

"Who are you then?" he shouted. "Who are you?"

* * *

P.S. His cigar makes me feel ashamed of myself. Just now I bit off the crisp tip, and then drew the first few puffs that are always so especially dry and especially fragrant. In a minute I was so amazed by the aroma that I took the cigar from my lips and looked at it carefully. Dannemann! My favourite brand! Really and truly? So he's once more—

* * *

Went to Davos yesterday. It's just as Thomas Mann describes it. Moreover it rained all day long. Nevertheless I had to go for a very special walk, during which Julika made me look at squirrels while my counsel kept handing me fir-cones to smell. As though I had denied the aromatic smell of fir-cones. Later, in a very special restaurant, I had to eat snails, which are a famous delicacy but make you stink of garlic afterwards. All the time I could clearly observe Julika and my counsel exchanging glances, waiting for me to let slip some admission, or at least burst into tears. None the less I greatly appreciated eating off a white tablecloth again. Since conversation flagged, I told them about Mexico—the mountains round about, though very small, reminded me of Popocatepetl and the Cortez Pass, and I have always found the conquest of Mexico one of the most fascinating stories.

"May be," said my counsel, "but we're not here for you to tell us about Cortez and Montezuma."

They wanted to show me the sanatorium where Julika lay during her illness; but it had since been burnt down, about which my counsel was heart-broken. After the meal there was coffee, kirsch, and cigars *ad lib*. I wondered what they were spending all this money for. The little outing cost about two hundred Swiss francs; my counsel and I went in the State prison van (meals for the driver and the police constable were extra), Julika by train. In better weather it would have been a pleasant bit of countryside, no doubt about it. Once, down in the valley, we overtook the train, Julika waved.

* * *

My greatest fear: repetition.

* * *

Frau Julika Stiller-Tschudy discovered the old scar over my left ear and wanted to know how I got it. She kept on about it. I said to her:

"Somebody tried to shoot me."

"No," she said pressingly, "seriously—"

I told her a story.

* * *

P.S. Julika, now that I have seen her more often, is quite different from what I thought at our first meeting. Just what she is like, I should find it hard to say. She has moments of unexpected grace, especially when my counsel is not there, moments of defenceless innocence, a sudden blossoming of the childhood years that were never lived, a face as it must have been the first instant it was awakened by the breath of the Creator. Then it is as though she were surprised herself—a lady in a black tailor-made costume and a Paris hat, generally surrounded by a veil of smoke—surprised that no man has yet known her. I can't understand this vanished Stiller. She's a hidden maid waiting under the cover of mature womanhood, at moments so beautiful it takes your breath away. Didn't Stiller notice? There is nothing womanly this woman does not possess, at least potentially, smothered over perhaps, and her eyes alone (when she stops believing I'm Stiller for a moment) have a gleam of frank anticipation that makes you jealous of the man who will one day awaken her.

*   *   *

Repetition. And yet I know that everything depends on whether one succeeds in ceasing to wait for life outside repetition, and instead, of one's free will (in spite of compulsion), manages to turn repetition, inescapable repetition, into one's life by acknowledging: This is I . . . But again and again (here, too, there is repetition) it needs only a word, a gesture that frightens me, a landscape that reminds me, and everything within me is flight, flight without hope of getting anywhere, simply for fear of repetition—

*   *   *

Once again (for the last time!) I made an attempt today to help my over-solicitous counsel to escape from his positively touching misunderstanding of my situation, which has caused him so much work, so much fruitless work and so much annoyance with me, with me who am really so grateful to him for his daily cigar—

"Are you familiar," I asked him as I once more bit the dry knob from the cigar, "with the story of Rip van Winkle?"

Instead of an answer he gave me a light.

"An American fairy tale," I said with the cigar in my mouth and hence rather indistinctly. "I read it once as a lad, decades ago that's to say, in a book by Sven Hedin, I believe. Do you know it?"

As I spoke (this is important) I held his silver lighter with the little flame without lighting the fragrant cigar, that one and only sensual pleasure available to me in my imprisonment on remand, no, notwithstanding my avid desire I repeated my question:

"You don't know it?"

"What?"

"The story of Rip van Winkle?"

Only by means of this trick—that's to say by holding the lighter, which I relit every time it went out, and with the cigar in the other hand, all the time on the point of lighting the splendid cigar, indeed once setting the cigar aglow, so that all I had to do was to draw on it, but every time prevented—prevented by Rip vanWinkle, whose story was obviously more acutely important than my cigar—only by means of this trick could I compel my busy defence counsel to listen at all.

The story goes something like this.

Rip van Winkle, a descendant of that intrepid van Winkle who opened up the country of America while serving under Hendrik Hudson, was a born lazybones but at the same time, it seems a thoroughly good fellow, who didn't fish for the sake of the fish but in order to dream, for his head was full of so-called thoughts, which had little to do with his reality. His reality, a good little wife whom everyone in the village could only pity or admire, didn't have an easy time with him. Rip certainly felt he ought to have a trade, a masculine trade, and he liked to pretend he was a hunter, which had the advantage of allowing him to roam around for days on end where no one saw him. He generally came back without so much as a single pigeon, carrying nothing but a bad conscience. His little house was the most neglected in the whole village, to say nothing of his garden. Nowhere did the weeds flourish so merrily as in his garden, and it was always his goats that wandered off and fell into the ravines. He bore it without bitterness, for he was philosophically inclined, unlike his ancestors who all gazed down from the old pictures with every appearance of being men of action. For days at a time he would sit outside his dilapidated little house with his chin in his hand pondering why he wasn't really happy. He had a wife and two children, but he wasn't happy. He had expected more of himself; he was fifty and he still expected more, even if his good wife and his companions smiled about it. Only Bauz, his shaggy dog, understood him and wagged his tail when Rip took down his gun to go squirrel hunting. He had inherited the gun, a heavy thing with a great deal of ornament, from his forefathers. They must have smiled to themselves when Rip talked about his hunting; what he had seen always exceeded what he had shot. And since his stories couldn't be roasted, his wife, the mother of two children, had soon had enough of them; she called him a lazy good-for-nothing, in front of everyone, which he couldn't stand. So in order to unburden himself of his stories, Rip used to spend almost every evening in the village tavern, where there were always a few people to listen to him, even if his stories couldn't be roasted. His splendid gun and the tired dog at his feet were witnesses enough when Rip talked about his hunting. People liked him, because he never spoke ill of anyone; on the contrary it seems as though he was always a bit afraid of the world and badly needed to be liked. He drank a bit too, no doubt. And if no one listened, that didn't matter either; in any case, Rip and his dog, which put its tail between its legs as soon as it heard Mrs. van Winkle coming, didn't go home before midnight, because every evening there was a palaver of which Rip understood as little as his dog, a palaver while he took off his boots, and of course it was obvious things couldn't go on like this, but that had been obvious for years . . . One day Rip and his faithful dog went squirrel hunting again, striding out as long as the village could see them; then, as usual, Rip made his first stop, taking a bite from his provisions while Bauz kept watch in case anyone should come round the hill. In return, as usual, Bauz got a small bone, and Rip lit his pipe in order to give his good old dog, who was loudly gnawing at the bare bone, a bit of a rest too. Finally they trotted on into the morning, into the wide sweep of hilly country above the glittering Hudson, a glorious region as may still be seen today, and there was no lack of squirrels. God knows why Rip went on telling everyone he was a hunter! Sunk in thoughts that no one ever got to know, he strolled through the forest. There were hares here, yes, even a deer! Rip stood still and looked at the surprised animal with reverence, his hands in his jacket pockets, his gun on his shoulder, his pipe in his mouth. The deer, which obviously didn't imagine for a moment that he was a hunter, went on calmly grazing. I've got to be a hunter! Rip told himself, suddenly thinking of the tavern in the evening and of his faithful wife, and he put the gun to his shoulder. He took aim at the deer, which gazed at him. He even pressed the trigger, only there was no powder in it! It was strange, the dog barked even though no shot had rung out, and at the same moment shouts came from the ravine: Rip van Winkle, Rip van Winkle! A very odd-looking fellow, panting under a heavy burden, came up out of the ravine that was as unexpected as it was rocky, bent down so that his face was out of sight, but his clothing alone was disconcerting, a cloth jerkin as in old-fashioned pictures and wide breeches with bright-coloured ribbons, yes, he even had a goatee beard such as Rip's forefathers had once worn. But on his shoulders he carried a handsome little barrel of brandy. Rip didn't take long to respond to his call. You're a polite person, said the fellow with the goatee. You're a helpful person. And with these words, which Rip was so pleased to hear, he hoisted the barrel onto his shoulders, so that Rip abandoned any further questions. First they went uphill, then down into another ravine, an area Rip had never seen before. Even Bauz, the faithful dog, felt ill at ease, rubbing up against his master's legs and whimpering. For there was a sound like thunder coming from the ravine! At last they got to the point when the hard barrel was lifted from Rip's aching shoulders and he could straighten up and look around. This is Rip van Winkle, said the fellow with the goatee, and Rip found himself in the middle of a group of old gentlemen wearing Dutch hats, with stiff, solemn faces and old-fashioned frills. No one said a word, only Rip nodded. It was, as it turned out, a group of skittle-players. Hence the booming and rumbling from the ravine! Rip had immediately to fill the jugs; each of the old gentlemen took a hearty swig, then they went silently back to their skittles and Rip, who liked to show himself polite, couldn't avoid setting up the skittles again. Only now and then, hurriedly, was he able to take a gulp from the jug. It was gin, his favourite liquor! But once again the skittles flew apart and every time with a ringing crack that echoed through the whole ravine. Rip had his hands full. And there was no end to the cracking and rumbling. No sooner had the heavy and rather wobbly skittles been straightened up again, so that Rip could reach for the gin, than the next gentleman stepped up to the alley, shut his left eye in order to aim, and bowled his stone ball, which boomed like a thunderclap. They were a pretty strange group of people and, as I have said, not a word was spoken, so that Rip too didn't dare ask when he was going to be released from this drudgery. Their faces between the Dutch hats and the old-fashioned frills, as worn by his ancestors, were so dignified. Only as Rip set up the skittles again he had the disagreeable feeling that they were grinning behind his back, but Rip couldn't turn round and look because while his hand was still on the last skittle, that was wobbling, he heard the booming rumble of the next ball and had to jump out of the way to prevent it from crushing his leg. It was impossible to see when this drudgery would ever come to an end. The barrel of brandy seemed to be inexhaustible, again and again Rip had to fill the jugs, again and again they took a gulp, again and again they went silently back to their skittles. There was only one thing for it: Rip must wake up! . . . The sun was already sinking into the brown haze of evening as Rip sat up and rubbed his eyes. It was time to go home, high time. But he whistled in vain for his dog. For a while, still half in a dream, Rip looked around for the ravine and the skittle-players with their Dutch hats and old-fashioned frills, but none of that existed! Beyond the forest the broad Hudson gleamed as always and if the dog had just come along faithfully wagging his tail, Rip would have thought no more about the dream. On his way home he would have turned over in his mind what he was going to tell them in the village. To be sure, these stories of his seemed to him a bit like the wobbly skittles that he had to keep putting up so the others could knock them down. Not a sign of Bauz! Finally, Rip picked up his gun from the grass, but just look, it was overgrown by junipers. Not only that, it was also rusty, the most miserable-looking gun in the world. The wooden butt was mouldy. Rip shook his head, turned the thing over in his hand a few times, then threw it away and rose to his feet. For the sun was already sinking. Rip just wouldn't believe that the bleached bones lying beside his knapsack were the last remains of his faithful dog Bauz. But what else could they be? It was all real, he wasn't dreaming, he rubbed his chin and tugged at a beard that reached down to his chest, an old man's beard. Years had passed. How many? Anyhow it was late. Driven by hunger, and no doubt by curiosity as to how many people he knew were still alive after that stupid game of skittles, Rip van Winkle came to his familiar village, whose streets and houses he didn't recognize. Nothing but strangers! Only his own house was still standing, as dilapidated as ever, empty and with no window panes, inhabited only by the wind. And where was Hannah, his wife? Gradually horror took possession of him. The old tavern, where you could always find out what you wanted to know, was nowhere to be found. Lost and lonely, bewildered, fearful and encircled by unknown children, he asked after his old companions. People pointed to the cemetery or shrugged their shoulders. Finally (in a low voice) he also asked about himself. Wasn't there anyone left who knew Rip van Winkle? They laughed. They knew all about Rip van Winkle, the squirrel hunter, and he heard really droll stories about the man who, as every child knew, had fallen down a ravine or been taken prisoner by the Indians twenty years ago. What could he do? He asked shyly after Hannah, the squirrel hunter's wife, and when they told him, yes, she died long ago of grief, he wept and tried to walk away. Who was he? they asked him and he thought it over. God knows, he said, God knows, yesterday I thought I knew, but today, now that I'm awake, how should I know? The bystanders tapped their foreheads with their fingers and all in vain he told them the extraordinary story of the skittles, the brief story of how he had slept away his life. They didn't know what he was talking about. But he couldn't tell the story any other way and soon the people walked off, only a young and rather pretty woman remained. Rip van Winkle was my father, she said. What do you know about him? For a while he looked into her eyes and no doubt he felt tempted to tell her he was her father, but was he the one they all expected, the squirrel hunter with the stories that always wobbled a bit and fell over when they laughed? In the end he said, Your father is dead. And so the young woman left him too, which hurt him, but no doubt it had to be. So had he woken up for nothing? He lived on in the village for a few more years, a stranger in a strange world, and he didn't ask them to believe him when he told them about Hendrik Hudson, the discoverer of the river and the country, and about his ship's crew that gathered from time to time in the ravines and played skittles, and when he said that was where they should look for their old Rip van Winkle. They smiled. It was true that on hot summer days they sometimes heard a dull rumble from the other side of the hills, a thudding as of skittles; but the grown-ups always took it to be an ordinary storm, and no doubt that's what it was.

So much for the fairy tale.

"Well?" asked my counsel when I had finished telling it and finally lit my cigar. "What has that to do with our matter? Your case is coming up for trial towards the end of September and you're telling me fairy stories—fairy stories!—is that what I'm supposed to present in your defence?"

"What else?"

"Fairy tales," he complained. "Instead of just for once telling me a plain and simple truth I can make use of!"

* * *

Of course Herr Dr Bohnenblust, the defending counsel provided for
me by the State, is right: If I tell him a hundred times what a fire in a
Californian redwood sawmill looks like, how the American Negress
makes up, or how colourful New York appears during an evening
snowstorm accompanied by lightning (it does happen), or how to
land without papers at Brooklyn harbor, it doesn't prove that I've
been there. We live in an age of reproduction. Most of what makes
up our personal picture of the world we have never seen with our
own eyes—or rather, we've seen it with our own eyes, but not on the
spot: our knowledge comes to us from a distance, we are televiewers,
telehearers, teleknowers. One need never have left this little town to
have Hitler's voice still ringing in one's ears, to have seen the Shah of
Persia from a distance of three yards, and to know how the monsoon
howls over the Himalayas or what it looks like six hundred fathoms
beneath the sea. Anyone can know these things nowadays. Does it
mean I have ever been to the bottom of the sea? Or even (like the
Swiss) almost up Mount Everest?

And it's just the same with the inner life of man. Anyone can
know about it nowadays. How the devil am I to prove to my counsel
that I don't know my murderous impulses through C. G. Jung,
jealousy through Marcel Proust, Spain through Hemingway, Paris
through Ernst Jünger, Switzerland through Mark Twain, Mexico
through Graham Greene, my fear of death through Bernanos, in-
ability ever to reach my destination through Kafka, and all sorts of
other things through Thomas Mann? It's true, you need never have
read these authorities, you can absorb them through your friends
who also live all their experiences secondhand.

What an age! It means nothing any more to have seen swordfish,
to have loved a mulatto girl, it could all have happened during a
matinée performance of a documentary film; and as for having
thoughts—good heavens, it's already a rarity in this age to meet a
mind that's moulded on one particular model, it's a sign of personality if someone sees the world with Heidegger and only with
Heidegger; the rest of us swim in a cocktail containing pretty well
everything and mixed in the most elegant manner by Eliot; we know
our way about everywhere and, as I have said, not even our accounts
of the visible world mean anything; there's no *terra incognita* nowa-

days (except Russia). So what's the point of telling all these stories? It doesn't mean you've been there. My counsel is right. And yet— I swear:

There was a mulatto named Florence, a docker's daughter, I saw her every day and occasionally talked to her over the fence, a fence made of tar barrels and overgrown with brambles that kept us well apart. There was Florence with her gazelle-like walk. I dreamt about her, certainly, the wildest dreams; but nevertheless she was there next morning in the flesh. There was a tapping of high-heeled shoes on the wooden porch, and I immediately looked out through the holes in the curtains of my single hut hoping to see Florence; I was generally too late. But then I waited until she came out again with a bucket, emptied the frothy contents against my fence, and nodded; for at this moment I rushed impetuously out into the garden. She said, "Hallo", and I said, "Hallo." And I daren't describe her white smile in her brown face. People are familiar with this smile too from documentary films, from the newspapers, and even from a variety show in this very town, I know, and her singular voice can be heard on gramophone records, almost her voice . . . Then, as I "happened" to be in the garden, Florence would ask, "How's your cat?" The fact was that once, months ago, I had asked Florence after my hated cat, the agile beast which I once shut up in a refrigerator because of its reproachful spitting; I have referred to the incident already. Of course Florence knew nothing about this refrigerator intermezzo, but she must have guessed at my inner conflict with this black cat (she was grey, her name was Little Grey, but at night outside my window she was black) and thought I ought to show her (the cat) more love. But it was Florence I loved and the cat was perfectly well aware of the fact. So was Florence, in all probability . . . When Florence was not at home and I could not hear her singular voice, I used to go round the district from bar to bar looking for her. Once I actually found her.

Everyone knows how Negroes dance. Her partner at the moment was a U. S. Army sergeant. The couple danced so well that a circle of spectators formed round them, and the enthusiasts in the circle began to clap their hands in an ever faster rhythm, and finally in a frenzy. The U. S. Army sergeant—a tall fellow with the slender hips of a lion, with two legs of rubber, with the half-open mouth of pleasure and the sightless eyes of ecstasy, a fellow who had the chest and shoulders of a Michelangelo slave—reached the end of his strength; Florence danced alone. Now I could have taken over—if I'd been able to. Florence was still dancing alone when another came and spun her around, scarcely touching her fingers, circled around her, then took hold of her with the palm of his hand and swung her almost to the parquet floor, and then picked her up by the waist and lifted her so that her head almost struck the low ceiling; as she was poised in mid-air Florence made such a regal gesture with her arms, a gesture of such joyful triumph, that I felt like a cripple with my inexpressive white man's body; then she landed on the parquet floor as weightless as a bird. Now there was nothing to be heard but a dull jungle drumming, a soundless tremor, a kind of frenzied silence, while she went on dancing. A third partner was used up, and a fourth. Then suddenly, without being in the least exhausted, Florence laughed and stopped. As unselfconsciously as a child, a very happy child, who has been allowed on the roundabout and is still beaming with pleasure, she made her way out between the little tables, no doubt to powder her nose, and saw me. "Hallo," she said, "Hallo"; she even added, "Nice to see you," and it almost consoled me for the bitter-sweetness of my confusion. For I knew very well that I could never content this girl.

This filled me with all the greater longing.

And then, one hot Sunday, I heard the long-missed tapping of her high-heeled shoes again and dodged behind the curtains. I saw her father, the docker, in a black suit that made him look like a cross between a waiter and a clergyman, walking round with a broom tidying up the back garden; the bushes were decorated with coloured ribbons, so was my tar-barrel fence, and Florence, dressed in an exaggerated evening dress, as gaudy as a parrot, was carrying armchairs out of the house. Florence's mother, a kind of mother earth, came with a gigantic cake, put it on the table with the white cloth, raised a black umbrella over it to keep it from being ruined by the sun, and placed flowers all round it. From behind my curtains I shared her excitement. While the docker was only concerned to have clean stairs and no litter in his garden and no dry twigs and certainly not an old tin (he threw it over my fence) and not even a match, in short, while the father was exclusively attendant upon his broom, mother and daughter had all four hands full; a great bowl of punch came out on to the table and under the umbrella, also glasses of every shape and size, and gradually the guests arrived too, families with children of all ages, all the women in gaudy evening dress, so that the back garden soon looked like an aviary, but all the men, of course, were in black with white shirts. One of them drove up in a Nash, and not a model from the year before last either; he also wore horn-rimmed spectacles. It was very hot.

Once the first greetings were over, the clan did not seem to have much to say to one another. The U. S. Army sergeant was also standing about. Even the tiny tots with their fuzzy hair and big eyes, the boys in white shirts, the girls with coloured ribbons round their short pigtails, all behaved with model good manners. The grown-ups sat down and crossed their legs; some of them were smoking cigars. Besides a few ladies who were no longer Negresses in colour, who were recognizable as Negresses only by the modelling of their faces, by their teeth, by their improbably slender fetlocks, but above all by the animal grace of their movements—the hand never moves without the movement flowing out of the arm, the head never turns without the movement rising up out of the back and radiating out into the shoulders; whether slow or quick, it is always a perfect movement, unconscious and without fidgeting, without rigidity in some other part of the body, it flows or hurries or rests, it is always in harmony with itself—in short, besides girls like Florence, who had already rid themselves of the frizzy hair, this clan also contained others, Africans with grey-black skin and greyish-purple lips, with hands like boxing gloves, fathers to whom their de-frizzed daughters were an embarrassment. The man with the new Nash no doubt set the tone; it was very hot, as I have said, but no one took off his black jacket, and this tediously conventional conduct, the standing around with cigars swapping small talk, the perfect behaviour of the countless children, which reminded me of performing animals in a circus, the stiff politeness between relations, the general uneventfulness, the restraint, and a joyless effort on the part of every family to keep its end up, despite unequal abilities, in the whole clan's demonstration of refined comportment, this utter caricature of white middle-class respectability without the faintest hint of Africa, was itself the great event for them, I believe: now they were really acting like white people.

When my doorbell rang and the docker invited me over for some punch, I went across, naturally not without first also putting on a white shirt and the darkest jacket I had. Everyone said, "Nice to see you," and in more personal conversation, "How do you like America?" The U.S. Army sergeant with the slender loins of a lion and the shoulders of a Michelangelo slave, I learnt, was only here on leave, normally he was in Frankfurt, so that the Russians shouldn't come too close to America. I asked in return, "How do you like Frankfurt?" and I could see from his studied expressions of admiration that he lumped all us Europeans together. Then, at last, came my glorious Florence, who gave me a glass of punch and said:

"This is Joe, my husband—!"

I congratulated them.

"And how's your cat?"

They were married that Sunday, and Joe remained on leave another three full weeks, that is to say Florence was not to be seen in her father's house for three more weeks. . . .

In love as I was, I couldn't let these weeks slip past without seeing Florence at least in church. I knew now which church she belonged to. It was called the Second Olivet Baptist Church and turned out to be a hut that was almost indistinguishable from the rest of the storage sheds, except for a wooden Gothic front dating, I should say, from the twenties of this century. On the stage inside, to left and right of the microphone, hung two large flags, the Stars and Stripes and a white flag, while for the rest, apart from a black piano, the room was as bare as a drill hall. The large congregation was murmuring in a curious fashion, and right at the front stood a Negro in a light-coloured Sunday suit, asking questions that always contained the word "sin." The congregation nodded, one or two called out, "Oh yes, my Lord, oh yes." The questions, begun in a casual, matter-of-fact tone, were repeated with slight variations, sounding more and more urgent with every repetition, although the voice grew no louder. Somewhere a young woman cried, "I know, my Lord, I know." Most people murmured, a few gazed indifferently into the air, but the woman yelled out and began to shout whole sentences and to moan so that you felt you ought to go to her assistance.

The questioner in his light-coloured Sunday suit, unflinching in the repetition of his questions, was no longer a person but only the human repository of a voice that poured out over the congregation, his questions were calls, songs, and finally yells that pierced me to the marrow, loud and agonizing. As though from a distance, like an echo, the murmuring congregation answered with lowered heads, some with their hands over their faces. The moaning woman had jumped up from her bench, a young Negress with a ladylike hat, with white gloves which she stretched up towards heaven and holding a red handbag. "My Lord," she screamed, "My Lord," and then, unhindered by anyone, she fell on her knees, disappeared from my sight and whimpered as perhaps people whimper in a torture chamber, sounds of extreme agony that were now indistinguishable from the sounds of voluptuous delight; her voice melted into sobs.

The prayer, the general prayer, came to an end as the questioner, after becoming more and more pressing, died away into a voiceless ecstasy. Then came a moment of breathlessness, of exhaustion; then relaxation, the heads in front of me bobbed up again, a matron at the piano played a few lazy rhythms, ushers came round distributing gaudy fans, presented, as you could read on them, by a hairdresser "around the corner," and everyone fanned himself . . .

I couldn't see Florence, but I caught sight of Joe in his uniform; he was leaning against the wall, his arms crossed, unmoved, as though looking down on these people from the heights of Frankfurt. It was frightfully hot. During this pause a jovial priest at the microphone reminded us that the Lord had also saved the poor children of Israel and the Lord knew very well how hard it was nowadays to earn a dollar, therefore the Lord was not angry with the reluctant, for the Lord had infinite patience, therefore the reluctant would be given another chance to put something in the bowl. Meanwhile the congregation was chatting gaily and freely, like a social gathering in which everyone feels at ease. When the collection had reached a point where the Lord could feel satisfied for today, the matron at the piano played an electrifying prelude, as though in a dance hall, softened the tone as soon as there was silence in the room, and accompanied the sermon with almost inaudible, almost soundless jazz that was just a low rhythm and fell almost imperceptibly but effectively silent when the preacher made solemn pronouncements: "The Lord knows we are poor people, but the Lord will lead us into the Promised Land, the Lord will protect us from Communism. . . ."

All around the fans presented by the hairdresser as an advertisement were waving and the dust dancing in the rays of the sun. It smelt of gasoline, sweat and scent. I sat stewing in the sunlight that glared in through a torn blind, next to a lady in black silk, next to an old Negro with ashen hair, an Uncle Tom, who restrained with trembling hand a lively grandchild who found it difficult to get used to me, the stranger. In front of me sat a young workman; he listened to the sermon as a soldier listens to the latest bulletin from the front. Beyond him I looked straight at the back of a very pretty girl's neck smothered in white powder. (Oh, this yearning to be white, this yearning to have straight hair, this lifelong striving to be different from the way one is created, this great difficulty in accepting oneself, I knew it and saw only my own longing from outside, saw the absurdity of our yearning to be different from what we are. . . .)

After the prayer, as we sat down again, the side doors opened and from the courtyard, from which came the horrid stink of gasoline, there appeared the choir of angels, some twenty Negresses in white dresses. Florence among them. As well as some twenty Negroes in white shirts and black ties, each of them carrying a black book. Now the stage was full. They started off triumphally, as though we had just entered the Promised Land, first the piano and then the voices; softly to begin with, a hum like a hot summer field, as though we were hearing from a distance a primeval river of lamentation, dull and monotonous as waves, then the sound slowly swelled until gradually it flooded everything, a cataract of voices, half anger and half exultation, a mighty song that sank again and trickled away without really ceasing, an endless river of longing, as broad as the Mississippi; a male voice rang out above the rest like a fanfare, hard, loud, and lonely; then there was only the strange buzz, the voiceless hum as over a burning hot summer field, the heat in the hall, the dancing dust in the sunlight that glared in through the torn blind, the smell of gasoline and sweat and scent.

* * *

After three weeks Joe disappeared.

* * *

Once more I heard the tap of high-heeled shoes, Florence was back, even though married, and she actually called up to my window; I rushed down the steep stairs, miraculously without stumbling, although I wrenched a newel post out of the banister, and over to the tar-barrel fence, where Florence was already standing the other side of the brambles.

"What's happened to your cat?" she asked.

She was even holding the creature in her arms.

"D'you know she's hurt?" she said. "Awfully hurt."

That was the wound on the snout.

"And you don't feel any pity for her?" she said. "You are cruel, you just don't love her."

And with that she handed the beast over to me.

"You should love her."

"Why should I?"

"Of course you should."

That was my affair with the mulatto girl called Florence, and even now, I think of Florence whenever I hear high-heeled shoes; unfortunately the cat always comes to mind as well.

Translated by Michael Bullock

From
HOMO FABER

A Report

My decision to change route on an official trip and make a private detour via Guatemala, merely to see an old friend of my youth again, was reached on the airfield at Mexico City and at the very last moment. I was already standing at the barrier, shaking hands all over again and asking Herbert to give his brother my best wishes, if he remembered me at all, when the usual announcement came over the loudspeaker: ATTENTION PLEASE, ATTENTION PLEASE (it was another Super-Constellation), WILL ALL PASSENGERS FOR PANAMA-CARACAS-PERNAMBUCO . . . I just couldn't face the prospect of climbing into another airplane, fastening another safety belt. Herbert said:

"It's time you got moving."

I am generally considered extremely conscientious over professional matters, perhaps excessively so, anyhow I have never before postponed an official trip for a passing whim, let alone changed my route. An hour later I was flying with Herbert.

"Well," he said, "that's sporting of you."

I don't know what it was really.

"Now the turbines are waiting for me for a change." I said. "I've waited for them often enough, now they can wait for me."

Of course, that was no way to look at it.

As soon as we reached Campeche the heat greeted us with slimy sunshine and sticky air, the stench of slime rotting in the sun, and when you wiped the sweat from your face it was as though you yourself stank of fish. I said nothing. In the end you stop wiping the sweat away and sit there with your eyes closed, breathing with your mouth shut, resting your head against a wall and sticking your legs out in front of you. Herbert was quite sure the train went every Tuesday, he had it in black and white in a Düsseldorf guidebook— but after waiting five hours we suddenly discovered it was not Tuesday, but Monday.

I didn't say a word.

At least there was a shower in the hotel, and a towel that smelled of camphor as is usual in this part of the world; when I went to take a shower, beetles as long as my finger fell from the moldy curtain—I tried to drown them, but they kept climbing up out of the plug-hole again, until I squashed them under my heel so that I could finally have my shower.

I dreamed of those beetles.

I had made up my mind to leave Herbert and fly back the following afternoon, friendship or no friendship . . .

I felt my stomach again.

I was lying stark naked.

It stank all night long.

Herbert also lay stark naked.

In spite of everything, Campeche is a town, a human settlement with electric current so that you can shave, and telephones; but there were zopilotes perched on every wire, waiting in rows for a dog to die of hunger, a donkey to collapse, a horse to be slaughtered, then they would come flapping down . . . We arrived just as they were tugging a long tangle of entrails this way and that, a whole pack of blackish-purple birds with bloody guts in their beaks, they wouldn't fly away, even when a car came along; they dragged the carcass off somewhere else, without rising into the air, just hopping and scurrying, and all this right in the middle of the market place.

Herbert bought a pineapple.

As I said, I had made up my mind to fly back to Mexico City. I was in despair. I have no idea why I didn't do so.

Suddenly it was midday.

We were standing outside on an embankment, where it stank less but was even hotter, because there was no shade, eating our pine-

apple; we leaned forward because of the dripping juice, then we bent
down over the stones and rinsed our sugary fingers; the warm water
was also sticky, not sugary but salty, and our fingers smelled of
seaweed, of motor oil, of shells; of unidentifiable rotting matter, so
that we immediately wiped them on our handkerchiefs. Suddenly
there came the roar of engines. I stood paralyzed. My DC-4 for
Mexico City was flying directly overhead, then it curved round and
out to sea, where it seemed to dissolve in the hot sky as though in a
blue acid.

I said nothing.

I don't know how that day passed.

It passed.

Our train (Campeche-Palenque-Coatzocoalcos) was better than
expected—a diesel engine with four air-conditioned cars, so that we
forgot the heat and along with the heat the stupidity of this whole
journey.

"I wonder whether Joachim will recognize me?"

Every now and then our train would stop during the night on the
open track, no one knew why, there was no light anywhere, from
time to time a distant flash of lightning revealed that we were passing
through a jungle, or sometimes a swamp, the lightning flashed
behind a tangle of black trees, our locomotive hooted into the night,
we couldn't open the window to see what was going on . . . Suddenly it started off again—at 20 m.p.h., although the ground was as
flat as a pancake and the line dead straight. Still, we were glad it was
moving at all.

At one point I asked: "Why did they get divorced?"

"Don't know," he said, "She became a Communist, I think."

"Was that the reason?"

He yawned.

"I don't know," he said. "It wasn't a success. I never inquired."

Once, when our train stopped again, I went to the car door and
looked out. Outside was the heat we had forgotten, humid darkness
and silence. I stepped down onto the footplate, the stillness was
broken by flashes of lightning, a buffalo stood on the track in front
of us, that was all. It stood as though stuffed, because it was dazzled
by our headlights, obstinately immovable. The sweat at once ran
over my forehead and down my neck again. The locomotive hooted
and hooted. All around us was undergrowth. After a few minutes the

buffalo (or whatever it was) moved slowly out of the glare of the headlights, then I heard a rustling in the undergrowth, the snapping of branches, then a plop and it splashed around in the water out of sight.

After this we drove on.

"Have they any children?" I asked.

"One daughter."

We settled down to sleep, our jackets under our heads, our legs stretched out on the empty seat opposite.

"Did you know her?"

"Yes," I said. "Why?"

Soon afterward he fell asleep.

When morning broke, we were still in the scrub; the early-morning sun shone over the low jungle horizon and white flocks of herons rose with a flapping of wings in front of our slow-moving train; there was brushwood without end, as far as the eye could see, with every now and then a group of Indian huts hidden among trees with aerial roots, an occasional isolated palm, but for the most part deciduous trees, acacias and others I didn't know, above all bushes and antediluvian ferns; the place was teeming with sulphur-yellow birds and the sun shone once more as though behind smoked glass, you could see the heat-haze.

I had been dreaming (not of Hanna!).

The next time we stopped on the open track it was Palenque, a little halt at which no one got out or in except us, a small shed beside the line, a signal, that was all, not even a double track (if I remember rightly); we asked three people where Palenque was.

The sweat immediately began to pour again.

The train drove on, leaving us standing there with our luggage as though at the end of the world, or at least at the end of civilization, and of the jeep that was supposed to take the gentleman from Düsseldorf straight to the plantation there was, of course, not a sign.

"Here we are."

I laughed.

All the same, there was a narrow road, and, after a pretty exhausting half hour, children emerged from the bushes and later a donkey-driver, who took our luggage, an Indian of course. All I kept was my yellow briefcase with the zip-fastener.

For five days we were suspended in Palenque.

We were suspended in hammocks, with beer within reach all the time, sweating as though sweating was our purpose in life, incapable of coming to any decision, quite contented actually, because the beer there was excellent, YUCATECA, better than the beer in the uplands. We lay suspended in our hammocks and drank, so that we could sweat better, and I couldn't think what we really wanted.

We wanted a jeep.

If we didn't keep telling ourselves this all the time, we forgot about it, and apart from this we said very little all day long, a curious state.

A jeep, yes, but where from?

Talking only made us thirsty.

The landlord of our tiny hotel (the Lacroix) had a Land Rover, obviously the only vehicle in Palenque, but he needed it himself to fetch beer and guests from the railway station, people interested in Indian ruins, pyramid-lovers; at the moment there was only one of them there, a young American who talked too much, but fortunately he was out all day—looking at the ruins, which he thought we ought to look at too.

Not on your life!

Every step set the sweat pouring, which immediately had to be replaced with beer, and the only way to exist was to lie motionless in the hammock with bare feet, smoking; apathy was the only possible state; even a rumor that the plantation across the frontier had been abandoned months ago did not stir us; Herbert and I looked at one another and drank our beer.

Our only chance was the Land Rover.

It stood outside the hotel day after day.

But, as I have said, the hotelkeeper needed it.

Only after sunset (the sun didn't really set, it simply wilted away in the haze) did it become cooler, so that we could at least joke. About the future of the German cigar. I found the whole thing ludicrous, our trip and everything. Native uprising! I didn't believe that for a moment; the Indians were far too gentle, too peaceable, positively childlike. They squatted for whole evenings in their white straw hats on the earth, motionless as toadstools, content without light, silent. The sun and moon were enough light for them, an effeminate race, eerie but innocuous.

Herbert asked what I thought had happened.

Nothing.

What should we do? he asked.

Take a shower.

I showered from morning to evening. I hate sweat, because it makes me feel like a sick man. (I've never been ill in my life, except for measles.) I think Herbert was rather hurt that I had no suggestions to make, but it was much too hot. He himself made the craziest suggestions.

"Let's go to the movies," he said.

As if there was a movie house in this little cluster of Indian huts! He got quite angry when I laughed at him.

There was not a drop of rain.

Lightning flashed every evening, it was our only entertainment in the evenings. Palenque had a diesel motor that generates electricity, but it was turned off at 9 P.M., so there we were in the darkness of the jungle and all we could see was the lightning, bluish like a quartz lamp, and the red glowworms, and later a slimy-looking moon, there were no stars to be seen, it was too hazy for that . . . Joachim simply didn't write any letters, because it was too hot, I could well understand that; he lay suspended in his hammock like us, yawning, or he was dead . . . There was nothing to do, anyhow, but wait till we could get a jeep and cross the frontier and see for ourselves.

Herbert yelled at me:

"A jeep! Where from?"

A few minutes afterwards he was snoring.

Apart from this, silence reigned most of the time, once the diesel generator had been turned off; a horse grazed in the moonlight and in the same enclosure a deer, but the deer made no sound, there was also a black sow and a turkey that couldn't bear the lightning and squawked, and also some geese that started cackling when the turkey set them off, there would be a sudden alarm, then silence again with lightning flashing across the flat landscape, only the grazing horse we heard all night long.

I thought about Joachim.

But what was I thinking?

I was simply awake.

Only our ruin-lover chattered a lot; it was quite interesting when you listened to him—about Toltecs, Zapotecs, and Aztecs, who built temples yet hadn't discovered the wheel. He came from Boston and was a musician. At times he got on my nerves, like all artists who think themselves loftier or more profound beings simply because they don't know what electricity is.

In the end I, too, fell asleep.

Every morning I was wakened by a curious noise, half mechanical, half musical, a sound which I couldn't explain, but loud, but as frenzied as crickets, metallic, monotonous; it must be mechanical in origin, but I couldn't guess what it was, and later, when we went to breakfast in the village, it was silent, nothing to be seen. We were the only guests in the only inn where we always ordered the same thing—*huevos a la mexicana,* terribly peppery, but presumably wholesome, together with tortillas and beer. The Indian proprietress, a matron with black pigtails, took us for archaeologists. Her hair resembled plumage; it was black with a bluish-green sheen. She had ivory teeth, that showed when she smiled, and soft black eyes.

"Ask her," said Herbert, "whether she knows my brother and when she last saw him!"

There wasn't much to be got out of her.

"She remembers a car," I said. "That's all."

The parrot didn't know anything either.

GRACIAS, HEE-HEE!

I spoke Spanish to him.

HEE-HEE, GRACIAS, HEE-HEE!

On the third or fourth morning, while we were having breakfast in the usual way, gaped at by a crowd of Mayan children who didn't beg but merely stood by our table and every now and then laughed, Herbert developed the fixed idea that somewhere in this miserable hamlet, if we only looked hard enough, there must be a jeep— behind some hut, somewhere in the thickets of gourds, bananas and maize. I left him to it. It struck me as crazy, like everything else, but I didn't care, I lay suspended in my hammock and Herbert didn't show up all day long.

I was even too lazy to take films.

Apart from beer, YUCATECA, which was excellent but flat, there was only rum in Palenque, rotten stuff, and Coca-Cola, which I can't stand.

I drank and slept.

Anyhow, I spent hours thinking of nothing.

Herbert, who didn't return till dusk, pale with exhaustion, had discovered a brook and bathed; he had also discovered two men with curved sabers (so he asserted) walking through the maize, Indians with white trousers and white straw hats, just like the villagers—but carrying curved sabers.

Not a word about the jeep, of course!

I believe he was scared.

I shaved while there was still electric current, and Herbert told me all about his time in the Caucasus again, his horror stories about Ivan, which I knew already; later since there was no more beer, we went to the movies, accompanied by our ruin-lover, who knew his Palenque—there really was a movie, a shed with a corrugated-iron roof. The first picture was Harold Lloyd climbing up and down walls in the manner of the twenties, the feature, love and passion among the Mexican smart set, adultery with a Cadillac and a Browning and plenty of evening dresses and marble. We doubled up with laughter, while the four or five Indians squatted motionless in front of the crumpled screen, their great straw hats on their heads, perhaps satisfied, perhaps not, you can never tell, they are so impassive, Mongolian. . . Our new friend, a Boston musician, as I mentioned, an American of French origin, was thrilled with Yucatan and couldn't understand why we were not interested in ruins; he asked what we were doing here.

We just shrugged our shoulders and looked at one another, each one leaving it to the other to say that we were waiting for a jeep.

I don't know what he must have thought of us.

Rum has the advantage that you don't break into a sweat as after every glass of beer; on the other hand you wake up with a headache next morning, when the incomprehensible noise starts off again, half piano, half machine gun, and accompanied by singing—it went on every day between 6 and 7 a.m., and every day I decided to look into it, but I always forgot about it as the day wore on.

You forget everything here.

On one occasion—we wanted to bathe, but Herbert couldn't find his legendary brook and we suddenly found ourselves among the ruins—we came across our musician at work. Among the stones, which were supposed to represent a temple, the heat was unbearable. The only thing he was worried about was keeping the drops of sweat off his paper! He scarcely greeted us; we were disturbing him.

His work consisted in placing tracing paper over the stone reliefs and then rubbing a black crayon this way and that for hours on end, a crazy way of obtaining a copy of anything; but he insisted that you couldn't photograph these hieroglyphs and grinning deities, they would be dead at once. We left him.

I'm no art historian.

After climbing around the pyramids for a while out of sheer boredom (the steps are far too steep, the relation between height and width is exactly the reverse of what it should be, so that you get out of breath), I lay down, dizzy from the heat, in the shadow of some so-called palace, with my arms and legs stretched out, breathing.

The humid air . . .

The slimy sun . . .

I had made up my mind to go back by myself if we didn't get hold of a jeep tomorrow. It was more sultry than ever, damp and musty; birds with long blue tails were flitting in all directions; someone had used the temple as a toilet, hence the flies. I tried to sleep. The flitting wings and animal cries made the place sound like a zoo; you couldn't tell what creatures were whistling and screeching and warbling, it was a din like modern music, they might have been monkeys, or birds, or maybe some feline species, it was impossible to tell, they might have been in heat or terrified, you couldn't tell that either.

I could feel my stomach. (I was smoking too much.)

At one time, in the eleventh or thirteenth century, a whole city is supposed to have stood here, said Herbert, a Mayan city.

So what?

To my question whether he still believed in the future of the German cigar, Herbert returned no answer; he was snoring, having finished talking about the religion of the Mayas, art and stuff like that . . .

I let him snore.

I took my shoes off, snakes or no snakes, I needed air, I had palpitations from the heat, I was astounded by our tracing-paper artist, who could work in the blazing sun and gave up his holidays and his savings to bring home hieroglyphs which no one could decipher.

People are funny.

A race like these Mayas, who hadn't discovered the wheel and built pyramids and temples in the jungle, where everything becomes smothered in moss and crumbles with damp—what for?

I couldn't understand myself.

I should have landed in Caracas a week ago and today (at the latest) I ought to have been back in New York. Instead of that I was stuck here—for the sake of saying hello to a friend of my youth, who had married the girl friend of my youth.

What for?

We were waiting for the Land Rover that brought our ruin-artist here every day and took him back again around evening with his rolls of tracing paper. I decided to wake Herbert and tell him I was going off on the next train to leave Palenque.

The flitting birds . . .

Never an airplane!

Every time I turned my head to one side to avoid seeing the smoked-glass sky, it was as if I was in the sea, our pyramid an island or a ship, with the sea on all sides; and yet it was nothing but undergrowth, unending, greenish-gray, flat as an ocean—undergrowth.

Above it the full moon, lilac in the daylight.

Herbert was still snoring away.

It's amazing how they got these blocks of stone here, when they weren't acquainted with the wheel and therefore had no pulleys. They didn't know the arch either. Apart from the decorations, which didn't appeal to me anyhow, because I like functionalism, I found these ruins extremely primitive—unlike our ruin-lover, who liked the Mayas precisely because they had no technology, but gods instead. He thought it delightful that they began a new era every two hundred and fifty years, smashed up all their pots and pans, put out all their fires, then relit them all over the country from the fire in the temple and made fresh pots and pans. A people that simply abandoned their cities (intact) and moved on, for religious reasons, and after fifty or a hundred miles built a completely new temple city somewhere in this unchanging jungle—he thought it pregnant with significance, though uneconomic, a sign of great depth of spirit, that was his serious opinion.

Sometimes it made me think of Hanna.

When I woke Herbert, he sprang to his feet. What was the matter? When he saw that nothing was the matter, he started snoring again—to avoid being bored.

Not a sound of an engine!

I tried to picture what it would be like if there were suddenly no more engines as in the days of the Mayas. One has to think about something. I felt a rather childish amazement at the way in which they had shifted these blocks of stone: they simply built ramps and then dragged the blocks up them with an idiotic expenditure of manpower, that was what made it so primitive. On the other hand their astronomy. According to the ruin-lover, their calendar reckoned the solar year at 365.2420 days, instead of 365.2422 days; nevertheless, for all their mathematical knowledge, they never evolved a technology and were therefore condemned to decline and disappear.

Our Land Rover at last!

The miracle happened when our ruin-lover heard that we had to cross over into Guatemala. He was wildly enthusiastic. He took out his little calendar and counted the remaining days of his vacation. Guatemala, he said, was teeming with Mayan settlements, some of them barely excavated, and if we could take him with us he would do everything in his power to get the Land Rover, which we couldn't get, on the strength of his friendship with the landlord of the Lacroix Hotel—and he did get it.

(At a hundred pesos a day.)

It was Sunday when we packed, a hot night with a slimy moon, and the queer noise that had wakened me every morning turned out to be music, the clatter of an antiquated marimba, hammer taps without resonance, a ghastly kind of music, positively epileptic. It was some festival connected with the full moon. They had practiced every morning before going to work in the fields, so that now they could play for dancing, five Indians who struck their instrument with whirling hammers, a kind of wooden xylophone, as long as a table. I overhauled the engine to avoid a breakdown in the jungle and had no time to watch the dancing; I was lying underneath our Land Rover. The girls were sitting in rows around the market place, most of them with a baby at their brown breasts; the dancers sweated and drank coconut milk. As the night passed, more and more seemed to arrive, whole tribes; the girls were not wearing their everyday clothes, but American dresses in honor of their moon, a fact that agitated Marcel, our artist, for several hours. I had other worries. We had no arms, no compass, nothing. I'm not interested in folklore. I packed our Land Rover, after all someone had to, and I was glad to do it in order to get out of here.

* * *

July 9th–13th, in Cuba.

My reason for going to Havana: to change planes, because I want at all costs to avoid flying via New York, KLM from Caracas, CUBANA to Lisbon, I stay four days.

Four days doing nothing but look.

EL PRADO.

The old street with the old plane trees, like the Ramblas in Barcelona, the town out for its evening stroll, an avenue of beautiful people, incredible, I walk and walk, I have nothing else to do.

The yellow birds, their uproar at dusk.

Everyone wants to clean my shoes.

The Spanish Negress, who sticks her tongue out at me because I am admiring her, her pink tongue in her brown face, I laugh and say hello—she laughs too, showing her white teeth in the red flower of her lips (if one may put it like that) and her eyes, I don't want anything from her.

"How do you like Havana?"

My anger because they keep taking me for an American, merely because I am white; the pimps walking along in step with me:

"Something very beautiful! D'you know what I mean? Something very young!"

Everyone strolling, everyone laughing.

Everything like a dream.

The white policemen smoking cigars; the sailors smoking cigars—boys with narrow hips in white trousers.

CASTELLO MORRO (founded by Philip II).

I have my shoes cleaned.

My resolve to live differently.

My joy.

I buy cigars; two boxes.

Sunset.

The naked boys in the sea, their skin, the sun on their wet skin, the heat, I sit and smoke a cigar, storm clouds over the white town, dark purple clouds, the last rays of sunshine lighting up the tall buildings.

EL PRADO.

The green dusk, the ice-cream vendors; the girls sit (in groups) on the wall under the street lamps laughing.

TAMALES.

This is maize wrapped in banana leaves, a snack which they sell in the street—you eat it as you walk along to save time.

My restlessness. Why do I feel restless?

There was nothing whatever for me to do in Havana.

My rest in the hotel—again and again—with showers, then unclothed on the bed, the draft from the electric fan, I lie smoking cigars. I don't lock my door; outside in the corridor a girl is singing as she does the cleaning, another Spanish Negress, I smoke incessantly.

My desire.

Why doesn't she come in?

My fatigue. I am too tired to get an ash-tray, I lie on my back and smoke my cigar so that its whitish ash doesn't fall off, vertically.

PARTAGAS.

When I walk in the Prado again it is like a hallucination again—crowds of beautiful girls, the men very handsome too, splendid-looking people, a mixture of Negro and Spanish, I can't stop staring. Their erect and flowing walk, the girls in flared blue skirts, their white headscarves, their Negresses' heels, their bare backs are precisely as dark as the shadows under the plane trees, consequently at first glance you see only their blue or lilac dresses, their white headscarves, their white teeth when they laugh and the whites of their eyes; their earrings flash.

THE CARIBBEAN BAR.

I am smoking again.

ROMEO Y JULIETA.

A young man, whom I first take for a pimp, insists on paying for my whisky, because he has become a father.

"For the first time!"

He embraces me, keeps repeating:

"Isn't it a wonderful thing?"

He introduces himself and wants to know my name and how many children I have, especially sons. I say:

"Five."

He immediately insists on ordering five whiskies.

"Walter," he says, "you're my brother."

We have hardly clinked glasses when he is off to buy the others a whisky, to ask them how many children they have, especially sons. It's all like crazy.

At last the storm. As I sit alone under the arcades in a yellow rocking chair there is a rush of water on all sides, a sudden cloudburst with a gale, the avenue is suddenly empty of people, as though an alarm had sounded, the flapping of blinds, outside the rain spraying up from the sidewalk: a sudden bed of narcissi (especially under the street lamps), white.

Myself rocking and watching.

My delight at being here and now.

From time to time rain sprays in under the arcade, petal confetti, then the scent of hot foliage and a sudden coolness on the skin, from time to time flashes of lightning, but the waterfall is louder than any thunder, I rock and laugh, wind, the rocking of the empty chair beside me, the Cuban flag . . .

I whistle.

My anger with America!

I rock and shiver.

THE AMERICAN WAY OF LIFE!

My resolve to live differently . . .

Flashes of lightning; afterward it's as though you were blind. For a split second you see the sulphur-green palm trees in the gale, clouds, violet with the bluish glow of an oxyacetylene torch, the sea, the flapping corrugated iron; the reverberation of this flapping corrugated iron, my childish delight in it, my sensual pleasure—I sing.

THE AMERICAN WAY OF LIFE.

Even what they eat and drink, these palefaces who don't know what wine is, these vitamin-eaters who drink cold tea and chew cotton-wool and don't know what bread is, this Coca-Cola people I can no longer abide . . .

And yet I am living on their money.

I have my shoes cleaned.

With their money.

The seven-year-old, who has polished my shoes once already, now like a drowned cat; I take hold of his fuzzy hair.

His grin . . .

His hair isn't black, more of an ashen gray, a brownish gray, young, it feels like horse hair, but frizzy and short, you can feel the childish skull underneath, warm, like stroking a shorn poodle.

He only grins and goes on polishing.

I love him.

His teeth . . .

His young skin . . .

His eyes remind me of Houston, Texas, of the Negro cleaning woman who knelt beside me in the washroom after I had my attack of sweating and giddiness, the whites of her large eyes that are altogether different, beautiful like animals' eyes. The whole of her flesh.

We chat about different makes of car.

His nimble hands . . .

There is nobody else in sight but this boy and myself, all around us the Flood, he squats there shining my shoes with his rag so that it makes a slapping sound.

THE AMERICAN WAY OF LIFE.

Their ugliness in comparison with people like these here, their pink sausage skins horrible, they only live because there is penicillin, that's all, the fuss they make as though they were happy because they're Americans, because they have no inhibitions, and yet they're only gawky and noisy—fellows like Dick, whom I have taken as a model!—the way they stand around, their left hands in their trouser pockets, their shoulders leaning against the wall, their glass in the other hand, easygoing, the protectors of mankind, their backslapping, their optimism until they are drunk and then hysterical weeping, sell-out of the white race, their vacuum between the loins.

My anger with myself!

(If only one could live over again.)

My night letter to Hanna . . .

The following day I drove out to the beach, it was cloudless and hot, midday with a gentle surf, the wash of the waves and the chink of the shingle, every beach reminded me of Theodohori.

I weep.

The water is clear, you can see the bottom, I swim with my face in the water so that I can see the bottom, my shadow on the bottom—a violet frog.

Letter to Dick.

What America has to offer: comfort, the best gadgets in the world, ready for use, the world as an Americanized vacuum wherever they go, everything is turned into a highway with the world as a wall of posters on either side, their cities that aren't cities at all, lighting, next morning you see the empty scaffolding, humbug, infantile, an advertisement of optimism spread out like a neon carpet in front of the night and death . . .

Later I hired a boat.

In order to be alone.

Even when they're in their bathing costumes you can see they've got dollars; their voices (as on the Via Appia) are unbearable, wherever you go you hear their rubber voices, the moneyed masses.

Letter to Marcel.

Marcel is right. Their fake health, their fake youthfulness, their women who don't admit to growing older, the way they use cosmetics even on corpses, their whole pornographic attitude to death, their President who has to laugh on every magazine cover like a pink baby, or else they won't elect him again, their obscene youthfulness . . .

I rowed a long way out.

Heat-haze over the sea.

Very much alone.

I read my letters to Dick and Marcel and tore them up, because they were not objective; the white scraps on the water; the white hairs on my chest . . .

Very much alone.

Later, like a schoolboy, I draw a woman in the hot sand and lie down inside this woman, who is nothing but sand, and talk aloud to her.

"You wild girl!"

I don't know what to do with this day, with myself, it was a queer day, I didn't recognize myself, I had no idea how it had passed, an afternoon that looked absolutely like eternity, blue, unbearable, but beautiful, but endless—until I am once more sitting on the Prado wall (in the evening) with closed eyes; I try to imagine that I am in Havana, that I am sitting on the Prado wall. I can't imagine it, terror.

Everybody wants to clean my shoes.

Nothing but beautiful people, I gaze at them admiringly as at strange animals, their white teeth in the dusk, their brown shoulders and arms—their laughter, because they're glad to be alive, because it is a holiday evening, because they are beautiful.

My lust for looking.

My desire.

Vacuum between the loins.

I exist now only for shoeshine boys!

The pimps.

The ice-cream vendors.

Their vehicle: a combination of old baby carriage and mobile canteen added to half a bicycle, a baldachin with rusty curtains; a carbide lamp; all around, the green twilight dotted with their flared skirts.

The lilac moon.

Then the business with the taxi. It was still early in the evening, but I couldn't bear to wander along any more like a corpse in the parade of the living, I wanted to get back to my hotel and take a sleeping pill; I beckoned a taxi, but when I pull the door open the two ladies are already inside, a black one and a blonde. I say "Sorry!" and shut the door; but the driver jumps out and calls me back, "Yes, sir!" he cries and pulls the door open again, "For you, sir!" I have to laugh at so much service and climb in.

Our delicious supper.

Then the fiasco.

I knew it would happen sooner or later, afterward I lie in my hotel—sleepless but relaxed, it is a hot night, from time to time I shower my body that is leaving me, but I don't take a sleeping pill, my body is still just good enough to enjoy the wind from the electric fan that turns this way and that, wind on my chest, wind on my legs, wind on my legs.

My haunting fear: cancer of the stomach.

Apart from this I am happy.

The din of birds at daybreak, I take out my Baby Hermes and at last type my UNESCO report on the assembling of the turbines in Venezuela, which has just been completed.

Then sleep till midday.

I eat oysters because I don't know what to do, my work is finished, I am smoking far too many cigars.

(Hence the pains in my stomach.)

The way I simply sit down on the Prado wall and get into conversation with a strange girl, in my opinion the same one who stuck her pink tongue out at me the day before yesterday. She doesn't remember. Her laughter when I tell her I'm not an American.

My Spanish too slow.

"Say it in English!"

Her long thin hands . . .

My Spanish is just enough for negotiations connected with my work. It's funny: I don't say what I want to say, but what the language wants. Her laughter at this. I am the victim of my limited vocabulary. Her astonishment, her positively kindly eyes when I myself feel astonished—at my own life, which seems, when put like that, so insignificant.

Juana is eighteen.

(Even younger than our child.)

Suiza—all the time she thinks it means Sweden.

Her brown arms stretched out backwards as a support, her head against the cast-iron street lamp, her white headscarf and black hair, her unbelievably beautiful feet; we are smoking; my two white hands interlaced over my right knee.

Her unaffectedness.

She has never left Cuba.

This is only my third evening here, but everything is already familiar—the green dusk with the neon signs, the ice-cream vendors, the checked bark of the plane trees, the birds with their twittering and the net of shadow on the ground, the red flowers of their mouths.

Her life's goal: New York!

The bird droppings from above.

Her unaffectedness.

Juana is a packer, a *fille de joie* only on weekends, she has a child, she doesn't live in Havana itself.

Again the young sailors sauntering past.

I tell her about my daughter who has died, about the honeymoon with my daughter, about Corinth, about the viper that bit her over the left breast, about her funeral, about my future.

"I'm going to marry her."

She misunderstands me.

"I thought she was dead."

I explain.

"Oh," she laughs, "you're going to marry the girl's mother, I see."

"As soon as possible."

"Fine!" she says.

"My wife lives in Athens."

Her earrings, her skin . . .

She is waiting here for her brother.

My question whether Juana believes in mortal sin, or in gods; her white laugh; my question whether Juana believes that snakes (speaking quite generally) are guided by gods, or by demons:

"What's your opinion, sir?"

Later the fellow with the stripped Hollywood shirt, the youthful pimp, who has accosted me previously, her brother. He shakes my hand: "Hello, *camarada!*"

It doesn't mean anything, we are all good friends, Juana puts her cigarette under her heel and crushes it, her brown hand on my shoulder:

"He's going to marry his wife—he's a gentleman!"

Juana disappeared.

"Wait here," he says and looks back over his shoulder to keep me where I am. "Just a moment, sir, just a moment!"

My last night in Havana.

No time on earth in which to sleep!

I had no particular cause to feel happy, but I did. I knew that I am going to leave everything I am seeing, but that I shall not forget it: the arcade by night, where I rock and look, or listen as the case may be, a cab-horse whinnies, the Spanish house front with the yellow curtains flapping out of black windows, then the corrugated iron again from somewhere, it's reverberation going through my marrow, my pleasure at all this, my sensual delight, wind, nothing but wind shaking the palms, wind without clouds, I rock and sweat, the green palm tree is as pliant as a willow wand, the wind in its fronds makes a sound like knives being sharpened, dust, then the cast-iron street lamps that begin to whistle, I rock and laugh, their flickering and dying light, there must be a considerable draft, the whinnying horse can scarcely hold the cab, everything is trying to fly away, the sign on a barber's shop, brass, its tinkling in the darkness, and the invisible sea sending its spray over the wall, then every time thunder in its depths, over the top of this it hisses like an espresso machine, my thirst, salt on my lips, a gale without rain, not a drop will fall, it can't because there are no clouds, nothing but stars, nothing but the hot, dry dust in the air, air like an oven, I rock to and fro and drink my Scotch, one only, I can't take any more, I rock and sing. For hours on end. I sing! I can't sing, but nobody hears me; the cab-horse on the empty macadam road, the last girls in their flying skirts, their brown legs when their skirts fly up, their black hair that also flies out behind them, and the green Venetian blind that has torn itself free, their white laughter in the dust and the way it skids over the surface of the street out toward the sea, the raspberry light in the dust above the white town in the night, the heat, the Cuban flag—I rock and sing, nothing else, the rocking of the empty chair beside me, the whistling cast iron, the eddy of petals. I sing the praises of life.

Translated by Michael Bullock

From GANTENBEIN

Yesterday, at a party at Burri's, people were once more talking about Communism and imperialism, about Cuba, someone talked about the Berlin wall, opinions, counter-opinions, passionate, a game of chess, this too, move and counter-move, a party game, until someone, silent till then, told us about his flight. Holding no views. Just like that: an action involving bullets that struck his comrades, and a fiancée who stayed behind. When asked later what news he had of his fiancée, he said nothing. We all fell silent—then I ask myself, sucking my cold pipe in the silence, confronted by this real story, what I am really doing:—making sketches for an ego! . . .

—having woken up again, my hair still uncombed, but having had a shower and dressed, even if still without jacket or tie, I suppose, because the first actions are mechanical, helpless habit, I only know that I am once again sitting on the edge of a bed, yes, I have once more woken up, but I am still encircled by dreams which, if I look at them closely, I fear, will prove not to be dreams at all but memory, not memory of the night, however, but memory as such, the sediment of experience, and yet I am awake, as I have said, even washed and free of emotion, perhaps even whistling, I don't know exactly, it's unimportant, and if at this moment I am softly whistling, it's only so as not to have to speak, even to myself, I have nothing to say to myself now, I have to get to the airport, heavens above it's high time, so I assume, and yet I am in no hurry, as though this had already happened before, long ago, I'm surprised that no pneumatic drill is chugging, I listen, silence, nor are any hens clucking, I listen, there's no cheap music-hall to be heard, memory, steaming and puffing in a night-time goods station, that was once upon a time, whistles and echoes of whistles, I hold my breath, silence, for the space of a breath I sit as motionless as a statue, in the pose of a man pulling out a thorn, I'm not pulling out a thorn, however, but putting on a shoe, the second incidentally, every now and then there's the sound of a lift, but I'm not even sure if this sound of a lift doesn't come only from memory, the memory of a night, another one, it doesn't worry me, I merely see that my tie is still hanging over the chair, on the other hand my watch is on my wrist, yes, it's time, so I assume, time as always, time to set out into the future, I am resolved and shaved, actually gay, without exactly showing it, once again awake, free from longing, free, evidently I have meanwhile lit a cigarette, anyhow the smoke is making me blink, and if it isn't I who am smoking, I don't know who is smoking, I only know when my plane leaves, a Caravelle I hope, yes, the weather, I'll see about that once I've left this room, I mustn't leave anything behind, no words now either that remain behind, no thoughts, I'm sitting on the edge of a bed tying my right shoe, I've had an idea for half an eternity already . . . for a moment, now before I put my foot down on the carpet, I pause: again and again, I know it already and yet I am startled into immobility, I am Enderlin, I shall die as Enderlin.

So I drive out to the airport.

In the taxi, my hand in the shabby loop, I see outside the world, shop fronts, advertisements, monuments, buses—

Déjà vu!

I try to think something.

For instance:

What I could have said the other day during our conversation about Communism and capitalism, about China, about Cuba, about atomic death and about mankind's food situation in the event of its multiplying tenfold, particularly about Cuba, I was in Cuba once—but now I'm here, being asked how many cases I have, as I show Enderlin's passport and am given a green card, *Flight Number Seven-O-Five*, the plane is late, I hear, due to fog over Hamburg, while here the sun is shining.

Will she confess to her husband?

Enderlin is not the only one waiting here, and I try to entertain him, which isn't easy, because he is secretly thinking of the night, and I can't think of anything to say about that—

A model airport!

I buy newspapers:

Another atom bomb test!

—Enderlin can't think of anything to say about that.

Will he confess to anyone?

I try to think something—this inner life of love, to tell the truth, is boring, too familiar—for example, how this hall is constructed, reinforced concrete, the shape is convincing, stylish, light and floating. Beautiful. As regards the construction: in technical language, I believe, that's called a three-pinned arch . . . but Enderlin isn't interested in that, I see, Enderlin would like to fly. The faster, the better. Enderlin is once more passing the time left to him on earth with coffee, later with cognac. His luggage has been handed in, so I am free and unencumbered, apart from his briefcase, which I put on the counter. I look round: other people are now flying to Lisbon, others to London, others are coming from Zurich, loudspeakers are booming: *This is our last call,* but not for Enderlin. I reassure him, I heard it quite clearly. Enderlin is jumpy, I am merely bored, because it really is impossible to have a conversation with Enderlin. I make sure I don't forget his briefcase. Enderlin buys perfume, in order not to go home empty-handed, Chanel 5, I know that. Is Enderlin really thinking of his home? Anyhow Chanel 5. Others are called for Rome-Athens-Cairo-Nairobi, while there is evidently still fog in Hamburg, yes, it's boring. . .

I imagine hell:

I'm Enderlin, whose briefcase I am carrying, but immortal, so that I have to live through his life again, or if you like only a part of his life, a year, if you like even a happy year, for example the year that is just beginning, to live through it again in the full knowledge of what is coming and without the expectation that is alone capable of making life bearable, without the openness, the uncertainty compounded of hope and fear. I imagine it as hellish. Once again: your conversation in the bar, gesture by gesture, his hand on her arm, the way she looks at him, his hand that for the first time strokes her forehead, later a second time, your conversation about fidelity, about Peru, which he describes as a land of hope, everything word by word, first of all the talk about the opera, which you then miss, the whistles from a night-time goods station, whistles and echoes of whistles, and nothing can be skipped, not a sound, not a kiss, not a feeling and not a silence, not a fright, not a cigarette, not a visit to the kitchen to fetch water that won't quench your thirst, no shame, not even the telephone conversation from the bed, everything over again, minute by minute, and we know what follows, we know and have to live it again, otherwise it's death, live without hope of things happening differently, the business of the key in the letterbox, you know it will go off all right, afterwards the public wash at the fountain, the workmen's bar, sawdust on the stone floor, not one minute is different from the way I know it was, not a minute is left out, not a step and not an espresso and not the four rolls, the wet handkerchief in my trouser pocket, Enderlin waves, it's the same taxi, but I know that later he will get out to feed pigeons, all that over again, including the fright with the note, the mistake, the melancholy, the sleep accompanied by pneumatic drills tearing up the sunlit surface of a street outside, and later the waiting at the airport, *Flight Number Seven-O-Five*, fog at Hamburg, and what follows: Goodbye in the hope that there will be no story, reunion, end and embrace, parting, letters and reunion in Strassburg, difficulties on all sides, passion, enchantment with no future, yes, with no future—but I know the future: the happiness in Colmar (after looking at the Isenheim Altar and on the way to Ronchamp) is neither your last, as you fear, nor your highest; nevertheless, it has to be lived again, just as it was, including the goodbye in Basle, the goodbye for ever, just as it was, yes, but with the knowledge of what follows. All the presents you gave each other have to be given over again, packed and tied with ribbon again, undone and admired and thanked for with delight. Misunderstandings that ruin half a journey have to take place again, quarrels about which you cannot laugh until later, everything has to be thought and felt again, every conversation spoken again, although I know how often it will be repeated, and the same letters have to be taken out of the letterbox again, torn open with a beating heart, and all plans have to be planned again in the knowledge of how differently things will turn out, for weeks you look for a plot of land, you negotiate, you buy and have worries that prove unnecessary, hopes that fill you with bliss, I know that nothing will ever be built, nevertheless the plot of land has to be measured, all for the birds, but you can't change destiny, although you know it, and again I go to the door and cordially greet the man who comes between us, again I ask what he would like, whisky or gin, again my jokes, my suspicion, my magnanimity, my innocent victory, again your trip when the car broke down, my worried night, again the familiar times of indifference, I write him my greetings again on a picture postcard, those moody greetings that I wrote without knowing, just the same, but now I know, and again the coffee boils, only to grow cold after your confession, I know, I know, and yet I have to curse again and stride up and down the room and curse, just the same, once again the glass that shatters against the wall, the pieces that I sweep up, just the same, yes, but everything with the knowledge of what happens next: without the curiosity as to what happens next, without the blind expectation, without the uncertainty that makes everything bearable—

That would be hell.

Enderlin, leafing through a newspaper, pretends not to be listening; the situation is tense; he enjoys not knowing what will be in the paper tomorrow, not knowing for sure—

That would be hell.

Experience is a foretaste of it, but only a foreteaste; my experience doesn't tell me what is going to happen, it merely reduces my expectation, my curiosity—

Flight Number Seven-O-Five.

The plane has just landed, I heard, and will be taking off again in half an hour, and now I'm curious after all to see what Enderlin will do; whether he will really fly without ringing her again, without seeing her again.

You don't want a story.

You don't want a past, don't want any repetition.

Enderlin, I see, is now paying for his cognacs, there were three of them, the barman knows that, Enderlin pretends to be in a hurry, and yet there's another half an hour before passengers can go aboard, and even the man who hasn't made up his mind can be in a hurry . . . I see the plane, a Caravelle, that is just having its tank filled. A fine plane. In two hours Enderlin will be at home, if he really flies. What does at home mean? Anyhow the plane is having its tank filled, time to sit down again, to cross his legs, even to open his briefcase and take out a book; anyway, the beginning is good, in my opinion. A technical book that Enderlin would have to read in any case, and he will read it too, no doubt about that, perhaps in the plane, if Enderlin really flies, and at home there's post waiting for him, no doubt about that, perhaps very pleasant post. . .

Let's hope she never writes!

Now, so I imagine, she is no longer lying in that bed either, but has dressed in clothes Enderlin has never seen, a pair of slacks perhaps; she is convinced that Enderlin is already soaring high above the clouds, and for her part falls from the clouds when his phone call comes.

"Where are you?"

"Here," he says. "At the airport."

Outside there is a booming, the sound of jets, and also the loudspeakers, which, however, are not called Enderlin, there's time to talk, much too much time; there's nothing to say. . .

I knew it.

When Enderlin leaves the glass booth, determined to fly, I see that our Caravelle is still taking in petrol; the white-clad mechanics are still on the plane, and the doll's face with a blue tie and raspberry-red lips and a little blue cap on silver-blonde hair, a stewardess from whom Enderlin makes enquiries, can't alter the fact that it is indeed (I knew it) our Caravelle that is still taking in petrol. The luggage is just being loaded on to a conveyor belt. More determined than ever not to see her again, the woman who is occupying his feelings, Enderlin is the first to take up a position in Front of *Gate Number Three,* alone, glancing at his wrist-watch, which he compares with the public clock in the hall, as though every half minute mattered— as though he were making an escape. . .

I understand his escape from the future.

Beware of names!

Sooner or later comes the day when you know what to talk about, even if it is only that you say whom you met yesterday, an acquaintance whose name you mention because it is of no importance. You are still the only reality far and wide, other people are puppets of your mood; you still hold the strings in your hands and anyone who would disturb the situation just doesn't come into your conversation, or comes into it in such a way that he doesn't disturb it. You are still careful and say: a Pole, a refugee, who lived with us and was my sister's boy friend. Or: my first husband. Or: a colleague of mine; an aunt of mine; a young girl I once met on the Via Appia. All nameless. This is all right for a time, then it becomes too complicated, and the doctor who is my friend becomes Burri. Why should I conceal his name? That's the man who always comes to play chess. The process goes on, names are like weeds, the seed spreads in all directions and the jungle grows; you don't see it yet; you go on talking, until suddenly Burri has a former wife. Anita? You laugh: how small the world is! You lie on your backs and chat about Anita, who now was Scholl's mistress, and Scholl is the first person you both know, Hannes Scholl, who went to Baghdad. You lie on your backs and smoke. How is Scholl getting on in Baghdad, you wonder. You never bothered about it before, but now it is a pretext to talk, and it's strange to think that suddenly there is someone in the world, even if a long way from here where you are lying side by side on your backs, who knows you both without having the least idea that you are a couple. What would Scholl have to say about it! It's strange how often henceforth you talk about this Scholl—till one day he writes from Baghdad that he is coming back to Europe soon. He writes to both of you, each of you, since he knows you both and would like to see you both. Is that necessary? The process continues, it's impossible to prevent the circle from forming; the best thing would be to lie where you are and say nothing, but that's impossible. Every now and then you go out into the street and a man named Hagen says good morning to you. How do you know this Hagen? He's a friend of her brother's. You've got a brother? One ought to flee. Where to? Ibiza is no longer what it used to be. When were you in Ibiza? One ought to go to Africa. You laugh! I know a man who has a farm near Nairobi and is scared of Mau-Mau, his name is Ramsegger, you've guessed it, James Ramsegger. How do you know his name? His wife didn't want to go to Nairobi, which you can understand, and is now living in London with a Pole who has also cropped up in your conversations already; now his name is Vladimir, and since he's in the ballet it can only be the same Vladimir whom I know through Frau Löwbeer. Isn't that funny? I don't mention Frau Löwbeer; but a dressmaker, as an advertisement, tells you she also works for Frau Löwbeer. Is that necessary? Unexpectedly everything hangs together, and the future turns out to be the past. You lie on your backs and smoke, in order not to mention any names. In vain! In Vienna there's a concert in a private house; her brother is playing the first violin and I am introduced to him. Is that necessary? In Strassburg, when you meet for a secret weekend, Frau Löwbeer steps out of the lift that is to take you to your room. Nothing fails to happen. Even Burri, the man whose name wasn't mentioned, now enters into the service of the demons; suddenly at a party he meets the woman who loves Enderlin and talks to her about Enderlin, his friend. Why is that necessary? You lie on your backs and smoke and tell each other your past, just so that the world, that has no idea about you, shan't know more about it than you do yourselves; this brings further names to light. Pity! The demons scarcely let a week pass without catching you: Scholl, back from Baghdad, forces you to have your first lunch *à trois*. Further: the professor who has just got half the Nobel Prize for chemistry and stares out of every newspaper is her father. Further: on the occasion of a private view, which is unavoidable, you are at last introduced to each other in public; her husband, who has no idea, is also there; the ever-cheerful Frau Löwbeer arrives later— etc.

Mankind seems to be a family, as soon as one is a couple; everyone else seems to know one another in this way or that, and only the couple, who have come from making love, don't yet know each other from outside; you still smile, because no one who knows you has any idea; you still walk upon soles that do not touch the ground. For how long? Every third person encircles you; every dream is ground down.

Flight Seven-O-Five.

Enderlin (I see him looking out through the glass pane, his face in the blue reflection of the pane) is now no longer the only one waiting; a whole herd, all with green or red cards in their hands, is crowding in front of the doll's face of the stewardess, who isn't allowed to open the door yet; Enderlin is no longer at the front—

He is still free to choose.

I'm in favour of flying.

At last the door opens and the herd moves, some hurry, others wave back, the doll's face repeats:

Flight Seven-O-Five.

I can imagine both:

Enderlin flies.

Enderlin stays.

I'm gradually getting tired of this game that I now know: to act or not to act, and in any case I know it is only a part of my life, and the other part I must imagine; action and inaction are interchangeable; sometimes I act merely because inaction, equally possible, also makes no difference to the fact that time is passing, that I am growing older . . .

So Enderlin stays.

I don't . . .

Why he and not I?

Or the other way round:

Why I?

Either way:

One will fly—

One will stay—

It's all the same:

The one who stays imagines how it would have been if he had flown, and the one who flies imagines how it would have been if he had stayed, and what he really experiences, either way, is the split that runs through his person, the split between me and him, whatever I do, either way—unless the Caravelle, which now has a free runway and is starting to move, for some inexplicable reason explodes and the bodies are identified; but our Caravelle, I see, is climbing and climbing . . .

I imagine:

In the taxi, his hand in the loop, Enderlin is proud that he hasn't chosen inaction, at the same time bewildered; his body is sitting in the taxi, but desire has left his body—it is with me, as I fly, high above the clouds—and Enderlin doesn't really know why he is going to this woman, who suddenly has no present any more; the only present is the endless drive into the town, bumper to bumper, Enderlin is sitting as though he were in a hurry, and the driver, eyes to the front, as though the future were always in front, is doing all he can to move forwards, while Enderlin, now lighting a cigarette, is secretly glad of every red light, every convoy, every delay; there's no hurry about the past . . .

I imagine:

my fingers touching her forehead for the first time; her surprised face that no longer exists, not like that . . .

I imagine:

Enderlin after paying his taxi, confused for a moment because he has no luggage, horrified, as though it had been stolen, his luggage that is now flying over the clouds, but then reassured and positively delighted to be without luggage, but at a loss, but with both feet on the ground, actually on the pavement, so that really nothing can happen to him, Enderlin doesn't know exactly where he is in the unfamiliar city, but roughly, Enderlin remembers the kiosk, provided it's the same one, and if he doesn't now go in the wrong direction her house can't be far way, Enderlin calls himself an ass, he could have gone there in the taxi, but no, he suddenly told the driver to stop, obviously in the belief that he could still choose inaction. So why does he need to find her house, yes, why? Enderlin at the kiosk: he asks the way to her street, so as not to go there, but they don't know, obviously it's a different kiosk, and Enderlin is really at a loss. Why didn't he fly! All the same, Enderlin recognizes the advantage in not having (like me) to eat on the plane, and it's a pity he hasn't my hunger; Enderlin has the choice of eating French or Italian, even Chinese, because he has plenty of time, a whole evening in a foreign town, no one knows where Enderlin is at this moment, even she doesn't know, since he isn't going to call on her, he doesn't even know himself, no, the kiosk is the same, but the bar next to it is missing. Why is he walking? He might just as well sit down on the pavement. Why doesn't he simply go into a restaurant? Suddenly everything is so senseless, including eating, when one isn't hungry, I understand; Enderlin strolls not to look for her house, but to find it by chance. Until he has, he can't sit alone in a restuarant and read the menu, the wine list, to celebrate having seen her house again— without ringing the bell . . .

I imagine:

Her house from outside . . .

Enderlin hasn't seen it from outside before, not yesterday, when he went in to fetch her for the opera, it was just any house, not yet a monument, and this morning, when Enderlin left it, he must have seen the front door with its brass fittings, but afterwards he didn't look back; really all Enderlin remembers is the front door.

I imagine:

The front stucco, four storeys, string courses of sandstone, built in the eighteeneth or seventeenth century, renovated (I know there's a lift inside) in the spirit of the preservation of ancient monuments, height of each storey aristocratic except on the fourth floor, gargoyles, roof with pantiles; light in places on the fourth floor—

Or:

The front faced, travertine, height of each storey democratic, a modern building but with a tiled roof to tone in with the Old City, on the ground floor is a confectioner's that surprises me; the string courses of sandstone are on the next house, so are the gargoyles; a front door with pointed arches, probably built in the fifties of our century, reinforced concrete, but lacking the shapes of modern architecture; light in places on the fourth floor—

Or:

The house has no fourth floor at all (I'm sure it was on the fourth floor) on this side and one can't walk round the house; a front that was once genteel, now dilapidated, Biedermeier, later devalued by the proximity of the goods station with its whistling and puffing, business nameplates on the first and second floors, mullioned windows; light in places on the third floor—

Possibly:

A postman, who is just coming out of the door, asks Enderlin, speechless, pretends to have come to the wrong place and walks on—without even saying thank you . . .

(Possible but not probable.)

Certainly:

I remember the swaying reflection of a streetlamp in the wind, swaying all night long, reflection in the curtains and on the ceiling, to be exact: when the streetlamp didn't sway its light didn't pass over the balustrade of the window, and only when the wind blew did the public light beat into our room like spray into a ship, and in the reflection from the ceiling lay a woman, that's to say, looked at from outside it will be the windows just above this streetlamp, whether they're on the third or the fourth floor . . .

I imagine:

Enderlin has rung the bell.

(—while I in the plane, wedged in between strange elbows with the familiar tray in front of me, am just taking the knife and fork and spoon out of the cellophane, looking at the oxtail soup and cold chicken and fruit salad.)

I imagine:

An evening without lovemaking, for a long time not even a kiss, you are meeting from outside, which forces you to make conversation, until you scarcely misunderstand each other any more, yes, it's terrifying . . .

I order wine.

We are flying, according to a handwritten report from our captain, 9,000 meters above sea level at an average speed of 800 kilometers per hour.

The wine is too cold.

I imagine:

Your wine is warmer. . .

I drink mine nevertheless.

I imagine:

You are living, you people on earth. . .

The stewardess, when she finally takes my tray, is smiling. Why? They always smile, one knows that, and they're always young, even if ten years have passed between the cigarette I have just finished and the next which I light from it.

I imagine:

Ten years—

I imagine:

So there you rest, a couple with bodies dead to love all night long in your joint bedroom, apart from short trips like this one. So there you live. Whether it is a flat or a house, furnished in this way or that, probably a mixture of antique and modern with the usual Japanese-made lamp, in any case there is a shared bathroom, the daily sight of utensils for the varying care of two bodies, one female, one male. Sometimes you are filled with longing. Neither of you has anyone with whom you are more familiar, no, not even in memory; not even in hope. Can one be more closely linked than you? One cannot. But sometimes you are filled with longing. What for? It makes you shudder. What does? You live through the endless, swiftly passing years lovingly, a couple, tenderly, without showing your feelings before your guests, because you really are loving and tender, a real couple with two bodies dead to love that rarely seek each other again. Only after a trip perhaps, a separation for the duration of a congress, does it happen that in broad daylight, soon after getting back, before the cases have been unpacked and the essential news exchanged, you make love. What business is that of other people's?

It's refreshing, but it's not worth a confession. Then once again, as in the old days, you have an hourless day in a dressing-gown and with gramophone records. Then again the gentle disappearance of all curiosity on both sides, not uttered and scarcely shown; only camouflaged behind the demands of the day. Thus you live away your lives. Your letters, when you happen to be separated, almost frighten you, fill you with bliss, as you write with a storm of forgotten words, in a language you have ceased to speak. From an hotel room with an empty double bed you ring each other up, cost no object, from London or Hamburg or Sils, to chat in the middle of the night, urgent with love. Then you hear your past voices once again and tremble. Until you meet again at home. What remains is affection, the quiet and deep and almost unshakable affection. Is that nothing? You have survived almost everything, except the end, it's nothing new to you that one of you runs off in the middle of the night, that anger breaks out again, that it doesn't help if you don't speak to each other for two days, you're a couple, at any time free, but a couple. There's nothing much to be done. Often there comes the thought: why just you? You look round for other men, for other women. Not much comes into consideration, or everything. Nothing will be wilder than your love in the old days, at best it will be just the same. Was it wild? You don't speak about that. In tender protection of the present. Or else with reproach, which is false like every reproach against life. Who can help habituation? How it once was is known only to a mirror in an impossible hotel room, a rusty-silvery-smoky mirror that never stops showing a pair of lovers, many-armed, man and woman, nameless, two bodies drunk with love. Which of you saw it remains a secret. Both? That wasn't you two in particular. Why does it pursue you, what that mirror shows? It might be another man, another woman, you know that and look at each other, you two in particular, trying to achieve magnanimity through irony, in vain. How can you bear the fact that you understand each other so well, better and better, so sexlessly, as though you weren't still, seen as bodies, a man and a woman? Then you suddenly seek grounds for jealousy. Without it, God knows, your deadly comradeship would be complete. A stupid incident on the beach, a natural, easy embrace among pine trees, which remain the unforgettable thing about it, an infidelity that happened years ago, cursed in anguish, then of course forgotten, her name or his name is preserved in silence like the Crown Jewels, uttered only in extreme conversations, hence rarely, once or twice a year, so that it shan't get worn out like the love of your bodies. Oh that name! It alone produces once more the wild feeling for the other one, the sweet, the hot, the immoderate feeling, or at least the reverse side of it. The rest is affection, a great blessing really; only madness dares shake it with sudden suspicion during a sleepless night. Then what is wrong? You pretend to be tired, you put out the light, because what can be wrong? Then, while the other is asleep again, you make plans of the sort prisoners make, during the night you are resolved to take action, to break out, recklessly and childishly, it isn't desire but the longing for desire; then you pack your bags. One time she, another time he. It balances itself out. Adultery doesn't lead far, it remains part of marriage. You are a couple, fundamentally certain that you will never more lose each other, a couple with bodies dead to love, and it's no good packing your bags; a phone call by the beloved voice is enough to make you turn back, to confess or not; then you live in the everyday again, which is truth, with pyjamas and a toothbrush in your foamy mouth in front of the other, with classical nakedness in the bath that does not excite, intimate, you talk in the bathroom about the guests who have just left, and about the intellectual world that links you. You understand each other, without having to agree. You are alive, you develop your views, but you know each other's body as one knows one's furniture; then you go to bed, because it's two o'clock again and tomorrow is a strenuous day. Now isn't Now, but Always. There are moments of excitement, tender excitement, but one of you is tired or full of thoughts that are only now, whereas your bodies are always. Then you're alone in a house, the two of you, but you're often alone, so often. There's nothing to it. Marriage has got you again and you give each other a kiss that is like a full stop. You are filled with longing—not for each other, because you're both there, you long for something beyond each other, but you long jointly. You talk about a trip in autumn, a trip together, you suddenly long for a country that actually exists, you could go there in autumn. No one will stop you. You don't need a rope ladder in order to kiss, and no hiding place, and there are no nightingales and no lark to warn you it is time to leave, no myrmidons force you together, no prohibition, no fear that your amorous sin will be found out. You are approved of. All that prevents you is your bodies. Now you smoke another cigarette, you talk, you read the newspaper in bed. You don't enquire into your story; that is well known, so to speak. The calendar of your early times has long since been emended; a selection of names and dates and places, at first bold in its incompleteness, then carefully completed, has been closed for years. Why should you now, at two in the morning before a strenuous week-day, explore your past again? Confession with its joys has been used up, trust is complete, curiosity abandoned, the other's early life is a book you think you know as you know a classic, a bit dusty already and only when you move house and are faced with the empty rooms, which echo, do you pick up such books again and are surprised to find out who you have been living with all these years. You can't be surprised throughout all the years. Now you put out your cigarette. The past is no secret any longer, the present is thin because it is worn out day by day, and the future means growing old. . .

I am flying.

Please fasten your seat belts, we're coming in to land again, *stop smoking, thank you,* I not only stop smoking but also imagining, now is now, I wait for the usual bump as the plane touches down, that's the present, *we hope you have enjoyed your flight and that we shall see you again,* the present is already past again, *thank you.*

But I'm waiting with interest:

to see who has come to meet me at the airport.

I look:

if she has black hair and water-grey eyes, big eyes and lips that are full but never cover her upper teeth, and a tiny birth-mark behind her left ear, then it is I who didn't fly when it came to the point.

I'm growing older—

Via Appia Antica.

She could be my daughter, and there's no sense in our meeting again. I should like to, I've fallen for her, but there's no sense. We are standing on a Roman burial mound, afternoon, actually they're waiting for us in town. The whole time I see nothing but her eyes, a child, once I ask what she is thinking, and her eyes look at me and I know already that she is not a child. We dare not sit down on the summery earth lest we become a couple. I don't kiss her. There's no sense, we both know that, it doesn't have to be. In order to do something, she looks for a clover, a four-leaved one, as is appropriate to moments of happiness; but in vain. An aeroplane is droning in the sky; our gaze remains in the branches of the pine. With her leather bag hung on her shoulder and a three-leaved clover in her hand, she stands and turns round in the wind, which rumples her hair, and looks out over the brown countryside, Campagna with proliferating suburbs, which would have provided a pretext to talk about town-planning; she keeps silent. I give her a resinous pine cone. I really can't guess what she is thinking and repeat my question. She says: The same as you! But I'm not thinking anything. Her eyes: they are shining with present that can't be touched. Where shall we now throw these resinous pine cones? Once I jokingly press her head to my head, without kissing, and we both laugh. What about? There is simply no target for our resinous pine cones; so we take them with us. No doubt people can see us from far away, as we stand on this burial mound, a man and a girl, now arm in arm. Jokingly? For something to say I say: Shall we go? Because of the climb, I take her bag, she gives me her hand, sticky with resin, once I take hold of her foot, because it doesn't find the foothold between the tufts of dry grass, and then we are at the bottom, clap the dry earth from our hands longer than necessary. In the car, after we have been driving for quite a while, with the roof down, so that she can bathe her reddish hair in the wind, I ask for her address just as I am changing gear, that's to say casually. And she writes it down on a letter from my pocket. I drive slowly, because of the old Roman road surface. Now, as she looks at me silently from the side, I could say something about the road surface: about the legions who marched over this surface, the thousands of years and so on. I don't say it, because I've said it often before. On the other hand I ask: What can one do with a daydream? as we are held up by a red light, my hand on the quivering gear lever, and she answers: Take it! And then, after I have changed gear, we drive on—

Basta!

Today I threw away the pine cone, which was still lying in my car, because it had no scent any more, and her address too; one day I shall see her again, I know that, by chance in the street, a young woman, chatting animatedly about this and that, about her marriage and so on.

* * *

I'm sitting in a bar, afternoon, so I'm alone with the barman, who is telling me his life story. A first-class raconteur! I'm waiting for

someone. As he rinses the glasses he says: That's how it was. I drink.
So it was a true story. I believe you, I say. He dries the rinsed glasses.
Yes, he says again, that's how it was. I drink and envy him—not for
having been a prisoner of war in Russia, but for his doubt-free
relationship to his story . . .

"H'm," he says. "Just listen to that rain again!"

I don't respond to this, but drink.

"Every story is an invention," I say after a while, without on that
account doubting the horrors of being a prisoner of war in Russia,
as a general principle: "every ego that expresses itself in words is a
rôle—"

"Herr Doktor," he says, "another whisky?"

Herr Doktor!

"Our greed for stories," I say and notice that I have already drunk
a great deal; this is evident from the fact that I don't finish my
sentences, but assume that I have been understood thanks to my
insight: "—perhaps a man has two or three experiences," I say, "two
or three experiences at the outside, that's what a man has had when
he tells stories about himself, when he tells stories at all: a pattern of
experience—but not a story," I say, "not a story." I drink, but my
glass is empty. "One can't see oneself, that's the trouble, stories only
exist from outside," I say, "hence our greed for stories." I don't
know whether the barman is listening to me after being six years in
the Urals, and take a cigarette in order to be independent. "Have
you a story?" I ask, after he has just told me what he obviously
considers to be his story, and say: "I haven't one." I smoke—I watch
him take my empty glass from the zinc, dip it in the rinsing water,
and pick up another, a fresh, dry one. I can't prevent him from
pouring me another whisky: precisely because I'm watching I can't
prevent him . . . I think of the man on the Kesch, a story which until
today I have never told anyone, although it pursues me constantly,
the story of a murder I didn't commit. I twist my glass round as I ask:

"Have you ever been on the Kesch?"

"Kesch," he asks, "what's that?"

"Piz Kesch," I say, "a mountain."

"No," he says. "Why?"

Nonsense! I think. Why should he be the man I met in 1942 on
the Kesch? I fall silent. Nonsense. I drink.

"Sooner or later everyone invents for himself a story which he regards as his life," I say, "or a whole series of stories," I say, but I'm too drunk really to follow my own thoughts and this annoys me, so that I fall silent.

I'm waiting for someone.

"I knew a man," I say, in order to talk about something else, "a milkman, who came to a bad end. He ended up in a lunatic asylum, although he didn't think he was Napoleon or Einstein; on the contrary, he definitely thought he was a milkman. And he looked like a milkman. In his spare time he collected stamps, but that was the only fanatical streak he had; he was a captain in the Fire Brigade, because he was so reliable. In his youth, I believe, he was a gymnast, anyhow a healthy and peaceable man, widower, teetotal, and no one in our community would ever have guessed that he would one day have to be put in a lunatic asylum." I smoke. "His name was Otto," I say. "Otto." I smoke. "The ego this good man had invented for himself remained uncontested all his life long, especially as it demanded no sacrifices from his environment; on the contrary," I say, "he brought milk and butter into every house. For twenty-one years. Even on Sundays. We children loved him, because he often used to let us ride on his three-wheeler," I smoke. I go on with my story: "It was one evening in spring, a Saturday, as Otto, smoking his pipe as all through the years, was standing on the balcony of his detached house, which, although it was on the village street, had so much little garden round it that the pieces couldn't hurt anybody. You see, for reasons unknown even to himself, Otto suddenly seized a flowerpot, a geranium if I'm not mistaken, and threw it pretty well vertically down into his little garden, which immediately caused not only broken pieces, but also a sensation. All the neighbours immediately turned their heads; they were standing on their balconies, in their shirtsleeves just like him, enjoying their Saturday, or in their little gardens watering the flowers, and they all immediately turned their heads. This public sensation, it seems, so vexed our milkman that he hurled all the flowerpots, seventeen in number, down into the little garden, which after all, like the flower-pots themselves, was entirely his own property. Nevertheless they took him away. After that Otto was considered mad. And no doubt he was," I say. "It was impossible to talk to him any more." I smoke, while my barman gives a suitable smile, though he isn't sure what I'm getting at. "Well," I say, stubbing out my cigarette in the ashtray on the bar counter, "his ego was worn out, that can happen, and he couldn't think of another one. It was horrible."

I don't know whether he understands me.

"Yes," I say, "that's how it was."

I take my next cigarette.

I'm waiting for someone—

My barman gives me a light.

"I knew a man," I say, "another one, who didn't end up in a lunatic asylum," I say, "although he lived completely and utterly in fantasy." I smoke. "He imagined he was dogged by bad luck, a decent man, but one for whom everything went wrong. We were all sorry for him. No sooner had he saved up some money than there was devaluation. And it went like that all the time. No tile ever fell from the roof when he wasn't passing. The invention that one is dogged by bad luck is one of the favourites, because it's comfortable. Not a month passed for this man without his having cause for complaint, not a week, scarcely a day. Anyone who knew him a bit was afraid to ask: How are things? And yet he didn't really complain, he merely smiled about his legendary bad luck. And in fact things were always happening to him that other people were spared. Simply bad luck, there was no denying it, in big things as in small. And all the time he bore it manfully," I say and smoke "—till the miracle happened." I smoke and wait until the barman, mainly occupied with his glasses, has asked what kind of a miracle. "It was a blow for him," I say, "a real blow, when this man won the big prize in the lottery. It was in the newspaper, so he couldn't deny it. When I met him in the street he was pale, dumbfounded, he didn't doubt his invention that he was a man dogged by bad luck, but he did doubt the lottery, in fact the world altogether. It was no laughing matter, he actually had to be comforted. In vain. He couldn't grasp the fact that he was not dogged by bad luck, wouldn't grasp it and was so confused that on his way back from the bank he actually lost his wallet. And I believe he preferred it that way," I say. "Otherwise he would have had to invent a different ego for himself, the poor fellow, he couldn't have gone on seeing himself as a man dogged by bad luck. Another ego is more expensive than the loss of a full wallet, of course; he would have had to abandon the whole story of his life, live through all its events again and differently, since they would no longer have gone with his ego—"

I drink.

"Shortly afterwards his wife deceived him too," I say. "I felt sorry for the man, he really was dogged by bad luck."

I smoke.

Outside it is still raining. . . . I no longer know what it was I was trying to say with this story and I look at my barman. Perhaps it is him after all? I think, although he denies it; I can't remember any more what he looked like, my man on the Kesch, perhaps for that reason I shall never get rid of him; I smoke, think about it in silence, smoke.

That was in 1942, a Sunday in April or May, we were stationed at Samaden, Grisons, a cloudless day, I had weekend leave, but I didn't go home, I wanted to be away from people and went up into the mountains. Actually, soldiers on leave were strictly forbidden to go into the mountains alone, because of the danger; but I went notwithstanding, and up the Piz Kesch. I had spent the night in a hay barn, where it was cold as hell, no hay, draught blowing through a clear, starry night; I wanted to avoid the Kesch hut, because there were probably officers there to whom I, a simple gunner, would have had to report my destination, which was just what I didn't want to do. What I wanted was real leave, leave from all compulsion to report. Since I was as cold as hell all night, I was up and about early, long before sunrise; against the grey scree of the mountainside no one could see me, field-grey as I was, and I climbed pretty quickly, and when I reached the snow it was still crisp and hard. I rested on the Kesch Gap just as the sun was rising, not a soul in sight, I breakfasted on dry Ovomaltine. I had an ice ax with me, that was why I hadn't wanted to be seen by anyone in the valley, a lone climber with an ice ax. I was glad to have this shiny little ax; I might have managed without it, since the ice quickly softened in the sun, but in the shade I had to cut steps. I had taken off my floppy battle tunic and slung it from my belt; every now and then I stopped and peered round to see if anyone was coming, an officer perhaps. Once on the peak, they couldn't stop me any more, I thought, at most they might ask if I didn't know the regulation and then say no more about it, moved by the comradeship between fellow mountaineers. But I saw no one, anyhow not on the snowfield, and when I wasn't actually hacking away with my ax I heard nothing either. I was as much alone as on the moon. I heard chunks of snow rolling down over the rocks, nothing else, from time to time the ring of my ax against the sharp rocks, wind, nothing else, wind over the chine. Later, when I reached the peak, I found myself alone with the cross on the summit, happy. It was getting warmer and warmer, and after I had built up a shelter of loose stones behind which I was out of the wind, I actually took off my sweaty shirt and rolled my tunic into a pillow. Later I slept, tired after the night, I don't know how long; at least I shut my eyes and dozed, having no other plans. The man who had suddenly spoken to me, a civilian—he said *Grüssi!* which he imagined to be Swiss; obviously a German—didn't want to disturb me, as he said, when he saw my amazement; but naturally I immediately sat up, at first without saying a word. He had evidently been here some time; he put down his rucksack a little way away. I said good morning, as I rose to my feet so that we were now standing side by side. He wanted to know, a pair of field-glasses to his face, which was the Bernina. You're a soldier! he said, when he saw my impossible drainpipe trousers, with a certain smile, and as I showed him what he wanted to know I soon noticed how well he knew the district. A lover of the Engadine obviously, a foreigner, but a connoisseur; at least he was familiar with the names, Bernina and Palü and Rosatsch, but also with the names of the villages down in the valley. He was carrying a map in the approved manner, although maps had been confiscated at that time, and also a Leica. His stubborn insistence on imitating our national speech and making it sound like a form of baby talk, an attempt to curry favour without any talent for catching the alien intonation, patronisingly benevolent without noticing that it set my teeth on edge, did more to make conversation difficult than the wind. Naturally I answered in High German, even if with an Alemannic accent, but without success. He even knew what a kitchen cupboard was in Swiss: *Chuchichäschtli.* This in passing; it had nothing to do with the conversation. A lot of soldiers here, yes. He was trying hard, I could see, to take my military uniform seriously. Perhaps the embarrassment is my fault, I thought, as he offered me his field-glasses, and in return I offered him my waterbottle, filled with Veltliner. I now saw through his field-glasses that he had used my tracks. No one else came. I thanked him for the field glasses. He stayed for about half an hour, and we chatted above all about the mountains, also about the flora, of which he spoke in a tone of great appreciation. I had an inhibition (why, actually?) against looking him in the face, as though prepared for some tactless remark that embarrassed me in advance, and I couldn't think of much to say. I don't know what he thought of me, anyhow he thought me gauche; he was very surprised indeed when it turned out that I knew Berlin. The more fluently the conversation now went, more fluently because he reverted to his own natural intonation, the more urgently I waited for the moment when he would pick up his rucksack. My advice as to how he could best get down to the Madulein proved superfluous. He had spent the night in the Kesch hut, which he praised as though I had built it. A lot of officers, yes, very nice lads. I left it to the wind to answer his question as to whether we were trained in mountaineering. That he would get to Madulein by four, he left me in no doubt. All the same, he now packed his rucksack, not without bequeathing me an apple. I felt somewhat ashamed. An apple up there was something. After he had buckled on his rucksack, I was no longer prepared for it; we had already shaken hands when he was seized by that outburst of frankness the exact wording of which I have forgotten. The Reich, that was enough for me; the meaning was plain. I said nothing, nor did I contradict him; I simply stood in silence, my hands in the pockets of my field-grey drainpipe trousers, which I hated, looking out over the land which soon, as he said, would also belong to the Reich. What I saw: rock, blackish, in places also reddish, snow in the midday light and scree, slopes covered in grey scree, then meadows, treeless, stony, streams glittering in the sun, pastures, cattle that looked in the distance like tiny grubs, a valley with a wood and cloud shadows; close by, the black choughs. It was only after a while, after he had put away his Leica and finally disappeared round a rock with a cordial wave and wishing me a good time in the army, that I felt angry at not having told him to shut his trap and began to take an interest in his special characteristics; I now stepped out onto the projecting ledge, but too late: I didn't see him again until he came round the ridge, now a hundred feet below me, so that all I could see was his green felt hat. He slipped, but managed to steady himself; then he climbed more carefully. I shouted to him, to make him raise his face again; but he heard nothing. I wanted to tell him kindly not to dislodge stones. They kept rolling down, which obviously didn't worry him; he was up above. The more I forbade myself to get indignant about what he had said, the more wildly indignant I now became over the way this idiot climbed. Stones were rolling down again! I whistled through my fingers; he probably took it for the whistle of a marmot that would also soon belong to Hitler's Reich, and looked around. I stood out on the rock until he reached the Kesch Gap, a little black man in the snow; he was probably taking photographs again, anyhow he spent a long time tramping to and fro. I picked up my battle tunic, suddenly resolved to climb down and catch up with him. What for? I remained on the peak. All the same, I watched him till he left the snowfield, and went on watching him on the scree slope; on the meadow he was camouflaged by his loden jacket and I abandoned my senseless watching.

Later I fell asleep—

When I woke, probably because I was cold, I was dismayed by the thought: I pushed that man over the rocks. I knew I hadn't done it. But why didn't I? I hadn't dreamed it either; I merely woke with the waking thought: A push with the hand as he bent down for his rucksack would have been enough.

Then I ate his apple.

Of course I'm glad I didn't do it. It would have been murder. I have never talked to anyone about it, never, not even tête-à-tête, although I didn't do it . . . I saw no one far and wide. A few black choughs. No eye-witness. No one. Wind and no listening ear. That evening at Samaden during roll call I would have stepped into the back row, head to the right, dress by the right, hand on the seam, at attention, good and straight, afterwards I'd have drunk beer. No one would ever have noticed from looking at me, I don't think. Since then I have talked to a lot of murderers, in a dining car or during the interval at a concert or elsewhere; you can't tell by looking at them . . . When I had eaten the apple I stepped out onto the projecting ledge to see how far he would have fallen. A snowdrift, harshly glittering, then nothing. The choughs, black, were soaring soundlessly above the distant glacier, black and close. A low north wall, pretty well vertical. I looked at my watch; time to go down. I picked up my floppy battle tunic, belt, ice ax. The snow was now pretty soft, and I admit that I too occasionally sent a stone rolling down. By the time I reached the Kesch Gap I had really forgotten the man already. Apart from the fact that the descent in the soft snow at times demanded my full attention, I hardly need say that I also had thoroughly real worries which it was more sensible to think about, beginning with the beast of a sergeant-major, who would try to put me on guard duty again, but above all the profession that had been left at home, my profession wasn't soldiering. In the Kesch Gap in the afternoon light, when I saw his footprints running this way and that across the snow, I couldn't remember what he had really said up there, where now the white cross stood all alone on the summit, only that one could have done something that I hadn't done. And that, one might have thought, was the end of it; precisely because I didn't do it. But I was interested to see where he would most likely have fallen. Just to have a look. Although I had come to the little glacier, I trudged northwards under the Piz Kesch. not far; only to see; only a few steps. The snow here was so soft that I sank to my knees; I was sweating. I should have had skis. I knew the run down over the glacier. Without a pack and a carbine on one's back it must be magnificent. Right towards Sertig, left towards Bergün. I didn't get far trudging around; besides, it was time I was going. Three o'clock! By this time he must already be far below in the valley, taking a look at Madulein, on the other side of the watershed; if he walked as sturdily as he talked, he must already have reached the first pines. While I was here sinking up to my knees in the snow! All the same, I was now more or less under the low wall, and as I didn't know how I should feel at the sight of a shattered skull, I pondered in a matter-of-fact way on whether the man would really have fallen on this slope. I climbed up a few yards, to get a better view of the wall and also to be able to stand better; a chasm below me made me anxious. I was panting. Perhaps he might have got wedged among the rocks, only his Leica would have fallen in the snow, or perhaps not. Seen from nearby, it wasn't really a wall; probably he would have got stuck up above in the couloir. I didn't know why I was worried about what hadn't happened. Here, where the wind of the summits didn't reach, it was deathly quiet, only the soft dripping of melted snow, since the afternoon sun was now shining into the couloir. It was hot, and not for the first time I cursed our army's impractical battle tunic. The rock, now in the afternoon light, looked like amber, the sky overhead violet, the little glacier by contrast bluish, at least the cracks, the snow more like milk, only my deep footprints in it looked glassy blue. Everything motionless. Only the choughs, black, were soaring high overhead. The cross on the summit wasn't visible from here. I went back to the Kesch Gap. My hope of being able to slide in places was disappointed; I tried it again and again, but the snow was too mushy. I followed his tracks to the end of the snowfield, but even on the slaty rubble I could still make them out, marks of slipping, but also other marks, footprints like rubber stamps, I saw that he had first-class climbing-boots; it was only on the meadows that I lost his trail for good.

That was all.

That evening at Samaden, during roll call, I got into the back row, but in vain; I was put on guard duty, and there was nothing doing with the beer and nothing doing with sleep either, I had a hellish sunburn, fever. Although I slowly became convinced that the man on the Kesch was no harmless tourist I said nothing about it. I was on guard in the village square, so I had nothing to do but look, with my carbine on my arm, to look and see whether a green felt hat crossed the square. Naturally my belletristic hope was not fulfilled. I did sentry-go in vain, ten steps this way, ten steps that. At that time, 1942, there really weren't any tourists. I should have recognized him, but he didn't come through Samaden—

So forget it!

Forget what?

In the following years, as everyone knows, a great deal happened. Real things. I never thought of it again, it was no time for trifles, God knows, and certainly not for figments of the imagination, for imaginary murders, when, as I soon knew, there were enough of the other sort every day. So I thought no more about it and never told anyone about that blue Sunday on the Piz Kesch; it was too ridiculous. Nor did I ever go on the Piz Kesch again. Nevertheless, as it turned out later, I haven't forgotten it, whereas I have forgotten so much that I have really done. That's strange. It seems that more than anything else it is our real deeds that most easily slip our memories; only the world, since it knows nothing about my non-deeds, has a predilection for remembering my deeds, which really only bore me. The temptation to exaggerate one's deeds, whether good or evil, springs from this boredom. I can't bear to listen to anyone reminding me that I did this, that or the other, whether it is shameful or praiseworthy. It is only as an unforgettable future, even if I displace it into the past as an invention, a figment of the imagination, that my life doesn't bore me—as a figment of the imagination: if I had pushed the man on the Kesch over the cornice . . .

I didn't do it.

The hand of the law will not descend upon my shoulder.

So forget it!

Not till much later, while reading a newspaper, did I suddenly think of it again. I read there, among other things, that the Germans had planned to set up a concentration camp in the vicinity of Klosters, Grisons; the plans were ready, and it's safe to assume that such plans were not prepared without a thorough study of the terrain. Who reconnoitred the terrain round Klosters? Perhaps it was the man who, on that Sunday in 1942, also made an excursion to the Piz Kesch to enjoy the view, and whom I didn't push over the cornice—

I don't know.

I shall never find out who he was.

Another time I couldn't help thinking about it when Burri, then a young doctor, came back from Greece, where he had been working for the International Red Cross, and when he told us all the things he had seen, among other things how a starving Greek child, who tried to steal a loaf from a Wehrmacht car in the middle of Athens, was grabbed by a soldier and shot in the middle of the street. Naturally Burri had seen other things too; not every soldier merely shot a Greek child or a Polish child. I know that. I simply asked him what that particular soldier in Athens looked like, asked as though I might have recognized him—

What for?

We just chatted the way people do on the top of a mountain, like comrades, so to speak, two men who are the only ones for miles around, comradely but sparing with words, the continual wind of the peaks makes long sentences impossible. Without formalities, naturally, a handshake without any introduction. Both of them have reached this peak, that's enough; both have the same wide panorama. Handshake or no handshake, I don't even remember that for sure now; perhaps I kept my hands in my trouser pockets. Later I ate his apple, that's all, and looked down over the cornice. I know for sure what I didn't do. Perhaps he was a good fellow, a splendid fellow even; I keep telling myself to take the weight off my mind, that I didn't do it. Perhaps I've actually met him again, without knowing it, after the war, dressed differently and so that with the best will in the world we couldn't recognize each other again, and he is one of the many people whom I esteem, whom I couldn't like to be without. Only sometimes I'm so uncertain. Suddenly. And yet it's twenty years ago. I know it's ridiculous. Not to be able to forget an act one never performed is ridiculous. And I never tell anyone about it. And sometimes I completely forget him again . . .

Only his voice remains in my ear.

I empty my glass.

Time to pay.

"Yes," I say. "The Russians!"

My barman too, I see, has meanwhile been thinking of other things. . . His story of the Russian mine, linked by a short circuit with my story that didn't happen—forget it.

"Herr Doktor," he asks, "another whisky?"

"Tell me," I say, while he is emptying the ashtrays and running a wet rag over the zinc, which I have evidently dirtied with ash, "— have you ever been on the Piz Kesch?"

"No," he says. "You've already asked me that."

I've drunk too much. . . The lady who has meanwhile come in and reminds me with her searching look round that I have been waiting for somebody for an hour and a half is, I realize, the wife of this somebody, who has unfortunately had to leave town, and has come to apologize for him, as I slip down off my stool to take off her wet coat. To be polite. To show I forgive her husband. As a matter of course. Really I ought to apologize; I've quite forgotten to wait. To be polite:

"Will you have a drink?"

I am just a bit confused, because I've never seen her husband, who is in London while I ought to have been waiting for him, and I'm now seeing his wife.

"Is it still raining?" I ask.

Actually I was just going to settle up.

"But I don't want to keep you!" she says, sitting down on the stool at the bar. "I really don't want to keep you—"

"What will you have?" I ask.

"No," she says, "what a downpour!"

First she has to tidy her hair, and since she has evidently noticed that I have already drunk too much, she orders a ginger ale. What shall we talk about now? I immediately take her for an actress, I don't know why. I'm seeing this woman for the first time, probably also for the last time. In order not to be impolite, I don't enquire what she does for a living; she may actually be a well-known actress, and my question would be a downright insult. So I nibble pretzels, as many as I can get hold of from left and right, and listen as she tells me why Svoboda, her husband, has had to leave town, give her a light between whiles and accept her apology again with a wordless gesture. She smokes rather hurriedly as she talks about her husband. Her hair, wet with rain, gleams black. I am determined not to fall in love. Her eyes are blue and big. From time to time it is up to me to say something, in order not to appear awkward or sullen. My uncertainty whether to take her for an actress or not is making me feel more and more embarrassed, as she now, I don't know why, talks about Peru. I ask myself what part I would give this woman. My silence filled with glances manifestly gives her the feeling of being understood; anyhow, she too becomes rather embarrased. She drinks her ginger ale as though she were suddenly in a hurry. She doesn't want to keep the strange gentleman. I enquire about Peru, but she really doesn't want to keep the strange gentleman, she came to apologize for her Svoboda, and tries gradually to pay, which I don't allow. Certainly not! I say, and since Pepe, the barman, is now playing deaf and keeping in the background, we don't get round to paying and have to go on chatting. What about? I enquire about her husband, whom I should have met. Her husband, as I have said, is at present in London. Now, as though in response to an alarm signal, I am suddenly very sober; only the strange gentleman, whom she doesn't want to keep, is still drunk, not badly, but enough for me to differentiate myself from him. Peru, he says, is the land of hope! Whereas I think he's talking rubbish, she listens big-eyed; it seems to please her, so they chat about Peru, which I don't know. She has travelled through Peru with her husband. I have to confess something to myself, namely that there is rarely a woman whose conversation interests me if she doesn't interest me in some degree as a woman. That's why I keep watching her mouth. When I hear in passing that she is faithful, I don't know why she said that; I wasn't listening. Her face is lively and beautiful when she is speaking, and I watch her in silence (while the strange gentleman is speaking) smiling, till she blushes, tosses back her hair and carefully taps the almost non-existent ash from her cigarette, pretends to be deciphering an advertisement over the bar, *Johnnie Walker highest awards,* blinking her eyes, because her own smoke is rising into her face, *guaranteed same quality throughout the world,* her face well worth looking at from the side too, her hand not strange; even her hair, that most curious substance in a human being, does not strike me as strange. . . She looks at her tiny watch.

"Oh," she says, "three o'clock already!"

But I've got plenty of time.

Actually she has plenty of time too.

"Won't you really have a whisky?" I ask, and since Pepe, like every barman, is quick to sum people up, he has already taken a fresh glass, so all I can say is: "Two then."

I ask myself what's going to happen next—

Three in the afternoon is a terrible hour, an hour without a slope, flat and with no outlook. I remember my distant childhood, when I was ill in bed and it was three in the afternoon, picture books, stewed apple, eternity. . . . Simply for something to say, I ask whether she has any children, which is really none of my business. We watch the barman doing his stuff: ice, whisky, soda. . . The strange gentleman, as he later (ca. 3:30) takes hold of her bare arm, is embarrassed not in relation to her, but in relation to me. She doesn't look at me, as I had expected, with a mocking expression: What's the idea? Nor does she withdraw her warm arm, and as she doesn't say anything there is nothing for it but to persist in the strange gentleman's action. I honestly regret that I feel nothing as I do it. More than that: I'm staggered. And when the strange gentleman finally takes his hand away, because I need it to take hold of my whisky before it gets warm, she has already noticed my secret dismay, I think, and misunderstood it. Anyhow, she now, as she also picks up her glass, draws rather too deep a breath, as though something had happened to her, and pushes the hair back from her forehead, looks at me—me!—with her big blue eyes, without seeing that I would like to be alone. We smoke, outside it is still raining, we smoke. I can feel it, now I am going to relapse into the melancholy that suits men so, that renders them irresistible. It's no good my keeping a close watch on the strange gentleman. As I expected (I know him!) he now talks with playful frankness, more intimately than I feel like doing, getting right down to the problems of life. Should a woman who has a profession have a child? What is meant by marriage? I see through the game. To utter words before they have any meaning in relation to one's own personal life story, that's the point, words like love, man and woman, sex, friendship, bed and profession, fidelity, jealousy, species and individual and so on and so on. And since my own views, thus diluted into general principles, bore me to death, the strange gentleman spices them with little examples, which he makes up. Let us suppose, he says, that two people like us fall into each other's arms. Or: We agree that it shan't develop into an affair, we swear in advance that there shall be no repetition. He goes a step further in order to make the example, meant to illustrate a principle more vivid; he invents dialogues that enable him to address her with the familiar *Du*, the example demands it, and she understands that the strange gentleman only means it as an example when he says, We. Or, you and I. Or, you knew that we should part, and I knew it too. She smokes as he talks, she understands that he is speaking in inverted commas, and she smokes away, and when he picks up my glass again to show that we are in this dreary bar and nowhere else, he addresses her with the formal *Sie* again. The game is over. And she remains silent for a long time now, intoxication rises from her half-open mouth like a bluish veil over her face that is full of understanding for his views, for the universal validity of his views in general principle. They are not in love, oh no, that's clear. But the game of using *Du* has brought an experience that somewhat changes the conversation; this can't be reversed by reverting to *Sie*. I occasionally look at my watch, to warn the strange gentleman; but in vain. The *Sie*, no matter how strictly it is adhered to henceforth, has acquired a magic that dispels boredom. So I talk now about innocuous things, world events, in a monologue. Every now and then, as though the smoke were forcing her to, she half closes her eyes like a woman in an embrace, and it would be only natural if the strange gentleman, either with a joke or a mute doglike gaze, should take hold of her bare arm again, her hand, her hand with the cigarette lying by the ashtray, her further shoulder, the back of her neck. He doesn't do it. If I weren't keeping watch on him he might try it—involuntarily. . . .

Now I really did want to settle up.

"Pepe?" I called out.

In order to treat us like a couple, the barman had made himself indispensable over by the window, was acting as though he had never seen traffic in the rain before, and pretended to be deaf, no matter how often I banged with the coin on the zinc. Suddenly I was very bored indeed again. For that very reason I only dared tap very softly, un-urgently.

"You must go," she said.

"Unfortunately," I admitted.

"So must I," she said.

I banged with the coin again.

Why the strange gentleman, who was boring me even more than her, since I wasn't listening to his remarks for the first time, suddenly started talking about the charm of homosexual men, I don't know; I wasn't listening very closely, because I was trying to catch the attention of the inattentive barman—she agrees with him, oh yes, regarding the charm of such men who like to dress up (I remember now, we were talking about a particular actor, then about actors in general) and who have a feeling for women's costumes, a feeling for perfumes. She is wearing a yellow costume. He admits that he likes her costume, but adds this: if he liked it less, he wouldn't have the slightest idea how it could be improved. He swears to that. By contrast, that kind of man, he thinks, would immediately—and he does it purely as an example—would immediately take hold of her collar, alter something and transform it as though by magic. He does it. Her amazement makes her even more beautiful, I can see that, different from hitherto. . .

Now I pay.

I don't want a love story.

I want to work.

She had her handbag, black, which went splendidly with the yellow costume, black like her hair, under her arm already, as I put the change in my pocket and she said how glad she was to have met me. After this I held her coat for her. To invite her to dine with me would have been very natural, especially as her husband was away; I didn't do so while she tied her scarf round her hair. I also said how glad I was to have met her, as I now, before she slipped into her coat, saw her whole figure for the first and, as I hoped, last time. Most love stories need never happen, I believe. Have you got everything? I asked, as though I already knew how forgetful she was. She liked

that. I don't know whether it was the strange gentleman who now—
she looked so bewildered each time he addressed her with the
intimate *Du*—stroked her forehead, jestingly so to speak, ar-
bitrarily, altogether mockingly, in order affectionately to stress the
absence of destiny; anyhow, it happened. Our parting out in the
rain, when a taxi finally stopped, was swift and formal. Not until
she was sitting in the dry, inconsiderately preoccupied with her black
handbag, was one struck by what one calls emotion. She saw it in
my face, I believe, and after the surly driver, surly because he wasn't
really allowed to stop here, had driven off with the lady in the rain,
while I waited in vain to see if she would wave with her glove, I was
paralysed by the fear that my freedom of action might be at an
end. . .

I pulled my cap over my head.

I turned on my heel—I don't want to be the ego that experiences
my stories, stories that I can imagine—I turned on my heel in order
to part, as quickly as possible, from the strange gentleman.

Translated by Michael Bullock

From SKETCHBOOK
1966–1971

QUESTIONNAIRE

1. Are you sure you are really interested in the preservation of the human race once you and all the people you know are no longer alive?

2. State briefly why.

3. How many of your children do not owe their existence to deliberate intention?

4. Whom would you rather never have met?

5. Are you conscious of being in the wrong in relation to some other person (who need not necessarily be aware of it)? If so, does this make you hate yourself—or the other person?

6. Would you like to have perfect memory?

7. Give the name of a politician whose death through illness, accident, etc. would fill you with hope. Or do you consider none of them indispensable?

8. Which person or persons, now dead, would you like to see again?

9. Which not?

10. Would you rather have belonged to a different nation (or civilization)? If so, which?

11. To what age do you wish to live?

12. If you had the power to put into effect things you consider right, would you do so against the wishes of the majority? (Yes or no)

13. Why not, if you think they are right?

14. Which do you find it easier to hate, a group or an individual? And do you prefer to hate individually or as part of a group?

15. When did you stop believing you could become wiser—or do you still believe it? Give your age.

16. Are you convinced by your own self-criticism?

17. What in your opinion do others dislike abut you, and what do you dislike about yourself? If not the same thing, which do you find it easier to excuse?

18. Do you find the thought that you might never have been born (if it ever occurs to you) disturbing?

19. When you think of somebody now dead, would you like him to speak to you, or would you rather say something more to him?

20. Do you love anybody?

21. How do you know?

22. Let us assume that you have never killed another human being. How do you account for it?

23. What do you need in order to be happy?

24. What are you grateful for?

25. Which would you rather do: die or live on as a healthy animal? Which animal?

* * *

QUESTIONNAIRE

1. Do you still find marriage a problem?

2. When are you more in favor of marriage as an institution, when you consider your own marriage or when you consider other people's?

3. Have you more frequently advised others:
   (a) to separate? or
   (b) not to separate?

4. Do you know of reconciliations that have *not* left a scar on one or both of the partners?

5. What problems are solved by a happy marriage?

6. How long on average can you live with your partner without losing your self-integrity (meaning that you no longer venture even in secret to hold views that could shock your partner)?

7. How do you explain to yourself the urge, when contemplating a separation, to look for blame—either in yourself or your partner?

8. Would you of your own accord ever have invented marriage?

9. Do you feel in harmony with the mutual habits of your present marriage? If not, do you believe your partner is happy with them, and on what do you base your assumption?

10. When do you find marriage most of a strain:
    (a) in everyday matters?
    (b) on journeys?
    (c) when you are alone?
    (d) in company with others?
    (e) when just the two of you are together?
    (f) in the evenings?
    (g) in the mornings?

11. Does marriage produce common tastes (as the furnishing of the marital home seems to suggest), or does the purchase of a lamp, a carpet, a vase, etc., always mean a silent capitulation on your part?

12. If you have any children, do you feel a sense of guilt toward them when a separation occurs? That is to say, do you believe

that children have a right to unhappy parents? If so, up to what age?

13. What induced you to marry:
    (a) a desire for security?
    (b) a child?
    (c) the social disadvantages of an irregular union, for example, difficulties in hotels, gossip, the tactlessness of others, complications with officials or neighbors?
    (d) custom?
    (e) simplication of household arrangements?
    (f) consideration for your families?
    (g) the experience that irregular unions can equally lead to habit, boredom, disenchantment, etc?
    (h) the prospect of an inheritance?
    (i) a trust in miracles?
    (j) the feeling that it is only a formality anyway?

14. Would you like to add anything to the marriage oath as used in church or registry office ceremonies:
    (a) as a woman?
    (b) as a man?
    (Please give precise wording)

15. If you have been married more than once, at what point did your marriages most closely resemble one another, at the beginning or at the end?

16. If you find after separation that your former partner does not cease blaming you, do you conclude from this that you were more loved than you had realized, or do you feel relieved?

17. What do you usually say when one of your friends gets a divorce, and why didn't you say it to the person concerned before?

18. Can you be equally frank with both partners in a marriage when they themselves are not frank with each other?

19. If your present marriage can be called happy, state briefly to what you atrribute this.

20. If you had to choose between leading a happy marriage and following a call that might endanger your marital happiness, which would you consider more important:
    (a) as a man?
    (b) as a woman?

21. Why?

* * *

LUNCH IN THE WHITE HOUSE, 2 May 1970

The officer sitting watchfully in the anteroom is as friendly as a concierge satisfied with our passes; we are announced. The black taxi driver had, on the other hand, seemed sullen when we told him our destination. We have to wait. The officer looks bored, his cap on the table, a revolver in his belt. I notice that I cannot sit down: I am tensed up, though my curiosity, now I am here, is less than I had persuaded myself it would be. A female secretary goes into the washroom; an old Negro empties the ashtrays in the corridor. No sign of alarm. Now and again young men in shirt sleeves go along the corridor to get a Coca-Cola from the vending machine, talking of nothing in particular. The atmosphere inside the house is not at all tense. Administration. The daily round of a world power. . .

> Two days ago the Americans marched into Cambodia, the usual pictures on television: tanks from behind, swarms of helicopters, soldiers with tilted helmets, in full kit, loaded with provisions, weapons, ammunition, provisions; working or standing around looking lost, waiting for orders where to go in the jungle. According to the reporter, they don't yet know they have crossed a border—nothing in the vegetation to show it. When the reporter tells them, their faces betray no signs of excitement. Only when asked how they feel, does one soldier say into the microphone: "This is a mistake, I'm sure." Another: "We're going to make history, that's all I know."

We wait in the corridor, which is narrow, not to be compared with a corridor at IBM. No chrome, no leather. We sit in cushioned lower-middle-class comfort. No trace of ministerial grandeur. It could be a dentist's waiting room, apart from the photographs: Nixon in Hawaii with a floral wreath around his neck, he is laughing; Nixon with the astronauts from Apollo 13 after the averted disaster, he is laughing and waving; Nixon with his wife on a staircase, he is waving and laughing; Nixon leaving his airplane, waving; Nixon in the garden as family man, not waving but laughing; then the official Nixon again, shaking children's hands; Nixon at a gala dinner with Negroes to his right and left, a bevy of Uncle Toms in dinner jackets; the same dinner again . . .

> Nobody can say for certain how large the Black Panther party is. "The Black Panther party regards itself as a socialist organization and believes that means of production should be in the hands of the people. They declare that men only live creatively when free from the oppression of capitalism." As whites we are warned against going into Harlem; all the same, we drive to Harlem and walk around on foot, the only whites in the Apollo Theater. We are not molested; in the street, as long as the white man doesn't gape, no hostile looks. Much the same goods on sale, and the same language, too,—but a different continent. No slogans on the walls. It is difficult to say what has changed in twenty years, but a lot has. In the movies: the white heroes being laughed at.

Our host sends apologies: it will take him another few minutes. Easy to understand that, with a new area of warfare only two days old. I am still wrapped in wonder about this corridor; apart from the Nixon pictures in frames as cheap as they are tasteless, there is nothing to suggest we are on the premises of a firm spending billions a day on war. Not until I go in search of a washroom do I find, in a side corridor, a picture of Nixon in Vietnam: soldiers listening solemnly to his fatherly words . . .

> I have come here as a tourist, chiefly to see American painting in its own environment, studios on the Lower East Side. Along the road one runs into demonstrations: Vietcong flags waving in front of the Public Library, loudspeakers, a great helicopter circling over the park, where young people, male and female, are squatting on the ground or on railings, others lying under the trees, young people with guerrilla beards and Jesus hair, groups with guitars, policemen stationed around the park. The youngsters shout: "Peace now, peace now"; the policemen are

silent, their eyes averted, their truncheons hanging from loops around their hands. "Peace now, peace now, peace now." Nobody is being threatened, the policemen look redundant, the surrounding skyscrapers need no protection. Some call out: "Revolution now," but they are backed by the constitution. Nothing happens to them, but the doctrine urging war has lost its pull. Some call out: "All power to the people," making their two-fingered sign, then suddenly fifteen thousand voices shout: "Peace, peace now, peace, peace, peace."

Henry A. Kissinger, our host, greets us heartily and invites us into his anteroom. We know him from Harvard days; as professor of government he was already President Kennedy's occasional adviser. Now he is at the White House full time, adviser for military affairs. He is in his middle forties, thickset, inconspicuously cosmopolitan; an academician of the German sort, even if he puts his hands in his trouser pockets. The phone call that again calls him away for a while comes from Nelson Rockefeller, and so we wait, not only with understanding but with an embarrassed awareness of how precious his time is. Two secretaries are sitting in his anteroom, just starting on their lunchtime hot dogs. Another picture of Nixon here: the President (seated) listening to Henry A. Kissinger, his adviser (standing), surrounded by flags. Henry A. Kissinger, now free, introduces us to a lady who does not come from the White House, an actress, at the same time referring jokingly to Siegfried Unseld as "my friend and left-wing publisher." Another picture of Nixon here, a portrait with a dedication to Henry A. Kissinger: "Grateful for ever"; I don't get the date, for just then Henry A. Kissinger wants to know what I am working on now, a novel or a play? None of us is actually very hungry, but there are other reasons than that for a meeting over lunch: the task of ordering one's meal is a welcome way of postponing the questions that can't be avoided—questions about the American invasion of Cambodia. We all decide on mineral water. Once the White House waiter leaves us, Henry A. Kissinger starts off with a personal account: he daily receives letters threatening his life. The man from the Secret Service who in consequence shadows him constantly is nowhere to be seen. Is he perhaps the waiter, or are we regarded as completely trustworthy? Then on to the problem of the generation gap: it is all our fault, a failure on the part of fathers and teachers, who yield to every empty threat, capitulate, resign themselves, etc., instead of proclaiming what they themselves think is right and showing the way. Henry A. Kissinger relates how, in one university, where he had gone for discussions with the students, he was accused of being a "war criminal"; around one-half of the assembled students supported the accusation by rising from their seats and remaining on their feet. Henry A. Kissinger was still prepared to go on with the discussion, but when the appellation "war criminal" was shouted again, he left the room. Quite a few of the students, he says, wrote to thank him for his gesture and to apologize for the incident.

> "War Crimes and Individual Responsibility," a memorandum by Richard A. Falk, deals with the massacre of Song My on 16 March 1968, when more than five hundred civilians were wiped out: "The U.S. prosecutor at Nuremberg, Robert Jackson, emphasized that war crimes are war crimes no matter which country is guilty of them." The charter of the Nuremberg tribunal defines not only massacres, deportations, acts of torture, etc., as crimes; it also contains an Article VI: "Crimes against peace: Planning, preparation, initiation or waging of a war of aggression in violation of international treaties, agreements or assurances."

As far as the invasion of Cambodia is concerned, not only are we laymen, but we know it. Henry A. Kissinger has been working on the theory of the subject the layman sums up facilely as war for decades; hence his composure two days after the invasion of Cambodia. The food is good but ordinary, thus providing no distraction. What shall I talk about—simply in order *not* to put to Henry A. Kissinger the question that millions of Americans are asking? He is friendly, perhaps even pleased to be lunching with lay people, and he asks my publisher about his publishing business; but Siegfried Unseld, normally only too glad of an opportunity to speak at length about his firm's plans, cuts his account short in order to put a question of his own, which Henry A. Kissinger (with whom he stands on intimate, first-name terms since the time of the Harvard seminar) answers easily: the action in Cambodia will last a fortnight, till the rains come. Our host's attempt to bring the conversation around to marriage also fails. There is another silence. A President's adviser is in a more difficult position than a publisher or a writer; he cannot, in order to avoid speaking of his profession, switch to a more general and more important topic—for instance, war. For that *is* his profession, and no amount of personal modesty on his side and tact on ours can help out. Henry A. Kissinger says that the Cambodia decision of course gave him no pleasure. It was a case of choosing the lesser evil (lesser for whom?) and—obviously I had heard wrong the first time—the lesser evil would last six weeks at the most. Henry A. Kissinger, who keeps to a diet, talks sparingly and without eagerness: he is under no compulsion. The President is at his country house today. In order to keep the conversation going, I could have told him what the Americans I had met think about it, but Henry A. Kissinger has guessed it even before I speak: they are all students, professors, painters, writers, intellectuals. He says: "Cynics have never built a cathedral." The protests throughout the country cannot divert the responsible people from their course; they alone know the facts, which are secret. Henry A. Kissinger is an intellectual who has taken on responsibilities, and he relies on the fact that it was not "we" who started this war in Vietnam—by "we" he means President Nixon's administration. A thankless inheritance. To come back to the invasion of Cambodia: the U.S.A. has absolutely no interest in Cambodia; all they want to do is to establish a negotiating position. He asks us what we would like for dessert. According to the opinion polls, 63 percent of Americans today favor the invasion, 25 percent are against. (*The New York Times* is against.) I order fruit salad, and am glad when a young man in shirt sleeves interrupts with a murmured message: "The President is calling." A quarter of an hour on our own, we eat our dessert in silence; what our host can tell us Nixon has already said on television:

> No infringement of Cambodian neutrality, for this neutrality has already been infringed by the Vietcong. No aggression against Cambodia, for in the district concerned there are no local inhabitants, only Vietcong, whose bases are being destroyed. The monsoon period will prevent the Vietcong reestablishing these bases for six months. No escalation of the war: on the contrary, it is all part of the preparations to withdraw American troops; after the rains the South Vietnamese troops will be able on their own, etc.

The restaurant in the White House: solidly cozy, like a clubroom—brown paneled comfort. Here there is no picture of Nixon, but four oil paintings of old ships, three of them in distress . . . "The President is calling" . . . Here I am eating fruit salad in a place where millions of American citizens never get a chance to talk. What is so funny about that? A host in daily peril of his life, but he shows neither fear nor indignation. An occupational risk. Perhaps he even feels flattered: a bit reminiscent of Julius Caesar. What will they be talking about on the telephone? I have a mental picture of Henry A. Kissinger standing with his right hand in his trouser pocket, while we sit eating fruit salad. I wonder why I am reluctant to argue with a man in peril of his life: as if it would protect him, were I to remain silent while he says what he likes. "Intellectuals are cynical and cynics have never built a cathedral." Men think like that in our government offices, too; it is in keeping with this brown-paneled clubroom.

> A number of professors from Harvard call on Henry A. Kissinger a few days later to sever their connections with him; they say the Cambodia invasion was irresponsible, and the way the decision was made, undemocratic.

Of course, we should like to be shown over the White House, but we could be taken around by somebody else whose time was less precious. Obviously our host, after we have had our coffee, wants no further table talk about Cambodia, and we are honored that Henry A. Kissinger now offers personally to show us around the residence. (At certain times anyone can view it.) The palace guard, no more numerous than keepers in a museum, give no military salutes; our host, one hand in his trouser pocket, gives some short, informal greeting, and the uniforms subside again in the very act of rising. This gives us, too, a faint aura of belonging. All the same, I don't dare to light my pipe, but hold it in my hand or between my teeth without smoking. White walls, red carpets. I am uncertain what to think. . . . So this is where power dwells; it suggests a being that likes quiet and clean surroundings, beginning with the ashtrays; respects tradition; loves the silent grounds, the green lawns, and the flowers according to season; it probably has no relish for street fights, even when the victims have only themselves to blame, and massacres like Song My must arouse only horror. Even the noise or ordinary street traffic is distasteful: it cares for no noise of any kind that could disturb its meditations; it cherishes the view to a distant obelisk, the splash of a fountain. Whoever belongs in this household of power, whether as military adviser or as custodian, walks without haste, and obviously also without concern, so that one thinks of cries like "Revolution now!" only with a smile. Lincoln and others were shot dead, finally Kennedy; what disturbance has that caused? Their portraits in oil on the walls create a mood that immediately compels the visitor to speak softly; even the portrait of Lyndon B. Johnson, not yet looking down on us from Beyond, makes us feel that here modesty is called for. Only Henry A. Kissinger, who talks less than the usual guide, does not remove his hands from his pockets, thus wordlessly assuring us that everything in the house of power is completely natural, civilized, humane, because informal. He even makes a joke about Jacqueline; that is quite in order. Power, it seems, comes above all of a good family and possesses good taste—in china, for instance, and in furniture. This gives everything that happens here an aristocratic air. Every President has his own china, which later, when he is no longer in office, is put on view in a glass case; thus each succeeding President admires the china of his predecessors, and all are united through a taste for china. We walk along without asking much, less meditative than discreet; as we go up the marble staircase I do not, for instance, put my hand on the banister. The paintings that form part of the furnishings of power keep to the previous century; no Rothko, Roy Lichtenstein or Stella, no Jim Dine, no Calder, etc. A hankering for tradition, but it begins with Lincoln and Washington; there is no knight's armor. Birds are Nixon's main love. There are no Gobelins depicting military victories, or if there are I do not see them; there is no military strutting here, in fact no strutting at all. Power wears a respectable face, and has no desire to shock. Only the reality is huge—not the mansion in which this being lives and entertains. Another view over the park: even the jumbo jet one can just hear does not really fit in. Here history walks on wall-to-wall carpets. There is nothing to remind one of oil, of the computers in the Pentagon, the CIA, the United Fruit Company, etc. Here a large desk, and I take my pipe from my mouth: this—so I believe—is where the President, at the moment Richard Nixon, works. Behind the empty seat stands the Stars and Stripes, to each side of it the flags of all the armed forces. The desktop is empty, everything cleared away, but authentic. The only object that makes it believable that historic decisions are made here is also the only one that is not an antique: a telephone, white. We feel as if we were standing in the Escorial, where one must tell oneself: So this . . . !

> Nixon speaking to the press (8 May) on the U.S. invasion of Cambodia: "Decisions, of course, are not made by a vote in the Security Council or in the Cabinet. They are made by the President with the advice of others. I, as Commander in Chief, I alone am responsible. . . . I made the decision. I take the responsibility for it. I believe it was the right decision. I believe it works out. If it doesn't, then I am to blame."

In order not to ask: What help is it to the victims of a catastrophe, a civil war, or a world war, if Richard Nixon, the Commander in Chief, personally takes the blame and possibly destroys himself like Hitler? I ask his adviser what sort of a mind the President has. A very good mind, I am told, better than Kennedy's or Johnson's. But what sort of a mind? I am told it is an analytical mind. The tour of inspection moves on. . . .

> Two days later, 4 May 1970, during an antiwar demonstration at Kent State University, Ohio, four students are shot dead by the National Guard, who claim to have acted in self-defense against snipers, an allegation contradicted by all eyewitnesses. Pictures in *Life* show the National Guard shooting into the crowd from a distance of thirty yards, thus not threatened even by stonethrowers. Without preliminary warning. They lost their nerve, it is said, because their supply of tear gas had run out. Nixon says: "The needless deaths should remind us all once more that when dissent turns to violence it invites tragedy," a statement on which *The New York Times* remarks: "Which of course is true, but turns the tragedy upside down by placing the blame on the victims instead of the killers." Nixon is writing personal letters of sympathy to the parents.

We next inspect a little room in which the President can retire for a rest, no larger than an actor's dressing room, with a narrow couch, armchair, closet, and wash basin. The only thing missing: a makeup table. So this is where Nixon rests between appearances. . . . Gradually my inhibitions begin to fade; what we are looking at has nothing to do with reality. Why in fact are we viewing it all? The White House is not all that large, yet our walk seems endless. White walls, red carpets, they give the corridors an air almost of gaiety; what a pity, I almost feel, when our host breaks in with the remark that this is where Chancellor Willy Brandt, for example, was recently received. As he speaks, I am still reflecting on his words at lunch: "What happens in Cambodia after we leave Vietnam is not our problem." I nod: So this is where Willy Brandt had to eat. In front of a colleague to whom he introduces us the joking tone emerges again: "My friend and left-wing publisher." I know now that an open spirit dwells in this house. This colleague, like the young men we saw in the waiting room, is in shirt sleeves, neat, relaxed; the first reports from Cambodia appear to be good, in line with expectations. (At Harvard, in 1963, Henry A. Kissinger could be even more open, an intellectual who did not carry great responsibilities; he showed more concern then.) I wanted to ask a question, but the moment has passed; we are now inspecting a room where Henry A. Kissinger usually sits with the Soviet ambassador. I nod, as if my confirmation were required. The room reminds me of the Tarasp Kurhaus: a lot of easy chairs in little groups, all uncomfortable but solid, stylish, presumably genuine antiques. Now Henry A. Kissinger has both hands in his pockets, as though to show that he is not responsible for the internal architecture. Nor is Nixon. The apartment that the President in office can furnish to his own taste is on the floor above; all we are seeing are the state rooms, which, as I said, are open to all American citizens at certain times. Democracy has no secrets from its voters. . . . This (and now I am already nodding before I know what I am required to confirm) is where the Cabinet meets. A convincing room. Around a long, wide, and heavy table stand leather chairs, not too opulent, just right: chairs that oblige one to sit upright. Here it could be argued whether Cambodia should be invaded or not. But it is only infrequently, I am told, that the Cabinet meets, and then it is just a bore. Henry A. Kissinger smiles; he only wanted to show us the room. The decisions are not made here, he says. . . .

> Walter J. Hickel, Interior Secretary, complains in a published letter that the President consulted him only three times within a year. He writes: "Permit me to suggest that you consider meeting, on an individual and conversational basis, with members of your Cabinet. Perhaps through such conversations we can gain greater insight into the problems confronting us all. . . ."

My question would have been: What does Nixon really want from power? There are aims that can only be achieved by first gaining power (the abolition of poverty in the world's wealthiest country, the integration of the Negroes, peace without exploiting other countries, etc.). What is Richard Nixon's aim? But the question is superfluous; his aim was to become President of the United States, and he has achieved his aim by virtue of having no other—power as the aim of power—and I can believe without question that Nixon genuinely desires peace, if there is no other way of remaining in power. . . .

Everything is getting out of hand: garbage, youth, hair, drugs, Negroes, riots, students, protest in the streets, the fear of America. New skyscrapers, but the guitar is getting out of hand. In the fall, when they once again marched on Washington, there were reckoned to have been a quarter of a million of them assembled around the White House. "Peace now, stop the war, peace now." There were no fatalities; President Nixon had the windows closed and (as he himself later announced) watched football on television. Six months later, on 9 May 1970, they besieged the park again—"Out of Cambodia,"—this time only a hundred thousand (many have ceased to believe they will be listened to), but Nixon had a sleepless night, according to the press; early in the morning the President went to the Lincoln Memorial, where he talked to some of the students and demanded their understanding: it was his responsibility to ensure that the United States remain the leading power. The students say he then talked about sports. According to the press, the President breakfasted on ham and eggs. War helps against crises, but what helps against young people who are getting out of hand? Four hundred universities are staging strikes in protest against the shooting of students at Kent State.

In the park, which—as we have frequently seen through the windows—is very beautiful, but answers no questions, Henry A. Kissinger says he will not remain in office much longer: he has hardly any private life of his own. Now we see the White House from outside: just as one knows it from pictures. Out here in the open I at last light up my pipe, while we walk along, hearing only our footsteps on the gravel. What to talk about? A fine summer day. People who make decisions or advise on decisions affecting millions of human beings cannot afford to ask themselves afterward whether the decision was right; the decision has been made, and we must await what follows. It would really be the opportunity for a joke, but none occurs to me.

This morning in Jimmy's Coffee Shop: conversation with a cheerful waiter, who takes me for a German and in consequence tells me that he was neither for nor against Hitler, "but perhaps we have to see that Hitler was a great philosopher." Seeing my hesitation, he switches to McCarthy, "who was considered to be a fool," but today one feels that, if McCarthy had been listened to at the time, "we wouldn't have all the trouble with Vietnam." He himself, the waiter, is actually Greek, and a patriot there as well: he finds Pattakos all right, "only some Communists can't stand him." Incidentally, we are not alone: the man selling tobacco next door is for Hitler. Why? Hitler had great faith. What was that? "He believed that the Germans are a superior race." He himself, the tobacconist, is a Puerto Rican with crinkly hair, and he incidentally thinks the United States should have occupied Europe after the war. This reminds me of a conversation I had in 1952 in a California motel. "Depression is worse than war," the landlord assured me, though by that he meant a war in old Europe. Why in Europe? "Because they are used to having wars over there."

In the park there is nothing to see, and our silence is all the more conspicuous; I am glad when Siegfried Unseld begins to talk of his publishing business. Every firm has its problems. Henry A. Kissinger, unassuming, as extraordinary minds usually are, almost vainly unassuming, an expert who has considered all the potentialities of weapons of destruction and only wants what is best (namely, the least possible destruction of the world), he knows what at this moment only a few in the world know (it is only the historians who will eventually know) and prefers to listen, if somewhat absentmindedly, to someone else. I have met no other man whose potential error could have such vast consequences. A surgeon whose knife once slips, an engine driver, even a member of parliament who is not up to his job, a police chief who follows the wrong clue, an air pilot with a hundred sixty passengers, or a Herbert Marcuse, a publisher, etc.—these are responsibilities a single man can assume. But a White House adviser? I begin to understand why Henry A. Kissinger has his hands in his pockets wherever he goes; his responsibilities are in no sort of proportion to his person, which wears an ordinary suit like us. The more disastrous the potential error, the less the individual man can do about it. Without my saying a word of all this, Henry A. Kissinger remarks that he can bear responsibility much better than ineffectualness; then, speaking to the other side, adds something that I do not clearly hear. We are walking very slowly. Henry A. Kissinger has no idea what he will do when he leaves the White House. Return to the university? He feels that would hardly be possible. Our walk on the gravel will soon be an an end, and it seems there is nothing more to ask. Why did Henry A. Kissinger, before the election Richard Nixon's declared opponent, become his adviser? My wife's question is more suited to the occasion, however: How had his scientific theories been vindicated or altered by being applied in practice? That, says Henry A. Kissinger, is a question he is often asked: he has no time to think of it. A terrible remark, but we are now passing through a revolving door. I hear only: "When you are once on the tightrope, there is no way back. . . ." Then (emerging from the revolving door): ". . . no policy without the risk of a tragedy." Tragedy for whom?

* * *

QUESTIONNAIRE

1. Do you fear death and, if so, at what age did you begin to fear it?

2. What do you do about it?

3. If you do not fear death (because you think materialistically, because you do not think materialistically), are you frightened of dying?

4. Would you like to be immortal?

5. Have you ever believed yourself to be dying? If so, to what did your thoughts then turn:
   (a) to what you would leave behind?
   (b) to the world situation?
   (c) to a landscape?
   (d) to a feeling that it had all been in vain?
   (e) to the things that would never get done without you?
   (f) to the untidiness of your drawers?

6. Which do you fear more: that on your deathbed you might abuse someone who doesn't deserve it, or that you might pardon all those who don't deserve it?

7. When yet another acquaintance dies, are you surprised by the ease with which you accept the fact that others die? And if not, do you feel the dead person is one up on you, or do you feel one up on him?

8. Would you like to know how it feels to die?

9. If there was an occasion when you wished yourself dead, but did not die, do you afterwards conclude you had been wrong— that is to say, do you then take a different view of the circumstances that made you feel that way?

10. Do you ever think: Serve you right if I died?

11. If there are times when you do not fear death, is this because you are finding life difficult at the moment, or because you are enjoying life at the moment?

12. What is it about funerals that upsets you?

13. If you have pitied or hated somebody and then hear that he has died, what do you now do with your pity or hatred for him?

14. Have you friends among the dead?

15. When you see a dead person, do you feel you ever knew him?

16. Have you ever kissed a dead person?

17. If you think of death, not in a general way but personally in relation to your own death, are you always dismayed, and do you feel sorry for yourself or for the person who will survive you?

18. Would you rather die in full awareness, or be cut off suddenly by a falling brick, a heart attack, an explosion, etc.?

19. Do you know where you would like to be buried?

20. When breathing stops and the doctor confirms death, are you confident that at this moment the person has no more dreams?

21. What agonies would you prefer to death?

22. If you believe in a place to which departed spirits go (Hades), do you find comfort in the thought that we shall all be reunited in eternity, or is this the reason why you fear death?

23. Can you imagine an easy death?

24. If you love someone, why do you not wish to be the one left behind, but prefer leaving the sorrow to your partner?

25. Why do dying people never shed tears?

Translated by Geoffrey Skelton

WILHELM TELL

A School Text

Probably Konrad von Tillendorf, a younger man and plump for his age, residing at the time at Castle Kyburg, or possibly another man who was called Grisler, serving in the same capacity, a knight, at any rate, with no eye for landscape, rode on a warm summer's day in the year of 1291, through the region which is nowadays designated as the aboriginal or *Ur*-Switzerland.* A föhn was probably blowing; the range of mountains which the plump knight saw before him seemed closer than necessary. So as not to be discourteous to young Rudenz who was to go with him to Uri, he took the trouble, more than once, to praise the blossoming cherry trees. It was hot and blue. The longer he rode the more silent the plump knight became; these mountains on both sides were getting the upper hand. He often wondered that there was such a thing as a path in this land, but there, in fact, was a path which, as the plump knight knew, leads even to Rome, though always around one more rock. He wondered that people lived here[1] but did not say so. The narrower the valleys, the more easily are its people offended; the plump knight already sensed as much, and once more praised a blossoming cherry tree. At midday, in Brunnen am See, they had to get back into another skiff. An arduous land. Sir Konrad or Grisler felt uneasy in the skiff and gripped the bench with both hands though the heavy skiff barely rocked; he sat oppressed, staring at

*The original Switzerland, consisting of the present-day cantons Uri, Schwyz, and Unterwalden. (Translator's note.)

the valley of Uri which looked to him like the end of the world. These cliffs on the left, cliffs on the right. He was not traveling for pleasure, but as the emissary of King Rudolf's heirs, that is to say, in his official capacity, and therefore wore his velvet cap. It was hot even on the lake. Not a blustering kind of föhn, but a föhn. The boatman rowed hard and in silence and acted as if he personally had made these dreadful rocks, and showed no sign of humor. The plump knight knew, of course, that the Uri of those days was a state under direct protection of the emperor, that is to say, he was at that moment on foreign soil. He did not mention that he would not wish to live in Uri. He only said he had a headache. The skiff made little headway. Young Rudenz, a nephew of Baron von Attinghausen, took it upon himself to point out this and that, whatever it was the local people imagined to be particularly noteworthy. Now and then the plump knight, nodding politely the while, dipped his hand into the chilly water of the Vierwaldstätter See (Four Forest Lake) to make his headache go away. He noticed neither the summer meadow of the Rütli[2] nor the rock which was to become the famous Tellenplatte[3], but looked straight ahead to where he suddenly thought he could make out the St. Gotthard. It was the only time the boatman, whose name was probably Ruodi, briefly grinned. Snow on the mountains in summer. Though on clear days one could see snow from Castle Kyburg, it nevertheless surprised him: snow in summer. He said nothing about it. The people of Uri seemed proud of this snow. Once he asked the good boatman how much longer it was going to take him to Flüelen. No answer. Now young Rudenz, who was embarrassed when his forest people appeared unmannerly, unpacked a small repast from the leather pouch so as to divert the Hapsburg official from this peculiarity of forest people, probably cheese and bread, also hardboiled eggs which, as soon as Ulrich von Rudenz put them on the bench before the noble guest, immediately fell off and rolled to and fro in the skiff. Even this did not make the good boatman smile, for he was known as the best and ablest of the boatmen of Lake Uri, and that this *Fötzel* (fucking foreigner) had asked how much longer it was going to take him to Flüelen was something he did not forget as long as he lived. Unfortunately, the emissary of King Rudolf's heirs had no appetite whatsoever, which looked as though he held the local cheese in contempt. The journey in this skiff seemed to him endless. More and more often he closed his eyes so he wouldn't see any more mountains and only heard the harsh beating of the waves, the slapping underneath the skiff, and the groaning oars. He tried to think about his diplomatic mission, both hands gripping the bench, but could not rid himself of the feeling that they were going in the wrong—the diametrically wrong—direction. . . . "Here we are, sir!" said young Rudenz—a flock of huts in green meadows, with apple trees. So this was Flüelen. Inasmuch as the emissary of King Rudolf's heirs had not imagined Flüelen at all, it did not surprise him. He thanked the good boatman, who was still offended because he had been asked how long it would take him to Flüelen; his eyes were positively uncanny. It was as if the man had meanwhile grown a goiter. Another, who was holding the horses in readiness, had a real goiter. As they road along the River Reuss toward Altorf the plump knight asked whether there was much inbreeding in these valleys. The information given him by young Rudenz has not come down to us. However the High Commissioner is understood soon thereafter to have reined in his horse to say, "All these mountains all around, these mountains!" His headache had not gone when they arrived in Altorf.

———

1. "Give ear unto the beginnings of the three lands of Uri, Schwyz, and Unterwalden, even how they have come honorably into being; Uri is the first of the lands that received favor from a Roman Empire, there to clear the ground and to dwell. Thereafter did the Romans come unto Unterwalden; to these also the Empire granted to clear there and to dwell. That became their freedom and their right. Thereupon people have come from Sweden to Schwyz, for there were, in their homeland, too great a number. They also received from the Empire freedom and the right to settle, clear, and dwell. Thus sat these lands a long while and for many a year in good quiet until there came near unto these lands the counts of Hapsburg." (*Das Weisse Buch von Sarnen* [The White Book of Sarnen], circa 1470.) Thereto Karl Meyer: "The account of the Roman ancestry of the people of Uri and Unterwalden might well preserve the memory of an earlier Romance populace; the presumptive descent of the Schwyzers from the Swedes, on the other hand, rests solely upon the similarity of the name Schwiter (as the Schwyzers continued to call themselves as late as about 1350), and Sweden." Latin: Svitenses and Svetenses. In our own day one may still meet persons in Texas or Turkey who confuse Switzerland with Sweden, more particularly as one imagines both countries to be snowed in and democratic. Compare also Hans Tschäni, *Profil der Schweiz* (Profile of Switzerland): "The first people are .

presumed to have lived in the region of present day Switzerland since the last ice age (50,000 to 40,000 B.C.). They were hunters and cave dwellers. In the sixth century B.C. it was inhabited by Ligurians. We are here dealing with lake dwellers, builders of stilt houses. The next inhabitants of the Jura and the midlands were the Helvetians of Celtic orgin. After their exodus they were defeated by Caesar at Bibracte, 58 B.C., and Helvetia was occupied by the Romans. After 500 the Alemans advanced into northern and eastern Switzerland."

2. Rütli, which according to tradition (though without proof) is the location of the Oath of the Confederacy of 8/1/1291. See Aegidius Tschudi: "In this manner was the above-mentioned alliance first made and sworn by the aforenamed three valiant persons in the land of Uri, which gave rise to the Confederacy, and the land Helvetia (now named Switzerland) brought back unto its ancient station and freedom."

3. To this day a popular goal of school excursions. Compare Karl Meyer: "If the name Tellenplatte were really only the name of a rural locality, and older than the name of the archer Tell, and was only subsequently identified with the liberator, this fact in itself would not disprove the historical authenticity of the archer, but only the correctness of Tell as the archer's name: in this case the name Tell could have been attributed to the marksman in the belief that the site of our national salvation derives the name Tellenplatte from him."

* * *

When Sir Konrad or Grisler, sometimes also mistaken for a certain Count von Seedorf,[4] woke up the next morning, went to the low window, and saw no sky but only cliffs and firs and stones, he worked up his courage by drinking milk. He probably had a touch of liver and didn't know it; hence his tendency to melancholy. He praised the milk. He felt sorry for the people who were born here, in this valley; the sun shone on the rocks high up but the valley lay in shadow, and when he looked up at the sky it seemed to him as if he had dropped into a cistern. Immediately, even before he drank his milk, he sent a servant over to Attinghausen,[5] to announce his arrival as the Imperial High Commissioner, and to say it was urgent. The plump knight wished for the shortest possible stay in Uri. Even this first hour, while he waited for an answer from Attinghausen, seemed very long. A premonition of what was awaiting him in these forest regions, the plump knight seems by no means to have had. Kneeling in the chapel, he prayed not for his own person but crossed himself in a general hope for better times. His headache had gone and even this seemed a good omen to him. Unfortunately the servant reported back that the Baron von Attinghausen was unwell and would be unable to receive the Imperial High Commissioner before next week. This also he took to be a good omen. What if the old man of Attinghausen had happened to have just died. Not wanting to be idle, he took his first ride through the surrounding country and paid an official visit to a construction site between Silenen and Amsteg where a tower was at that time being erected to guard the path to the Gotthard.[6] The sun had meanwhile come to the valley but the mood on the site was disagreeable. An old construction foreman whom they used, in those days, to call a "Fronvogt" or overseer, a Tyrolese whose alien intonation alone made him an object of hatred to the people of Uri, had, presumably out of personal spite, because they called him a fucking foreigner, called the stronghold "Twing Uri" (Hold Uri Down). This, as Sir Konrad or Grisler could understand, must irritate the good people of Uri. The Tyrolese was dismissed on the spot—but too late; the vicious name stuck for all time.

---

4. The burial of the name under historical data is understandable since the name of the chief commissioner who, according to the chronicles, was administrator of Uri and Schwyz comes down through the historiographies of neither Uri nor Schwyz, but solely by means of a foreign historical tradition. (Karl Meyer, *Die Urschweizer Befreiungstradition,* 1927.) "One can hardly fail to recognize that there are two figures which have become fused into the High Commissioner Gessler, namely a despot who rules the land of Schwyz from his stronghold at Schwanau and was slain in that vicinity (i.e., near Küssnacht), and a despot in the land Uri (the Count von Seedorf according to the Lucerne chronicle by Diebold Schilling) who enforces the appleshooting and is shot to death on the Tellenplatte." (August Bernoulli, 1881.)

5. The Baron von Attinghausen, Lord of the manor and of serfs, who himself enjoyed the Freedom of the Empire, thereby legally on equal footing with the House of Hapsburg, was the magistrate of Uri, and possessed the most powerful stronghold in the valley. "The Confederates *(Eidgenossen)* represent only part of that nation of free peasants with whom our patriotic fantasy populates the Urschweiz. The local society conformed to the social structure of the middle ages, i.e., it was subdivided according to estate. The majority—on the bottom rung—was composed of bondsmen who, though they could not be sold like slaves, owed their lords socage service and taxes. . . ." (Marcel Beck, 1970.) In

consequence it was correct of the Imperial Commissioner to negotiate with the Baron von Attinghausen, not with his bondsmen.

6. "As King Rudolf and his sons, respectively, held the right of excise in the pass valleys, these strongholds ensured the safety of the merchants and supported the trade and customs policy of the Hapsburgs which was very important fiscally." (Karl Meyer, *ibid.*) As to the significance of the strongholds for the consolidation of sovereignty, compare E. Lamprecht, *Deutsches Wirtschaftsleben* (German Economy); also E. Schrader, *Das Befestigungsrecht in Deutschland bis zum Beginn des 14. Jahrhunderts* (Rights of Fortifications in Germany to the Beginning of the Fourteenth Century).

* * *

Evenings in Altorf were the worst, these evenings with a certain Lady von Bruneck and young Rudenz who, though much too young for the elderly virgin, lusted after her inheritance. Evenings with bats in a tower. They played dice. Even when he had no headache the plump knight was in bed by nine. He had not imagined this mission would be so boring. He obviously had no sense that he was then on the very soil of *Ur*-Switzerland,[7] which is to say, of the birthplace of our freedom.[8] Like the foreigner Sir Konrad or Grisler in either case was, there were many things that puzzled him. The cowherd who brought the daily milk did it with a look that made you wonder if he hadn't pissed into it. Like every foreigner from that day to this, the plump knight noticed a lot of peculiarities which are not typical, or to which only natives know how to do justice.[9] He was afraid, sometimes, of these mountain people; their soul remained closed to him. If he went out riding and stopped to question a herder and talk about the weather, the man would suddenly begin chatting with his cattle, and hit at the dumb beast with a stick to make it move and glance back, as if it were none of the foreigner's[10] fucking business, the weather of Uri. So he rode for days on end without talking to anybody. He saw their huts between the cliffs. It seemed preposterous to him that people should live in such a country and he felt sorry for them. When he saw the stupid cliffs and stones everywhere, these sheer slopes of stones, he understood that they were surly although he, Sir Konrad or Grisler, had not done them any harm. He praised their cattle. They were short, on the average, and strong. For the first few days he thought all of them had goiters. They all had short, thick, massive necks, these short, these massive necks, with little skull in back, a low and square-edged forehead and, below that, two eyes with a biting glance. They never really looked at one, they looked one over. They had a hard life, and were proud of it. They were Christians. Men carried the hay on their heads, entire clouds of hay, and you saw only their legs crooked with the power in their calves. They knew how to make cheese and didn't need the world to teach them anything. A humorous word was enough to put them out of humor. Frugal like their fathers and their grandfathers before them, they built their huts like their fathers and grandfathers; what was not as it had always been seemed to them dubious if not straight from the devil himself who, incidentally, played a major role in these valleys. Anyone even daring to come into these valleys was already suspect; the cowherds, who spent summer alone on their alp, would rather talk with spirits than with a stranger.[11] Only once did the plump knight get up onto an alp, and wondered, uncomprehending: not a single tree, the muck of cows, moors, thistle, grass in between the stones, wind, flies on the black muck, creek with pebbles, above all stones, and it wasn't only the cattle that gaped goggle-eyed, but also the cowherd whom he asked for milk. The herder gaped and stopped his work at the stove and gaped and didn't speak.[12] Thereafter the courtly Konrad or Grisler stayed below in the valley. A well-to-do, well-set-up peasant named Walter Fürst, who owned a large farm in the valley, at least bid him a good day and offered a chair; he, the peasant himself, remained standing in distrust. They had a charter[13] and were in the right. They could not imagine an empire as something that could be of use to them. The peasant disliked even the foreign cut of a beard, for in Uri they wore their beards in a different fashion and were in the right. If they admitted that the path over the St. Gotthard brought them much advantage and profit through all kinds of trade with the Hapsburgian countries, they owed their thanks to God, to no one but God, who let go an avalanche now and then, but for the rest did not butt in like the gentlemen of Hapsburg. Sir Konrad or Grisler or whatever his name was, the plump emissary of King Rudolf's heirs, needn't say anything whatsoever; they did not want him to. In the end he picked up his knight's cap from the bench, not accustomed to someone scratching the hair on his chest when you were talking to him, and arose smiling—no reason to smile—and wanted to shake hands with the peasant; they didn't want even that[14]—the Urner was still scratching the hair on his chest.

7. "Urschweiz" ("Ur-Swiss") is a posthumous designation. The conspirators against Hapsburg (Stauffacher-Gesellschaft [Stauffacher Company]) did not call themselves "Schweizer" (Swiss), but "Eidgenossen"* (Confederates). It was in the Austrian camp that Schweizer was first used as a nickname for all the forest peoples, including the non-Schwyzers. Compare Felix Hemmerli, *De nobilitate et rusticitate dialogus*, 1449: "The Schwyzers were simply the first offenders against their overlord; and all those who, one after the other, offended with them inherited their name."

8. Freedom in the sense of national sovereignty.

9. Respect for the Swiss character, that is to say a positive interpretation of ways and behavior that unnerve the foreigner, is found in Swiss literature as well as in Swiss journalism.

10. *Fötzel* is, despite modern tourism, an expression still much used in central Switzerland; it denotes the foreigner's a priori inferiority. There exists, to the best of my knowledge, no standard work on xenophobia and the hotel business to date. The xenophobia of the peasant, a natural phenomenon, particularly in narrow valleys, has by no means disappeared, despite tourism (1964: 32,325,000 overnighters in the Confederacy, i.e., Switzerland). Servility toward the foreigner insofar as he is solvent does not stand in contradiction to the peculiarity of the Swiss character.

11. "At Rinderbüel in the Madran Valley, lies buried under a mighty avalanche of stones, a whole alpine dairy farm. There, one evening, as the alp people were milking cows, something called down from the sheer, uncanny threat of the cliff wall that overhung the huts, "I'm going to let go." The cowherd put both hands to his mouth to make a funnel and through this speaking tube called back, "You can hold on a bit." The next evening the voice rang out again, "I got to let go!" and once more the fearless cowherd answered, "Come on, you can hold it a bit longer!" The third evening had settled in on the hushed alp, and the last cow was being milked, but all the cattle were still standing chewing their cud when the screaming came down again from the overhanging rock wall in a terrible voice, threatening, imploring, "Jesus, I got to let go!" The cowherd was just removing the one-legged milking stool from under the cow. He stood up with the full pail in his hand and called, "So let go!" And in that moment the rock burst with a crash and came thundering with a scatter of sparks all around and buried the whole beautiful alp with the cowherd and the servants under rubble and stone blocks high as houses." (Josef Müller, *Sagen aus Uri* [Legends of Uri].)

---

*Literally: sworn companions.

12. "A cowherd on his alp had finished his boiling, and a large kettle full of precious mild goatsmilk smiled up at him. And he thought, "Now I'd sure like to give some poor fellow his bellyfull." Hardly had he thought this when someone came to the door of the hut, rested his hands on the little half-door and looked into the hut. But the cowherd was afraid to say something to him. After a while the stranger went away and as he passed up the slope behind the hut he screamed horribly. The cowherd ought to have spoken to him and offered him some goatsmilk, said the woman who was telling the story, and that might have lifted the curse." *(Ibid.)*

13. This refers to the charter of freedom which King Heinrich, son of Friedrich II, and his Imperial Administrator in Germany had given to the people of Uri, May 26, 1231. The valley of Uri was formerly subject to the superior court jurisdiction of the office of the Imperial Commissary of Zurich.

14. The intent of the Confederates of 1291 to incur no obligation to any alliance of nations but to limit themselves to the proceeds from traffic through the passes, was not preserved unbroken into the 20th century. Only after an epoch of armed aggression and expansion which placed might before right, and only after the defeat at Marignano in 1515, did the Ur-Swiss way of thinking, the renunciation of participation, their claim to independence by strict non-integration (neutrality) win out once again. In 1970 Switzerland is still known as a preeminent store of gold, and a non-member of the U.N.

*   *   *

Although the misdeed had not taken place on Uri soil, everyone in Uri knew all about it, and the way Father Rösselmann, the priest, managed to tell the story, the peasant in Altzellen was, of course, in the right when he found the Lord High Commissioner of the Hapsburgs sitting stark naked in a tub washing his sweaty hair and had beaten him murderously to death with a spade.[15] The plump knight was no doubt horrified to hear this story about a colleague of his and at first he said nothing . . . it's just that it was hard to find officials for these forest regions; whoever in any way excelled and therefore found good favor with the gentlemen of Hapsburg so that he could, to some degree, have some choice of position would wish himself to Innsbruck or Zurich, to Baden maybe, but never Sarnen or Lowerz or up on the Rotzberg.* This Lord von Wolffenschiessen, it was understood in court circles, had been transferred to Unter-

*Literally: Mount Snot.

walden as a punishment, because he'd been carrying on with the pages.[16] And so it surprised the plump knight that this Wolfenschiessen, of all people, and a likable colleague in his way, was supposed to have tried to seduce, even to rape, one of the women of Unterwalden. Had there been, he cautiously inquired of Father Rösselmann, any witness besides God. For he simply couldn't make it out.[17] What also puzzled the plump knight, when he was trying to imagine the misdeed, was that a man who wants a woman should go and undress by himself and sit in a tub. But Father Rösselmann insisted as though he himself had been present and no one in Uri doubted that this was a matter of attempted whoring coincident with the act of tyranny; otherwise the Altzellen peasant, known to be a pious man, would not have reached for the spade and murderously split the bathing High Commissioner's skull wide open which, as Father Rösselmann let it be understood, could happen again at any moment. . . . And so he was forewarned, this emissary of King Rudolf's heirs, as from one Christian to another. . . . There were more such Hapsburgian misdeeds, Father Rösselmann said when he sensed that the plump knight, though shaken, still privately doubted who, in this incident, was in the right; there were more such Hapsburgian misdeeds. For instance, did he, the emissary of King Rudolf's heirs, know the story of the equally good and pious Melchtal? No, he did not. Should Melchtal, the son, have put up with King Rudolf's heirs unhitching his oxen from his plow? Well, he defended himself and in the process inadvertently broke the little finger of one of the Hapsburgs' armed men. And what did the High Commissioner do then? He raged, he had them fetch the aged father and gouged his eyes out.[18] This story, no less grisly, Father Rösselmann also related as if he had been there and it was not doubt, but the expression of his horror when the plump knight said, "You're sure?" He put a hand up to his own eyes he was so horrified how very much these forest people are always in the right,[19] nor did it make any difference that the story of Melchtal was, in that year of 1291, already quite an old story.

---

15. "There was a worthy man in that time dwelling at Altzellen, and he had a pretty wife. But he who, at that time, governed there, wanted to have her, whether she would or no. And this he told to her. She however did as a proper woman does and begged him to let her alone and

unmolested for she never would be his. But her words were in vain. The gentleman thought to have his wanton way with her and came to Altzellen into her house. Her husband had gone to the woods. The gentleman forced the woman to prepare him a bath and said to her that she must bathe with him. The woman prayed God to keep her from disgrace but the Lord Commissioner stepped into the bath and ordered her to sit herself in it with him. She despaired that her husband did not come, and, because God has never yet deserted his own when they cry to him in their need, the man came and asked what it was that weighed so upon her. She said, 'The master is here and has forced me to make him a bath. He sits there now and wants me to come to him to do with me that which he would like to do. But I would not and have prayed God to save me from disgrace.' The man grew angry, went, and at once beat the master to death with the ax and saved his wife from disgrace. It was God's will that he came home." (*Das weisse Buch von Sarnen,* about 1470.) Compare the chronicle by Aegidius Tschudi a hundred years later: "And so he demanded she should prepare him a bath of water, because he had grown sweaty and tired with walking," which was not in itself an indecent proposal; nevertheless this good peasant woman is frightened, according also to Aegidius Tschudi; only it isn't God who sends her good man home but she fetches him out in the field. "The older the stories are, the simpler do they seem to be; the later, the more circumstantial. The later writers have more to relate than the earlier." (Georg von Wyss, 1858, *Zur Geschichte der Urschweiz* [The History of the Urschweiz]). No chronicle mentions the Right of Hospitality due to the Commissioner of the Land. All the chronicles agree that the High Commissioner, Sir Wolffenschiessen, sat in a bathtub while the peasant woman remained dressed and the only witness that the commissioner demanded more than a bath remains the good peasant woman herself.

16. In the chronicles there is no reference to the homosexuality of the above-mentioned commissioner, which can however also be explained by the fact that homosexuality was taboo in the Urschweiz.

17. As recently as 1943 it came to unpleasantness in these parts when we sweaty soldiers took off our shirts at a village well and wanted to wash at least our naked chests. The village priest came running to the captain to complain about our depraved carryings-on which would ruin the morals of the village women, and when the captain, a city man, insisted that we might, after a day's march, be allowed to wash, the priest assured him he and his faithful had never in their lives taken a bath and stood well in the grace of God.

18. "Now there was at Sarnen a Lord von Landenberg in the name of the Empire. He heard it said that there was one in the Melchi who had a pretty yoke of oxen and so his Lordship sent one of his servants and had the oxen unhitched and brought to him. To the poor man he sent word the peasants should themselves draw the plow, he wished to have the oxen. The servant did as his master had bidden him, went there and

wanted to unhitch the oxen to drive them to Sarnen. But the poor man had a son who did not wish to have it so. He would not let the oxen go, and when his Lordship's servant took hold of the yoke he lashed out with the stick and broke a finger of his Lordship's servant. The servant became angry at this, went home, and complained to his master how it had fared with him. His Lordship, enraged, threatened evil to the peasants. The son fled but the Lord High Commissioner had the father fetched, carried him to Sarnen unto his castle, and there blinded him, took from him what he had, and caused him great sorrow." *(Das weisse Buch von Sarnen.)* Here again Aegidlus Tschudi, though a hundred years later, is able to be more precise: "For some small cause wherein his son, Arnold von Melchtal, was said to have transgressed and incurred punishment," that is to say the seizure of the oxen took place as a penalty for a previous misdemeanor. Furthermore, in Tschudi it becomes comprehensible why the poor father ("Heinrich von Melchtal, a wise, sensible, honorable, propertied man") is blinded: he keeps silent as to the whereabouts of his disobedient son. "The blinding with which the old Melchi peasant was punished is one of the most frequent means of punishment in the middle ages." (Karl Meyer, *ibid.*)

19. The tendency of oral tradition to justify its own collective is natural. Compare Johannes Dierauer, 1887: *"Der Eigenliebe des Volkes schmeichelnde Geschichten"* (Stories to Flatter a People's Self Love). Compare further oral tradition in modern times, e.g., how Switzerland imagines itself to have behaved during the Second World War. A quarter century later, those events are already forgotten or at least not handed on, which might burden our conviction that Switzerland is immune against fascism. The oral tradition even contradicts documentation of the kind not available to the medieval chronicler. The publication of documents therefore not infrequently produces shock, for example the so-called *Bonjour* report about the neutrality of Switzerland in the Second World War, written for the Bundesrat (Federal Council), published in 1970 only after some initial hesitation. If we, like the *Ur*-Swiss of those days had only oral tradition (the pub, grade school, etc.), there would, for instance, have been no pro-Hitler upper bourgeois and officers etc. in the Switzerland of 1933 to 1945 after a mere quarter century of oral tradition. *Das weisse Buch von Sarnen,* the earliest chronicle of the Confederacy in the Forest Regions, was written no less than 180 years after the events. (Compare *Quellenwerk zur Entstehung der Schweizerischen Eidgenossenschaft* [Source Book of the Origin of the Swiss Confederacy], issued by Geschichtsforschende Gesellschaft der Schweiz [Historical Research Society of Switzerland], part III Chronicles, volume 1 [*Das weisse Buch von Sarnen*], 1947.)

* * *

A first meeting with the man who later became famous as Wilhelm Tell in numerous poetical works[20] probably took place above Amsteg one day when Sir Konrad or Grisler, but more likely Konrad von Tillendorf,[21] happened to be hunting. The plump knight, who was having another of his headaches that day, sat by the River Reuss and let the others hunt. He would have liked to take his boots off and hang his naked feet into the icy water which, in the thirteenth century, was the best remedy against headaches. Unfortunately he was not alone. The Lady von Bruneck who was once again keeping him company talked incessantly into the rushing of the Reuss. Now and again he nodded, knew more or less what she might have been saying, and collected the small and bigger pebbles between his boots to throw into the fast flowing creek as though he wanted to demolish the mountains. To climb the Bristen or the Windgälle had not as yet occurred to medieval man. So there one sat, near Amsteg, which, as everyone knows, is a hole. High up, a blue sky. Once he said, "Nothing against the people of Uri!" and as she couldn't understand him either, he had almost to roar, "Nothing against the people of Uri!" It just wasn't the place for conversation and as a matter of fact dear Sir Konrad (as the gregarious damsel called him) was glad. He didn't know what was the matter with him. By now he could see nothing except fir trees and stones. Again he asked her Ladyship if this was what you call a föhn. Then he tried to think something—anything. Her Ladyship found the spot with moss absolutely enchanting—this whole landscape, these firs, these stones, these waterfalls, this air. It was as if time stood still. When after a long silence he discovered that he was still throwing pebbles, but now the large ones, into the spraying brook, panic took hold of him; not that he sensed his imminent murder but because he looked at all these pebbles and couldn't think of anything to think. They made him stupid. Hence his remark, "Nothing against these people of Uri. . . ." His servant, Rudolf the Harras, who tended the two horses, had settled himself at a suitable distance in case his Lordship might wish to move closer to her affable Ladyship, and had apparently fallen asleep so that he didn't notice the native haymaker or cowherd who came striding broadly down the steep slope, a crossbow slung over his right shoulder and with a boy by the other hand. It was the Lady von Bruneck who whispered, "Somebody's coming!" It can be assumed that the knight, who now turned, was not the one to give a first greeting. Haymaker, cowherd or poacher, it was in any case a native, a short man, thickset, rugged, with naked

knees, in a whitish smock with the hood haymakers use so the hay
they carry on their heads will not tickle their necks; he was not,
however, carrying hay that day, but a crossbow lightly over his
shoulder. And he came striding broadly, with his beard, rugged,
coming down over the steep slope; the little boy looked cheerful,
walking by his side. Konrad von Tillendorf, taken aback by the
apparition, waited with no urgency, and in vain, for some simple
greeting. The native came to a stop, lifted the crossbow from his
shoulder and bent it with the help of his foot, took an arrow from
the quiver, showed the boy how to set the arrow on the crossbow,
and looked about for birds. But nothing was flying. What a pity. The
knight would have liked to watch an arrow and a bird meet in
midflight. Now when the lively little boy noticed that there was a
knight and a lady sitting by the Reuss, Konrad von Tillendorf
couldn't help himself: he nodded and now the crossbow father
looked too[22] but didn't nod, stuck the arrow back into the quiver
like a poacher caught in the act and walked on with his broad stride
down the meadow, the crossbow back on his shoulder, as if nothing
had happened. The boy looked back twice. . . . He would have liked
to ask the rugged poacher what it's like further up there, when you
climb the St. Gotthard, whether there's snow etc. That wasn't a
poacher, remarked her Ladyship, but a hunter, a professional archer.
She thought she knew everything about everything, this Bertha, who
is not even authenticated.[23] She thought herself chic in her dress
from Lucerne, and sat upright drawing stalks through her narrow
mouth.

---

20. Even in the U.S.A. there originated operas and melodramas. One,
for example, with a score by Benjamin Carr (1768–1831), who was first
to publish the patriotic tunes "Hail Columbia" and "Yankee Doodle";
the famous actor John Hodgkinson (1767–1807) played the title role in
New York and Boston.

A libretto by the New York director William Dunlap (1766–1839)
under the title *Die Bogenschutzen oder die Bergler des Schweizerlandes*
(The Archers or the Mountain Folk of Switzerland) is considered the
first American work about Tell.

Wilhelm Tell's success seems to have been in a version by James
Sheridan Knowles (1784–1862). In Philadelphia the piece was offered
no less than 26 times between 1825 and 1830 and remained a favorite in

the American repertory over the next four decades. There exists furthermore a copperplate (anonymous) with the title *Die Helden der Freiheit* (The Heroes of Freedom) representing George Washington and William Tell.

21. Versions of record: Tilndorf, Tilendorf, Tillendorf, Thillingsdorf, Tellindorf, Dillendorf. Compare Karl Meyer: "In this case the much hated High Commissioner of the Urschweiz was called Tillen for short and the one who overmastered him the Tillen-shot or Tillen-killer or Tillen-Willi." *(Die Urschweizer Befreiungstradition.)*

22. In reference to the learned controversy as to the historicity of the character whose crossbow, as we so well know, has become the symbol for the quality of things Swiss, August Bernoulli writes (about 1872): "The fact that we don't know the real names of either the marksman or the victim is surely no reason to doubt the matter itself." Compare also Robert Walser: "I am convinced, for instance, that, to come back to Wilhelm Tell, the Swiss who loves liberty owes much to the High Commission, housed in his relatively interesting residence, insofar as the latter has spurred the former on to action etc."

23. Friedrich Schiller based his invention of a Lady von Bruneck on the assumption that the notorious High Commission was named Gessler (or Gesler)—which is not so—consequently that he had occupied Brunegg. Nevertheless, the possibility cannot be dismissed that there existed a Lady von Bruneck or Brunegg in Uri except that she played no part in the confederation sworn in 1291 and does not appear in "The Tradition of the Freeing of *Ur*-Switzerland," since she committed no heinous crimes against the forest people.

* * *

July came. Day in and day out the plump knight yearned for the flat land. He was still waiting for the Baron von Attinghausen to be finally able to receive him for negotiations regarding rights of way, duties, renunciation of powers etc.[24] He personally had no interest in extending the Hapsburgs' rule over this valley or Uri. On the contrary, that could have meant that he, Sir Konrad or Grisler, would be transferred to this valley for life—a thought that threw him backward onto his bed in broad daylight. . . . There lay the knight—his boots on his legs, hands behind his neck, his gaze turned to the ceiling, when the servant came and reported that the land magistrate from Schwyz was then staying over at Attinghausen.[25] Could there be some mistake, the plump knight asked so as not to have to jump from the bed in his anger at these forest people. They receive a subject of King Rudolf's heirs while they keep him, Sir Konrad or Grisler, the emissary, waiting around for weeks. This, he thought, was really something, but he only set his boots down on the floor and went on sitting on the edge of the bed, too tired, at that moment, to believe in a conspiracy.[26]

He merely shook his head instead of getting on his horse then and there and riding over with his armed men to arrest this Stauffacher, who was already known to the Hapsburgs.[27] He stepped in front of a mirror, pulled down his lower eyelid with his finger, to check if the bile had begun to discolor his eye—he knew what that meant: jaundice. . . .

----

24. "There existed at the time no conflict between the rulers and the territories that could not have been argued amicably, i.e., in the courts. The chronic dispute of the people of Schwyz with the cloisters of Einsiedeln and Steinen—before Morgaten—had in each case been decided by means of bloodless proceedings in which, to be sure, it was mostly the other side which had a complaint to file." (Marcel Beck, in an interview with *Sonntags Journal,* Zurich, 1970.)

25. "At that same time was there one in Schwyz named Stauffacher who lived at Steinen this side of the bridge. He had built himself a good stone house. On a day Gessler, in those days High Commisioner there in the name of the Empire, rode past and called for Stauffacher to ask to whom belonged the pretty lodging. Stauffacher answered him, oppressed and speaking low, "It is yours my Lord and my fief." And he dared not say it was his own so much did he fear the High Commissioner, who rode on. But Stauffacher was a wise man and had a clever wife. He turned the matter over in his mind, and feared the High Commissioner might take his life and goods." (*Das weisse Buch von Sarnen,* about 1470.) Compare A. Coulin: *"Befestigungshoheit und Befestigungsrecht"* (Fortifications, Their Sovereignty and Law).

26. "The secrecy in which the liberating deeds took place, the killing, as in an ambush, of the two Austrian High Commissioners, the secrecy of the consultations on the Rütli and at Treichi, Stauffacher's anxiety and his evasiveness when face to face with the High Commissioner, the flight of the Schwyzer and of the two Unterwaldners (Melchtal, Baumgarten) to the imperial valley of Uri—it is only in the course of time that all these things have acquired the brilliancy of glorious actions. Originally they were felt, like all secret actions in the Middle Ages, to be not unobjectionable." (Karl Meyer, *Die Urschweizer Befreiungstradition.*)

27. "As the head of the College of Swiss Magistrates, Rudolf Stauffacher gets into a dispute with the Hapsburg Commissioners right

after the passing of the country into the rule of King Rudolf's line, when he taxes the Cloister of the Cistercian nuns of Steinen. He defies Sir Hartmann von Baldegg, Rudolf's highest House and Imperial official, who defended the tax-free status of cloisters, and the nuns' appeal to the queen." (Karl Meyer, *ibid.*)

* * *

Once a child asked him, "Are you the Toggeli now?" probably because the jaundice was beginning to discolor his face. As Sir Konrad or Grisler, himself a father, amused and without any of the knight's grand manner, asked him what a Toggeli might be, the child ran away in terror and he understood only that he ought not to have laughed. The child screamed as if the Lord High Commissioner held a whip and had mistreated him. Later the knight asked young Rudenz what the child could have meant. Rudenz blushed as if the child had said something improper or too appropriate and, playing the man of the world, assured him there were no more Toggelis[28] nowadays.

---

28. Golzern was an alp in the old days. On what is now called the Metzgerberg stood a hut and there lived and worked three servants or three brothers, the chief herder, a cowherd, and the boy. There was little work to be done because the cattle on the pasture hardly needed tending and were never stabled. Once when they didn't know what to do with their high spirits and boredom they went and whittled a crude head out of a piece of wood, dressed it up in rags and stood the puppet behind the table. They made fun of this Toggle or Tunsch (also called Tunggel) and called him "Häusäli." My source thinks it means "Hanseli" or Johnny. When they were eating their whipped cream they asked, "Haüsäli, you want a bite?" and smeared a big chunk under his nose and around his snout. By and by they put a spoon in his claws and showed him what he was supposed to do with it. And be damned if that Toggel didn't begin to feed himself! First they were scared, but got used to it bit by bit and started their tricks again. Once when they were playing cards the herder asked, "Häusäli, you want to play too?" and put the cards in his paws. At first he was only supposed to hold the cards and his partner looked them up himself and played them. Little by little, however, the Tunsch held the cards firmly and played for himself. What a laugh!

From then on he always played along . . . and whoever had him for a partner was sure to win. The monster nourished himself well and grew. Every Sunday they had to carry him over to the neighboring Chrottäbiel to take the sun, and he was so fat that all the three of them together could hardly lift him. When they went to Oberstafel they took him along and again in the fall when they returned to Golzern. But it was always the herder who carried on the worst. Summer was over, the mountain meadows paled, winter had posted its advance sentries on the mountain peaks. That meant coming down from the alp. When the cows were rounded up and everything ready, Häusäli turned up too, but not to celebrate a heartwarming goodbye. With a grim and severe gesture the Toggel ordered the herder as headman on the alp to remain, the others he allowed to take off but not to look back until they had reached the Egg. And so they did. The herder stayed, the others went off with the cattle, and when they had reached the Egg they looked back and, shuddering and horrified, saw the Toggel stretch the herder's bloody skin across the roof of the hut. Since that time the place is called Metzgerberg (Butcher's Mountain). (Josef Müller, *Sagen aus Uri* [Legends of Uri].)

* * *

The conference at Attinghausen somewhere around the end of July came and went without results. They sat in a hall by no means rustic. The old man wore a cap of Lombard velvet, sat in a chair whose carved back rose above him, said nothing and coughed his little hacking cough. So as not to come riding roughshod the emissary of King Rudolf's heirs began by speaking in a general way: about changing times. Although one was unable to imagine an end to these Middle Ages the plump knight said, certain changes could hardly be kept from coming, were even desirable, there were certain institutions upon this earth capable of improvement etc. The old man of Attinghausen looked as if he were stuffed, though with no sign of a stroke. He said, *"Wie vor des chünges zyten."* ("As in the days before the king.")[29] A servant brought wine from Lombard. As always when he wanted to seem more relaxed than he was, Konrad von Tillendorf had the bad habit of crossing his legs and fiddling with his glove. It wasn't only a matter, he said, of tariffs,[30] but got no further with his speech. "As in the days before the king." Nothing else came under consideration for Uri. "As in the days before the king." He had hoped young Rudenz would mediate. But no. Uli (as his uncle called him) supported the old man in his silence, and Sir Konrad or Grisler talked much too much. As he became conscious of this and fell silent one could hear the Reuss because the Baron von Attinghausen was silent as well. He had already said it at the beginning: "As in the days before the king."[31] It is possible that the plump knight began little by little to smile: a people that only thinks toward the past! After the old man and land magistrate of Uri had mumbled that, as a matter of fact, one did not recognize King Rudolf's heirs, the plump knight might then and there have stood up. He finally took a little sip of the Lombard wine before, and not without smiling, he came back to the question of recognition; he took to be a fact that the Hapsburgs existed, the result of historical events, but the old man went on shaking his head, "as in the days before the king," thus and no other way. "As in the days before the king."[32] Now he said nothing more, this plump knight, who was thinking to himself: that's an old man's way of thinking, his grandchildren will think differently.[33] What he could no longer stand was this Baumgarten story about the bawdy Commissioner who had demanded a bath etc., and that Melchtal story with the gruesome punishment for a little finger etc.[34] When, becoming slowly impatient, he plainly called Baumgarten a murderer, he had finally to take in that Herr von Attinghausen was hard of hearing. Instead of being outraged by this foreign view of the matter, the old man nodded. He nodded as if it had been the bathing Commissioner who had been called a murderer. For a moment he was embarrassed so that he unconsciously plucked at his glove, then he inquired of young Rudenz as to the degree of his uncle's deafness. He was not deaf, was the answer, only hard of hearing, which however changed nothing in his viewpoint. The very fact however that this influential old man had not understood approximately one tenth of all that King Rudolf's heirs had submitted to this neighbor of theirs with his Imperial Freedom, gave the plump knight new hope; he drew his chair closer and recited everything over again—this time in a loud voice. . . . Again he was wrong: the old man of Attinghausen, a landowner and with Imperial Freedom, would not be roared at, least of all by Hapsburg.[35] The conference was at an end.[36] The plump knight, when he left the castle of Attinghausen, stretched out his hand (without a glove): it was raining. It was not a föhn, so it couldn't be the weather.

---

29. This refers to the time of the interregnum: 1245 (dethronement of Frederic II by the pope) to 1273.

30. "During the Rudolfian period the older (Austrian) Hapsburg line had brought almost every neighbor of Uri under its sovereignty: 1273

Schwyz and Nidwalden, 1264 the Glarus valley . . . but above all, Hapsburg-Austria gained the Gotthard route; 1283 the Gotthard valley Ursern; then the Rotenburgian rights governing Lucerne and surroundings, . . . the Gotthard customs, uniformly consolidated in Lucerne, formed the backbone of the Hapsburg's financial system in the ancestral lands. The valley of Uri and its trade routes became an imperial enclave in the middle of Hapsburg's possessions at the Gotthard, and doubtlessly came, like the rest of the imperial communities of our country, under the supervision of Hapsburg's house official who, in our regions, took care of House and Imperial Administration in a Personal Union. (Karl Meyer, *Gründung der Eidgenossenschaft im Lichte der Urkunden and Chroniken* [The Origin of the Swiss Confederacy, in the Light of Documents and Chronicles], 1930.)

31. The belief in what is traditional, an essence of *Ur*-Swiss thinking, whereby one fears innovations more than backwardness, has survived to this day. Compare for instance house rules for the penitentiary in Regensdorf in the canton of Zurich: "The personnel addresses the prisoners by their numbers. The prisoners go to the privy one by one to empty and rinse their chamber pots and return to their cells at once. Persons who are not blood relatives have no visiting rights. The visit is limited to thirty minutes and is supervised. Communication by mouth and in writing between prisoners is prohibited. Silence is enforced as a matter of principle. On the way to church, during services, entertainments, and the like, as well as on the way back to the cell, all conversation is prohibited. Absolute quiet is to be observed on the way to and from work. Prisoners in solitary confinement walk single file. A distance of three meters is maintained. Talking is prohibited. On a communal walk double file is permissible at a distance of about two meters. Decent conversation is allowed. It is incautious to discuss personal matters with other prisoners. Above all the address of a wife and other relatives should not be given to other prisoners. Censorship of incoming and outgoing mail is the responsibility of the director. Mail from former prisonmates may be placed in the personal file without notifying the addressee—."

32. " 'Vor des chünges zyten' ("as in the days before the king") was the *status debitus* which they have in mind in the *arenga* of their statement of confederation." (Karl Meyer, *ibid.*)

33. "Untenable, because undialectical" is the statement by Friedrich Engels: "The people of *Ur*-Switzerland have twice brought themselves to the attention of history. The first time when they so gloriously freed themselves from the Austrian tyranny; the second time at this moment, when they battle with God for the Jesuits and the fatherland. The glorious liberation out of the claws of the Austrian eagle in itself stands up very badly when we look at it in the light of day. There was only one time in its career when the house of Austria was progressive and that was

in the beginning, when it allied itself with the Philistine burghers of the towns against the nobility and attempted to found a German monarchy. It was progressive in the most bourgeois manner, but all the same it was progressive. And who most decisively obstructed this? The *Ur*-Swiss. The fight of the *Ur*-Swiss against Austria, the glorious oath upon the Grütli, Tell's heroic shot, the forever memorable victory of Morgarten; it was all the struggle of stubborn herdsmen against the pressures of the evolution of history, the struggle of stiff-necked, immovable local interests against the interests of the entire nation, the struggle of the primitive against education, of barbarism against civilization. . . . Two invasions have been attempted in more recent times against this simpleminded morality and primitive power. The first was that of the French in 1798. But these French, who have spread some civilization, at least, everywhere else, foundered against the Swiss. No trace of their presence remains, not one iota of the old habits and virtues were they able to eliminate. The second invasion came 20 years later and bore some fruit at least. It was the invasion of the English travelers, the lords from London, and the innumerable candlemakers, spice dealers, and bone merchants who followed after them. This invasion at least put an end to that old hospitality and the honest mountain dwellers in their alpine huts who had hardly known what money was, transformed themselves into the greediest, most loutish gougers anywhere in existence. . . . The greatest pride of these squares *Ur*-Swiss was at all times that they never deviated by a hair's breath from the customs of their ancestors, that they had preserved unaltered over the centuries the simpleminded, chaste, upright, and virtuous ways of their fathers. And that is true; every attempt at civilization has rebounded from the granite walls of their cliffs and their skulls. Who, on the 14th of July, 1789, defended the Bastille against the onslaught of the people, who, from behind their walls, shot down the workers of Faubourg St. Antoine with shrapnel and bullets? The *Ur*-Swiss from the Sonderbund (Separatist League),* grandsons of Tell, Stauffacher, and Winkelried. Who on the 10th of August, 1792, defended the traitor Louis XVI in the Louvre and in the Tuileries against the righteous anger of the people? The *Ur*-Swiss from the Sonderbund. Who, with the aid of Napoleon, suppressed the revolution of Naples in 1798? The *Ur*-Swiss from the Sonderbund." (Written 1847.)

34. *The White Book of Sarnen* (about 1740) as well as the *Chronicle of Aegidius Tshcudi* (1505–1572), as well as every Tell-play, back up the summary complaint against Hapsburg's High Commissioners ("they exerted great pressure upon the people") with only two concrete cases: Cunrad von Haumgarten and Arnold von Melchtal. The case of Stauffacher, who built a stone house without governmental permission and was called to account for it, is less applicable since Stauffacher was

---

*League formed in 1845 by seven Catholic cantons; defeated in 1847.

not punished in consequence of his excuse yet nevertheless fled to Uri to engage in conspiracy.

35. By "freedom" the Confederates of 1291 understand chiefly: freedom from Hapsburg. "We will be free as our fathers before us," the watchword with which Friedrich Schiller has endowed us and which is still in solemn use in today's Switzerland, in no way addresses itself to the local conditions of ownership, that is to say it is by no means a matter of freedom of the working man any more than the oath of Rütli concerned itself with the freedom of the native bondsmen: *ita tamen quod quilibet homo iuxta sui nominis conditionem domino convinienter subesse debeat et servire.* What was meant then was the freedom of the local barons and their independence, the defense of which, with body and soul, is the duty also of the simple people. The Swiss army (military service is obligatory for every Swiss) serves that *Ur*-Swiss idea of freedom to this day. Compare the general strike of 1918, when our army was called out against the socialist workers. How very much alive after six centuries is this unconditional will to independence, can be seen not only in the military expenditures (1970: 1.8 billion Swiss francs), but in the intellectual life of Switzerland as well; "Then it [the Swiss Writers' Association] will, after all its sophistications, suddenly find itself before the clear and basic question: where, in fact do you stand with respect to national defense? For it? Against? Even if against, no member of the Swiss Writers' Association would have to leave the country or lose the protection of our constitution. I think this makes it worthwhile, once again, to declare one's allegiance to the state." (Werner Weber, *Neue Zürcher Zeitung,* 5/31/1970.) Compare prison sentences for conscientious objectors.

36. The oldest extant historical works from the regions surrounding the Vierwaldstätter Lake date from the 15th century. . . . "Events of considerable importance may have taken place without a glimmer shining through the documents that have come down to us. . . ." (Karl Meyer, *Die Urschweizer Befreiungstradition.*) There exists no report, for instance, of any conference at Attinghausen in the year 1291 when the notorious High Commissioner was in Uri. If it could never have become known on the Hapsburg side because the representative of King Rudolf's heirs was shot to death on his journey home, the forest people, for their part, if they questioned their magistrate, could discover very little about what it was that Hapsburg had offered them. The deaf old man could only exhort them to unite. He died soon after.

*   *   *

The first day of August 1291 was a muggy day[37] and as the plump knight had not the faintest inkling that it was the day on which the forest people not only drove their cattle to pasture and made cheese and in the evening whetted their scythes etc. but also accepted an historical mission comparable with the missions of very few nations in history,[38] he breakfasted as usual: cheese with bread and some milk. Once more he rode to the building site at Silenen-Amsteg to set his bureaucratic conscience at rest. No trace of strike or sedition. He rode on. In the beginning young Rudenz sometimes escorted him but not any more. Since that hunt above Amsteg, Uli could not be dissuaded from the delusion that Sir Konrad had stolen his rich heiress of Bruneck away from him and would have nothing more to do with the foreigners. And so Sir Konrad rode alone. There was still snow on the mountains. He saw haymakers and herders who, being bondsmen, didn't know anything either and took this first of August, 1291, for just another day of socage which, as a matter of fact, it was. No solemn premonition filled the air, only the summer hum of blowflies around the sun-warmed dung. A muggy day and Konrad von Tillendorf would have liked to take a bath in the Reuss but not wishing to shock the pious forest people, he rode back to Altdorf. Lunch with Lady von Bruneck. In the afternoon he had to lie down on his bed. It was definitely the liver.[39] He lay and thought about things. One knew in the meantime that King Rudolf was dead. He thought about what and how he was going to report the political situation in this muggy imperial valley to his masters, King Rudolf's heirs. A blowfly which hummed in the chamber and wouldn't be caught, hampered the plump knight from thinking politically: all he could do was hope. It was, incidentally, not a blowfly but a bumblebee. Toward evening when the peasants were more likely to have time, he would have another consultation with Zurfrouen and Fürst, with one at least of the two, but received the same answer from both farmsteads: father had gone up on the alp today to visit a sick cousin—still the plump knight evidently came away with no suspicion, merely annoyed by the stupid excuse of these peasants whom, as he did admittedly say, the devil should take, wherever they happened at the moment to be.[40] If they would not negotiate, well then they would not. He'd had it up to here. Rudolf the Harras, his servant, should order a boat for the day after tomorrow, departure from Flüelen in the early morning. He thought them thick-headed and hide bound and crafty, these forest people, but not capable of revolution.[41] And so he spent the rest of the day, which is still celebrated in Switzerland and by the Swiss abroad, without foreboding; among other things he played with a black cat, attended to his neglected beard etc. Another evening with the Lady von Bruneck. They threw dice. As always it smelled of hay and one could hear how the servants whetted their scythes; bats flitted. Her Ladyship was sorry that Sir Konrad was ready to leave for home the day after tomorrow; Sir Konrad, on the other hand, was glad that by the day after tomorrow he'd be back among human beings. He didn't, of course, say so in these words but protested he would never forget this summer in Uri. . . . The old man of Attinghausen had been buried, the most important of the peasants were visiting sick cousins on the alp and so there was only one thing left which he, in his capacity as High Commissioner, had still to take care of: the customary ceremony with the hat on the pole.[42] One day, he hoped, would be enough for this ceremony.

---

37. The dating of the Oath of the Confederacy by Melchior Russ and Etterlin, "about 1292," "about 1294," as also in the first Tell-play "about 1296" as also by the chroniclers Brennwald and Tschudi, "1314," "1307," have turned out, according to the newest research, to be erroneous.

38. "It would mean thoroughly to misunderstand the Documents of Confederation of 1291 to construe them as anything but the will of the country people in that general ruin to stand back to back, to secure house by house, path by path, footbridge by footbridge by their own effort and God's help. This was no oath under some night sky and way out on the Rütli . . . it is an alliance which, as tradition tells us, was discussed by the broad light of day, in the middle of Brunnen, under the white glare of the August sun, set down in Latin, sworn to, and sealed in due and legal form: an act of state of the clearest formulation, clearest content and immediate validity. What promised this alliance an eternal duration was not some unheard of idea but solely the eternally existing unchanging need and God's help. What do its simple words mean! They mean the founding of the first modern national and constitutional state. By this action the confederates accepted a mission comparable to the mission of only very few nations in history. As the nation of Israel was given the task of forming a theocracy, the Greeks a free polis of free citizens, in order to oppose to the great oriental monarchies the worth of the little people and the worth of man, in this same way did these men raise, in the midst of a warlike era, the simple demand for safety of life and property." (Eduard Renner, *Goldener Ring über Uri*, 1954.)

39. Hepatitis (jaundice) can be caused by a virus but is in any case a

psychosomatic phenomenon, i.e., a certain tendency to depression which afflicted the Imperial Commissioner in this land of Uri may be the consequence as well as the cause of jaundice.

40. Whether the conspirators (Confederates) did in fact meet at the Rütli on that day as is generally assumed, or in Brunnen under the white glare of the August sun, as Eduard Renner asserts, is uncertain but changes nothing in the spirit of the conspiracy as it documents itself in the Bundesbrief (Statement of Confederation) nor in the roster of its participants of which the chroniclers leave no doubt. Stauffacher, Melchtal, Fürst, the "Eidgenossen," all well-known land owners. The idea that a nation of herdsmen conspired together is of a later date and misunderstands the medieval spirit of the conspiracy of 8/1/1291 which led to the founding of Switzerland.

41. "Does the Statement of Confederacy of 1291 signify a revolution? The *Waldstätte* merely wanted Justice, the old justice." (Karl Meyer, *Die Gründung der Eidgenossenschaff im Lichte der Urkunden und Chroniken*, 1930.) That the Rütli oath has no revolutionary character follows from the passage quoted above: "—in such a manner, however, that everyman shall be kept on his estate to be subject to his master and duly to serve him." The liberal historian explains why this sentence was included in the original document of the alliance "in the name of God." It was "out of consideration for those leaders and the gentry of the Forest districts who, like the Barons of Attinghausen, were either themselves lords of the manor and of bondsmen or, as stewards of estate and cellar of the secular and ecclesiastical nobility, interested in the preservation of seignorial rights and serfdom. One need only think of the knights of Silenen, the stewards of Erstfelden, the stewards of Stans, the stewards of Wolffenschiessen . . . the influence of this class which cooperated in the liberation movement is palpable elsewhere in the Statement of Confederacy. All these families pressed for the adoption of such an article because there existed, beside the political liberation movement in the Urschweiz, another movement of social emancipation that leaned to the left. The gentry of the Urschweiz wished to maintain their social position." (Earl Meyer, *ibid.*)

42. As regards the planting of that hat on that pole as a symbol of dominion and ownership, compare R. Schröder, *Deutsche Rechtsgeschichte* (History of German Law): "we are not dealing, as Friedrich Schiller leads one to believe, with an infamous invention on the part of this particular Commissioner but with a perfectly legal medieval ritual. The author of *Das weisse Buch von Sarnen*, about 1470, seems already to have forgotten this fact: 'he issued a decree that whoever should pass must bow before the hat as though it were the master himself standing there. . . .' Such ritual salutations are preserved to this day. Compare the service regulations of the Swiss army."

* * *

A regrettable incident occurred in that last hour. Sir Konrad von Tillendorf, notorious to this day under the name of Gessler, was just having his second boot handed him when the report came: someone had not saluted the hat on the pole. He sighed, as always when he was putting on these boots, and they had to report it to him twice; someone had not etc. This did not suit the plump knight at all. He wanted to get as far as Immensee today. He was so annoyed by the incident he didn't say a word; an hour later and the hat would no longer have been on the pole. He asked for his doublet, then the belt. His men-at-arms had unfortunately apprehended the man. He put on the gloves appropriate to official functions and was annoyed not so much at the man who, he hoped, had perhaps simply overlooked the hat on the pole, but at himself because he had not left at dawn. He had overslept. He considered how the regrettable incident might be most quickly settled. Without spectators it would have been simple: mercy before justice. All day yesterday nothing had occurred and he had no interest in playing up an individual case, this plump knight who still hoped to get as far as Immensee that day. There was a föhn, a light föhn, which could get worse from one hour to the next; he was already worried about crossing the lake. When he came to the square where the hat still hung on the pole the curious were already milling around. His men-at-arms, officious in front of their knight, drove the crowd back with their lances although nobody was trying to free the arrested man; they only wanted to watch. As often at such events, on horseback it was not so easy to get the horse into the right spot and keep it as quiet as you might wish, facing in the direction you wish etc. It danced and pranced and went so far as to drop some turds. When he recognized the man with the crossbow and the boy he remembered at once and his face lit up; the Lord Commissioner even smiled. He evidently thought the case could be settled with a joke: "You never greet anybody, I know! You just don't." But the forest people stared darkly and self-righteously. Although he was on horseback and therefore had a certain overview it was not clear to him how the majority stood toward the outsider. Did they resent it that the haymaker was not behaving like the majority or were they pleased? He himself, the haymaker with the

crossbow on his shoulder, looked uncertainly toward his countrymen instead of answering when he was asked his name. Someone
pushed out in front of the bunch, a small peasant with a red face and
menacing fists. When asked why the man was so excited a silence
fell. They all seemed to know—perhaps it was the fugitive peasant
from Altzellen whom these Uri people were pulling quickly back
into the crowd. . . . Now it was a matter of keeping his own men-at-
arms from committing the sort of foolishness to which armed men
are liable. It doesn't take much to make armed men feel threatened.
Therefore the plump knight ordered them with a sharp voice he did
not ordinarily use: Quiet, hands off, quiet! before he turned to the
haymaker who was meanwhile looking grim as well. Why didn't he
salute the hat was the question the knight put to him. The haymaker, however, surrounded by his countrymen in the center of the
square of Altdorf where his monument stands today, could not utter
a word, not even to answer the question that was trying to meet him
halfway, whether perhaps he simply hadn't seen the hat on the pole.
He was not used to answering questions in front of an audience and
did not look at the Commissioner, who was perhaps getting a bit
impatient, so much as at his countrymen. It was with them he would
have to go on living. He wanted to get as far as Immensee today! the
plump knight said, in order to hurry the haymaker's answer, which
did not help. He had a reddish beard and freckled skin, a choleric,
probably, who didn't always have an easy time of it with other
people. Why did he always carry a crossbow like that on his right
shoulder, asked Sir Konrad just to start him talking. That didn't
help either. There were some who seemed to be grinning. The
tension as to whatever his Lordship the High Commissioner was
going to come up with next was so great that it transferred itself to
the horse, and Tillen (which might, possibly, have been his nickname) could control it only by reining it roughly in, which cannot
help giving a rider the appearance of a brute and a bully. Startled,
the man with the crossbow now said, "My Lord, it's just something
that happened, not out of disrespect, forgive me, if I had wit would
they call me the Tell,[43] begging your mercy, it won't ever happen
again." A mistake then; the plump knight was glad to believe it since
the procedure was thereby shortened, and stroked his horse to calm
it. But the people of Uri were disappointed with this submissive
speech; the haymaker felt it and corrected himself: he was a free

man, he said, and didn't salute any Hapsburg hat! The plump knight was still stroking his horse, even smiled, for what hung on the pole was no Hapsburg hat but the imperial hat to which reverence was due even in a valley like Uri with its imperial freedom. Most of the people knew this, only the good haymaker obviously did not. Circumstances admittedly were somewhat complicated in those days. Now the matter was to all intents and purposes settled except that the crossbow father, because he'd had to be publicly lectured and could not bear the shame, corrected himself once more: and he'd salute no emperor's hat either, never, ever, a free man of Uri etc. This was unnecessary, but he'd said it. The man suddenly had a red face and even said it again, louder than before. Perhaps he too felt the föhn.[44] Some said, "God help him!" Others waited worldlessly for the arrest. The boy too felt that his father was confused and had committed some blunder and wanted to help and praise his father: he could hit a bird in flight. Nobody, at that moment, had questioned this.

When the Lord High Commissioner on his horse did not say anything whatever, momentarily at a loss how to be rid of this strange customer, the boy said his father could hit an apple at thirty paces. Nobody had questioned that either. Somehow or other Konrad von Tillendorf took it for a joke to save the situation: so let the crossbow-father go shoot[45] an apple from the head of his smart-alecky boy who was beginning to get on his—that is to say the plump knight's—nerves. He said it as he was already tightening the reins to ride out of the square—he couldn't understand why the Lady von Bruneck, who was still present, began to beseech him: Dear Sir Konrad! She took him seriously. She spoke of God. And now Father Rösselmann came up to also take it seriously. They had been waiting for some outrage all along, now they had one: father forced to shoot apple from child's head. Everybody was crowding in wanting to have seen it: father forced to shoot apple from child's head. The haymaker, seeing himself in the center of public sympathy, could hardly do otherwise: he took an arrow from the quiver, placed it on the crossbow to show his countrymen he was no windbag. Obviously he didn't hear what the Commissioner was meanwhile saying—nobody heard it; he only noticed in the confusion that he had forgotten something and took the arrow off the bow again and held it between his teeth while he bent the bow with the help of his foot (the way he had done recently near

Amsteg) and replaced the arrow on the bow, before an apple could be found. The silly smile on the face of the plump knight who still thought he had made a joke naturally embittered the forest people; again it was that peasant from Altzellen who could hardly be restrained in his rage, the one who had already beaten one high commissioner to death with his own hands. Now young Ulrich von Rudenz, nephew of the Baron von Attinghausen, too was speaking in the name of the people, in the name of his bondsmen, while the Commissioner only fiddled with his gloves obviously thinking he had the simple solution: reprieve for lack of apple. But the boy seeing his father in the center of public attention, did his bit, he actually found a green apple in his trouser pocket.[46] A lane was already forming, the crossbow-father kneeling before the lane was formed. That was the moment for Father Rösselmann who now also knelt down and begged for mercy with folded hands after the Commissioner, frightened by the course things were taking, had already twice said, "Joking apart!" But it was precisely the joke which enraged the forest people; they prayed God for the success of the apple-shooting.[47] It was almost too late when Sir Konrad or Grisler leaped from his horse; the kneeling archer was already taking aim, his eyes screwed up, when Sir Konrad or Grisler went to him and without another word took the arrow from his trembling crossbow—this fellow would have been capable of taking a shot at the green and quite small apple to prove his honor as a marksman.[48] It was an embarrassing moment for all: for the plump knight who had suddenly lost control of the situation, and for the praying crowd, but not least for the archer who felt he had been made fun of. His neck looked swollen; crossbow still bent, he had a confused uncanny air when the Lord High Commissioner, groping for the right word at that moment, regarded the beautiful arrow and returned it to him; the question whether he made these arrows himself, where it was that he lived, whether he had many children etc. remained unanswered—it was only asked out of embarrassment—the man seemed deaf with fury and stayed on his knees, though the apple-shooting was no longer in demand. Only the smart-alecky littlle boy was still calling to his father: he wasn't afraid in the least, he was saying, his father could hit a bird in flight etc. People were already beginning to leave the square when the Lord High Commissioner, now back on his horse, asked not without irritation, "What's this second arrow for?" Later, some were of the opinion that was not what happened: that the archer had a second arrow stuck in his jerkin from the beginning to revenge himself against the Commissioner if the master shot failed.[49] But the plump knight didn't mean the arrow stuck in the jerkin, which was, of course, the arrow he had taken from the crossbow with his own hand and returned to the archer; now he saw the archer taking a second arrow from the quiver and place it on the crossbow, hence his question: "What's this second arrow for?"[50]

The man blushed when he noticed the first arrow in his jerkin and didn't know what to say. He himself didn't know why he had not taken this arrow but a second one in order to show off his master shot, just for spite. Konrad von Tillendorf understood this confusion perfectly well but demanded that he now put both arrows in the quiver and get up— he was free. . . . Unfortunately the two men-at-arms had heard what the man, wanting still to impress his countrymen, had just said: that he knew very well what he'd wanted the other arrow in the jerkin for: he would have shot the commissioner dead, yes, right there in front of everybody.[51] The plump knight hesitated a moment; should he ask this choleric, "Is that what you said?" But the man could not recant or his countrymen would consider him a windbag his life long, and if he didn't deny and didn't challenge what the armed men said they had heard him say, there was no way, as everybody feared, to settle this without a trial, without imprisonment. So it was time and advisable now to take the man away.[52] The men-at-arms laid hold of him and because they did it in the medieval manner, that is to say not with kicks and cudgeling but by the strength of their arms, the forest people found it very unjust. What, after all, had this father with his crossbow and his child done? Many had not even heard the belated threat with the second arrow, others didn't take it too seriously.[53] But it was nine o'clock in the morning and Sir Konrad von Tillendorf, as already mentioned, wanted to get as far as Immensee that day—

---

43. *Das weisse Buch von Sarnen*, which is the first to name the archer in writing, shows variations in spelling: Thael, Tall, Tal, Tallen, whereas it calls the famous rock "Tellen-blatten." The traditional words of this hero of liberation used also by Schiller, "were I witty (prudent) I would be called by another name and not the Tall," can be understood only as a pun, that is, if we derive the nickname of the archer from "dahlen, tallen," which means to say and do simple and childish things.

44. It is statistically proven that during the föhn (a downward mountain wind warmed by friction), disturbances of psychic balance take

place, irritability etc., increased traffic accidents and marital crises, even suicides.

45. It is not to be assumed that the High Commissioner, whoever he may have been, knew the Toko story by Saxo Gramaticus. "According to the Danish chronicler Saxo Gramaticus (died 1204) Toko, the vassal of the Danish king Harald Blauzahn (10th century), made boast of his marksmanship and was thereupon forced to shoot an apple from the head of his son. The immediate derivation from the historical work of Saxo's, which used to be taken for granted, is unlikely, since it does not exist in manuscript, but only in a first printing of 1514. . . ." (Karl Meyer, *ibid.*) Beside the Toko story there exists the story of Heming Aslakson in Icelandic, as well as English, Estonian, and Finnish sagas with the same motive of an apple shooting. Compare Helmut de Boor: *"Die nordischen englischen und deutschen Darstellungen des A-pfelschusses"* (Nordic, English, and German Representations of the Apple-shooting) in *Quellenwerk zur Entstehung der Schweizerischen Eidgenossenschaft* (Sources Relating to the Orgin of the Swiss Confederation) III, Chronicles, volume 1, 1947.

46. "But to begin with, it is in fact an apple? Again Saxo and Ths. (the Thidreks saga) agree on this point while Hem. (Hemmings-Thattr) deviates in setting the nut as target, Eindr. (Eindrida-Thattr ilbreids) the manmade pawn. Here too, however, the identity of the two oldest sources with the German-English group (Henning Wulf, Tell, William) may be decisive: we take the apple to be the most ancient target." (Helmut de Boor, *ibid.*)

47. In all versions of the Nordic saga as well as the Swiss one, the apple shooting is successful. There are no variants, for example, in which Tell does place his child in jeopardy but shoots the inhuman Commissioner, nor a version in which a faulty shot kills the child, and no version in which the indignant populace forcibly sabotages this inhuman performance.

48. The art of sharpshooting is still cultivated in Switzerland and is part of Swiss nationhood, even though the rifle may have lost much in military importance. There is hardly a village without its sharpshooter's association. In the first half of the 20th century the Swiss often won the world championship in all three positions (standing, kneeling, prone) with the carbine as well as with the army rifle. It is only in recent times that they have been upset, principally by the Americans, Finns, and Soviet Russians in a sport which, for the Swiss, is more than a mere sport.

49. It is a fact that this version, which corresponds to the Scandinavian saga, is more convincing and offers more to an oral tradition, but this does not prove its correspondence to the factual events. Compare the

history of miscarriages of justice based on plausible testimony of witnesses.

50. According to tradition Wilhelm Tell's first answer is perfectly prudent, an excuse: "that it's the marksman's habit" (Chronicle by Aegidius Tschudi). It is only after the guarantee which insures his life that his words become bolder: he would have shot down the High Commissioner if necessary. It is true there is no lack of discrepancy between the sagas, as Karl Meyer has pointed out. The Danish Toko does not try excuses but immediately answers with his speech of defiance. But whereas Toko must follow his defiance, that he intended the remaining arrows for the king himself, with the performance of yet another daring stunt—namely skiing down a cliff (which corresponds somewhat to the Nordic discipline of the ski jump) which Toko successfully survives, the Norwegian version of the apple-shooting saga again ends with Egill not punished for these same defiant words: "But the king valued this in him and all found that he had spoken bravely."

51. Compare Peter Bichsel, *Des Schweizers Schweiz* (The Swiss Man's Switzerland) 1969: "I simply cannot imagine that the ancient Confederate Swiss were more ideal characters than my neighbor and I."

52. While *The White Book of Sarnen* reports only the arrest and the threat by the Commissioner ("that he would put him in a place where he would never more see the sun and moon"), the later chronicler Aegidius Tschudi supplemented: "so that I may be safe from you," which makes the measure taken by the Commissioner plausible, Tell has, at all events, uttered a hypothetical threat of murder.

53. Even in a constitutional state one would have to count on disciplinary measures following the conduct described by the chroniclers. Much more modest provocations (without threat of murder), for instance against a teacher or judge in office, let alone against a major or colonel etc., are punishable. The words of Tell as handed down to us have not, after all, become the yardstick of our freedom of speech.

* * *

Everyone in Uri could imagine how things went for the High Commissioner out on the lake. The lake was green that day, green with a white froth which the wind tattered. The rowing was a desperate business, for the skiff rocked on the hard and pointed waves, often positively reeled. It splashed from all directions. But there was some headway made, even though the two men-at-arms were not skilled oarsmen, thanks to the wind at their backs, which came in gusts. After a quarter of an hour Sir Konrad or Grisler was completely drenched. It even seemed to him that they got on faster than that time with the boatman called Ruodi who was not available today. With both hands gripping the bench, eyes straight ahead, the plump knight looked forward to the open land or at any rate tried. His armed men on the other hand (both from the Thurgau) were afraid they would never make it and for the time being silently cursed the knight. With four of them together with Harras and that crossbow fellow from Uri, whom they could have pressed into service, it would have been easier, but their capricious knight hadn't wanted that and so they sat here, the three of them, in this heavy skiff. The waves came with crests of froth which sloshed into the skiff, then overtook them so that the two rowers who faced backward had the impression they were not getting ahead while the plump knight who faced forward comforted them: The Rütli was already in sight. But to check whether the knight's reassurance was correct the rowers would have had to turn and that was quite impossible because one could hold course on this raging lake only by incessant rowing. And it was not even a heavy storm, merely the föhn. The sun was shining. When Sir Konrad or Grisler, in order to spur on the two Thurgauers, promised them a free weekend, they did not look at him, they no longer believed in a weekend; the only reason their hair did not stand on end was that it was wet. Their helmets they'd thrown into the skiff. The plump knight did not feel perfectly easy either, with the water sloshing into the skiff and in the distance the perpendicular cliff of the Axen. There was no other boat in sight that day on the green lake. Nevertheless Sir Konrad von Tillendorf held in his silent conviction that he had acted properly in simply leaving the man with the crossbow behind on the shore, guarded by his groom for a while, until the skiff was well out on the lake. What goes on in the head of a man who shoots apples! Shortly before Sisikon, where to this day they point out the famous Tellenplatte and where a chapel bears witness that God was on the side of the people of Uri, things were undoubtedly getting worse and worse; the waves were driving the skiff toward the rocks. The skiff had barely missed being smashed in pieces. This had always been an ill-famed spot (as the locals knew, only the foreigners did not) where many a man had battled when the föhn blew. No wonder stories had sprung up around[54] the spot. It was a great and arduous labor for the two oarsmen.[55]

54. "The details of the lake crossing and the rescue at the Tellenplatte, what became of the crossbow, placed in the back part of the ship and which the fleeing Tell took away with him etc., point to the combinations by which later revisionists attempted to justify, provide motivation, and fill the gaps. Like Tschudi they wished to picture the Tell story to themselves in every detail." (Karl Meyer, *Die Urschweizer Befreiunestradition.*) Compare *Eidgenossische Chronik* (Swiss Federal Chronicle) by Melchior Rust (written 1482–1488): "What happened to Wilhelm Tell on the lake." The historian August Bernoulli (1891) believed "that the saga originally ended with the shooting of the High Commissioner at the Tellenplatte." The version which opposes this and which Friedrich Schiller has made famous abroad no doubt corresponds to the skiing feat of the Danish Toko saga.

55. "The High Commissioner and his servant crossed the lake toward Brunnen with much distress and labor," it says in Aegidius Tschudi's story, that is to say they managed without Tell, as those on shore could see.

* * *

By the time they reached Brunnen[56] the two oarsmen were completely exhausted, their legs wobbled under them, and they left it to the knight to thank God. Luckily the sun was shining. He hung his doublet and trousers on a tree so that they looked like a scarecrow and gazed back one last time toward Uri. Once and never again! The men-at-arms showed the calluses on their four hands so as not to have to row on to Küssnacht that day. The other possibility was to go by land, an arduous ride, he knew, when you had a headache, and he had a bad one just like that first day, though he had not felt it in his terror out on the lake. By now, thought Sir Konrad von Tillendorf, one more day didn't matter. They spent the night near Brunnen by the lake which sealed his fate,[57] but was more comfortable—one night in dry hay.

56. In a strong föhn a landing at Brunnen is said to be extremely difficult. *The White Book of Sarnen* does not mention a landing at Brunnen, and only rejoins the Commissioner in the Hollow Lane near Küssnacht, whereas the chronicle by Aegidius Tschudi assumes a successful landing in Brunnen.

57. If the Commissioner had ridden on that day it would at least be unlikely that the archer from Uri, who pursued him on foot, in part over difficult mountains, would have arrived at the Hollow Lane in time.

* * *

Sir Konrad or Grisler, but ever more probably Sir Konrad von Tillendorf,[58] reached the Hollow Lane[59] around noon, hungry for a good meal at Immensee; he was thinking of fried fish[60] when he felt a sudden pain.[61] In the first moment the stabbing pain seemed almost familiar to him and he still thought he could hide it when it doubled him over. It is uncertain whether he had time to recognize the man with the reddish beard and bare knees who now stepped out from the bushes, upright and with his broad stance, the crossbow in his right hand, before everything turned black before his eyes; only a rattle in his throat as the two servants tried to support him but could not. They had to lay the plump knight down on the ground. What it was that the archer in the hedge enunciated in those moments of first aid (for which neither of the men-at-arms was trained) found scant attention in that time and place; one of the servants merely said, sonofabitch![62] but the latter had already disappared into the bushes. A farm wagon or stretcher was not easy to come by as the peasants were in their fields at that hour. When he came to once more and opened his eyes, the plump knight found himself alone in the landscape—he did not understand what had happened, whence this pain, why these continual cowbells and this blood on his hand, blood with pine needles. Although he lay with his eyes open, he no longer recognized the mountains which might have eased him,[63] nothing left but what was nearest: leaves in the midday sun, woods with shade glistening between the tree trunks (the sun probably on cobwebs), and moss, quiet with the hum of summer a long as his throat did not rattle. He wanted to raise himself to look for his horse—he suddenly remembered the horse which grazed in a clearing—and felt a pain that at once threw him backward. In Schwyz they probably already knew about this glorious deed;[64] as everything turned black again in front of the plump knight's eyes, still he heard cowbells—

---

58. "Tillendorf died between the spring and fall of 1291, which means in that critical time when the High Commissioner of the chroni-

cles which precede the Confederacy must have succumbed." (Karl Meyer, *ibid.*)

59. "No other road leads to Küssnacht" (Friedrich Schiller) is based on the error of the earlier chronicles that the High Commissioner resided at Küssnacht; the fact is that the event proceeds in the opposite direction.

60. The region is known to this day for its fish cuisine: "Zuger Röteli," "Felchen a la Zug," etc.

61. "And as they came riding along he stood there behind a bush, bent his crossbow, and shot an arrow into His Lordship." *(Das weisse Buch von Sarnen.)* "And as they approached the Hollow Lane he [Tell] heard all manner of plots by the Commissioner against him. He, however, had bent the crossbow and shot the Commissioner through with his arrow so that he fell from the horse and was dead from that hour on." (Chronicle by Aegidius Tschudi.)

62. It was not without justification, though it caused a general outrage, that the Palestinian assassins who from their ambush shot at an El-Al plane as it was taking off from Zurich on February 18, 1969, invoked Wilhelm Tell. The killing of the High Commissioner at Küssnacht as described by the Swiss chronicles corresponds to the methods of El Fatah.

63. The claustrophobia of the notorious High Commissioner at the time of the founding of the Swiss Confederacy is not unusual for a medieval man. The physician and poet Albrecht von Haller (1708–1777) was the first in his famous didactical poem *"Die Alpen"* (The Alps) to create an enthusiasm for mountains which was not granted to medieval man. What in Albrecht von Haller's work retains the character of an apologia, later, especially in J. W. von Goethe and others, becomes natural feeling which romanticism sometimes raises to exaltation until, primarily through the English (first conquest of the Matterhorn by E. Whymper in 1865), we reach the advent of alpinism. Only through the mass tourism of the 20th century does the pleasure of mountains become fully popular, thanks, not least, to the cable car and ski lift.

64. Even though historians are unable to prove either the name of the archer or the name of the Commissioner, a killing of a commissioner near Küssnacht is hardly in question. That we are here dealing with a deed of heroic glory is taught in the Swiss grade schools to this day. If we compare the Tell story to the Nordic sagas which come closest to it, e.g. the Toko story and Egill story, which are admittedly somewhat older (which means that plagiarism in the reverse sense is impossible), the discrepancies, as Karl Meyer has already mentioned, are in fact considerable: both Nordic heroes, Toko as well as Egill as, by the way, also some others who hit an apple or a nut, do not, after accomplishing their master shot, turn themselves into treacherous murderers whereas the peripatetic Nordic saga (the apple shooting) turns the treacherous killer of Küssnacht into a hero.

*   *   *

It was over an hour before the two men-at-arms finally came with a farm wagon on which to load the knight whose throat no longer rattled. The Hollow Lane, of course, was not suitable for farm wagons and the undertaking was not so simple, particularly as he was still breathing. Unfortunately there were some children running behind and they saw a knight the way they never imagined a knight, his face all smeared with blood and pine needles, because he'd probably tried to chase a blowfly away with his hand. He lay with his eyes open but died upon the bumpy transport to Immensee, the arrow stuck in his already diseased liver.

Translated by Lore Segal and Paul Stern

From
MILITARY SERVICE RECORD

We gave our oath of allegiance on September 3, 1939, at Arbedo, Ticino. I wrote about it in a little journal, "Pages from the Knapsack." An incident on that day, mentioned only in passing in my naïve little journal, appears different in retrospect. Apparently at that time I didn't want to admit to a shock.

The captain who administered the oath is named Wyss and is commanding our battery for the first time. On the train he is already going from car to car addressing people who bear the number 73 on their service topcoats, giving orders in advance. Obviously nervous. The seriousness of the situation (Hitler invades Poland) concerns everyone, but apparently this captain in particular; he doesn't know us and is dependent on us. He is not little, but just short enough that hardly any of the men have to look up to him.

After our oath is sworn, there's a lot to do in preparation for moving out: loading of ammunition, grouping of the four gun crews, and so on. Then, in the course of this day, things are far enough along so that Captain Wyss has time to inspect our ranks. From platoon to platoon, man to man, each must display both his hands, first the upside, then the underside, as if the captain were a palm reader. Along with that, each man must state his profession: milker, mechanic, manual worker, blacksmith, bricklayer, farm hand, store clerk, office employee, locksmith, hod carrier. A captain who wants to know his soldiers. So I show him my hands, first the upside, then the underside, and I say, "Cand. arch, ETH." That's how we're called. I am not aware at this moment that Captain Wyss, who is scrutinizing the college student, works in the same field, as a building technician—without a college diploma, but apparently well-positioned. "Cand. arch.," I am obliged to repeat. And since this designation seems to annoy him, I say, "student at the Federal Polytechnic Institute." Apparently it is my hands that displease him: "college student" is what he can see, he says. I am suspect. The next man: packer. Now, those are hands.

After everyone has shown his hands, it's parade march in columns of four abreast on somewhat stony terrain, with Captain Wyss stationed on top of a little hill in the manner of the generals in the old oil paintings. Columns of four abreast, heads swinging round in salute. Suddenly there is shouting. The company comes to a standstill, as if turned to stone, rifles shouldered, all eyes front—myself included. France and England have declared war: maybe my mind is on that. The shouting goes on (I no longer recall words). By the time I grasp that it is I being addressed, the voice is practically hoarse. "You, yes you!" When I am lined up in front of him, he is no longer shouting; he is white as chalk. Who do I think I am? Then the usual speech about attitude toward service. It is possible that as outside man I arrived late on the turn of the column. The heavy shoes pinch his feet too, says Captain Wyss. Then, speaking again after seeming to have regained his composure—and this I remember word for word: "In case of actual war, I have very specific postings for people like you!" In response to my question whether I might answer, he bawls the question have I understood or not and the order, "Back in line!" What I have understood is that Captain Wyss can have me dispatched, under the oath of allegiance.

I never asked myself at that time, Will our army fight? No doubt about it then. Possibly a drunk might say, "Let them come, the Bosch, just let them come!" For the rest, no bravado, only the certainty that the Swiss army would not go the way of the Czech army, no indeed, rather it would emulate the astonishing Finns against the Russians. When the first reports of victory for the German *Wehrmacht* came on our radio, I was on Kitchen detail fetching the kettle of soup and sacks of bread, so hadn't heard anything. They came angrily with their mess tins, muttering. Only if asked did they volunteer with an angry laugh that the Germans have always been big talkers. The swift collapse of Poland was a disappointment, but then Poland was far away. And later the even swifter collapse of Holland and Belgium . . . Holland and Belgium didn't have mountains as we did. One knew perfectly well that the German

Wehrmacht would not be stopped at our border. Nobody, nary a lieutenant nor a captain, made that claim. In this respect we thought ourselves without illusions. But we would fight. We didn't need any official announcements to that effect; it was a foregone conclusion borne out of Swiss history. Official announcements of this kind were not addressed to us but rather to Hitler, lest he labor under illusions. Otherwise to what purpose our day and night exercises? France occupied, and suddenly the Germans were near Geneva. But we would fight. From setback to setback until protected by the mountains. The new concept: *reduit.* That's where they would get stuck with their panzer units.

I remember how this concept relieved me. I don't remember its ever being discussed among enlisted men. This or that exercise did strike us as dilettantish. But at least we trained in the mountains—from time to time in the Engadine, then in the Ticino again. No doubt about it, those cliffs and scree deserts and gorges, those dangerous roads and avalanche-threatening slopes in winter would be our allies. Some of our technical equipment compelled the belief that in combat what counts is the man. Especially in the mountains. The captain didn't have to tell us that; we experienced it ourselves every time we took up position. I don't remember ever having looked upon our army with irony at that time. In general the terrain alone was too sobering. On flat land—at that time sitting under the apple trees near Zurich—I could readily picture the German *Wehrmacht* (up to then known only from photos), swarms of armored cars, and so on. But not here. Here one almost forgot them. No question that our general staff took its own concept seriously. There was visible evidence: construction of dugouts in the mountains (for which I once had to draft blueprints in a military office) and munitions magazines in the rock, bombproof at a glance. How supply lines were supposed to function after the bridges had been blown up, and, come to think of it, how the general staff imagined we could fight after the loss of our industries and cities—such things, of course, they couldn't explain to us. (The enemy, after all, was listening in.) Our families under German occupation while we are in the mountains . . . : our imaginings needn't get so detailed, in the hope that it really wouldn't come to that.

Translated by Alice Carey

From MONTAUK

Recently (though now it is already years ago) I chanced to see him again from a distance in Zurich (on the Limmatquai); a weighty man now. We had been at school together in Zurich. No idea whether he saw me too; he did not turn around, and I felt guilty because I just remained standing where I was and did not at once go after him. So the last view I had of him was only from the back. Without a hat. Broad shoulders. He is very tall, unmistakable in a crowd, and I had seen him just before from the front. He was looking straight ahead, obviously deep in thought, but then he looked down at the curb, as if he had also recognized me. He knows and I know what he has done for me. I did not even call out across the street to make him turn. What does W. want with my eternal gratitude? And anyway I know that, all in all, I cannot measure up to him. In class he was always at the top, though he was not a grind. He was more intelligent than the rest of us but could not take his intelligence lightly, so he was conscientious as well. He was always rather embarrassed when the teachers praised him, and unwilling to be regarded as a model pupil, he could at times be very insolent to them. After school I used to walk home with him: it was out of my way, but worth it—from him I first heard about Nietzsche, Oswald Spengler, Schopenhauer. His parents were very rich, but that he considered unimportant, nothing to be self-conscious about. After graduation he could, for instance, have toured the world, but he was as little interested in that idea as in a car of his own. He disliked such superficialities. He had a philosophical bent; I was amazed by all the things he had in his head. He was also very musical, which I am not; he spent whole evenings playing me records of Bach, Mozart,

Anton Bruckner, and others whose names I had never even heard; nobody is completely unmusical, he said. I was at that time writing for newspapers, and I felt proud when my little pieces were published; my urge to assert myself was, I believe, the first thing about me that disappointed him. Of course he understood that I had to earn money, but the things I wrote embarrassed him. He encouraged me to draw, since in this direction he thought me not untalented. His feeling for the graphic arts was also unusual, and it was not just the result of reading; it came entirely from his own sensibilities. In spite of his encouragement, however, I had no confidence in my drawing abilities, but I did learn from him what to look for in pictures. In philosophical concepts he was soon so far ahead of me that I could not converse with him on equal terms; he hardly ever mentioned whom he was reading at the time, so it may well be that I credited him personally with things that really belonged to Sigmund Freud. Not that he deliberately deceived me. It was just that he saw no point in mentioning sources of which at the time I had never even heard. And so he encouraged me to draw. He himself gave up playing the cello, because in spite of all the practice he put in, he could not satisfy his own high standards; his hands were too clumsy. In all sorts of ways W. made life difficult for himself. His parents of course knew that he would never take over the family business, though he did in fact in later years become a director, but only very reluctantly. For a time he studied medicine, then passed his preliminary examinations; I never really understood why he felt obliged to give it up, but it was certainly not for frivolous reasons. Later he started to paint, and I admired what he produced; it was anything but dazzling, but it had an elemental quality. He was an unusual person; no doubt things were more difficult for him than for the rest of us. He was also physically my superior. His parents had a tennis court in their garden and, since I had little money to spare, W. gave me his old rackets so that we could play together. He was not a bit interested in winning; it was simply that he played better, and I was able to learn from him what he himself had learned from a coach, and more: he also taught me to lose, not to play just for points. It didn't matter to him what he himself had learned from a coach, and more: he also taught me to lose, not to play just for points. It didn't matter to him, of course, since he scored all the points anyway, but it was hopeless for me. I enjoyed those hours very much, and when he was obliged sometimes to tell me that the court was too wet to play on, I was unhappy. I dreamed of W. When I visited him, a maidservant would open the door and politely ask me to to wait in the hall until she had inquired inside, and then of course I had the feeling that I was intruding, even if W. did not send me away. W. seldom called on me, but if I did not call on him for weeks at a time, he was surprised. He was a warmhearted friend, in fact my only friend at that time, for beside him anyone else seemed unthinkable; no one could ever have measured up to W. His parents, who viewed him with some concern, were always friendly to me; when W. asked them whether I might stay for supper, they always said yes. It was, incidentally, the first rich family I ever came to know, and nicer than others I have known since. On the whole I felt rewarded. It was more difficult when I wanted to give things to W.—for his birthday or at Christmas. He was always touched, but embarrassed, for his taste was better developed than mine, and things had often to be returned for exchange. At that time I had my first girl, and of course I could not exchange her. She was afraid of W., I believe, and unwilling to recognize his superiority, which grieved me. This was forty years ago. I often asked myself what W. got from me. We walked a lot; we went swimming together. He also had an extremely sensitive eye for the beauties of nature. Mechanical things—overhead cables and so on—offended him almost physically. Through him I came to appreciate Caspar David Friedrich, Corot, later Picasso and African masks, but he was never at all pedantic about it. Much of what he knew he kept to himself. I had walked all over Greece, and of course I told him about it, but when I did so, I had the feeling that W. would have seen more. It was a feeling that he himself, I think, shared; he would listen, but then could not resist interrupting me to point out something worth seeing that I should certainly not have seen but for him, something of immediate interest, an unusual moth, for instance. He simply saw more. There was only one thing for which I was never grateful: his suits, which were a size too large for me. My mother could of course shorten the sleeves, the trousers too; but all the same, they never really fitted me. I wore them only in order not to offend W.; he meant it well, knew that I could not afford suits of my own, and the material, when he passed on a coat or a jacket to me, was always still in perfect condition. Why he did not continue wearing the things himself was none of my business. He was in no way a fop or a slave to fashion. But his parents had a tailor who, I think, came to the house from time to time. And anyway, he gave me other things which he had not worn himself—gramophone records, for instance, a whole symphony. He never gave presents blindly, as the newly rich tend to do; the gift was never irrational or extravagant for my circumstances. He had an inkling, without my ever having to tell him, of how little a young reporter and reviewer earns. He had sensitivity enough, he was indeed embarrassed on my behalf by the luxury of his home—quite unnecessarily, in fact, for I never identified W. with luxury. He seemed to me, in his room with a view over the garden, the city, and the lake, more like a Diogenes—his rarefied spirit giving him independence. He rode on streetcars like anybody else. In all things he never chose the easy way; he was always hard on himself. In October, when the water is cold, he would swim across the lake and back. Later, W. paid for my whole course of studies: sixteen thousand francs (worth more then than now) spread over four years, which is to say four thousand francs a year. Actually I am sorry I have even mentioned the suits. I was not annoyed when suddenly, in the middle of a conversation, he would recognize his own jacket again and remark how well English materials wear and it was a pity and so on; I found it rather comic—nothing more. For a long while he kept inviting me to concerts, and not only at the last moment because his mother couldn't use the tickets. He really did believe that no one could be unmusical through and through, and indeed I often was thrilled—in a low-brow sort of way, as I could see from his face; at such times W. was silent—not supercilious, just embarrassed. All the same, he continued inviting me to concerts, but never to the theater. He was by no means blind to the theater, but his attitude was far more critical than mine. Altogether he was more critical than I was, even toward himself. I often found him in a state of genuine despair. He was a person who could not take things lightly—himself least of all. His despair was not hysterical. He could describe clearly and sensibly the problems he found insoluble. Anything I could then say to him would only emphasize how much alone he was. The worries of an ordinary mortal—like, for example, my worries over a Jewish fiancée during the thirties—could not be compared with his; even I could feel that. His troubles were exemplary, mine merely personal, and these were capable of solution, in various ways which he confided to me. Not that W. lacked sympathy; but there was no one who could help him with his own concerns, certainly not his father, a kind but sober man, or his mother, who regarded herself as an intellectual and whose cultural wanderlust he saw as escapism. Many years later, when we had not seen each other for a long time (I had been spending a year in America), I told him of my impending divorce. W. asked no questions, but his silence was enough to show me how self-righteously I had depicted the matter to him. We were tramping through woods, and W. tried to talk of something else, but in that moment I had no eye for moths. To stay on the subject of my divorce, I asked him about his own marriage. Although I had long been familiar with the story he unfolded, what he now told me was more to the point, richer in complications, and its deeper insights could not be applied to my own particular case. It would have been more than tasteless if I had attempted to bring the subject back to my own difficulties. His divorce permitted no comparisons. All the same, I did eventually get divorced. At the time I did not notice that during these years we were almost always alone together, never among a group, which would have enabled me to see my friend pitting himself against others. This was due as much to myself as to him, although he did indeed dislike social occasions. I did not suffer from the sense of his superiority as long as we were alone; I was used to it. As I said, I felt rewarded, singled out, as in the days when I was permitted to walk home from school with him. He gave me the Engadine. Even today I cannot drive through that area without thinking of W. And I do not just mean that otherwise a journey to the Engadine would have been beyond my means. He knew the Engadine intimately. He was also the better climber. His family had a mountain guide who had given him instruction year after year. Without W. I should never have climbed those mountains. He knew when and where there was a danger of avalanches and how to negotiate a tricky stretch of territory; he tied the red avalanche thread to his rucksack, inspected the slope carefully, tested the snow, then swept off down the valley on his skis, and all I had to do was to follow in his bold tracks as best I could. Once, when I broke a ski in a heavy fall, W. bought me a new pair so that we could continue with our tour—not the most expensive brand, which would have embarrassed me, but all the same a better brand, with better bindings, than I had had before. He did this without any fuss, though not without a certain constraint as he put the money down on the counter; he would have been embarrassed if I had shown signs of being impressed by money. Of course I thanked him. I was never a practiced skier and am to this day amazed by his patience with me. Naturally W. was always ahead, though not by conscious effort; he never tumbled, and when I eventually caught up with him, out of breath and white from many falls, he would always say: Take your time. He never minded waiting. In the meantime he had been enjoying the landscape, and now he pointed with his stick as he named the peaks and drew my attention to a nearby pink tree or to the incredible light, so uniquely characteristic of the Engadine. He loved the Engadine, the country of *Zarathustra,* which I had also read but had not, perhaps, completely understood. As the weaker member I was allowed to decide when to continue our descent. W. did not press me, though on his own he could long ago have been in Pontresina. But that did not matter. He was giving me his Engadine. I still love it today. What would have become of me without W. it is hard to say. Perhaps I should have had more confidence in myself—too much, I suspect. In a certain sense W. had always encouraged me—for example, to give up my writing and to study architecture. I did not expect W. to look over the few buildings I was responsible for. I suspect he would have been disappointed—rightly so, And he too would have suffered from his disappointment. For a number of years I did indeed talk a lot to him about architecture, though I never managed to convince him of the merits of my teachers. Later I spoke of Corbusier, of Mies van der Rohe, of Saarinen, and then he would put on an expression as if I were talking about music—of which, as W. knew, I basically understood nothing—or philosophy. W. knew the sort of person I was from our school days. He became a distinguished collector. After the event, but only after it, I would perhaps feel there were things I ought not to have put up with, but I never disliked him on that account: the mistake had been my own. In his parents' villa there were a number of paintings that must have seemed to W. quite dreadful, junk in heavy frames inherited from his father's family. Most of it was stored in the cellar. His father had something of the personality of the early pioneers, but was in no way artistic or even intellectual: I liked him very much, this man, as he sat there in front of the fire discoursing soberly on the hunt. Many of the paintings depicted stags and boars, pheasants, hounds. I cannot remember whether the well-meant proposal came from W. himself or from his father or his mother (who also made fun of these pictures). Anyway, the idea was that, if I was able to sell them, I should be allowed to share in the proceeds—that is to say, I could earn myself a little money without having to neglect my studies. The only stipulation was that the sale should not be conducted from the villa. The name and address would attract buyers who might perhaps raise their eyebrows. The proposal made me rather uneasy, but on the other hand I felt it only right that I should do a favor for the family to which I owed so much. A garage was rented in another part of the city. The family also undertook the advertising—an insertion in the newspaper three times a week: *Bargain / Old Paintings from a Private Collection.* I was given a list of minimum prices; if I could sell at a higher price, my percentage would increase accordingly. After all, there were two or three little Flemish paintings in the collection, so one could still talk of a school, even if they were unsigned. In any event, W. thought it might be amusing for me to play at being a salesman, to get to know people. So there I stood, three afternoons a week, alone in a garage full of paintings, waiting about for hour after hour. And in fact a few antique dealers did turn up, mostly men in reduced circumstances, but shrewd. Not even the frames interested them, and usually I was not even asked the price. The advertisement continued to appear. A lawyer connected with W.'s father's firm brought a large Magadalene with naked breasts, suitable for a bedroom. The stags and boars were heavier going. I drew attention to landscapes that were of interest not only to hunters, landscapes with windmills against the light or with reeds. When asked where the paintings came from I was never to answer with a name, but was simply to say that it was a PRIVATE COLLECTION. On the other hand, I did talk about a school of Flemish painters, until one day a shabby old man, a customer, laughed in my face. Did I really believe that? It was springtime, I remember, and at six o'clock I was glad to ride away on my bicycle, even if I had sold nothing. How were things going? W. wanted to know, quite interested, though only from a human point of view, since he did not need the money. On the other hand, W. was quite right in pointing out that the garage also gave me a chance to do some reading. The whole enterprise lasted, I think, three weeks—not very long. And I did actually earn something from it, though I always settled quickly for the minimum price. So I was not much of a salesman; I felt besmirched, as if I were God knows who, yet I had to admit that my father, a former architect, had also become a real-estate agent toward the end of his life. W. knew that, of course. It did not bother him. He had no prejudices of that kind. Later, making a joke of something that was in fact anything but, when I was unable to conceal that I felt in some way besmirched, I caused W. some distress, as I could see from the deeply pained look on his face. But, after all, his family had not forced it on me. I had accepted their proposal, as I had to admit to myself. It never came to a showdown. In those years, if I am not mistaken, W. had hardly any other friends, certainly none of his own age; he revered his cello teacher, an elderly sculptor in Zurich, a scholar who was a friend of the family. He had a girl friend, but took care that I should not get to know her; a very non-middle-class girl whom he never married and he could never forget. A tragic affair of the heart of which W. spoke to me over a long period of years. Once, at his invitation, I joined him in a three-week walking tour through the Jura. W. was feeling the need to describe his inner conflicts. What he had to say—and indeed found so difficult to say that he could not even begin until the second day—revealed once again the variety of his emotions, his unusual intensity, his sense of responsibility toward the girl he loved as well as toward himself. And it was an unconventional sense of responsibility too. I felt honored that W. should let me into the secret of his complicated worries, even though I never set eyes on his mistress. Of course I had no advice to offer. Paternity also affected W. more than most. Things became difficult between us when I again took up my writing, when my things were published or presented on the stage. I knew what W. would think of them. In consequence we met only rarely, and then without mentioning them. I was also reading an increasing number of works that W. had not read, and I was unable to convert him to any of them. My interest in certain authors tended to arouse his skepticism against them: Brecht, for example. When it turned out that we admired the same authors—Strindberg, for instance, or Gide—W. was unwilling to talk about them; he had discovered them for himself and reserved them for himself. Of course, the fact that I had now abandoned architecture did not make me an author in his eyes, and so, as I said, we never talked about my writing, less and less about literature at all. W. had a different approach to literature. I realized that he could never read my books. He had different criteria, to which they could never measure up. All the same, he did make the effort. He once saw a play of mine *(Die Chinesische Mauer)* and wrote me a letter that could not have come at all easily to him, since his feelings about the play, though expressed in a friendly way, were obviously mixed. Many years later he went to see another of my plays *(Biedermann und die Brandstifter)*—at least, that is what somebody later told me. But he said nothing about it. We were by this time mature men. Even more difficult for him, I suspect, was my interest in politics. This we hardly ever discussed. The social conflicts of which I was becoming increasingly aware W. saw in the framework of a larger context. He did indeed listen to what I had to say, but then he would raise the conversation to philosophical levels, in which I was no longer sure of my bearings. I remember that during the Second World War, when we Swiss, though neutral, also had to black out our cities, W. thought it both ridiculous and unnecessary that his parents' villa, which lay on the edge of the city, should be subject to these tedious regulations; for how could the lights of a single house betray the whereabouts of a whole blacked-out city? He was against Hitler but also skeptical of democracy, with every vote having an equal value. Of course, W. had been spoiled by his environment, and he suffered inwardly for that very reason. He was impressed that I, his former school friend and never above average in class, was now earning my own living, however modestly. He saw it, I know, as his personal problem. To imagine that he was incapable of earning a living likewise was of course absurd, but it worried him now and again. If W. could have been satisfied with achievements of the sort other people have to be content with in order to earn a living, it would have been easy enough for him to earn his. And he knew it too. Altogether I had little to say to my friend. If, as sometimes happened, I criticized him, what was the result? W. listened carefully, but my criticism turned out to be as nothing compared with his own criticism of himself. There was no trace of conceit in him. On the contrary, he regarded himself as a defeated man. Toward me, as I well knew, he was indulgent. Standards such as hardly anybody could ever live up to he demanded exclusively from himself, not from me. Of course, he passed judgment on people, and his judgment was even severer than that of others—it was fundamental and was therefore complicated. But he never divulged it, neither to third persons nor in private. He had no wish to destroy anyone. His verdict on a person remained his own secret, if sometimes it cost him an effort, as one could feel. My megalomania must have caused him distress. At such times he would involuntarily draw his eyebrows together, but say nothing. I could only guess at his true opinion, and he relied on one's guessing only as much of it as one could at the moment bear. Greedy for appreciation from a person whose opinion was more fundamental and more penetrating than that of the general public, I was of course very susceptible when, for example, he would suddenly shower me with praise for my skill in lighting a stove in a mountain hut or in repairing my bicycle or, in later years, driving my Fiat, preparing a crab paella, and things of that sort. The praise was completely genuine: W. was incapable of praising dishonestly. W. was best man at my wedding, I at his. Even in later years we found enough to talk about when we went on long walking tours together, without his ever having to mention my books. W. experienced a great deal—though I do not mean adventures of a practical kind; it was rather than he lived so intensely that he could make misfortunes that would seem trivial in others' lives assume exemplary significance, whether it was a burst water pipe, his late arrival at an auction sale, or the behavior of his daughter's foster mother. It could be hard work, but all the same I always realized why I admired W. so much: the wealth of implications in his descriptions left one feeling that one had never experienced very much oneself. I shall never forget how he described the last weeks of his old father. The villa, which I no longer visited, became ghostly, his continuing to live in it himself a retribution. I eyed him from the side as we walked and walked, and he continued talking: a Lenz among the mountain tops. He did not compare himself to that wild poet, nor to Strindberg, Hölderlin, van Gogh, or Kleist, but he felt closer in spirit to them than to ordinary mortals like ourselves: a tragic figure. Today I can still remember his telephone number, though it is at least fifteen years since I last dialed it. And it has never happened, or at least very seldom, that I have failed to remind myself: Today is W's birthday. On his fiftieth birthday I sent him a telegram from Rome. I cannot say exactly when I ceased to think of him. The fact that in the meantime I had become prosperous could not have escaped his knowledge. What would he think about that? Occasionally I heard about him from a mutual friend, a painter—for instance, that his large art collection was keeping him fully occupied. Not even this painter had ever set eyes on the collection, which must have been a unique one. Afterward it occurred to me that I myself had never set eyes on the companions of his life, with the exception of the upper-middle-class woman he had married and of whom he often spoke even after their divorce. His first partner, I know, had been a nurse. Whenever W. spoke of these women, it was always in a tone of great earnestness, even when he kept their names to himself: he would just talk, for instance, of a Spanish girl in Barcelona, and so on. He was not afraid of major conflicts. I did once bridle when his mother told me what a burden his wife's illness was on him: it kept him so much from his work. I expressed sympathy for the sick wife as well. I am not suggesting that W. was just an egoist. Not only was he more self-sacrificing than most people; he also had more to sacrifice. On one occasion it was almost comic. We had not met for some years when, as so often before, we made a tour together in the Alps, *Grosser Aubrig*. Since on doctor's orders I had been off alcohol for six months and had taken an hour's walk daily, I managed the climb much more easily than W. I must admit I enjoyed not having to make him wait. It was he who lagged behind. We were not far from the summit, but W. did not wish to go on. To see our relationship thus would, I know, be too primitive. He just happened, on this last tour of ours, to be out of form. He had recently (while I was in the hospital) been going through difficult times. And after all, we were not sportsmen, but two men in our fifties. I never dared to talk to him about my work. His silent suspicion that I was succumbing to public success had become my own suspicion. I was grateful to him for that. Actually I have never been able to take pleasure in my own writings without first putting W. entirely out of my mind: enjoying them behind his back, so to speak. Beneath his blue eyes I never felt comfortable about them. I betrayed them, at least through silence—a silence which was mutual. Our last meetings were in 1959. The woman with whom I was then in love had studied philosophy; she had written about Wittgenstein and obtained her doctorate with a thesis on Heidegger. W., who was seeing her now for the first time, could not have known that; he had already heard her name, but he did not know her poetical work. She too found it difficult to open up with

W., just as it was difficult for Wittgenstein's *tractatus logicus*, which
W. did not know. I kept silent, not wishing to disturb them with my
half-knowledge. For a woman who was living with me to understand philosophy was something he evidently could not accept. He
did not feel comfortable in our apartment. In spite of the champagne, which I knew he liked. And she knew how much I owed to
this man—I had told her often and in detail about that, without,
however, really managing to describe my friend adequately to her.
And now here he was, a man large in stature, somewhat heavy.
There was no philosophical debate. W. just sat back in his chair in a
way I had never seen before: pure man! Not that, like everybody else,
he flirted with the woman, who was rather vexed; he just sat regarding her as she tried to talk. We had already had our first glass, so
that was not the trouble. No one was leading the conversation. Since
the lady evidently considered herself to be a writer (though her
books had not been mentioned), W. felt impelled to talk about
literature, not asking, but stating—although, as he said, he had
found little time recently for reading, since he was so busy catalog-
ing his collection. In his eyes Hölderlin was certainly greater than
Hans Carossa, but all the same he still saw Hans Carossa as a
writer. The woman, who had nothing to say to that, asked him
about his collection and wanted to know why W. would not show it
to us, not even to her. His assertion that he had the right, if he
wished, to destroy the treasures of ancient China as well as the
works of medieval masters and living painters, since he had not just
bought them with money but had made them his own through
choosing them and spending years of his life on them—this was not
said jokingly. His view found no acceptance with us. All the same, as
I later heard, the woman had pleased him in a certain way. Somebody told me that W. had later wondered how Frisch had found such
a companion. I never repaid the money that had made my studies
possible; I think that would have hurt him—it would, so to speak,
have nullified his generosity. When I recently recognized W. in the
street in Zurich, I felt a sense of dismay: there was an awareness in
me of what I owed to him, but no feeling. I did not write to tell him
that I had recognized him in the street. Today I am no longer even
interested to know what W. thinks of our long association. It is this
above all that distresses me. I feel that my friendship with W. was

basically a disaster for me, but that W. himself was in no way to blame. If I had been less submissive, the outcome would have been better—for him as well.

* * *

At dawn, years ago (1958), I was walking along the coast road while she still slept; not barefoot, but even in espadrilles one's feet can begin to burn. Impelled by a sense of urgency, I was walking swiftly. Though not consciously looking, I saw the anchored row of ships waiting to be broken up, fishing boats far out in the dusk. At first I just went out in front of the house and sat down on the jetty, looking up now and again at the house. Was I hoping she would come looking for me? When one is asleep an hour is nothing, but for the watcher it seems long. Then I went for a stroll, to keep myself from getting cold. Suddenly bored. At the point where the narrow coast road bends around the cliff and one loses sight of the little harbor and the house in which she was then sleeping, the small terrace on the top floor, there I sat down again on the wall, my arms spread out on either side of me, hands flat on the rough mortar, sandaled feet swinging. Then, brushing the mortar from my hands, I again walked on, before this day should dawn. I set off like someone with a message to deliver, an urgent one, but got no farther than LA SPEZIA. Too early in the day for coffee. Not a soul up and about, at least no person in his right mind, shutters still closed. They were not yet even setting up the daily market. No buses; one could walk in the middle of the road. Unable to think, I was glad to sit shivering on a public bench. I did not know where the future lay. Later, at the railroad station, after studying the timetable without my reading glasses, I looked to see how much money I had in my pocket. Back to her or away? Near her I could see only her, but near her, I knew, madness began. Yet still I thought it could be decided as by the toss of a coin: heads or tails. But it was already decided. Derisively, I threw up a real coin, one hundred lire—then picked it up without looking to see whether it was heads or tails. I waited only until I could get a cup of coffee in this town of LA SPEZIA . . . Two months earlier, in PARIS, at exactly this same twilit hour, our first kisses on a public bench and then in the market, where we drank our first coffee, with butchers in bloody aprons at the next table—too gross a portent. Her journey to Zurich; a distraught woman on a railroad platform; luggage, umbrella, bags. A week in Zurich as lovers and then, in clear recognition, the first parting. Hair really can stand on end: I saw it happen with her. A clear recognition, bearable no more than four weeks. My journey to Naples. She at the station; her arms had strength. Where should we go? The place we found to live in came to us by pure chance, and again the portent was too gross: PORTO VENERE, where we arrived in a taxi like a couple of refugees . . . Before I got up, I shook the sand out of my espadrilles and used the coin to pay for my coffee. We lived for seven months together, and then I fell ill with hepatitis. I was forty-eight and had never before been a patient in a hospital. I enjoyed it at first, everything white and service included. But then came the fear of losing my memory. For the first time. During the night a sentence that I must say to her. The sentence. It seemed to me right, and therefore it was important, since I was unable to write, that I should learn it by heart. Each morning I was given a transfusion in my right arm: it lasted three or four hours, dripping from a bag above my head. So as not to forget, I repeated to myself, every quarter of an hour, the sentence that had come to me in the night. I did not always know what it meant: it was just a group of words. After the senior physician had paid his visit and I had been hearing other words, it was vitally important to recall that group of words. Following the transfusion I always felt weak, but not only that: my vision was also disturbed. However, I had to jot the sentence down before I went off to sleep. Toward evening, my senses restored, I read the sentence. It was not a sentence at all—the subject so indecipherable I could not even guess at it, and no sign of a verb. I felt frightened. She came to visit me, and I could not say it. Could I hear at least? I did not notice that she was wearing a new summer dress. She was disappointed. She had spent the whole day searching Zurich for a new dress to cheer me up. She had also bought flowers for me, larkspur, which I like. They were in the apartment, she said, three bunches of them. I could not understand all she said, and I sent her away. Yellower than a real Chinaman, I authorized the purchase of two Volkswagens—one for her and one for me—for when I came out of this hospital. Fortunately there was someone passing through who could accompany her to Rome. Not just anybody, but Hans Magnus. I sent her away, in the summer of 1959, and shortly afterward I recovered. I could walk again: half an hour to the sulfur baths and half an hour back again, gradually longer. My memory also returned, and I knew she was in Rome. When I was able to stay on my feet for four or five hours each day, I realized I did not want to live without her, *Roma non risponde*. I could not understand why through the whole night I was unable to get her, and during the day it was the same. ROMA NON RISPONDE. I could think of many reasons why, but none of them convinced me. What most upset me was that ringing tone, then the inevitable voice saying: *Roma non risponde*. Since I kept falling asleep over the telephone, I fetched a blanket and set the alarm clock, so that I could ring her every hour. It was a sick man who had sent her away, I knew. The doctor had allowed me to dress and go down to the street for a few minutes to wave to them as they drove off. Had she not got my letters? I was no longer yellow. I wanted her. *Roma non risponde, Roma non risponde*. At last, however, I heard her voice at the other end, and a few days later we met at the Swiss-Italian border and drove in separate Volkswagens to Zurich. She told me what had happened in Rome. In Zurich an experiment with separate apartments, she living in the house where Gottfried Keller had lived when he was a government official, with doors of walnut and fittings of brass. What got into me? In Siena, in the fall of 1959, I stood in front of the post office like an awakened sleepwalker, for a while incapable of crossing the sunny square. The letter had been sent off, express—a fat letter. I had proposed marriage to her. Yes. I could not imagine her reply. No. The friend who was waiting for me in a nearby bar found me rather confused and did not know why. What was the earliest I could expect her answer? During this fall I was not allowed to drink, not even coffee: in such a sober spirit had I proposed marriage to her. In Assisi I went to the post office first and then to the cathedral, where a marriage ceremony was being performed, a Roman Catholic one; in Florence to the post office before seeking a hotel with my friend. Should I take my courage in my hands and ring her? My letter, which at that time I knew by heart, had arrived—that I learned from her only after my return to her in Zurich. What could I have been expecting from marriage only six months after the tardy ending of my first, respectable marriage? I went with her to Frankfurt. In the lecture hall, during her first reading at the university, I sat holding her coat upon my knees. On subsequent occasions she preferred to go to Frankfurt alone. Once on the railroad platform, where I had gone to meet her, she stopped when she saw me, utterly confused. What was in the telegram she received the following day and found so upsetting? That remained her secret. The fact that I went that winter to another woman, between our two apartments, did not free me from my subjection. My children also loved her, I thought. Later we moved together to Rome, via giulia 102, where it was noisy. Her Rome. Rumors of our marriage appeared in the newspapers, mentioning an Italian church I had never even seen. Could they not understand that she was a free person? When staying with friends, hers or mine, we were always put in the same room without question. We belonged together, or at any rate seemed to—it was hardly a secret now. In an Italian restaurant a German came up to our table. I watched their delight over this chance meeting and listened to them talking for a full half hour. She did not introduce me, and I did not introduce myself, since I knew she would not like it. Nor did he, Peter Huchel, venture to introduce himself, although he had recognized me. It was often rather comic. Once, when I visited her in Naples, she did not show me the house in which she was then living—not even the street. I could understand that. She disliked having people who were close to her meet one another. She did not want me to attend meetings of the writer's group, *Gruppe 47:* that was her territory. She had several territories. Now and again her secretiveness annoyed me. What was she afraid of? Once we visited Klagenfurt and she showed me the fountain with the dragon, famous from her description. I was the first man (she told me) she had ever shown it to. Me she showed to her family. On another occasion, in Rome, she divided past and present. She suddenly stopped, as if struck by a brick, and held the back of her hand to her steep forehead: No, please let's not go down the alley, please not! I asked no questions. One compromises oneself through revealing one's secrets—that is true. A gathering of all the people who have played a role in one's life or might one day play a role in it—that is a dreadful thought. To see them taking stock of one another, reaching agreement after an exchange of contradictory impressions, understanding one another—that would be the death of all self-understanding. Her radiance: we were seated before a real-estate agent in Rome who had the apartment of a baronessa to rent, and he was giving us to understand that the baronessa might perhaps prefer an American diplomat as tenant. *Dottore,* she said, looking as downcast and hesitant as a princess who has not been recognized, *senta,* she said, *siamo scrittori.* We got the apartment, with a balcony and a view across Rome. Frequently she was away for weeks on end, while I waited in her Rome. Once, when I knew she was on the way back to Rome, I could not wait a moment longer and drove to the outskirts of the city to keep watch for her on a roadside bank. I was waiting for her blue Volkswagen. To welcome her. In case she did not recognize me at the roadside I had my own car standing ready, pointing toward *Roma/Centro*. Occasional Volkswagens drove up, some of them blue, so I waved. Perhaps she had stopped for a meal in Siena, *Ristorante di Speranza*. I had plenty of time. When she came, she did not in fact see me, but it did not take me long to catch up to her. I saw her round head, her hair, from behind. Obviously she did not understand the hooting behind her, and some time passed before I could overtake her in the way the police do when stopping a vehicle. So she was also a bit frightened. I had been a fool, and I knew it. Her independence was part of her radiance. Jealousy was the price I had to pay for it, and I paid it in full. Lying on the summery balcony with its view across Rome, I slept with my face in my own vomit. By suffering I only increased my tender longings. But when she was there, she was there. Or was I deceiving myself? What was between us had never been a marriage of petty-minded domesticity. What did I find so torturing about it? I sat in my room, not listening deliberately, but hearing her talk to someone on the telephone. Her voice sounded cheerful, she laughed, the conversation went on a long time. I had no idea to whom she was speaking when she said: I am going to London the day after tomorrow. Without mentioning that we were going to London together for my play. Once I did the impermissible: I read letters that were not addressed to me. Letters from a man. They were considering marriage. I was ashamed and said nothing. When I did ask, she did not lie. She wrote: If anything changes between us, I shall tell you. There was another occasion when I thought I could not go on without her. I was driving north, a route I knew by heart: ten hours to Como, where I usually spent the night, but this time I drove on without a break. She did not know I was on my way to join her. I drove on—to Airolo in Switzerland, where it was night. Full moon. A drive across the St. Gotthard would be lovely now. Shortly afterward I met thick fog. Only with great difficulty could one make out the border stones along the highway. And later it began to rain. I considered whether it would not be more sensible to spend the night in the hostel, but I did not get out of the car. I was not feeling at all tired. On the contrary. Shortly after the hostel, where the road slopes downhill, my right headlight failed. I did not stop, but just reduced my speed. Twenty kilometers an hour. More was quite impossible, since I had only my left headlight and had to be able to see the stones to the right of the highway in order to know where I was. It was pouring rain. I was now the only driver on the road, not at all tired or even sleepy (or so I thought) after fourteen hours alone at the wheel. When suddenly I saw the white stones on my left instead of my right, I knew that I had run off the road. I braked sharply. The car came to a halt, tipping forward slightly. I did not get out to see how far the car was hanging over the precipice, but put it into reverse. It worked. I drove on. Very slowly, stopping now and again to wipe the windshield. The fog persisted, even after the rain eased up. In Andermatt all the hotels appeared to be closed—it was now after midnight. So I drove on, after getting out at last to see what lights I still had: the left headlight and two weak little parking lights. I could not give up now. I had drunk nothing (a Campari in Siena, three espressos in Como, a beer in Airolo), and I was feeling all right. Approaching drivers protested at my headlight, but I could not switch it off and rely on their seeing the two weak parking lights. I hoped I would not run into the police. At about three in the morning I reached home, *Uetikon am see.* Nothing had happened, nothing at all: I've come from Rome!—that was all. I was there. Why had I not at least telephoned? I did not know. I had not thought of it, had just been hoping she would be there. She was there. That was thirteen years ago. Ingeborg is dead. The last time we spoke together was in 1963, one morning in a café in Rome. She told me that she had found my diary in a locked drawer in that apartment, *Haus zum Langenbaum.* She had read it and then burned it. We did not show up well at the end, either of us.

Translated by Geoffrey Skelton

From
MAN IN THE HOLOCENE

At dawn, before the brief peal from the church bell, Geiser took his packed rucksack, his hat, raincoat, and umbrella, and left the house. The rucksack is not too heavy, and by the time he reaches the woods his heart has stopped pounding. In the village there is nobody to catch sight of him and ask where Herr Geiser is going, climbing the mountain with his rucksack in this weather.

Geiser knows what he is doing.

The pass lies 1,076 meters above sea level, and Geiser knows the way, at any rate as far as the top of the pass, from expeditions in previous years; besides, he has a map; he knows that one must keep to the left where the path forks, and that there are barns along the route in which one can shelter in case of a heavy thunderstorm, and more barns on the pass itself—

A path is a path even in fog.

At least there has been no thunder.

The path is not steep at the beginning; the slope is steep, but the path is almost horizontal, parts of it covered with slabs, a safe path even in fog, when one can hear the roar of the waterfall though one might not see it.

Farther on, the path grows steeper.

Later, Geiser gives up looking out for a chapel—below the path, to the right, if memory serves; perhaps it was invisible in the fog.

The woods must begin to thin sometime.

He has forgotten whether the path leads over two or over three bridges before it leaves the woods. When one can hear a stream close by, even if it cannot be seen, one ought in spite of the fog to be able to make out the railings of a bridge—or perhaps he just crossed a bridge without noticing it—

The high bridge has railings.

(Unless it has been swept away!)

The field glasses jogging against his chest are not really heavy, only useless. All he can see in the fog: the nearest tree trunks (their foliage hidden in fog), bracken, a few meters of the path ahead, somewhere a red bench, rocks indicating a gorge, then, all of a sudden, the railings.

The tubular uprights are twisted.

After one hour precisely Geiser takes his first rest, though he does not remove his rucksack or sit down. The climb is of course more laborious than in previous years, but his heart stops pounding.

He has plenty of time.

Many of the slabs that form the path look very heavy; it must have been hard work finding all these slabs, dragging them to the right spot, and fixing them in such a way that the path would stand firm in all storms—the trouble he himself is having with them, treading step by step from one to the next, is nothing by comparison; at times the steps are rather too high, which robs one of breath and proves discouraging.

The umbrella is a nuisance.

Now and again the path forks, but none of these can be the fork marked on the map, and Geiser feels no need yet to consult his map: the important fork, at which he must veer left, is somewhere above the first barns, and Geiser has not yet seen any barns. Despite this, he feels briefly unsure of himself—perhaps the fog prevented him from seeing the barns—until he realizes that it was only a short cut; the paths, both the steeper and the other one, come together again, so going back and taking the steeper path was a waste of effort after all.

The day is still young.

Even if in the fog it is impossible to know exactly where one is, the path is leading upward at every curve; the important thing is to keep going, without haste, step by step, regularly and without haste, so as never to run short of breath.

The barns at last—

A silly dog barking.

After half an hour, earlier than planned, Geiser takes another rest, without removing his rucksack, no desire for Ovomaltine; however, he does sit down on a mossy rock, drenched through in spite of his umbrella, but confident:

His plan is workable.

At the fork—the other path leads to a spring pasture, to a group of houses on the farther side of the valley, where, according to the map, it comes to an end—he chose correctly, also at a second fork not shown on the map. A white-red-white mark on a rock confirmed it. Later, the path became narrower, and it had no slabs.

Geiser has made two resolutions:

1. to keep to a path at all times,
2. to give up at any sign of heart trouble, and on no account to exhaust himself.

Once already Geiser has tripped over a root branch; a little blood on his skin, mixed with rain, a graze on his right arm, in which he is holding the umbrella, but not enough to make it necessary to undo his rucksack for a bandage. A walking stick would have been more useful than the umbrella, an oilskin better than the gabardine raincoat, which becomes heavy when wet.

The rain has not eased up.

An unbridged stream—not a proper stream, but a stretch of flowing water that is just the result of persistent rain and is not marked on the map, water flowing over debris, wide, but nowhere so deep or swift that one could not wade it in knee-high boots—this has cost him a lot of time, since Geiser is wearing ordinary walking shoes.

Half an hour at least. He walked up the slope and then down it, looking for stones he could trust, stones as large as possible, which would not tip or roll over when he set foot on them, and close enough for him to step across. But it was more or less the same everywhere. In the end there was nothing left but to risk it. One of the stones in which, after lengthy examination, he put his particular trust did then tip over—he did not fall, but he got a shoe full of water. This happened at nine in the morning, that is to say, while the day was still young.

Nearer the pass the ground becomes more even—

Ten years ago (Geiser is now approaching seventy-four) and in sunshine, it had been just a pleasant walk, an outing of two and a half hours there and back.

His memory has served him correctly:

a wide pass, pastures, rectangular dry-stone walls, and woods with clearings, the trees mostly deciduous (though beeches, not birches), and a few scattered houses (not barns, but deserted summer houses), and the path disappears in the open pastures, as is usual.

It would be time for a rest.

The thought that nobody could possibly know where Herr Geiser is at this particular moment pleases him.

No cattle—

No birds—

Not a sound—

To survey the landscape and find out before taking his rest what still lay ahead of him—the map shows a path with plenty of crosshatching, which means rock—Geiser went on farther. No path, and no view down into the other valley, just woods, growing ever steeper, undergrowth covering mossy debris, on which he kept stumbling, and in the end he found himself unable to move without slipping. Besides the gasping for breath there was now anxiety, haste, irritation with himself, and sweat, and where the undergrowth began to thin, the slope became even steeper; it was scarcely possible for him to remain upright. His progress turned into a crawling on all fours, an hour of which can use up more energy than three hours on a path, from one root branch to the next, and suddenly great walls of rock—

One false step and it is all over.

Geiser would not be the first.

Suddenly it has all become a question of luck.

By the time Geiser regains the open pasture of the pass, glad that there has been nobody to see him, it is noon. A gray noon. Beneath a large fir tree, where the ground is almost dry, though unfortunately teeming with ants, Geiser changes out of his sweaty shirt and waits for his confidence to return, his self-reliance, the feeling of not being lost.

He is not conscious of hunger.

A year ago two younger people, who had also lost their way, were not discovered for three weeks, even by a helicopter; it was only when someone noticed a number of birds circling over the woods, always in the same spot, that they were found.

Geiser has forgotten his Thermos.

The weather does not seem to worry the red ants in the least; their silent industry in a heap of fir needles—

He could do with his afternoon nap.

When one is not moving, one begins to feel chilly. Geiser has changed out of his wet socks as well, but his wet trouser legs still feel like cold poultices.

He has not forgotten the map, however.

The path leading seven hundred meters downward on the other side of the pass, to the right of the gorge according to the map, is bound to be a steep one, and when Geiser gets up to put on his rucksack, he fees the wobble in his knees. However, it has stopped raining. For a while, walking over the open pasture lands, he is not sure what he may decide to do.

AURIGENO/VALLE MAGGIA

Not far from the place where, three hours ago, Geiser was lost in the undergrowth, he sees this inscription on a rock in white paint, with an arrow pointing to the path, which leads right through the beech trees. A narrow path, stony in places, then one is again walking on woodland soil, which is kinder to wobbly knees, and as long as one does not tread on the roots, which are slippery in the wet, it is an innocuous path. In the woods one cannot see the gray clouds, the foliage is green, the ferns green, and to turn back, as Geiser was contemplating during his rest, would have been silly.

His plan is workable.

Geiser had figured on five to six hours (his son-in-law claims it took him just two and a half hours), making allowances for his age.

The first gully is nothing to worry about.

The second looks more troublesome, a steep hollow filled with debris, a tangled mass of boulders and shattered tree trunks, rivulets but no raging streams, one trudges through pebbles and mud, holding on to a rotting branch or a rock, not without some palpitations—but in the end one finds the path again. The warning in the guidebook ("Descent via the Valle Lareccio: care needed in bad weather") seems somewhat exaggerated when one is actually there, even though the slope is getting steeper and steeper. But one does not have to glance down into the gorge. A zigzag path with good steps. The crosshatchings on the map are no exaggeration; on the far side of the gorge there are cliffs and a waterfall dissolving into spray—

A third gully presents no problems.

The house Geiser left at dawn, his house, standing now in a different valley, seems hardly to belong to the present any more when Geiser reflects that he has been living there for fourteen years.

Usually on a walk one thinks of nothing.

The important thing is the next step and the one after that, so that one does not twist an ankle, one's knees do not give way, one does not slip suddenly. The umbrella is no use as a walking stick, it frequently slides on the stones and offers no support when one's footing is uncertain. But the path is still good, just now and again the steps in the stones are too high for someone whose knees have already become wobbly.

At times Geiser is beginning to think—

Suddenly it is his calves that go on strike; a pain at every step like being pricked by needles. The Maggia valley may already be in sight, its green plain spread out below, but the houses on it still look no bigger than toys, and it is better just to keep his eyes on the path.

At one point the path leads uphill again—

A chapel with an overhanging roof, and even a seat under the shelter of the porch, provides a chance to sit down and shake off the cramp in his calves; it is marked on the map, which is always comforting: one knows from a map exactly where one is at a particular moment; in somewhat less than an hour he has descended more than four hundred meters, and now there is not far to go:

Another 313 meters downhill.

The ants in his rucksack do not disturb him; Geiser permits himself a little cognac, then a glance down into the gorge, where almost certainly no human being has ever set foot, and a glance upward: ridges and cracks, slopes so steep that one wonders how one ever descended them. It is a tangled sort of valley.

It is now around two o'clock.

What is there to think about?

—$EB : AE = AE : AB$

—the Bible and the fresco of the Virgin Mary do not prove that God will continue to exist once human beings, who cannot accept the idea of a creation without a creator, have ceased to exist; the Bible was written by human beings.

—the Alps are the result of folding.

—ants live in colonies.

—the arch was invented by the Romans.

—if the Arctic ice were to melt, New York would be under water, as would Europe, except for the Alps.

—many chestnut trees are cankered.

—only human beings can recognize catastrophes, provided they survive them; Nature recognizes no catastrophes.

—man emerged in the Holocene.

It is almost four o'clock when Geiser wakes up. He has heard only the last faint rolls of thunder; obviously there was a brief rainfall. Clouds encircling the steep mountains, but billowy clouds, full of light, almost sunshine. In a little while one may even see blue sky here and there. Drops falling from the trees, which are glistening, and a twittering in the glistening leaves.

The cramp in his calves has subsided.

The church in Aurigeno (from which a mail bus runs to Locarno) is not yet visible, but Geiser can quite distinctly hear its clock striking the hour; a harsh, hoarse bell, with hardly any reverberations.

The ants have disappeared.

After finishing the cognac (a small flask), placing his field glasses in the rucksack, and slowly tying the rucksack up again, Geiser remains seated for a while, not telling himself what he is thinking, what he has decided in his head.

Then he rises, straps the rucksack to his back, looks around to make sure that he has not left an Ovomaltine wrapping on the ground or on the bench in front of the chapel—which is not, incidentally, a chapel. It is just a fresco of the Virgin Mary with an overhanging roof.

Geiser almost forgot his umbrella.

The ascent is laborious, just as he expected, and Geiser knows that it is four hundred meters up to the pass. The confident knowledge that the three gullies are not insuperable, that the track is a good one on the whole and not dangerous so long as there is daylight, and that the zigzag path in front of him is not interminable—these things hearten him, even though a path known only from the descent can often be unrecognizable when one comes to ascend it. It is not his calves that are on strike now, but his thighs. When will he reach the second gully, the large one? There are stretches Geiser cannot remember; all the same, there they are, fairly steep, and now and again, in order to surmount a high step, Geiser has to provide help for his thighs by putting a supporting hand, the right one, on a knee; the left hand is holding the umbrella as a walking stick. With increasing frequency Geiser finds it necessary to sit down on the nearest bank to regain his breath, both hands grasping the handle of his umbrella, his chin resting on his hands.

What use would Basel be to him?

By the time he reaches the pass, it is already about seven in the evening and growing dusky; at the pass it is raining again.

It has been a long day.

Once more the open pasture, where the path disappears, where in the morning Geiser enjoyed the thought that nobody could know where Herr Geiser was at this moment—

Nobody knows it now, either.

—and once more the wide stretch of water without a bridge:

The water over the debris is flowing no more swiftly, but it is now dark, and not even the best flashlight casts much of a beam in the rain. What it principally shows is glittering needles of rain. Each time he felt distrustful of the next stone within stepping distance, Geiser turned back. Here and there a vigorous leap would probably have done it, but Geiser no longer trusted his legs. If nobody was to know about this expedition, it was important to avoid an accident of any kind, even something as simple as a fractured arm. Once he tried still farther up, then lower down. He took his time about it— no one at home, waiting and counting the hours—no giving in to hastiness. Everywhere the same wash of water; with the difference that it is easier in daylight to guess where the water is deep or shallow. The thought that if, on the bench in front of the Virgin Mary, he had not chosen to return, he might now be sitting on a train or in a restaurant, was not exactly helpful when Geiser was standing on a stone surrounded by water as far as the flashlight could reach, and when even to turn back was risky; a stone on which he had previously stepped seemed to have shifted, and water was washing over it. What now? In the end he did lose patience, and closed his umbrella: one needs both arms free to keep one's balance. Suddenly the water was up to his knees, and after he lost his prodding umbrella, it became difficult for him to stand upright in the water—but he made it without losing his flashlight, and a flashlight was more important now than an umbrella.

A path is a path even at night.

As long as one keeps on walking, exhaustion is almost a pleasant feeling in one's veins, and Geiser knows he must not stop now to sit down; otherwise he will find himself unable to get to his feet again.

There is always ground, even at night.

What can be seen in the glimmer of a flashlight is for the most part enough for him: slabs, indicating a path, the next step, then woodland soil with roots, tree trunks on both sides, but a drop either to the left or to the right, then once more slabs in the bracken, debris and thistles, at one point a dead tree root, and beyond it nothing but glittering needles of rain—bottomless night, forcing one to go, not forward, but back, and there is the path again, and the sharp bend Geiser had overlooked before, clear to see. At times Geiser has the feeling that he knows more or less where he is, that he should now be approaching the meadow with the barns. Instead, more woods. Perhaps he did not see the barns he was expecting because they lay beyond the radius of his flashlight. Even when rain is streaming down, one ceases to notice it after a while. For the past two hours Geiser has simply been walking, not even wishing to know where he is. Now and then a knee gives way, but only once has he fallen. Woodland soil and pine needles sticking to his hands, but nothing more. The path is leading downward, and that is the main thing. The barns he has been expecting for the past hour come suddenly into sight. Geiser might have taken shelter there, but what is the point, when he is shivering in wet clothes? It cannot get any darker than it has been so far. What will come next Geiser already knows: a zigzag through the woods, in which one must be careful not to miss a bend, and later on the bridge with its twisted tubular railings; after that the path becomes more even, a good path that cannot be missed, so long as the battery of the flashlight holds out—

Nobody will ever hear about his outing.

Every time Geiser found it necessary to stop for a while and wait until his heart ceased its heavy pounding, he switched off his flashlight to preserve the battery.

What use would Basel be to him?

The village was asleep, it was past midnight when Geiser reached home, unseen by anyone.

Translated by Geoffrey Skelton

PART II

PLAYS

From
NOW THEY ARE SINGING AGAIN

Part I

Scene I

(*H*erbert, an officer, and Karl, a soldier.)

HERBERT: In an hour it will be night. Time to move on. Our task is
accomplished.

KARL: Yes, in an hour it will be night.

HERBERT: What's with you?

KARL: Our task is accomplished.

HERBERT: You're looking around as if it were you yourself you had
shot.

KARL: Time to move on.

HERBERT: As soon as the priest is finished, as soon as he has covered
up the trench.

KARL: Our task is accomplished.

HERBERT: You've said that twice now.

KARL: In spring when the snow melts, in spring I have leave. In
spring when the buds and the sun come out, this trench too will
emerge. We can command the priest, "Dig a grave of such and
such a length, and quickly!" We can command, "Now fill up the
grave again, and quickly!" We can command all things in this
world, all things, but not the grass, not the grass that shall grow

over it, and quickly. They will see the trench of such and such a
length, in spring when the snow melts, in spring when I'm on
leave at my mother's, eating cake.

HERBERT: Have a cigarette. *Herbert gives him a cigarette.*

KARL: Crumble cake . . . thanks. They saved up flour and sugar over
an entire year for this crumble cake!

Herbert gives him a light.

Once, as a boy, I loved crumble cake more than anything.

HERBERT: Smoke your cigarette and stop blathering. You're tired,
Karl.

KARL: In spring I have leave.

HERBERT: We are permitted to do anything, except to be tired,
except to lose our heads. That doesn't work, Karl, not with us.

KARL: In an hour it will be night. Maria writes she hears the
swallows. At this time of year! She sees butterflies. At this time of
year! Maria writes the springs are awaiting our leave, they are
waiting under the snow . . .
"Springtime's bright new ribbon flies
Rippling on the air again . . ."
Do you know Mörike?

HERBERT: Perhaps better than you.

KARL: I love him.

HERBERT: "Fragrances of old begin
To touch the earth with each sunrise.
Violets dream today,
Soon they will appear.
Hark, a harp's faint tune from far away!
Springtime, it is thou.
It is thyself I hear."
Silence.

KARL: Herbert, can you tell me why we shot those twenty-one
people?

HERBERT: What's it to do with you?

KARL: I shot them.

HERBERT: They were hostages.

KARL: They were singing. Did you hear how they were singing?

HERBERT: Now they are silent.

KARL: They were singing. To the very end. *Herbert looks over.*

HERBERT: I see it coming. The old priest will create a legend out of this if we let him talk, if we let him live.

KARL: Herbert!

HERBERT: Well, what?

KARL: Do you mean to say that the priest also—

HERBERT: He digs as if he had planted a flower bulb, he digs that carefully. And what a precious bulb! In the spring, if all goes well, a tulip will come out.

KARL: Herbert, the priest is not guilty—

HERBERT: Did we ask the hostages whether they were guilty? He shovels over them as if he really believes in their resurrection. Now he's picking out each and every stone!

KARL: Herbert, the priest is not guilty—*Herbert turns back again.*

HERBERT: Have you noticed the beautiful fresco? There in the middle apse?

KARL: What kind of fresco?

HERBERT: A crucifixion and a resurrection, what else? A remarkable piece—Byzantine, twelfth century perhaps, in excellent condition. I can't help thinking of your father, Karl.

KARL: Why?

HERBERT: Our schoolmaster. If only he could see this, he would be in heaven. And would lecture on it. All these figures, he would say, stand here not in front of the accidents of a landscape, which gave birth to and determined them; they stand in front of a gold ground, that is to say, they stand before the absolute realm of the spirit—and so forth.

KARL: Why are you talking about him now, right now?

HERBERT: I can't help thinking of our schoolmaster . . . often. I can't see anything without knowing what his education would have to say about it. Anything beautiful, I mean. Indeed, he only talked about the beautiful. By the way, do you know how he is these days? *The priest appears.* Well, Batiushka?

PRIEST: They are buried.

HERBERT: And you?

PRIEST: I have buried them, as you commanded.

HERBERT: An obedient man.

PRIEST: May God rest their souls.

HERBERT: And you?

PRIEST: I don't understand.

HERBERT: What?

PRIEST: Why God has sent you.

HERBERT: So you believe that God sent us, do you? *Herbert steps in front of him.* Swear that you will not talk once we've gone away. Swear it.

PRIEST: I swear it.

HERBERT: Swear you saw nothing with your own eyes.

PRIEST: You blindfolded my eyes.

HERBERT: Swear it!

PRIEST: I saw nothing, I swear it.

HERBERT: And also you heard nothing?

PRIEST: They were singing.

HERBERT: Swear that you heard nothing or we will shoot you too.

PRIEST: Me?

HERBERT: I will count to ten. Understood?

PRIEST: Me?

HERBERT: One, two, three, four, five, six, seven—

PRIEST: I swear it. *The priest is allowed to go.*

HERBERT: Bah! Bah! I say to all these rogues of God.

KARL: Had we not run into him, Herbert, he wouldn't have become a rogue. You made him do it.

HERBERT: Fear, fear! They all fear us.

KARL: That is the power we have.

HERBERT: And the spirit, which is supposed to be higher than our power? Where is it, then? What else are we looking for? So where is it, this God who gets painted on all the walls over centuries, who gets talked up so big? I don't hear him.

KARL: An hour ago they were singing.

HERBERT: Fear, fear! They all fear our power. They swear oaths that are false. They are astonished that this God does not conquer us. We resorted to power, to ultimate violence, so that the spirit might confront us. Let me experience whether what they say is true. I fire at them. Let me just once see a resurrection! I have shot hundreds of people, and I have seen not one.

KARL: We've just become murderers.

HERBERT: We resort to power, to ultimate violence, so that the spirit might confront us, the true one. But the Blasphemer is right. There is no true spirit, and we have the world in our pocket, whether we need it or not. I see no limits to our power: that is our despair. *He turns.* The priest also gets shot.

KARL: Why?

HERBERT: Because I'm ordering it. I said, "Make a grave for these twenty-one people." He did it. I said, "Fill it up again." He did it. I said, "Swear by God that you heard nothing." He swore it. Now I say, "The priest gets shot."

KARL: I don't understand that.

HERBERT: And you who don't understand, you will do it.

KARL: Me?

HERBERT: I order you.

KARL: Herbert—

HERBERT: You have five minutes to do it. *Karl stands and is silent.* We can't believe in his oath. He swears by a God that doesn't exist; otherwise he couldn't swear falsely and get away with it. He will avenge himself for his own betrayal as soon as he is no longer in our gun sights, you can be sure of that! Because he fears us. And it's always the fear, above all the fear, that makes them think of revenge. I tell you, in five minutes he'd better be shot.

KARL: And if I say I won't do it?

HERBERT: You know what that means.

KARL: I know.

HERBERT: You wouldn't be the first one, Karl.

KARL: I know.

HERBERT: I myself will execute you if that's the way it has to be—in fact, right away. You can believe me, Karl. We've always done what we said we would. In this day and age not everyone can claim that. We can be counted on.

KARL: I know you.

HERBERT: Think it over.

KARL: And if I sing all the while?

HERBERT: I'll give you five minutes.

KARL: And if I sing all the while?

HERBERT: Afterwards there will be no more words. I'll give you five minutes. *Herbert takes himself off.*

KARL: Now they are singing again. *The priest appears and waits. Chanting can be heard.*

PRIEST: I'm supposed to report to you.

KARL: What do you want?

PRIEST: I'm supposed to report to you.

KARL: Tell me one thing.

PRIEST: What is it?

KARL: Never mind . . . You swore falsely. Why did you swear falsely? You denied your Lord God, whom you wear at your neck. For twenty years, so you say, for twenty years you have lived in this cloister, praying, serving—

PRIEST: I have.

KARL: And straightway the cock crew! That's roughly how it goes, right? And straightway the cock crew . . . Why did you do that?

PRIEST: Let each concern himself with his own guilt.

KARL: In an hour it will be night. Tell me one thing: If I go in this direction, on and on, woods, heath, on and on, if I swim through the rivers, on and on, if I wade through the swamps, on and on, all through the night, on and on, on and on, where will I be? *The priest is silent.* Speak! Where will I be? Speak! It will save your life. *The priest is silent.* I'm going. Go ahead and betray me! I'm going to my mother. Tell them that. I'm going to my mother! *Karl takes himself off.*

PRIEST: My place is here. I will not betray you. Your flight does not save me any more than you. Any path you may travel, any path will lead you back here.

Translated by Alice Carey

DON JUAN, OR THE LOVE OF GEOMETRY
and Postscript

Characters

DON JUAN
TENORIO, *his father*
MIRANDA
DON GONZALO, *Commander of Seville*
DONNA ELVIRA, *his wife*
DONNA ANNA, *their daughter*

FATHER DIEGO
DON RODERIGO, *a friend of Don Juan*
DONNA INEZ
CELESTINA, *the procuress*
DON BALTHAZAR LOPEZ, *a married man*
LEPORELLO
WIDOWS OF SEVILLE
THREE SWORDSMEN COUSINS

Place: A theatrical Seville
Time: A period of good costumes

Act One

Outside the castle.
Night. Music. A young man creeps up the steps and peers from the terrace into the castle. A peacock screeches. As someone is coming out on to the terrace, the young man hides behind a pillar.

DONNA ELVIRA: Don Juan? Don Juan?

DONNA INEZ: There's no one here.

DONNA ELVIRA: His grey is in the stable.

DONNA INEZ: I'm sure you're mistaken, Donna Elvira. What would a man be doing out in this darkness? I'm freezing anyhow, and when the peacocks screech as well, ugh, a shiver runs down my spine at the very thought.

DONNA ELVIRA: Don Juan? Don Juan?

DONNA INEZ: Palms in the wind. Like the clink of a sword on stone steps. I know how it is, Donna Elvira; I hear it every night, and when I go to the window it's nothing but the palms in the wind.

DONNA ELVIRA: He has come, I know that; his grey is in the stable . . . *They leave, and the young man emerges again to peer into the castle. He has to hide behind a pillar again, as an old man and a plump priest enter from the other side.*

TENORIO: Patience! It's easy for you to talk, Father Diego. But suppose the scoundrel doesn't come at all? It's already midnight. Patience! Don't stand up for my son. He has no heart, I tell you, just like his mother. As cold as stone. At twenty he says he isn't interested in women! And the worst of it is, he's not lying, Father Diego. He says what he thinks. His love—he tells me to my face—his love is geometry. You've no idea the worry I've had over that boy. You told me yourself, his name never crops up in any confession. And a creature like that calls himself my son, my only son and heir. At the age of twenty, he has never been with a woman, Father Diego; can you imagine that?

FATHER DIEGO: Have patience.

TENORIO: You know Celestina—

FATHER DIEGO: Ssh.

TENORIO:—Spain's famous procuress; she even numbers bishops among her clients, but not my son. And all the money I've paid out! Once he's inside the brothel, all he does is play chess. I've seen it myself. Chess!

FATHER DIEGO: Keep your voice down, Señor Tenorio.

TENORIO: Isn't interested in women!

FATHER DIEGO: There's someone coming.

TENORIO: That boy will be the death of me, you'll see, Father Diego; he'll give me a heart attack—*Enter Don Gonzalo, the Commander.*

FATHER DIEGO: Has he arrived?

DON GONZALO: It isn't midnight yet.

TENORIO: Don Gonzalo, Commander of Seville, don't think ill of my son. Don Juan is my only son. Don Juan will make a delightful son-in-law, if he comes, and I can't believe that he has simply forgotten the date of his wedding, Commander, I can't believe that.

DON GONZALO: The young man has a long ride, and hard days behind him. I don't think ill of your son; he fought magnificently—

TENORIO: Is that true?

DON GONZALO: I'm not flattering him just because you happen to be his father; I'm simply telling you what Spanish history will never deny: he was the hero of Cordoba.

TENORIO: I'd never have believed it of him.

DON GONZALO: I didn't believe it of him either, to tell you the truth. My spies gave me very dubious reports of the young man. They said he even made jokes about me.

TENORIO: The young scamp!

DON GONZALO: I called him to my tent, and when we were alone I asked him: Why are we pursuing this crusade? And as he merely smiled, I asked him: Why do we hate the heathens?

TENORIO: What did he answer?

DON GONZALO: He said he didn't hate them.

TENORIO: The young scamp!

DON GONZALO: On the contrary, he said, we could learn a great deal from the heathens. And the next time I saw him, he was sitting under a cork oak reading a book. An Arabic book.

TENORIO: Geometry, I know; devil take geometry.

DON GONZALO: I asked him why he was reading it.

TENORIO: In Heaven's name, what did he answer?

DON GONZALO: He merely smiled.

TENORIO: The young scamp!

DON GONZALO: I don't deny, Don Tenorio, that his smile often infuriated me. When I sent your young son to Cordoba to measure the enemy fortress, it was a monstrous order; I didn't think he would dare carry it out. I simply wanted to wipe the smile off his face. And to make him take me seriously. Next morning, when he came into my tent, without a scratch from his head to his heels, I couldn't believe my eyes as he handed me a sheet of paper bearing the length of the enemy fortress—in black and white— nine hundred and forty-two feet.

TENORIO: How did he do it?

DON GONZALO: Don Juan Tenorio, I said to him and embraced him in front of all the officers who had never dared to do what he had done, I was wrong about you, but henceforward I shall call you my son, my daughter Anna's bridegroom, Knight of the Spanish Cross, hero of Cordoba! *Music rings out.*

TENORIO: How did he do it?

DON GONZALO: That's what I asked him.

TENORIO: What did he answer?

DON GONZALO: He merely smiled—*Enter Donna Elvira, carrying masks.*

DONNA ELVIRA: The masquerade has begun! *She performs a few dance steps to the music.*

They're already dancing inside.

"I am the woman
And the moonlit pond tonight.
You are the man
And the moon in the pond tonight.
Night makes us one.
Face have we none,
Love makes blind
All but the bridegroom and his bride."

FATHER DIEGO: We are waiting for the bridegroom.

DONNA ELVIRA: The bridegroom is here!

TENORIO: My son?

DONNA ELVIRA: His grey is in the stable. I have only seen him from a distance, Señor Tenorio, but your son is the most graceful rider who ever swung himself down from a grey, hey-hup, and landed on his feet as lightly as if he had wings.

DON GONZALO: Where is Donna Anna?

DONNA ELVIRA: I am the bride's mother, but I feel more like a bride than my child. We are the last ones without masks. I hope he won't think I'm his bride! But you, my husband, must take a mask, custom is custom, and if I may make the request, please do not give names any more, otherwise there's no point in the whole masquerade. *Enter a masked couple.*

SHE: It is you, isn't it? I bet my life it's you. Let me see your hands.
HE: You must be making a mistake.
SHE: No other man has hands like yours!
HE: People are listening to us. *Don Gonzalo and Tenorio put on their masks.*
DON GONZALO: Let us go.
DONNA ELVIRA: A word with you, Father Diego. *The masked couple kiss.*
FATHER DIEGO: Who are that shameless couple? I know their voices. I could swear that's Miranda:
DONNA ELVIRA: You must speak to her.
FATHER DIEGO: To Miranda, the harlot, here in the castle?
DONNA ELVIRA: To Donna Anna. *The masked couple kiss.* The poor child is completely confused; she wants to hide; she's afraid of the man; she has been trembling in every limb, the lucky girl, since she has known that he is here—
FATHER DIEGO: The most graceful rider who ever swung himself down from a grey, hey-hup, and landed on his feet as lightly as if he had wings.
DONNA ELVIRA: Diego?
FATHER DIEGO: Go on.
DONNA ELVIRA: Why do you look so gloomy?
FATHER DIEGO: If our Spanish Church were not so obstinately devoted to welfare work, which swallows up very nearly a tenth of all the alms we receive, I too could leap from a grey, Donna Elvira, instead of slithering down off a mule.
DONNA ELVIRA: Diego!
FATHER DIEGO: Go on.
DONNA ELVIRA: I never swore infidelity to you. Father Diego—let us remain friends. You seem to forget that I am married, my dear; and if I ever fall in love with a youngster—which heaven forbid— the only person I shall be deceiving will be my husband not you
FATHER DIEGO: Elvira—
DONNA ELVIRA: I'm telling you that once and for all, my friend.
FATHER DIEGO: Ssh.
DONNA ELVIRA: Let us go to Donna Anna. *Donna Elvira and Father Diego go off, leaving the masked couple and the young man behind the pillar.*
SHE: Mistake! How can you say such a thing? If that is true, then

everything that happens between a man and a woman is a mistake. Do you think I don't know your kiss? I found you and recognized you. Why don't you admit it? Do you think you can deceive me with a mask? Must I take off my mask to make you recognize me? They will throw me out into the street once I am without a mask—*She takes off her mask.*

HE: Miranda!?

SHE: The whore—yes: to them.

HE: How could you dare—

SHE: I love you. Yes, I dared to come in here, and I found you among hundreds. I love you. Why do you start with fright? They embraced me, but it was like water passing through a sieve; nothing touched me till you held me with your hands. Why don't you speak? You had no experience with women, you said, and I laughed; that hurt you, I know, you misconstrued my laughter— and then we played chess.

HE: Chess?

SHE: Then I discovered your hands.

HE: I don't play chess.

SHE: I laughed because you know more than all the other men in Seville put together. I saw you immersed in your chess, the first man who had the courage to do what he really wanted, even in the brothel.

HE: My name is Don Roderigo.

SHE: Of all people!

HE: Why do you laugh?

SHE: Don Roderigo! You're jeering at me, I know, because he too has embraced me. Don Roderigo—I know him and all the others, who differ only in their names; I'm often surprised they themselves don't get mixed up about who they are. One is just like the other! Even when they embrace me in silence it is nothing but a manner of speaking. How boring they are, fellows like your friend Don Roderigo. You have no idea how different you are, that's why I'm telling you.

HE: And suppose I am Don Roderigo all the same? Suppose I swear it to you by all I hold sacred?

SHE: Then I shall laugh at all a Don Roderigo holds sacred and take your hands. I recognized them. Let me kiss them. They are the hands that will carry me to myself, hands such as only one man possesses, and he is you—Don Juan!

HE: Don Juan? *She kisses his hands.* He's over there. Look! *He points to the young man who has now stepped out from the pillar behind which he was hiding. Miranda sees him and screams as if stabbed with a knife. At the same moment a polonaise of masked figures enters, hand in hand: Miranda is drawn into the chain and goes out with the masked figures.*

DON RODERIGO: Juan, where have you suddenly sprung from?

DON JUAN: Listen, Roderigo.

DON RODERIGO: What are you doing wandering around the park? They're expecting you, my friend; everyone is asking about the bridegroom. Why don't you go in?

DON JUAN: If you are my friend, Roderigo, do me a favour, for you it's a small matter, not worth talking about; for me, everything depends upon it. I can feel it so clearly: Here and now, tonight, a decision will be reached which afterwards it will be impossible to reverse. I have known this for an hour, Roderigo, and I can do nothing about it. I can do nothing. Suddenly everything depends on a wretched grey horse, a decision affecting our whole life; it's terrible. Will you help me, Roderigo?

DON RODERIGO: I don't understand a word.

DON JUAN: Fetch my grey from the stable.

DON RODERIGO: What for?

DON JUAN: I must get away, Roderigo.

DON RODERIGO: Away?

DON JUAN: I'm still free. *Laughter from the castle; Don Juan takes his friend by the shoulder and draws him into the dark foreground.* Roderigo, I'm afraid.

DON RODERIGO: You, the hero of Cordoba?

DON JUAN: Forget about that nonsense!

DON RODERIGO: The whole of Seville is singing your praises.

DON JUAN: I know: they seriously believe that I crept off to Cordoba and measured the fortress; they imagine I would risk my life for their crusade.

DON RODERIGO: Didn't you?

DON JUAN: What do you take me for?

DON RODERIGO: I don't understand . . .

DON JUAN: Elementary geometry, Roderigo! But even if I drew it in the sand for them, those gentlemen wouldn't believe me; that's why they talk about miracles and Almighty God now that our mortars land on the target at last, and that's why they get angry when I smile. *He looks round anxiously.* Roderigo.

DON RODERIGO: What are you afraid of?

DON JUAN: I can't see her.

DON RODERIGO: Who?

DON JUAN: I've simply no idea what she looks like any more.

DON RODERIGO: Donna Anna?

DON JUAN: No idea. No idea at all . . . I rode all day. I was longing for her. I rode more and more slowly. I could have been here hours ago; when I saw the walls of Seville, I sat down on the edge of a reservoir and stayed there till darkness fell . . . Roderigo, let us speak frankly.

DON RODERIGO: Certainly.

DON JUAN: How do you know when you are in love?

DON RODERIGO: My dear Juan—

DON JUAN: Answer!

DON RODERIGO: I don't understand you.

DON JUAN: I don't understand myself, Roderigo. Outside the city walls by the reservoir, with my reflection in the black water— you're right, Roderigo, it's strange . . . I think I'm in love. *A peacock screeches.* What was that? *A peacock screeches.* I'm in love. But who with?

DON RODERIGO: With Donna Anna, your bride.

DON JUAN: I can't picture her—suddenly. *A group of gay masked figures flashes past.* Was she among them?

DON RODERIGO: Your bride is not wearing a mask. You are be-wildered by your happiness, that's all, Juan. Let us go in. It's past midnight.

DON JUAN: I can't.

DON RODERIGO: Then where on earth are you going?

DON JUAN: Away!

DON RODERIGO: To your geometry?

DON JUAN: Where I know what I know—yes . . . Here I am lost. As I was riding round the castle in the darkness, I saw a young woman at the window. I could have loved her, the first one I came across, any woman, just as much as my Anna.

DON RODERIGO: Perhaps it was Anna.

DON JUAN: Perhaps. And you expect me to swear an oath on that, like a blind man, when any woman can come along and say she's Anna?

DON RODERIGO: Quiet!

DON JUAN: You won't give me away, Roderigo, you haven't seen me.

DON RODERIGO: Where are you going? *Don Juan swings himself over the balustrade and disappears into the dark park. Don Roderigo puts his mask on again, while Father Diego and Donna Anna enter, both without masks.*

FATHER DIEGO: Here, my child, we shall be alone here.

DONNA ANNA: No.

FATHER DIEGO: Why not?

DONNA ANNA: A man—?

DON RODERIGO: "I am the man
And the moon in the pond tonight.
You are the woman
And the moonlit pond tonight.
Night makes us one,
Face have we none,
Love makes blind
All but the bridegroom and his bride."
He bows. God bless Donna Anna, the bride. *Don Roderigo goes out.*

DONNA ANNA: Perhaps that was he?

FATHER DIEGO: The bridegroom wears no mask.

DONNA ANNA: I'm so frightened.

FATHER DIEGO: Child! *The peacock screeches.* That is the peacock, my child; nothing to be afraid of. The poor peacock isn't looking for you; for seven weeks he has been wooing with that raucous voice and rattling his tail quills to make Donna Peahen hear him. But she seems to be as frightened as you are, I don't know where she is hiding . . . Why are you trembling?

DONNA ANNA: I love him—I'm sure I do . . .

FATHER DIEGO: And yet you want to hide from him? From the most graceful rider who ever swung himself down from a grey, hey-hup, and landed on his feet as lightly as if he had wings. Ask your Mama! Your Mama swears that no man ever had such a figure before, and even if I doubt your Mama's memory and as a priest must remind you that a slim figure isn't everything, oh no, there are also inner qualities which a woman often overlooks, spiritual qualities that outweigh a three-fold double chin—what I meant to say was, there is no doubt, my child, that it will be a slender youth who will appear before you at any moment, as proud as a peacock—*Donna Anna tries to run away.* Stay! *He pulls her back onto the bench.* Where are you going?

DONNA ANNA: I shall faint.

FATHER DIEGO: Then he will hold you in his arms, my child, until you come to your senses, and all will be well.

DONNA ANNA: Where is he?

FATHER DIEGO: In the castle, I expect. He is looking for his bride, as is the custom . . . The heathens used to call it the Wild Night. A vile custom, says the chronicler; anyone coupled with anyone, just as the urge took them, and no one knew that night whom he was embracing. For everyone wore the same mask and they were all stark naked, thinks the chronicler, male and female. Stark naked. That's how it was among the heathens—

DONNA ANNA: Someone is coming.

FATHER DIEGO: Where?

DONNA ANNA: It sounded like it.

FATHER DIEGO: Palms in the wind . . .

DONNA ANNA: I'm sorry, Father Diego.

FATHER DIEGO: That's how it was among the heathens, anyone coupled with anyone; but that was a long time ago. The Christians called it the Night of Recognition and the whole thing took on a pious significance. Thenceforth bride and bridegroom were the only ones who were permitted to embrace that night, provided they recognized one another from among all the masks—through the power of their true love. A beautiful significance, an estimable significance, wasn't it?

DONNA ANNA: Yes.

FATHER DIEGO: Only unfortunately it didn't work, says the chronicler so long as bride and bridegroom wore a mask like everybody else. There were too many mistakes, says the chronicler . . . Why aren't you listening?

DONNA ANNA: Someone is coming! *Donna Elvira comes out of the castle.*

DONNA ELVIRA: Father Diego!

FATHER DIEGO: What has happened?

DONNA ELVIRA: Come with me! Come quickly! Come! *Father Diego follows Donna Elvira back into the castle, leaving Donna Anna sitting alone in the darkness. The peacock repeats his raucous cry. Suddenly seized with horror, she takes flight over the same balustrade as Don Juan before her and vanishes into the gloomy park, to escape from him. Donna Elvira comes back.*

DONNA ELVIRA: Anna! Where has she got to? Anna! *Father Diego comes back.*

FATHER DIEGO: Of course she's a harlot, her name is Miranda, every man knows her name, a poor creature who has no business here. Of course her place is in the street. *He sees the empty bench.* Where is Donna Anna?

DONNA ELVIRA: Anna? Anna!

FATHER DIEGO: She must be inside . . . *Donna Elvira and Father Diego go in; silence; the peacock repeats his raucous cry.*

INTERMEZZO

Celestina and Miranda appear before the drop-curtain.

CELESTINA: Stop crying, I said. And don't talk sentimental rubbish. If you don't know how a whore should behave, here's your bundle.

MIRANDA: Celestina?

CELESTINA: You're dripping with soul.

MIRANDA: Celestina, where am I to go?

CELESTINA: In love! And you dare to show your face before me? In love with one man. Here's your bundle and that's the end of it! . . Didn't I warn you all, over and over again; leave your soul out of it? I know all that nonsense about true love. How else do you think I come to be running a brothel? I know the sob-stuff that starts when the soul comes into it. Once and never again I swore to myself. Haven't I been like a mother to you all? Good God, fancy a beautiful, mercenary creature like you starting to whimper like an animal and babble like a young lady. His hands! His nose! His forehead! And what else has your one and only got? Go on, tell me. His toes! The lobes of his ears! His calves! Go on, what else has he got that's different from everyone else's? But I could see it coming, those downcast eyes the last few weeks—that sentimentality!

MIRANDA: Oh, Celestina, he's not like all the others.

CELESTINA: Get out!

MIRANDA: Oh, Celestina—

CELESTINA: Get out, I say. For the last time. I won't have sentimental trash on my doorstep. In love with a personality! That's the last straw. And you dare to tell me that to my face, me, Spain's leading procuress. So you're in love with a personality?

MIRANDA: Yes. So help me God.

CELESTINA: *speechless.*

MIRANDA: Yes.

CELESTINA: That's how you thank me for your education.

MIRANDA: Oh, Celestina—

CELESTINA: Oh, Celestina, oh, Celestina! You think you can make fun of me, in the middle of the night, do you? You think you can lie to me like a man? God help you, yes, He'd better—because I certainly shan't, as sure as my name's Celestina. I know what I owe my name. Why do you think the gentlemen come to us? So that you can fall in love, so that you can make distinctions between one and the other? I keep telling you, day after day: there are girls outside too, women of every age and every degree of willingness, married, unmarried, whatever they like. So why do they come here? I'll tell you, sweetie: here, sweetie, the man recovers from his false emotions. That's what they pay for with silver and gold. What did Don Octavio, the wise judge, say when they wanted to close my house? Leave the good bawd alone, he said, and in public. So long as we have a literature that propagates so many false emotions, we can't do without her—we can't do without her, he said; and that means I am protected by the state. Do you think I should be protected by the state if I allowed anything improper to go on? I don't sell sentiment here. Do you understand? I don't sell girls who inside themselves keep dreaming of another man. Our customers have got plenty of that at home, sweetie; that's not what they come here for! Take your bundle, I say, and get out.

MIRANDA: What shall I do?

CELESTINA: Marry.

MIRANDA: Celestina—

CELESTINA: That's what you deserve. Marry! You could have been a magnificent harlot, the best one of the day, sought after and pampered. But oh no, you had to fall in love! I ask you! You want to be a lady. I ask you! You'll think about us, sweetie, when it's too late. A harlot doesn't sell her soul—

MIRANDA: *sobs.*

CELESTINA: I've told you what I think. Don't blub around on my doorstep, this is a "house of joy." *Celestina goes out.*

MIRANDA: I'm in love . . .

Act Two

A room in the castle.

Donna Anna, dressed as a bride, sits surrounded by busy women; Donna Inez is combing the bride's hair.

DONNA INEZ: That will do! I'll pin on the veil by myself, I'm the chief bridesmaid. Only we still need the mirror. *The women leave.* Why is your hair so wet? It's almost impossible to comb it, so wet. There's even earth in it. Where have you been? And grass . . .

DONNA ANNA: *stares into space without speaking.*

DONNA INEZ: Anna!

DONNA ANNA: Yes?

DONNA INEZ: You must wake up, my love, it's time for your wedding. They're ringing the bells already, don't you hear them? And Roderigo says the people are already out on all the balconies; he says it will be a wedding such as Seville has never seen before . . .

DONNA ANNA: Yes.

DONNA INEZ: You say Yes as though it was all no concern of yours.

DONNA ANNA: Yes.

DONNA INEZ: More grass! I'd just like to know where you went in your dream . . . *She combs, then she picks up the mirror.* Anna, I've seen him!

DONNA ANNA: Who?

DONNA INEZ: Through the keyhole. You ask who? He is striding up and down like a caged beast. Once he suddenly stopped, drew his sword and looked at it. As though before a duel. But he's all in white, Anna, all in shimmering silk.

DONNA ANNA: Where's the veil?

DONNA INEZ: I can already see it all; you raising your veil that is as black as night and the priest asking: Don Juan, do you recognize her? Donna Anna, do you recognize him?

DONNA ANNA: And suppose we don't recognize each other?

DONNA INEZ: Anna!

DONNA ANNA: Give me the veil.

DONNA INEZ: First look at yourself in the mirror.

DONNA ANNA: No.

DONNA INEZ: Anna, you're beautiful.

DONNA ANNA: I'm happy. I wish it was already night again. I'm a woman. Look at our shadows on the wall, he said; that is us: a woman, a man! It wasn't a dream. Don't be ashamed, otherwise I shall feel ashamed too. It wasn't a dream. And we laughed; he took me and didn't ask my name; he kissed my mouth and went on kissing, so I shouldn't ask his name either; he picked me up and carried me across the lake, I heard the water round his wading legs, the black water, as he carried me—

DONNA INEZ: Your bridegroom?

DONNA ANNA: He and no other will be my bridegroom, Inez. That is all I know. He and no other. I shall recognize him in the night, when he waits for me by the lake. No other man in the world has a right to me now. I know him better than I know myself.

DONNA INEZ: Quiet!

DONNA ANNA: Oh, if it were only night already!

DONNA INEZ: They're coming.

DONNA ANNA: Give me the veil! *Enter Don Gonzalo and Father Diego.*

DON GONZALO: The moment has come. I am not the man to make flowery speeches. Let me tell you with this kiss, my child, what a father feels on such a day.

FATHER DIEGO: Where's the veil?

DONNA INEZ: Just a minute.

FATHER DIEGO: Get ready, get ready! *Donna Inez and Donna Anna go out.* We're alone. What is troubling you? Speak openly, Commander. Why shouldn't we understand each other, a married man and a monk? *They sit down.* Well?

DON GONZALO: —as I was saying, we rode into the fortress of Cordoba, where Muhammed received me, the prince of the heathen, weeping over his defeat, and the courtiers all round were weeping too. All this, said Muhammed, is yours, Hero of Christendom, take it and enjoy it. I was astonished at so much splendor; there are palaces in Cordoba such as I have not seen in my dreams, halls topped by gleaming cupolas, gardens full of streams and fountains and the scent of trees, and Muhammed himself, weeping again, gave me the key of his library, which I immediately ordered to be burned.

FATHER DIEGO: H'm.

DON GONZALO: And this, said Muhammed, weeping yet again, this was my harem. The girls were weeping too. There was a strange scent of spices. All this, he said, is yours, Hero of Christendom, take it and enjoy it!

FATHER DIEGO: H'm.

DON GONZALO: There was a strange scent of spices.

FATHER DIEGO: So you said.

DON GONZALO: Take it and enjoy it, he said.

FATHER DIEGO: How many were there?

DON GONZALO: Girls?

FATHER DIEGO: Roughly.

DON GONZALO: Seven or nine.

FATHER DIEGO: H'm.

DON GONZALO: I don't want to take part in a sacred marriage ceremony, Father Diego, without first having confessed.

FATHER DIEGO: I understand.

DON GONZALO: You see, it involves my own marriage.

FATHER DIEGO: You frighten me.

DON GONZALO: For seventeen years I have been faithful—

FATHER DIEGO: That is celebrated. Your marriage, Don Gonzalo, is the one perfect marriage that we can show the heathens over there. It's easy for the heathens with their harems to make jokes about our scandals in Seville. I always say, if Spain didn't have one man like you, Commander, as an example of Spanish marraige—but go on.

DON GONZALO: All that is yours, he said—

FATHER DIEGO: Take it and enjoy it.

DON GONZALO: Yes—

FATHER DIEGO: There was a strange scent of spices.

DON GONZALO: Yes—

FATHER DIEGO: Go on.

DON GONZALO: The girls only spoke Arabic, otherwise things would never have gone so far. When they undressed me, how could I explain to them that I am married and what that means to us?

FATHER DIEGO: The girls undressed you?

DON GONZALO: That was what Muhammed had taught them to do.

FATHER DIEGO: Go on.

DON GONZALO: Father Diego, I have committed a sin.

FATHER DIEGO: I'm listening.

DON GONZALO: A sin in spirit.

FATHER DIEGO: In spirit?

DON GONZALO: I cursed fidelity!

FATHER DIEGO: And then?

DON GONZALO: I cursed the seventeen years of marriage!

FATHER DIEGO: But what did you do?

DON GONZALO: I didn't—

FATHER DIEGO: Don't tremble, Don Gonzalo, speak frankly; heaven knows about it anyhow.

DON GONZALO: I didn't—

FATHER DIEGO: We are all sinners.

DON GONZALO: I didn't do anything.

FATHER DIEGO: Why not? *Enter in gala dress: Donna Elvira, Tenorio, Don Roderigo, the three Cousins and various Girls, Boys bearing censers, Trumpeters.*

DONNA ELVIRA: My husband, we are ready! With incense and trumpets as seventeen years ago! Oh, to be young again—

DON GONZALO: Where is the bridegroom?

DONNA ELVIRA: I think he's magnificent!

DON GONZALO: I asked where he is.

DON RODERIGO: Don Juan, my friend, sends his apologies for having missed the great ball last night. Tired as he was from his long ride, he says, he wanted to rest awhile before presenting himself to his parents-in-law and his bride. And so it happened, he says, that he slept away the night in the park, until the cocks woke him. That is the message I am to give you. He is confused. He dare not appear at his wedding unless I can assure him that his sleep in the park has been forgiven.

DONNA ELVIRA: He dare not appear! He is the best behaved bridegroom I have ever met. I can think of nothing I would not forgive him. *Don Roderigo bows and goes out.* I surprised him in the veranda, I came upon him from behind. I asked him why he was biting his nails and he simply stared at me. Donna Anna? he asked in confusion, as though I were his bride, as though he couldn't remember what she looked like. As though I were his bride! He didn't even say goodbye when I picked up my skirt and left; he simply stared after me; I could see it in the mirror. He is so stupefied, so completely turned in upon himself—as though he were facing execution. *Trumpets sound; Don Roderigo comes in with Don Juan.*

TENORIO: My son!

DON JUAN: My father.

TENORIO: Custom demands that I say a few words, although God knows my heart is almost breaking, for I am seeing you for the first time as a bridegroom—for the first time, my honoured friends will understand what I am trying to say, for the first time and I hope, my son, for the last time . . .

DONNA ELVIRA: We understand.

TENORIO: Custom demands—

FATHER DIEGO: Keep it short.

TENORIO: God grant it may be so!

DON JUAN: *kneels and receives benediction.*

DONNA ELVIRA: How sweetly he kneels.

FATHER DIEGO: What did you say?

DONNA ELVIRA: How sweetly he kneels.

DON JUAN: *rises.*

DON GONZALO: My son!

DON JUAN: My father-in-law.

DON GONZALO: I am not a man of flowery speeches either, but what I say comes from my heart, so I shall be brief.

DON JUAN: *kneels down again.*

DON GONZALO: The time has come—

DONNA ELVIRA: He won't be able to think of anything else, Father Diego, let the trumpets sound; I know him, he won't be able to think of anything else.

DON GONZALO: The time has come—

TENORIO: God grant it!

DON GONZALO: God grant it! *The two fathers embrace; trumpets sound; the veiled bride appears, led by Donna Inez. An im-*

pressive ceremony ends with Don Juan, all in white silk, and the bride, in white silk with a black veil, standing facing each other with Father Diego between them, while everyone else kneels.

FATHER DIEGO: "Lord, who may be a guest in Thy tent?
Who may rest upon Thy holy mountain?
He who commits no sin and practises justice
And speaks the truth from his heart;
He who keeps his word even when his oath does him harm.
He who acts thus will be as steadfast as a rock." Amen.
Trumpets.
You, Donna Anna, daughter of Don Gonzalo of Ulloa, Commander of Seville. And you, Don Juan, son of Tenorio, banker of Seville. You two, clothed as bride and bridegroom, come out of the free decision of your hearts, resolved to speak the truth before God, your Lord and Creator, answer in a clear, full voice the question which I shall ask you in the sight of heaven and of those who are your witnesses on earth. Do you recognize each other face to face? *Donna Anna is unveiled.* Donna Anna, do you recognize him? Answer.

DONNA ANNA: Yes!

FATHER DIEGO: Answer, Don Juan, do you recognize her?

DON JUAN: *remains silent as though turned to stone.*

FATHER DIEGO: Answer, Don Juan, do you recognize her?

DON JUAN: Yes . . . that is . . . oh, yes! *Trumpets.*

FATHER DIEGO: Then answer the other question.

DONNA ELVIRA: How moved he is!

FATHER DIEGO: Since you recognize each other, Donna Anna and Don Juan, are you prepared and resolved to give your hand each to the other in the everlasting alliance of wedlock that shall keep and preserve you, so that Satan, the fallen angel, shall not transform the heavenly miracle of love into earthly pain: are you, then, ready to swear that no other love shall ever enter your hearts as long as you live, no other love than this which we shall consecrate in the name of the Father, the Son and the Holy Ghost. *All cross themselves.* I ask you, Donna Anna.

DONNA ANNA: Yes!

FATHER DIEGO: I ask you, Don Juan.

DON JUAN: —No. *Trumpets.*

FATHER DIEGO: Let us pray.

DON JUAN: I say No. *Father Diego begins to pray.* No! *All those kneeling begin to pray.* I said No. *The prayer dies away.* Please, friends, stand up.

DON GONZALO: What did he say?

TENORIO: The young scamp!

DON GONZALO: He said—No?

DON JUAN: I can't. It's impossible. I beg your forgiveness. . . Why don't you stand up?

FATHER DIEGO: What does this mean?

DON JUAN: I tell you, I can't swear that. It's impossible. I can't. We embraced each other last night, of course I recognize her—

DON GONZALO: What did he say?

DON JUAN: Of course we recognize each other.

DON GONZALO: Embraced, he said? Embraced?

DON JUAN: I didn't mean to talk about that.

DONNA ANNA: But it's the truth.

FATHER DIEGO: Go away, you boys, away with the incense!

DON JUAN: We met each other in the park. By chance. Yesterday in the darkness. And all at once everything was so natural. We ran away. Both of us. But in the darkness, because we neither of us knew who the other was, it was quite simple. And beautiful. And because we loved one another, we made a plan—now I can give it away: tonight, by the lake, we were going to meet again. That was our vow. And I was going to abduct the girl.

DON GONZALO: Abduct?

DON JUAN: Yes.

DON GONZALO: My daughter?

DON JUAN: I really had no idea, Don Gonzalo, that it was she—

DON GONZALO: Do you understand, Elvira?

DONNA ELVIRA: Better than you.

DON JUAN: If I hadn't been so strangely tired, so that I slept till dawn, on my word of honour, I should have saved you this great ceremony. What could I do? It was too late. I heard the trumpets and could think of no other way out, I thought to myself: I shall perjure myself. You will be indignant, but that's the truth: I said to myself, I shall treat your wedding as a joke, and then when night comes, when it is dark again. . . *He stares at Donna Anna.* God knows, I wasn't prepared for this!

FATHER DIEGO: For what?

DON JUAN: To find that it was you.

TENORIO: The young scamp!

DON JUAN: I can't swear to what I don't believe, Papa, just for the sake of incense and trumpets, and I don't believe myself any longer. I don't know whom I love. On my word of honour. That's all I can say. The best thing you can do is to let me go, the quicker the better. *He bows.* I'm dumbfounded myself.

DON GONZALO: Seducer!

DON JUAN *starts to go.*

DON GONZALO: Over my dead body! *He draws his sword.* Over my dead body!

DON JUAN: Why?

DON GONZALO: Over my dead body!

DON JUAN: You can't be serious.

DON GONZALO: Fight!

DON JUAN: I shouldn't dream of it.

DON GONZALO: As sure as my name is Don Gonzalo, you shall not leave this house except over my dead body!

DON JUAN: But I have no wish to kill.

DON GONZALO: Over my dead body!

DON JUAN: What difference will that make? *He turns to the other side.* You husband, Donna Elvira, wants to make me his murderer; please allow me to leave this way! *He bows to Donna Elvira and tries to go out towards the other side, but at this moment the three Cousins also draw their swords and he finds himself surrounded.* If that's what you want—

DON GONZALO: Death to the seducer!

THE THREE: Death!

DON JUAN *draws his sword.*

THE THREE: Death to the seducer!

DON JUAN: I'm ready.

DONNA ELVIRA: Stop!

DON JUAN: I'm not afraid of men.

DONNA ELVIRA: Stop! *She steps between them.* Four to one! And we scarcely know why the young man is so confused. Are you out of your minds? Will you please have some sense. And at once! *The swords are lowered.* Father Diego, why do you say nothing?

FATHER DIEGO: I—

DON JUAN: What could the Father say? He understands me best of all. Why hasn't he married?

FATHER DIEGO: I?

DON JUAN: For instance, Donna Elvira?

FATHER DIEGO: By God—

DON JUAN: He calls it God, I call it geometry; every man has something higher than the woman, once he is sober again.

FATHER DIEGO: What does that mean?

DON JUAN: Nothing.

FATHER DIEGO: What does that mean?

DON JUAN: I know what I know. Don't exasperate me. I don't know if the Commander knows.

TENORIO: The young scamp!

DON JUAN: It's breaking your heart, Papa. I know, you've been saying that for thirteen years; I shouldn't be surprised, Papa, if you were to die one day. *To the cousins:* Are we going to fight or aren't we?

DONNA ELVIRA: My dear Juan—

DON JUAN: I'm a gentleman, Donna Elvira, I shan't betray a lady's secrets. Have no fear. But I'm not going to be made a fool of, just because I'm young.

DONNA ELVIRA: Dear Juan—

DON JUAN: What do you want from me?

DONNA ELVIRA: An answer to one single question. *To the cousins:* Sheathe your swords, I am waiting. *To Don Gonzalo:* You too! *The cousins sheathe their swords.* Don Juan Tenorio, you came to marry Anna, your bride.

DON JUAN: That was yesterday.

DONNA ELVIRA: I understand that suddenly you felt afraid. So did Anna. You fled into the park. So did Anna. You were afraid of fulfilment. Wasn't that so? But then, in the darkness, you found each other, having no idea who you were, and it was beautiful.

DON JUAN: Very.

DONNA ELVIRA: Inexpressibly.

DON JUAN: Yes.

DONNA ELVIRA: You didn't want to marry the bride whom you had betrayed. You wanted to flee with the girl, the other one, you wanted to abduct her—

DON JUAN: Yes.

DONNA ELVIRA: Why don't you do so?

DON JUAN: Why—

DONNA ELVIRA: Don't you see how the girl is waiting for you, for you and none other, how radiantly happy she is that you, the bridegroom and the seducer, are one and the same?

DON JUAN: I can't.

DONNA ELVIRA: Why?

DON GONZALO: Why! Why! There's no why here! *He raises his sword again.* Death to the violator of my child!

DONNA ELVIRA: My husband—

DON GONZALO: Fight!

DONNA ELVIRA: My husband, we are in the middle of a conversation.

DON JUAN: I can't. That's all I can say. I can't swear. How do I know whom I love? Now that I know all that is possible—for her too, my bride, who was waiting for me and none other, and then happily went off with the first man who came along, who happened to be me.

DON GONZALO: Fight!

DON JUAN: If you can wait no longer for your marble memorial, begin! *He laughs.* I shall never forget you, Hero of Christendom, as you stood there in the harem of Cordoba. Take it and enjoy it! I saw you . . . Begin! I am his witness: the Moorish girls did everything they could to tempt him, our crusader of marriage, but in vain, I can swear to that; I saw him, so pale and stark naked; his hands trembled, the spirit was willing but the flesh was weak . . . Begin!

DON GONZALO *lowers his sword.*

DON JUAN: I am ready.

DONNA ELVIRA: Juan—

DON JUAN: As I told you, the best thing would be to let me go; I feel that my politeness is beginning to wear thin. *He sheathes his sword.* I shall leave Seville.

DONNA ANNA: Juan—

DON JUAN: Farewell! *He kisses Donna Anna's hand.* I loved you, Anna, even if I don't know whom I loved, my bride or the other one. I have lost you both, both in you. I have lost myself. *He kisses her hand again.* Farewell!

DONNA ANNA: Farewell—*Don Juan goes out.* Don't forget, Juan: by the lake, at nightfall—today—at nightfall—Juan? Juan! . . . *Donna Anna goes out after him.*

FATHER DIEGO: Is this evil-doer to get away like that?

DON GONZALO: Heaven smite him.

FATHER DIEGO: A priest can echo that. Heaven smite him!

DON GONZALO: After him! Get going! Surround the park! Let all the dogs off the leash and surround the park! Get going, all of you, get going! *Donna Elvira and Tenorio remain.*

TENORIO: It breaks my heart, Donna Elvira, to see how my son behaves.

DONNA ELVIRA: I think he's magnificent.

TENORIO: What sort of figure do I cut?

DONNA ELVIRA: Believe me, Señor Tenorio, that is the last thing which concerns us at the moment.

TENORIO: My own flesh and blood—hunted down with hounds! And I don't even believe that he seduced your daughter, a man with so little interest in women as my son. I know him! In the end it will all turn out to be a trick and a fraud to enable him to get back to his geometry, heartless as he is. He wouldn't even be surprised if I died one day—you heard him yourself—he wouldn't even be surprised! *The sound of dogs barking is heard; Father Diego comes back.*

FATHER DIEGO: You too, Señor Tenorio, get going! *Donna Elvira is left alone.*

DONNA ELVIRA: I think he's magnificent! *Don Juan rushes in.*

DON JUAN: I'll cut them down, the whole pack, I won't marry, I'll cut them down.

DONNA ELVIRA: Come!

DON JUAN: Where to?

DONNA ELVIRA: To my room—*Tenorio enters with drawn sword and sees Don Juan and Donna Elvira embracing as they take refuge in her room.*

TENORIO: The young scamp? *The pursuers enter with drawn swords and a pack of savage hounds dragging at the leash.*

DON GONZALO: Where is he?

TENORIO *clutches at his heart.*

DON GONZALO: Quick! Surround the park! *The pursuers rush out.*

TENORIO: I'm—dying . . .

INTERMEZZO

Miranda, dressed as a bride, and Celestina with sewing things, appear before the drop-curtain.

CELESTINA: One thing at a time, sweetie, one thing at a time. You won't be late. A wedding like that takes a long time, with all the speeches and the rest of it.

MIRANDA: No one must recognize me, Celestina; they would have me whipped and tied to the stake. God stand by me! *She has to stand still, so that Celestina can sew.* Celestina—

CELESTINA: If you tremble I can't sew.

MIRANDA: Celestina, do you really think I look like a bride?

CELESTINA: Exactly like one. *She sews.* I tell you, men are the blindest things God ever created. I used to be a tailoress, sweetie, you can believe me. Very few of them can tell the difference between fake lace and genuine till it's time to pay. I tell you, a man only sees the essentials.

MIRANDA: Celestina, I can hardly breathe.

CELESTINA: It's tight across the bust, I can see you're not a virgin. We'll simply open up the seam under the arm, that's easy. He won't notice, or not till it's too late. But don't tremble! Otherwise I shall prick you. What have you got on underneath?

MIRANDA: Underneath?—Nothing.

CELESTINA: That's always best.

MIRANDA: Well, it's too tight anyway.

CELESTINA: Fine gentlemen are funny about undies. All of a sudden they're upset by a pink or mauve and are put off by your taste. It's like when you're talking about novels and one of those coxcombs suddenly sighs: We belong to different worlds! and gazes out of the window. That's why I always tell you, don't discuss novels! Suddenly there's a chasm between you. And it's just the same with undies. There are men who wouldn't run away before any flag, but let them see a scrap of pink silk on the carpet and they're off. There's no arguing about tastes. No undies is the best; it takes them by surprise, but it never puts them off.

MIRANDA: Celestina—

CELESTINA: Stop trembling, sweetie, stop trembling!

MIRANDA: I don't know whether I dare go through with it, Celestina; I hope it isn't a sin, what I'm planning to do.

CELESTINA: Now it isn't tight any more, look, and yet the bust is still firm enough . . . What are you planning to do? And down at the bottom, sweetie, we'll make a hem, so that he sees your ankles. The ankles are important.

MIRANDA: Oh God!

CELESTINA: But first we'll pin up the veil.

MIRANDA: Oh God!

CELESTINA: Why are you sighing?

MIRANDA: Why is everything we do always a sham?!

CELESTINA: H'm. *She lifts the skirt.* Now for the hem.

MIRANDA: Not like that!

CELESTINA: You mean, I'm bending down?

MIRANDA: Celestina—

CELESTINA: Seven stitches will do the trick. *Miranda turns slowly round like a top, while Celestina stands and sews the hem of the lifted skirt.* I suppose you think he'll embrace you? Because he thinks you're Donna Anna, his bride. Kiss and embrace you! You're going to get the shock of your life, sweetie, but it'll give me a good laugh. All right, go ahead! It'll knock the silly ideas out of your head, that's why I'm helping you. Donna Anna? he will say when he sees you, and he'll feel guilty, that's all; he'll come out with a flood of lies and excuses and he'll have no time for embraces, to say nothing of pleasure. You overestimate married men, sweetie, you only know them as they are when they come to us. *The seam is finished.* There—

MIRANDA: Thank you.

CELESTINA: How does the bride feel? *The doorbell rings.* Another customer already!

MIRANDA: Leave me the mirror. *Enter a Spanish nobleman.*

CELESTINA: What can I do for you?

LOPEZ: I don't know if I've come to the right place.

CELESTINA: I think so.

LOPEZ: My name is Lopez.

CELESTINA: Be that as it may.

LOPEZ: I come from Toledo.

CELESTINA: Tired after the journey, I understand, you want a bed—

LOPEZ: Don Balthazar Lopez.

CELESTINA: We don't ask for personal particulars; all you need do here, sir, is to pay in advance.

LOPEZ: *looks around.*

CELESTINA: You've come to the right place, come in.

LOPEZ: *scrutinizes Miranda.*

CELESTINA: This girl has the day off. *Miranda is left alone with the mirror.*

MIRANDA: God stand by me! That's all I want: just to be recognized once as a bride, even if it's only a sham; I want him just once to kneel at my feet and swear that it is this face, Donna Anna, only this face that he loves—my face . . .

Act Three

Outside the castle.
In the first light of morning Don Juan is sitting on the steps eating a partridge; the hounds are still baying in the distance; Don Roderigo enters.

DON RODERIGO: Juan? Juan! It's me, Don Roderigo, your ever-faithful friend. *Don Juan eats and says nothing.* Juan?

DON JUAN: What's the matter, Roderigo, my ever-faithful friend? Why don't you even say good morning?

DON RODERIGO: Don't you hear?

DON JUAN: Barking? I heard it all night long, my dear fellow, from room to room. Sometimes further away, sometimes closer. I'm touched by their persistence.

DON RODERIGO: I've been looking for you all night. *Don Juan goes on eating in silence.* To warn you. *Don Juan eats in silence.* What are you doing here, Juan, sitting on the steps?

DON JUAN: I'm having breakfast.

DON RODERIGO: Listen, Juan—

DON JUAN: Have you been with your sweetheart?

DON RODERIGO: No.

DON JUAN: That's a mistake, Don Roderigo, my ever-faithful friend, a dangerous mistake. You should never leave a girl alone. Suddenly a stranger jumps into her room, hunted by hounds, and she discovers that you aren't the only man either.

DON RODERIGO: What do you mean by that?

DON JUAN: The truth. *He eats.* You have a charming sweetheart . . .

DON RODERIGO: Juan, you're limping.

DON JUAN: Like Satan himself, I know. That's what comes of jumping out of windows. *He eats.* There is no other way of getting to yourself. *He eats.* Women are insatiable . . .

DON RODERIGO: Juan, I must warn you.

DON JUAN: And I must warn you too.

DON RODERIGO: I'm speaking seriously, my friend. Something terrible will happen if you're not sensible, something frightful which you will regret as long as you live. Suddenly things have ceased to be a joke and there is blood everywhere. Blood that cannot be washed away. All night long I crept about the park, Juan, I trembled for you—

DON JUAN: *eats and says nothing.*

DON RODERIGO: I couldn't believe my eyes when I suddenly saw her in front of me, by the lake—like a specter of death!

DON JUAN: Who?

DON RODERIGO: Your bride.

DON JUAN:—Anna?

DON RODERIGO: She has been waiting for you, Juan, all night long. She's out of her mind. For hours she sits as motionless as a statue, for hours, then she flits along the bank again. I spoke to her. He is out there on the little island, she said, and I couldn't talk her out of the idea. The moment I'd gone she started calling your name. Over and over again . . . You must talk to her.

DON JUAN: I wouldn't know what to say, Roderigo, I'm not in the right state of mind to have feelings at the moment; and she knows that I've deserted her. What is there left to say? All I feel just now is hunger.

DON RODERIGO: Quiet! *Enter Don Gonzalo with drawn sword.*

DON GONZALO: Halt! Who goes there?

DON JUAN: He can scarcely stand any more. Tell him to give it up.

DON GONZALO: Who goes there?

DON JUAN: He is simply looking for death and his memorial; you'll see, he won't be satisfied till he has got them. *Enter the three Cousins, bloodstained, ragged and exhausted.*

DON GONZALO: Halt! Who goes there?

A COUSIN: Heaven smite the evil-doer.

DON GONZALO: Have you caught him?

A Cousin: We're all in, Uncle Gonzalo. Your damned hounds have torn us to shreds.

A Cousin: You whipped them, you idiot.

A Cousin: Idiot yourself, they attacked me.

Don Gonzalo: Where are the hounds?

A Cousin: I wasn't the one who slaughtered them.

Don Gonzalo: Slaughtered them?

A Cousin: We had to.

Don Gonzalo: Did you say, slaughtered?

A Cousin: We had to, it was them or us.

Don Gonzalo: My hounds?

A Cousin: We can't go on any longer, Uncle Gonzalo. Let heaven take its own revenge, we're done in.

Don Gonzalo: My hounds . . .

A Cousin: We must bind his wounds. *The three Cousins drag themselves off.*

Don Gonzalo: I shall neither rest nor slacken till the hounds too have been avenged. Tell my wife, when she wakes, that I shall neither rest nor slacken. *Don Gonzalo goes out on the other side.*

Don Juan: Did you hear? Heaven smite the evil-doer. A touching slogan. I'm sorry for every hound that gets slaughtered for it.

Don Roderigo: Let us not mock, friend.

Don Juan: I'm not mocking heaven, friend, I think it's beautiful. Especially at this hour of the day. One rarely sees it at this time of day.

Don Roderigo: Think of your bride!

Don Juan: Which one?

Don Roderigo: The one wandering about out there by the lake and calling your name—Juan, you loved her, I know you did.

Don Juan: I know it too. *He throws away the bone.* That was an unforgettable partridge! *He wipes his fingers.* I loved her. I remember it. In spring, when I saw Donna Anna for the first time, I went down on my knees, here on these steps. Mute. As though thunderstruck. That's the expression, isn't it? I shall never forget the way she came down these steps, one foot after the other, with the wind in her dress, and then, because I was kneeling, she stopped, likewise struck dumb. I saw her young mouth; under the black veil I saw the radiance of two blue eyes. It was morning as it is now, Roderigo; it was as though the sun were flowing through my veins. I hadn't breath enough to speak to her; a laugh was choking me, a laugh that could not be laughed because it would have wept. That was love, I think, that was it. For the first and last time.

DON RODERIGO: Why for the last time?

DON JUAN: It never comes back . . . If she were to come down the steps again, at this moment, with the wind in her dress, and I saw the radiance of her eyes under the veil, do you know what I should feel? At best nothing. Memory. Ashes. I don't want to see her again. *He stretches out his hand.* Farewell, Roderigo!

DON RODERIGO: Where are you going?

DON JUAN: To geometry.

DON RODERIGO: Juan, you can't be serious.

DON JUAN: The only thing left to me after this night. Don't feel sorry for me! I've become a man, that's all. I'm as fit as a fiddle, as you see, from my head to my toes. And sober with joy that it's all over, like a sultry storm. Now I shall ride out into the morning; the clear air will taste good. What else do I need? And when I come to a rushing stream I shall bathe, laughing with the cold, and my wedding will be over and done with. I feel freer than I have ever felt before, Roderigo, empty and alert and filled with the need for masculine geometry.

DON RODERIGO: Geometry!

DON JUAN: Have you never experienced the feeling of sober amazement at a science that is correct? For example, at the nature of a circle, at the purity of a geometrical locus. I long for the pure, my friend, for the sober, the exact. I have a horror of the morass of our emotions. I have never felt ashamed of a circle or disgusted by a triangle. Do you know what a triangle is? It's as inexorable as destiny. There is only one figure that can be made up out of the given parts; and hope, the illusion of unpredictable possibilities, which so often confuses our hearts, vanishes like an hallucination before these three lines. Thus and thus only, says geometry. Thus and not in some other way! No deception and no changing mood affects the issue; there is just one figure that is described by the name triangle. Isn't that beautiful? I confess, Roderigo, that I have never yet come across anything greater than this game whose rules the moon and sun obey. What is more awe-inspiring than two lines in the sand, two parallels? Look at the most distant horizon, and it is nothing in terms of infinitude; look at the distant ocean, it is distance, granted, and look up at the Milky Way, it is space—the mind goes up in steam at the thought, it is unthinkable; but it is not infinity—nothing demonstrates that save two lines in the sand, interpreted with intelligence . . . Oh, Roderigo, I am filled with love, filled with awe, that is the only reason I mock. Beyond incense, where everything is clear and serene and transparent, revelations begin; in those regions there are no passing moods, Roderigo, as in earthly love; that which is true today is also true tomorrow, and when I am no longer breathing it will still be true without me, without you. Only the sober man has an intimation of the holy; everything else is stuff and nonsense, believe me, not worth staying in. *He stretches out his hand again.* Farewell!

DON RODERIGO: And the girl by the lake?

DON JUAN: Another man will console her.

DON RODERIGO: Do you really believe that?

DON JUAN: Man and woman—why do you always want to believe what pleases you? At bottom people simply believe they can change the world by not laughing at it. Roderigo, my ever-faithful friend, I laugh at you! I'm your friend; but how do you know I shan't one day take it into my head to put our friendship in jeopardy? I can't stand friends who are sure of me. How do you know I haven't just come from your Inez?

DON RODERIGO: Drop that joke!

DON JUAN: How do you know it's a joke?

DON RODERIGO: I know my Inez.

DON JUAN: So do I.

DON RODERIGO: How?

DON JUAN: I told you: I've just been with her.

DON RODERIGO: That's not true!

DON JUAN: I'm curious, my friend, curious by nature. I wondered whether I should be capable of it. Inez is your sweetheart; you love her, and she loves you. I wondered whether she would be capable of it. And whether you would believe it when I told you.

DON RODERIGO: Juan—!

DON JUAN: Do you believe it or don't you? *Pause.* Don't believe it!

DON RODERIGO: You're diabolical.

DON JUAN: I love you. *He goes up to Don Roderigo and kisses him on the brow.* Don't ever believe it!

DON RODERIGO: If it were true, I should kill myself on the spot; not you, not her, but myself.

DON JUAN: That would be a pity. *He picks up his jacket, which is lying on the steps, and puts it on.* Now I know why I felt frightened when I saw my reflection in the water of the reservoir, in that mirror filled with the sweet blue of the fathomless sky. Don't be curious, Roderigo, like me. When we once leave the lie that gleams like a shiny surface, when we cease to look upon this world as the mirror of our wishes, if we seek to know who we are, ah, Roderigo, then there is no end to our fall and the wind whistles in your ears till you no longer know where God dwells. Never plunge into your soul, Roderigo, or into anyone else's soul; remain on the blue surface of the mirror like the gnats dancing over the water—that thy days may be long in the land, amen. *He has finished putting on his jacket.* With this thought I bid you farewell. *He embraces Roderigo.* It was good to have a friend, Roderigo, a friend who trembled for me last night; in future I shall have to tremble for myself.

DON RODERIGO: Juan, what has happened to you?

DON JUAN: *laughs.*

DON RODERIGO: Something has happened to you.

DON JUAN: I've used up all my love. *He starts to leave, but Don Roderigo holds him back.* It was a brief youth. *He frees himself.* Let go of me. *Don Juan goes, but at this moment he recognizes the figure of Donna Anna, who has appeared at the top of the steps in a bride's gown and veil.* What's all that for? *The figure comes slowly down the steps.* Donna Anna . . . *The figure comes to a stop on the third step from the bottom.* I've deserted you. Why this return? I've deserted you. Don't you know what all Seville knows? I've deserted you!

THE FIGURE *smiles and says nothing.*

DON JUAN: I remember. Oh, you! I see your young mouth smiling. As it smiled then. And under your veil I can see the radiance of your eyes. All as it was then. Only I am not the same man who kneeled before you here on the steps, and there is no going back.

THE FIGURE: My dear Juan—

DON JUAN: You shouldn't have come, Anna, you shouldn't have come down these steps. The sight of you fills me with the expectation of something that will never again exist. I know now that love

is not what I expected it to be on these steps. *Pause.* Go! *Pause.*
Go! I said. Go, in the name of heaven and hell. Go!

THE FIGURE: Why don't you go?

DON JUAN: *stands thunderstruck, looking at her.*

THE FIGURE: My dear Juan—

DON JUAN: Your dear Juan! *He laughs.* Do you know where he was
last night, your dear Juan? Your dear Juan was with your mother!
She could teach you a lot, but he deserted her too, your dear Juan,
who is so full of love that he jumped out of one window and fled
in through the next. He was with your mother, do you hear? They
hunted him with dogs, as though he didn't feel hunted enough
already, and I don't even know the name of the third one on his
wedding night, a young woman, nothing more, a woman like a
hundred women in the darkness. How your dear Juan enjoyed
forgetting you in that darkness without name or face, how he
enjoyed killing and burying that which had proved to be childish,
and passing on. What do you want with him who can do nothing
any more but laugh? And then, how dreary and without charm it
all was—it wasn't hope that lured him into the last bedroom, your
dear Juan, it wasn't her fair hair and her different way of kissing,
nor was it delight in her childish resistance; she defended herself
so fiercely, till she was overcome by the ecstasy of being weaker
than your dear Juan. Outside the dogs were barking. Oh yes, the
differences are enchanting, but their enchantment doesn't last
long, and in our arms they are all so much alike, very soon they
become terrifyingly alike. But this one, the last on the confused
night, had something that no other has or ever will have again,
something unique that stimulated him, something special, something irresistible—she was the sweetheart of his only friend.

DON RODERIGO: No!

DON JUAN: She didn't forget you, Roderigo, not for an instant; on
the contrary, your name burned on our brows, and we enjoyed the
sweetness of dishonour till the cocks crew.

DON RODERIGO: No!

DON JUAN: That is the unadulterated truth. *Don Roderigo rushes
out.* That is how I spent last night, while you were waiting for me
by the lake; so I shall kneel before you. *He kneels.* For the last
time, I know that. You have reappeared to take from me the last
thing I had left: my unrepentant laughter. Why did I embrace you

and not know you? You will leave me the picture of this moment, the picture of the girl betrayed who will continue forever to stand here in the morning sunshine, wherever I may go henceforward.

THE FIGURE: My Juan!

DON JUAN: How could you ever again believe that I loved you? I thought the expectation would never return. How could I believe it myself?

THE FIGURE: Rise!

DON JUAN: Anna.

THE FIGURE: Rise.

DON JUAN: I am not kneeling for forgiveness. Only a miracle, not forgiveness, can save me from the experience I have been through—

THE FIGURE: Rise!

DON JUAN: *rises.* We have lost each other, to find each other for ever. Yes, for ever! *He embraces her.* My wife!

THE FIGURE: My husband! *Don Gonzalo appears with drawn sword.*

DON GONZALO: Ah! There he is!

DON JUAN: Yes, father.

DON GONZALO: Fight!

DON JUAN: You have come too late, father; we have married again.

DON GONZALO: Fight!

DON JUAN: What for?

DON GONZALO: Murderer!

DON JUAN: Your father can't take it in; he sees our happiness with his own eyes, but he can't take it in!

DON GONZALO: Happiness—happiness, he says, happiness—

DON JUAN: Yes, father, leave us to ourselves.

DON GONZALO: —and you, you whore, you'll allow this criminal to talk you round again, if I don't stab him to death on the spot. *He threatens Don Juan, so that Don Juan has to draw his sword.* Down with him!

DON JUAN: Stop!

DON GONZALO: Fight!

DON JUAN: What do you mean, murderer? After all, they're only hounds, quite apart from the fact that I didn't kill them—

DON GONZALO: And Don Roderigo?

DON JUAN: Where is he?

DON GONZALO: With the death rattle in his throat, and lying in his own blood, he cursed you as the violator of his sweetheart.

DON JUAN: —Roderigo? *Don Juan is shaken by the news and stares into space, while the Commander's darting sword bothers him like an insect which he angrily brushes aside.* Stop, I say. *Don Gonzalo falls after a lightning thrust, before a fight has developed, and dies, while Don Juan, sheathing his sword, stares into space as before.* I am shattered by his death—I mean Roderigo's. Why did I have to deliver him up to the truth? He never understood me, my ever-faithful friend—I liked him with all my heart. I warned him: I can't stand friends who are sure of me. Why did I not keep silent? Only a moment ago he was standing here . . .

THE FIGURE: Death, death!

DON JUAN: Don't yell.

THE FIGURE: Oh, Juan!

DON JUAN: Let us flee! *Father Diego appears in the background, the drowned Anna in his arms, but Don Juan does not see him yet.* Let us flee! As we swore at night by the lake, oh, swore in such a childlike way, as though it lay in our power not to lose our way and each other. Why do you hesitate? I am holding your hand like a life that has been given to us for the second time, more real than the first, the childish life, fuller by our knowledge of how easily it may be wasted. Are you trembling? Look at me: I feel this morning sun and everything living with all the gratitude of a man condemned to die and pardoned—*He catches sight of Father Diego with the body.* What does this mean, Father Diego?— *Silence.* Answer! *Silence.* Which is my bride? *He shouts:* Answer!

FATHER DIEGO: She will never answer again, Don Juan, however loud you shout. Never again. She drowned herself. That is the end of your wedding, Don Juan, that is the harvest of your wantonness.

DON JUAN: No—

FATHER DIEGO: *lays the body on the ground.*

DON JUAN: That's not my bride. That's not true. I have married life, not a drowned corpse with dangling arms and hair full of water weed. What is this spectre doing in broad daylight? I say, that is not my bride.

FATHER DIEGO: Then who is your bride?

DON JUAN: This woman! The other one.

FATHER DIEGO: And why does she want to flee? *The figure starts to run up the steps, but at this moment the three Cousins appear.*

DON JUAN: Gentlemen, I welcome your arrival. My friend is dead—

A COUSIN: Dead.

DON JUAN: What about this woman?

FATHER DIEGO: Dead.

DON JUAN: And this man too. Who will believe that he spitted himself on my blade like a chicken. He will be resurrected as a monument.

A COUSIN: Heaven smite the evil-doer!

DON JUAN: And what has happened to my father?

A COUSIN: Dead.

DON JUAN: Is that true?

THE COUSINS: Dead.

DON JUAN: I confess, Father Diego, that I feel like an earthquake or a flash of lightning. *He laughs.* As to you, my cousins, sheathe your swords now so that you may survive and be witnesses at my wedding. Here are two brides and I must choose; one living, one dead, and Father Diego says that I am wedded to the corpse. But I say that she—*He steps up to the veiled figure and takes her hand.*—she and none other is my bride, she, the living one, she who has not chosen to die in order to damn me to the end of my days, she who has appeared once more to me in my confusion, so that I might recognize her, and I have recognized her.

THE FIGURE: Oh, Juan!

DON JUAN: Take off your veil!

THE FIGURE: *takes off her veil.*

FATHER DIEGO: Miranda? *Don Juan covers his face with both hands till he is alone, till the dead have been carried away, till the ringing of bells that accompanies the funeral procession has fallen silent.*

DON JUAN: Bury the poor child, but don't expect me to cross myself, and have no hope that I shall weep. And don't get in my way. Now I fear nothing any more. We shall see which of us two, heaven or I, makes a mockery of the other!

Interval

Act Four

A hall.
Don Juan, now a man of thirty-three, stands examining a banquet table laid with silver and candles. His servant, Leporello, is putting carafes on the table. Three Musicians are waiting for instructions. In the background is a large curtain.

DON JUAN: You will stay in the next room. Understand? And as to the Halleluiah, if anything happens, an accident or anything like that—for example, it's possible hell may open up and swallow me up—

MUSICIAN: Sir!

DON JUAN: —just go on playing. Understand? Keep on repeating the Halleluiah till there's no one left in the room. *He tugs his white gloves from his fingers while examining the table.* Right, get ready!

MUSICIAN: What about our fee?

DON JUAN: We'll discuss that later.

MUSICIAN: When there's no one left in the room—?

DON JUAN: Gentlemen, I'm expecting thirteen ladies who claim that I seduced them, and as though that were not enough I'm also expecting the Bishop of Cordoba, who is on the side of the ladies, as everyone knows, and I'm expecting a monument, which I have also invited, a stone guest—gentlemen, I don't feel up to discussing your fee just now, I simply don't feel up to it . . . *The Musicians withdraw.* It doesn't look bad.

LEPORELLO: The wine won't go far, sir; one little glass for each guest—

DON JUAN: That will be enough. I hope they'll lose all desire to drink pretty quickly, at the latest when the stone guest comes.

LEPORELLO: —Sir . . .

DON JUAN: We're bankrupt. *A doorbell rings outside.* Where are the place cards?

LEPORELLO: —Sir . . . You don't seriously think he'll come, do you, the fellow on the stone plinth?

DON JUAN: Do you seriously believe he will, then?

LEPORELLO: Me? *He tries to laugh contemptuously; when the bell rings for the second time, the laughter falls from his horrified face like a mask.* —Perhaps that's him!

DON JUAN: *places the cards on the table.*

LEPORELLO: —Sir . . .

DON JUAN: If it's that veiled lady again, tell her I absolutely refuse to see any more veiled ladies. We know all about them. They always try to save my soul, hoping I'll seduce them out of sheer pig-headedness. Tell the lady we know the procedure and are tired of it. *The doorbell rings for the third time.* Why don't you answer the door? *Leporello goes out nervously. The Musicians in the next room are tuning their instruments, producing a confused jumble of notes, while Don Juan carefully sets out the place cards; he comes to the last card and stops.* You, more living than all those who are alive, you won't be coming; you, the only one I loved, the first and the last, loved and did not recognize. *He burns the card over a candle. Ashes. Leporello returns.*

LEPORELLO: The Bishop of Cordoba!

DON JUAN: Blow these ashes off the table and ask the Bishop of Cordoba to wait a moment. But ask him politely! It's true the Bishop enjoys no credit with me, I mean I don't owe him anything; but I need him very badly. Without the Church, there would be no hell.

LEPORELLO: —Sir . . .

DON JUAN: Why do you keep trembling all the time?

LEPORELLO: There's a limit to everything, sir, there's no sense in overdoing things, I mean, inviting a monument to dinner, a dead man who has long ago mouldered away to dust, sir, I've always been a rogue when it paid me, and I'll do anything for a price, sir, I'm no coward, but what you asked for in the cemetery yesterday, sir, was roguery just for the hell of it, sir, inviting a monument to dinner—

VOICE: Don Juan?

LEPORELLO: Holy Mary!

VOICE: Don Juan?

DON JUAN: Just a moment.

LEPORELLO: He's coming.

DON JUAN: Just a moment, I said, just a moment.

LEPORELLO: Mercy! I'm innocent, I had to do it, I've got a family, God above, five children and a wife. *He throws himself on his knees.* Mercy!

DON JUAN: If you want to pray, go outside.

LEPORELLO: He called out; I heard him.

DON JUAN: Get up!

LEPORELLO: *stands up.*

DON JUAN: Now do as I tell you. Give the Bishop of Cordoba my compliments and ask him to come in, but do it with plenty of ceremony; I need another three minutes here.

LEPORELLO: Holy Mary!

DON JUAN: And don't forget to genuflect at the proper places. *Leporello goes out.* What's the matter out there at the back? *He walks over to the large curtain in the background; out steps Celestina disguised as a monument; only her head is still uncovered.* Why don't you put on the rest of it?

CELESTINA: This helmet is too tight.

DON JUAN: No one will notice that.

CELESTINA: Except me.

DON JUAN: *signs to her to go.*

CELESTINA: I've changed my mind—

DON JUAN: What about?

CELESTINA: You can say what you like, but it's blasphemy, and I'm not going to blaspheme for five hundred pesos, my good sir, not me.

DON JUAN: Celestina—?

CELESTINA: A thousand is the least I'll take. I'd get a thousand pesos if I sold you to the Duchess of Ronda, you know, and cash down.

DON JUAN: I call that blackmail.

CELESTINA: Call it what you like; I don't care what name you give it, all I care about is the money, and five hundred isn't enough for me.

DON JUAN: That's all I've got.

CELESTINA: Then I won't do it.

DON JUAN: *tears something from round his neck.*

CELESTINA: An amulet?

DON JUAN: The last thing I have left. Be off with you! If my descent into hell doesn't succeed I'm lost.

CELESTINA: It's not my fault you're bankrupt, Don Juan. Why won't you accept my offer? You'd be richer than the Bishop of Cordoba. I told you there's a castle with forty-four rooms—

DON JUAN: I don't want to hear any more about it!

CELESTINA: There's still time.

DON JUAN: For God's sake, stop your matchmaking! All Spain knows, and I tell you for the very last time, I shall never marry!

CELESTINA: Lots of men have said that.

DON JUAN: Silence! *Celestina disappears behind the curtain; Don Juan waits, but only Leporello enters.*

LEPORELLO: Sir—I've forgotten what I was supposed to say to him. He's so solemn, sir; he's striding up and down in the hall as though he couldn't wait for heaven to smite us.

DON JUAN: Give him my compliments and ask him to come in. *Leporello goes out, leaving both wings of the double door open. Don Juan prepares to receive the Bishop: he pushes an armchair into position, tries out where and how to genuflect: then he gives a sign to the Musicians. Solemn music begins to sound. Don Juan is standing in front of a mirror straightening his ruff, when a veiled Lady enters slowly through the open door. Pause. Don Juan notices her in the mirror and starts, without turning round.*

THE LADY: Why do you start with fright?

DON JUAN: Since I know the only thing worth knowing—that you are not Donna Anna, because Donna Anna is dead—why bother with a veil? *He turns round.* Who are you?

THE LADY: You refused to see me. Suddenly I found the door open . . .

DON JUAN: What can I do for you?

THE LADY: I once loved you, because you found a game of chess more irresistibly attractive than a woman. And because you passed by me like a man with a goal. Do you still have your goal? It was geometry. That was long ago! I see your life: it is full of women, Juan, and without geometry.

DON JUAN: Who are you?

THE LADY: I am now the Duchess of Ronda.

DON JUAN: You stepped into my mirror as black as death, Duchess. There was no need for all that black to frighten me. The more blooming a woman looks, the more she reminds me of death.

THE LADY: I am dressed in black because I am a widow.

DON JUAN: Through me?

THE LADY: No.

DON JUAN: What is it you want to see me about, Duchess of Ronda?

THE LADY: Your salvation.

DON JUAN: You are the lady who wants to marry me. You are the castle with forty-four rooms. Your perseverance is amazing, Duchess of Ronda. As to the rest, you are right: although a game of chess is more attractive to me than a woman, my life is full of women. And yet you are wrong! No woman has yet vanquished me, Duchess of Ronda, and I would rather enter hell than marriage—

THE LADY: I have not come as a woman.

DON JUAN: You put me to shame.

THE LADY: I've had men till I was sick of them; and there was nothing left for me to do but smile; then a man came along who imagined he couldn't live without my smile; he made me a Duchess and then he died.

DON JUAN: I understand.

THE LADY: Now I have this castle in Ronda—

DON JUAN: It has been described to me.

THE LADY: I see it like this: You can live in the west wing, I shall live in the east wing as I have been doing up to now. And in between there is a big courtyard, filled with silence broken only by a fountain. We need not meet at all, unless we feel like conversation. And on top of this there would be a ducal fortune, big enough not merely to pay off all your silly debts, but also big enough to silence every court in the world where you are accused of murder. In short, so long as you are living at Ronda no one will be able to distract you from your geometry.

DON JUAN: But?

THE LADY: There is no but.

DON JUAN: I admit, Duchess of Ronda, that your understanding of men is extraordinary. But what is the price for this salvation?

THE LADY: That you accept it, Juan.

DON JUAN: Is that all?

THE LADY: Maybe I still love you, but don't be scared; I have learnt that I don't need you, Juan, and that is the chief thing I am offering you; I am the woman who is free from the illusion that she cannot live without you. *Pause.* Think it over. *Pause.* All your life you have never loved anyone but yourself and yet you have never found yourself. That is why you hate us. You have used us, you have never loved us. We were an episode. Every one of us. But the episodes have swallowed up your whole life. Why will you

never believe in a woman, Juan, not once? It is the only way to
your geometry, Juan. *Leporello leads in the Bishop of Cordoba.*

LEPORELLO: His Eminence!

DON JUAN: Excuse me, Duchess of Ronda, His Eminence and I have
a business matter to discuss, but I hope soon to see you at table—
without a veil.

THE LADY: At Ronda, my dear Juan! *The Lady gathers up her skirt
and curtsies low to the Bishop; then she goes out, followed by
Leporello, who closes the door.*

DON JUAN: You see, Your Eminence, I don't get a moment's peace.
They all want to save me by marrying me . . . Your Eminence! *He
kneels.* Thank you for coming!

BISHOP: Rise.

DON JUAN: For twelve years the Spanish Church has persecuted
me—I am not kneeling out of habit, heaven knows, I am kneeling
out of gratitude; Your Eminence, how I have longed to talk to a
man!

BISHOP: Rise!

DON JUAN: *rises.*

BISHOP: What is this all about?

DON JUAN: Won't you sit down, Your Eminence?

BISHOP: *sits down.*

DON JUAN: I can't bear to see or hear any more about women, Your
Eminence. I don't understand Creation. Was it necessary to have
two sexes? I've been thinking about it—about men and women,
about the incurable wound of sex, about the race and the individual, that above all, about the lost position of the individual—

BISHOP: Let us come to the point.

DON JUAN: *sits down.*

BISHOP: What is this all about?

DON JUAN: To put it briefly: about the creation of a legend.

BISHOP: I beg your pardon?

DON JUAN: About the creation of a legend. *He reaches for a carafe.* I
forgot to ask, Your Eminence, would you like something to drink?
The Bishop refuses with a gesture. We haven't much time before
the ladies arrive, so you must forgive me if I speak plainly.

BISHOP: Please do.

DON JUAN: My suggestion is simple and clear. Don Juan Tenorio, whom the public has now come to look upon as your arch-enemy, who sits before you in all the splendor of his prime and is in the process of becoming immortal, indeed, I may say, of becoming a myth—Don Juan Tenorio, I say, is prepared and resolved to be dead as from today.

BISHOP: Dead?

DON JUAN: On certain conditions.

BISHOP: What kind of conditions?

DON JUAN: We are alone, Your Eminence, so I shall not mince words. You, the Spanish Church, will give me a modest pension, no more, a cell in a monastery, not too tiny a cell, if I may express a wish, and if possible with a view of the Andalusian Mountains; there I shall live on bread and wine, nameless, safe from women, in peace and quiet and satisfied with my geometry.

BISHOP: H'm.

DON JUAN: And in exxchange I shall give you, Bishop of Cordoba, what the Spanish Church needs more urgently than money: the legend of the evil-doer's descent into hell. *Pause.* Well, what do you say?

BISHOP: H'm.

DON JUAN: For twelve years now, Your Eminence, that monument has been standing there with the embarrassing inscription, HEAVEN SMITE THE EVIL-DOER, and I, Don Juan Tenorio, walk past it whenever I am in Seville, how long am I to carry on like this? Seducing, stabbing to death, laughing and passing on . . . *He rises.* Something must happen, Bishop of Cordoba, something must happen!

BISHOP: It will.

DON JUAN: What sort of example do I set our youth? The young model themselves on me. I can see it coming, I can see a whole era coming that will run into the void like me, but they will only be bold because they have seen that there is no judgment; I can see a whole generation of scoffers who believe they are like me, who are vain with a contempt that will become cheap, fashionable, vulgar, desperately stupid—I can see that coming!

BISHOP: H'm.

DON JUAN: Can't you? *The Bishop takes the carafe and pours himself out a glass.* Don't misunderstand me, Bishop of Cordoba; I'm not merely tired of women; I mean it in a spiritual sense too,

I'm tired of evil-doing. Twelve years of an unrepentable life: wasted in this childish challenge to the blue air that is called heaven! I have stopped at nothing, but you can see for yourself, Your Eminence, my evil-doing has merely made me famous. *The Bishop drinks.* I'm in despair. *The Bishop drinks.* For thirty-three years I have shared the fate of so many famous men: everyone knows our deeds, almost no one understands what they mean. I shudder when I hear people talking about me. As though I had ever cared about women!

BISHOP: All the same—

DON JUAN: To begin with, I admit, it's fun. My hands, they tell me, are like divining-rods; my hands discover wellsprings of pleasure which their husbands have failed to discover in ten years.

BISHOP: You are thinking of the good Lopez?

DON JUAN: I don't want to mention names here, Your Eminence.

BISHOP: Don Balthazar Lopez.

DON JUAN: I was prepared for anything, Your Eminence, but not for boredom. Their ecstatic mouths, and their eyes, their watery eyes, narrow with lust, I can't bear the sight of them any more! You do more than anyone else to foster my fame, Bishop of Cordoba; it's a joke: the ladies come away from your sermons dreaming of me, and their husbands draw their swords before I have even noticed the ladies, so I have to fight wherever I happen to be; practice makes perfect, and before I have even sheathed my sword the widows are hanging round my neck, sobbing so that I shall comfort them. I ask you, what alternative have I but to live up to my reputation, to be the victim of my reputation—there is one thing nobody in our polite Spain ever mentions: the crimes women commit against me! Or else I leave the widow lying there, turn on my heel and go about my own business; that's not easy either, Your Eminence, everyone knows the undying thirst for vengeance of the woman who has once hoped in vain to be seduced—*There is a knock at the door.* Just a moment! *There is a second knock at the door.*

BISHOP: Why are you looking at me like that?

DON JUAN: It's odd.

BISHOP: What's odd?

DON JUAN: This is the first time I've had a close look at you, Bishop of Cordoba; used you not be much plumper?

BISHOP: My predecessor, perhaps.

DON JUAN: All the same, I have a feeling I know your gloomy face. Where have we met before? *There is a knock at the door.* Very strange . . . *There is another knock at the door.* I was speaking about my misery.

BISHOP: Marriages violated, families broken up, daughters seduced, fathers stabbed to death, not to mention the husbands who have had to survive their shame—and you, who are responsible for all this, you dare to speak of your own misery, Don Juan Tenorio!

DON JUAN: You're trembling.

BISHOP: To be laughed at through the whole country as a cuckolded husband—have you ever been through that experience?

DON JUAN: Have you, Your Eminence?

BISHOP: A man like this good Lopez—

DON JUAN: Your Eminence seems to be a relation of his, to judge by the frequency with which you mention your good Lopez, who, as I know, has donated half a fortune to the Spanish Church to ensure that it shall never cease to persecute me; and now your good Lopez has even had my house surrounded by his hired ruffians. You blanch, Your Eminence, but it is a fact: I can no longer leave my house without running someone through—that is misery, Your Eminence, believe me, real misery. *Leporello has come in.* Don't disturb us now! *Leporello withdraws.*

BISHOP: To get back to the point—

DON JUAN: Please do.

BISHOP: The creation of a legend.

DON JUAN: You need only say yes, Bishop of Cordoba, and the legend will have been created. I have hired a woman who will play the dead Commander for us, and the ladies will scream their heads off when they hear his sepulchral voice. I shall reply with a sneering laugh that will send a cold shudder down your spine; there will be an explosion at the psychological moment, to make the ladies hide their faces—Your Eminence can see the ingenious machine under the table—and the place will stink of sulphur and smoke. All this will happen very quickly, of course; surprise is the mother of miracles. And then I thought you could deliver a few well-chosen words, as you are so fond of doing, something about the way heaven can always, be relied upon; and my musicians will play the Halleluia as I have ordered, and that will be that.

BISHOP: What about you?

DON JUAN: I shall have jumped down into the cellar—Your Eminence can see the ingenious trap-door in the floor—naturally not without a suitable scream to arouse pity and fear, as demanded by Aristotle. There will be a brown cowl and a sharp razor to remove my all-too celebrated moustache, waiting for me in the cellar, and a monk will go his way along the dusty road.

BISHOP: I see.

DON JUAN: On one condition: We must both maintain secrecy. Otherwise there will be no advantage to anyone. My descent into hell—the rumour will spread in a flash, and the less the few eye-witnesses have really seen, the greater the wealth of details invented by those who weren't there, the more impregnable the legend will be against doubt—my descent into hell will comfort the ladies, the husbands, the threatening host of my creditors, in short everyone will derive spiritual profit from it. What could be more miraculous?

BISHOP: I see.

DON JUAN: Don Juan will be dead. I shall have peace to get on with my geometry. And you, the Church, will have a proof of divine justice such as you will find nowhere else in the whole of Spain.

BISHOP: I see. *Leporello comes in again.*

LEPORELLO: Sir—

DON JUAN: What is it?

LEPORELLO: The ladies are here.

DON JUAN: Where?

LEPORELLO: In the courtyard. And they're rather indignant, sir. They all thought they were going to see you alone and so on. If I hadn't quickly bolted the door they would all be gone by now. They're flapping and cackling like an Andalusian barnyard.

DON JUAN: Good.

LEPORELLO: That's to say, to be exact, as you always tell me to be: just at the moment they're quite quiet, they're all eyeing one another from the side, all fanning themselves.

DON JUAN: Let them in! *After a glance at the Bishop:* Let us say, in five minutes. *Leporello goes out.* Your Eminence, tell me the name of the monastery.

BISHOP: You're very sure of yourself—

DON JUAN: Naturally the Church can only use a legend if it is successfully established. I understand your hesitation, Bishop of Cordoba, but don't worry: the story is credible, there's nothing original about it; it's an ancient theme in myths; a statue slaying the murderer occurs in classical mythology, so does the mocking of a skull which then sends the mocker into eternity; think of the Breton ballads our soldiers sing; we are working with tradition—

BISHOP *takes off his disguise and the dark glasses he has been wearing, and shows his true face.*

DON JUAN: Don Balthazar Lopez?

LOPEZ: Yes.

DON JUAN: So it is you.

LOPEZ: We have only met once, Don Juan, for an instant. A white curtain blew into the candle when I opened the door and found you with my wife; a sudden banner of red flames, you remember, and I had to put it out—

DON JUAN: Quite right.

LOPEZ: There was no time to fight.

DON JUAN *draws his sword.*

LOPEZ: Now that I know you plot to evade our vengeance, I shall take pleasure in exposing your blasphemous legend. Let the ladies come in! You will remain on this earth, Don Juan Tenorio, just like us, and I shall not rest until my vengeance is complete, until I see you too, Don Juan Tenorio, as a husband.

DON JUAN: Ha!

LOPEZ: Married to my wife! *Enter Leporello.* Even a master of chess, it seems, may sometimes move the wrong piece, and suddenly, certain of the victory he has craftily maneuvered, he checkmates himself.

DON JUAN: We shall see—*The thirteen ladies enter, highly indignant; when they see the supposed Bishop, they first fall silent; Lopez has put on his Bishop's mitre again and the ladies kiss the hem of his robe. They do this with dignity, then:*

DONNA ELVIRA: Your Eminence, we have been deceived—

DONNA BELISA: I thought he was on his deathbed—

DONNA ISABEL: So did I

DONNA VIOLA: We all thought so—

DONNA ELVIRA: Word of honour, otherwise I should never have come—

DONNA FERNANDA: None of us would—

DONNA ELVIRA: I, the Commander's widow—
DONNA FERNANDA: I thought he was on his deathbed too—
DONNA INEZ: So did I, so did I—
DONNA ELVIRA: I thought he had repented—
DONNA BELISA: We all did—
DONNA ISABEL: He wants to do penance, I thought—
DONNA VIOLA: What else—
DONNA ELVIRA: Your Eminence, I am a lady—
DONNA BELISA: And what are we?
BISHOP: Donna Belisa—
DONNA BELISA: Aren't we ladies, Your Eminence?
BISHOP: Be calm, Donna Belisa; I know that you are the good Lopez's wife.
DONNA BELISA: Don't mention his name!
BISHOP: Why not?
DONNA BELISA: The good Lopez, as he always called himself! And he didn't even fight for me, Your Eminence, he didn't even fight; at least all the other husbands fought; I am the only one here who isn't a widow.
BISHOP: Control yourself!
DONNA BELISA: The good Lopez!
DONNA ELVIRA: I was ready for anything, Your Eminence, for anything, but not for a parade of bedizened adulteresses who think themselves my equals.
THE LADIES: Ah!
DONNA ELVIRA: Go on, boil with indignation and fan your burning faces, you hypocrites, I know perfectly well what you all came to this notorious house for.
DONNA BELISA: What about you?
DONNA ELVIRA: Where is he anyhow, your lover? Where is he, so that I may scratch out his eyes?
DON JUAN: Here. *Don Juan steps into the circle like a torero.* Thank you, my loves, for all having come; of course, you're not all, but I think there are enough of your to celebrate my descent into hell.
LEPORELLO: Sir—?
DON JUAN: My loves, let us sit down. *The ladies stand, without fanning themselves, motionless.* I admit it is strange to see one's loves gathered together in one room, yes, very strange; I tried to

picture it to myself, but I couldn't and I don't know quite how to express myself at this solemn moment, when I see you all together, strangers to one another and yet not strangers, united solely through me, divided through me, so that no one looks at anyone else—*The ladies fan themselves.* Ladies, we have loved one another. *A lady spits at his feet.* I'm amazed myself, Donna Viola, how little is left of it—

DONNA ISABEL: I'm not Donna Viola!

DON JUAN: My apologies.

DONNA VIOLA: Viola he calls her!

DON JUAN: My apologies to you too.

DONNA VIOLA: I can't stand any more of this!

LOPEZ: How fleeting is that very feeling which, during the brief moment it lasts, brings us so close to eternity that as individuals we are blinded by it; yes, Donna Fernanda, that is bitter.

DONNA ISABEL: My name is not Fernanda either!

DON JUAN: My dear—

DONNA ISABEL: You called us all that: my dear!

DON JUAN: I never meant it personally, Donna Isabel—now I remember: Donna Isabel! You with the soul that was always overflowing, why didn't you sob straight away? *To the Bishop:* A man's memory is a strange thing; you're quite right, it's always the minor details we remember: a white curtain blown into the burning candle—

DONNA BELISA: Oh God.

DON JUAN: Another time it was a rustling in the reeds, and in my fright I drew my sword: it was a duck in the moonlight.

DONNA VIOLA: Oh God.

DON JUAN: What remain in the memory are objects: a cheap and nasty vase, slippers, a china crucifix. And sometimes smells: the scent of withered myrrh—

DONNA ISABEL: Oh God.

DON JUAN: And so on and so forth. And in the far distance of my youth, which was short, I hear the hoarse barking of a pack of hounds in the darkness of a park—

DONNA ELVIRA: Oh God.

DONNA CLARA: Oh God.

DONNA INEZ: Oh God.

DON JUAN: That's all I can remember. *The ladies have covered their faces with their fans.* Leporello, light the candles! *Leporello lights the candles.* I don't know whether I'm different from other men. Do they remember nights with women? I am dismayed when I look back upon my life, I see myself like a swimmer in the water— leaving no track. Don't they feel the same? And if a youngster were to ask me, what is this business with women like? to be quite honest, I shouldn't know what to say; it is something you forget, like food and pain, and only when it is there again do I say to myself: So that's what it's like, oh yes, that's how it always was . . . *Leporello has lit the candles.* I don't know, Don Balthazar, whether you want to take off your disguise now or later . . .

DONNA BELISA: What did he say? *The Bishop takes off his disguise.*

LOPEZ: My name is Lopez.

DONNA BELISA: You?!

LOPEZ: Don Balthazar Lopez.

DON JUAN: Treasurer of Toledo, if I am not mistaken, holder of several decorations; as you see, Señor Lopez has unselfishly volunteered for the unrewarding role of the jealous husband.

LOPEZ: The time for your mockery, Don Juan, is past. *A dull thudding is heard.*

DON JUAN: Quiet! *A dull thudding is heard.* Pray silence for Señor Lopez of Toledo. *A dull thudding is heard.*

LOPEZ: Don't be frightened, ladies; I know what is going on here; listen to me!

LEPORELLO: Sir—

DON JUAN: Quiet.

LEPORELLO: —the doors are locked. *The ladies scream.*

LOPEZ: Listen to me! *The ladies have run to the doors, which are locked; Don Juan has sat down on the edge of the table and is pouring himself a glass of wine.*

DON JUAN: Listen to him!

LOPEZ: Ladies—

DON JUAN: Forgive me if I drink meanwhile; I'm thirsty. *He drinks.* Go ahead and talk!

LOPEZ: He will not leave this house, ladies, not till he has suffered the punishment he deserves. I have seen to that. The hour of judgment has struck, the measure of his evil-doing is full.

DON JUAN: Hasn't it been full for a long time? *He drinks.* And yet nothing happens, that's the joke. Yesterday in the cemetery, Leporello, didn't we do everything to mock the dead Commander?

LEPORELLO: —Sir . . .

DON JUAN: Didn't I invite him to this table?

DONNA ELVIRA: My husband?!

DON JUAN: My good servant saw with his own eyes how your husband nodded his stone head, obviously as a sign that he was free today. Why doesn't he come? It is past midnight. What can I do to make heaven smite me at last? *The dull thudding is heard.*

LOPEZ: Stay here, Donna Elvira, stay here! *The dull thudding is heard.* It isn't true, it's an unparalleled piece of trickery; none of it is true, he is trying to make fools of you. Here, do you see this ingenious machine under the table? It's supposed to scare you with a loud bang and the smell of sulphur, so that you lose your senses, so that you believe Don Juan descended into hell, a divine judgment that is nothing but play-acting, an unparalleled act of blasphemy, so that he shall escape punishment on earth. To fool the whole of Spain, that was his plan, to set a legend in the world so that he should escape our punishment, that's what he's after, that's his plan, nothing but play-acting—

DON JUAN *laughs.*

LOPEZ: Do you deny it?

DON JUAN: Not in the least.

LOPEZ: You heard him, ladies.

DON JUAN: Nothing but play-acting.

LOPEZ: Here, you see this ingenious trap-door in the floor, ladies, here, ladies, see for yoursleves!

DON JUAN *laughs.*

LOPEZ: Nothing but play-acting!

DON JUAN: What else? *He drinks.* I've been saying that for twelve years. There is no real hell, no life to come, no judgment of heaven, Señor Lopez is quite right: it's nothing but play-acting.

LOPEZ: Did you hear, ladies?

DON JUAN: Here—*He rises, and goes to the curtain in the background and opens it to reveal the theatrical monument of the Commander.*—look. *The ladies scream.* Why do you tremble?

VOICE: Don Juan!

LEPORELLO: —Sir—sir . . .

VOICE: Don Juan!

DON JUAN: Nothing but play-acting.

VOICE: Don Juan!

LEPORELLO: Sir—it's stretching out its arm . . .

DON JUAN: I'm not afraid, my dears, you can see, I'm gripping its stone hand—*Don Juan grips the Monument's hand; an explosion and smoke; Don Juan and the Monument disappear through the trap-door; the Musicians play the Halleluia as ordered.*

LOPEZ: It isn't true, ladies, it isn't true; I beseech you, don't cross yourselves! *The ladies kneel and cross themselves.* Women . . . *All the doors open, revealing a hired ruffian at every door.* Why don't you stay at your posts?

RUFFIAN: Where is he?

LOPEZ: Now he has done it . . .

INTERMEZZO

Celestina and Leporello appear before the drop-curtain.

CELESTINA: I must talk to her alone. Stay by the coach! I know you: a bit of monastery garden, a few vesper bells, and you'll go all soft. Next thing we know, you'll start believing yourself that he's in hell. *A nun appears.* Sister Elvira? *Leporello leaves.* I have come because I have a guilty conscience, Sister Elvira. Because of what happened. I shouldn't have done it. When I see the effects it had I really reproach myself; when I see you praying all day long, just because you fell for the trick with the Stone Guest. I didn't believe any one would really believe it. Word of honour! And now the whole of Spain believes it. You can't tell the truth in public any more. That poor unfortunate Lopez! You've heard how he was banished because he dared to say in public that a fake played the Commander's ghost. Sister Elvira, it was I who played the Stone Guest, I and no one else. That poor unfortunate Lopez! You've heard how he hanged himself over in Morocco, poor fellow, after giving all his possessions to the Spanish Church, and now even the Church doesn't believe him. Why does truth have such a hard time in Spain? I've been travelling for three hours, merely so I could tell the truth, Sister Elvira, the simple truth. Are you listening to me? I am the last person who knows the truth about this silly story; it has really been a burden on my soul, ever since I heard that you had gone into a monastery because of that business. Between ourselves, Sister Elvira, he isn't in hell. Believe me! I know where he is, but I can't tell you, I've been bribed, Sister Elvira, handsomely bribed—otherwise I shouldn't be able to afford his servant . . . Sister Elvira, as one woman to another: Don Juan is alive, I've seen him with my own eyes; there can be no question of hell, no matter how much you pray for him. *Vesper bells; the nun goes out praying.* Hopeless! *Leporello comes.* Get up on to the box! I've no time for people who confuse faith with refusing to know the truth. Cross yourself!

LEPORELLO: Celestina—

CELESTINA: Don Juan is in hell.

LEPORELLO: And my wages? What about my wages?

CELESTINA: Get up on to the box!

LEPORELLO: "Voilà par sa mort un chacun satisfait: Ciel offensé, lois violées, filles séduites, familles déshonorées, parents outragés, femmes mises à mal, maris poussés à bout, tout le monde est content. Il n'y a que moi seul de malheureux, qui, après tant d'années de service, n'ai point d'autre récompense que de voir à mes yeux l'impiété de mon maître punie par le plus épouvantable châtiment du monde!"

Act Five

A veranda.
In the foreground stands a table laid for two. Don Juan is obviously waiting for the other person. After a while his patience snaps; he rings a bell and a Manservant appears.

DON JUAN: I asked not to be called away from my work until we can really start eating. Now I've been waiting for half an hour again. Aren't my days short enough? I know it's not your fault, Alonso. *He picks up a book.* Where is she? *The servant shrugs his shoulders.* Thank you. It's all right. Forget it. *The servant goes out; Don Juan tries to read a book, which he suddenly throws in the corner. He calls out:* Alonso! When we can really start the meal I'll be over in my cell. *Don Juan is about to go, but the rotund Bishop of Cordoba, formerly Father Diego, comes in from the garden carrying an aster.*

BISHOP: Where are you off to in such a hurry?

DON JUAN: Ah!

BISHOP: We've been waiting for you in the garden, my dear fellow. It's a staggering evening out there. How sorry I am that I can't stay tonight! Every time I stand out there under the arcade, where you see the Ronda gorge at your feet, with the sun shining behind the glowing asters, all red and purple, and the cool blue of the valley that is already in shadow, I always think to myself: This is a paradise that is lying at your feet.

DON JUAN: I know.

BISHOP: But it's autumn already . . .

DON JUAN: Will you have some wine, Bishop?

BISHOP: Please. *While Don Juan fetches a carafe and fills two glasses:* I was saying just now, what a talent the old Moors, who laid out gardens like this, had for living with their skin. All these courtyards with vista after vista, these cool, protected retreats, and the silence in them is not like the silence of the grave, it remains filled with the mystery of the blue distances behind the decorative tracery of grilles, you wander and luxuriate in the shadow, but the coolness is enlivened by the gentle reflection of sunshine on a wall; how ingeniously and delicately it is arranged, all to be enjoyed through the skin! Not to mention the fountains; what an art they had of making Creation play upon the instrument of our senses, what mastery in savoring the ephemeral, of bringing the spirit to the very surface of the body, what civilization! *He smells the aster.* The Duchess will be here at any moment.

DON JUAN: Will she.

BISHOP: She's feeling a little off-color, she says. *Don Juan hands him the glass he has filled.* How's the geometry going?

DON JUAN: All right, thank you.

BISHOP: I thought a lot about what you told me the other day— what you said about the dimensions, you know, and that geometry too arrives at a truth which it is no longer possible to visualize. That's what you said, wasn't it? Line, surface, area: but what is the fourth dimension? And yet you can prove intellectually that it must exist—*Don Juan knocks over his glass.* Don Juan, what's the matter with you?

DON JUAN: With me? Nothing. Why should there be? Nothing at all. *He fills the glass for the second time.* It's not worth talking about! *He knocks his glass over for the second time.* Why should anything be the matter?

BISHOP: Your health.

DON JUAN: Your health. *He fills his glass for the third time.* Every day I repeat my simple wish not to be called until we can really start eating. It's no use! First it was the gong which the Duchess didn't hear when the crickets were chirping in the valley; so I had another one made that booms right across the Ronda gorge. Seriously, the whole of Ronda knows when it's time to eat here. Everyone except the Duchess. I have trained my servants to look for the Duchess in person and tell her in person that the meal is ready, and not to call me until the Duchess is actually crossing the courtyard. You smile! These are trifles, I know, not worth talking about; that is precisely what makes them a torture. What can I do? I mean, I'm her prisoner, don't forget that, I can't leave this castle; if anyone saw me outside, my legend would be done for, and that would mean that I should have to live as Don Juan again . . . *He knocks over the third glass.* Let's say no more about it.

BISHOP: An exquisite sherry. *Don Juan maintains an angry silence.* An exquisite sherry.

DON JUAN: Sorry. *He refills the Bishop's glass.* Forget what I said.

BISHOP: Your health.

DON JUAN: Your health.

BISHOP: The Duchess is a wonderful woman. *He sips.* She is happy, but intelligent; she knows very well that you, the man, are not happy, and that is the only thing she complains of when we are alone together.

DON JUAN: She can't help it, I know.

BISHOP: But?

DON JUAN: Let's not talk about it! *Bishop sips.* Every day, when I come out on this veranda, every day, year in year out, three times a day, every time the feeling blazes up in me that I can't stand it any longer. A trifle! But I can't stand it! And when she does come at last I act as though it were really a trifle; we sit down at the table and I wish her a good appetite.

BISHOP: You love her.

DON JUAN: That on top of everything else. When she spends a week away in Seville, having her hair dyed, I won't say I miss her—.

BISHOP: But you miss her.

DON JUAN: Yes.

BISHOP: It is not good for man to be alone, it says in the Scriptures, therefore God created a companion for him.

DON JUAN: And did he think that then it was good? *The Servant appears with a silver tray.* We're not ready yet. *The Servant goes out with the silver tray.* Seriously, my dislike of Creation, which has divided us into man and woman, is more intense than ever. I tremble before every meal. What a monstrous mistake that the individual alone is not a whole! And the greater his longing is to be a whole the greater the curse that is upon him, he is so much at the mercy of the opposite sex that it can drain the last drop of his blood. What have we done to deserve that? And yet I should be grateful, I know. My only choice is to be dead or to be here. Grateful for this prison amidst the gardens of Paradise!

BISHOP: My friend—

DON JUAN: It is a prison!

BISHOP: With forty-four rooms. Think of all the others, Don Juan, who have only a small house.

DON JUAN: I envy them.

BISHOP: Why?

DON JUAN: I think they go mad and don't notice it any more . . . Why wasn't I allowed into the monastery?

BISHOP: Not everyone can enter a monastery.

DON JUAN: Be fruitful and multiply!

BISHOP: So it is written.

DON JUAN: You know that no excommunication inflicted by the Church, and no sword brandished by the world, ever made me tremble; but she, a woman who loves me, makes me tremble every day. By what means? I merely see that I can no longer smile at what is ridiculous. And that I am coming to terms where no terms are possible. She is a woman—perhaps the best of all imaginable women—but a woman, and I am a man. There is nothing to be done about that, Your Eminence, and certainly nothing can be done by good will. That simply turns the situation into a contest to see who can shame the other with his good will. You should see and hear us when we're alone. Never a loud word! We're an idyll. Once a glass was smashed against the wall, once and never again! We have achieved a frightful nobility; we suffer when the other isn't happy. What more do you want to make a perfect marriage? *Pause.* The only thing lacking now is for the woman to put the final noose round my neck . . .

BISHOP: What's that?

DON JUAN: To make me a father. What shall I do? She can't help it. We shall sit down at table as always and wish each other a good appetite. *Miranda, duchess of Ronda, appears.*

MIRANDA: Am I interrupting you, gentlemen?

BISHOP: Not at all, my dear Miranda. We were just chatting about Don Juan's descent into hell. *To Don Juan:* Have you seen the play in Seville? *To Miranda:* It's running at the moment.

DON JUAN: I never go to Seville.

MIRANDA: Did you say a play?

BISHOP: "The Scoffer of Seville," it's called, "Or the Stone Guest"; I had to see it the other day, because people say it was written by our prior, Gabriel Tellez.

MIRANDA: What's it like?

BISHOP: Not without wit. Don Juan actually does down into hell, and the audience shouts with horrified delight. You really ought to see it some time, Don Juan.

DON JUAN: See myself going down into hell?

BISHOP: What else could the theater do? Truth cannot be shown, only invented. Just imagine if the audience saw the real Don Juan: here on this autumnal veranda in Ronda! The ladies would give themselves airs and say: You see! And the husbands would rub their hands with malicious joy and laugh: Don Juan a henpecked husband! The unusual reaches a point where it looks desperately like the usual. And what about punishment, my secretaries would cry. There would be no end to the misunderstandings. And some young jackanapes who fancied himself as a cynic would announce: Don't you see that marriage is the true hell? And all sorts of other platitudes . . . No, it would be ghastly to hear an audience that only saw reality. *He shakes hands with Miranda.* Good-bye, Duchess of Ronda.

MIRANDA: Are you really going?

BISHOP: I must, I must. *He shakes hands with Don Juan.* Good-bye, Scoffer of Seville!

DON JUAN: Will it be printed?

BISHOP: I expect so. People take enormous pleasure in seeing a man do on the stage the things they would like to do themselves, and then being forced to pay the price which they would have had to pay.

MIRANDA: But I don't come into it, do I?

BISHOP: No.

MIRANDA: Thank God.

BISHOP: Nor do I, thank God—otherwise we should have had to ban it, and the threatre needs plays. By the way, I doubt whether it's really by Tirso de Molina; it seems to me far too pious, and the language isn't up to the standard of his other plays. But however that may be— *He puts the aster down on the table:* God bless your meal! *The Bishop goes out accompanied by Don Juan. Miranda is alone for a few moments; a gesture betrays that she is not feeling well. She finds the book on the floor; Don Juan comes back.*

MIRANDA: What happened to this book?

DON JUAN: Oh, that.

MIRANDA: Did you throw it in the corner?

DON JUAN: What's it called, by the way?

MIRANDA: And you asked if it was going to be printed. This is it: "El Burlador de Sevilla y Convidado de piedra."

DON JUAN: Then he has given it to us.

MIRANDA: Why did you throw it in the corner? *Don Juan pushes his chair into position.* Is it time to eat? *She sits down.* Were you angry? *Don Juan sits down.* You're being unfair to me, Juan—

DON JUAN: I'm sure I am, my dear, I'm sure I am.

MIRANDA: I really must lie down for a moment.

DON JUAN: Will you have some wine?

MIRANDA: No, thank you.

DON JUAN: Why not?

MIRANDA: I suddenly felt giddy again; I think we're going to have a child.

DON JUAN: A child— *The Servant appears.* We're ready— *The Servant goes out.*

MIRANDA: You don't have to say now that you're glad, Juan, but it will make me happy if one day I see that you really are glad. *The Servant comes in with the silver tray and serves dinner.*

DON JUAN: Buen' appetito.

MIRANDA: Buen' appetito.

They begin to eat in silence; the curtain slowly falls.

Postscript

Don Juan, like every figure, has a circle of spiritual relations; and however far removed from him they may be, Icarus or Faust are more closely related to him than Casanova. For this reason the actor need not worry in the least about whether he is having a seductive effect on the ladies in the stalls. His fame as a seducer (which accompanies him as fame, although he does not identify himself with this fame) is a misunderstanding on the part of the ladies. Don Juan is an intellectual, even though he is well built and does not wear glasses. What makes him irresistible to the ladies of Seville is entirely his spirituality, his claim to a male spirituality, which is an affront, because it has entirely different aims than woman and treats woman from the outset as an episode—with the well-known result, of course, that finally the episode swallows up his whole life.

An intellectual—in this sense:

"The Other lives in a world of things that are once and for all what they appear to be. Nor is it by chance that he puts them in question. They do not upset his composure . . . The world which the intellectual encounters seems to him to be there only in order to be put in question. Things as such are not enough for him. He turns them into a problem. And this is the greatest symptom of love. The result of this is that things only are what they are when they are for the intellectual. Woman often has an inkling of this . . ."

(Ortega y Gasset: *The Intellectual and the Other*.)

Don Juan is beautiful through his courage to taste experience. Not a *beau!* Nor a Hercules. He is slim like a *torero*, almost boyish. Like a *torero* he fights the bull; he is not the bull. His hands are strong but graceful; but not soft. People will ask themselves over and over again: Is he a man? He could have been a dancer. His masculinity moves on the borderline and he does not take it for granted. It is something precious which he possesses and therefore must not replace by a soldierly pose, for example; he has to defend it. His masculinity is something in danger. His face, however else it may be, has the alert eyes of a man in danger. Men in danger tend towards radicality.

As applied to the infidelity that is the most familiar label attached to every Don Juan this radicality means: he is not drawn from lust to lust, but repelled by what is not quite right. He always has to leave women not because he loves them, but because he loves something else (for instance geometry) more than women. His infidelity is not due to excessively strong impulses but to the fear of deceiving himself, of losing himself—his vigilant fear of the feminine in himself.

Don Juan is a Narcissus, no doubt of that. Fundamentally he loves only himself. The legendary number of his loves (1,003) is not repellent only because it is comic, and it is comic because it counts where there is nothing to count. Translated into words this number means: Don Juan remains without a Thou.

Therefore he is not a man who loves.

Love, as Don Juan experiences it, has to have the sinister repulsiveness of the tropics, something like humid sun over a marsh full of blossoming decay, panic, like the sticky silence full of murderous overfertility that devours itself, full of creepers—a thicket through which one cannot force one's way without a drawn blade; a place in which one is afraid to dally.

Don Juan remains without a Thou among men, too. Always there is only a Catalinon, a Scanarelle, a Leporello, never a Horatio. And once he has lost the friend of his youth, who was left to him from the brotherliness of his childhood years, he never forms another friendship; men avoid him. Don Juan is an unbrotherly man; partly because, among men, he feels feminine.

One might picture it like this:

Like most of us, brought up on poetry, he starts out as a youth believing that the love which takes possession of him one fine morning relates entirely to one person, unequivocally, to Donna Anna, who has inspired this love in him. The mere inkling of how great is the part played in this by the generic, to say nothing of mere experience, of how interchangeable is the object of his youthful longing; cannot fail to frighten and bewilder the youth, who has only just developed into a person. He feels to himself like a piece of nature, blind, ridiculous, mocked by heaven as a spiritual individual. From this wound springs his wild need to mock heaven, to challenge it by scorn and sacrilege—which, of course, always presupposes a heaven. A Nihilist?

In a society of mediocre dishonesty everyone (at least in our day) is called a Nihilist who tries to find out what is true.

His mockery: a more shamefaced kind of melancholy that concerns no one but heaven.

His shamefacedness seems to me important. Don Juan is shameless, never unashamed, and among men he would probably be the only one who does not laugh at a dirty joke, who cannot laugh at it. His sense of shame is directed inward, not outward; it is not prudery but sensibility; his tendency to play-act, to disguise himself to the point of self-denial, is part of this sense of shame. "Don Juan" is the role he plays.

El Burlador de Sevilla y Convidado de piedra, the first dramatic rendering, published in 1627 and attributed, probably incorrectly, to the glorious Tirso de Molina, begins with a scene which succinctly introduces Don Juan—not as he becomes but as he is and remains until Hell swallows him up. And thus, without preparation and without development, we also see him in later versions; Don Juan is simply there, a meteor . . . One has to ask oneself whether any attempt to develop Don Juan as a person in the process of becoming is only possible at the cost of ending up with no Don Juan at all, but a man who (for one reason or another) enters into the role of a Don Juan.

That is to say, a reflected Don Juan!

In that case his medium would certainly not be music—according to Kierkegaard the only possible medium for the immediate Don Juan—but the theatre, whose essence lies in the fact that mask and true being are not identical, so that mistaken identity occurs as in the old Spanish cloak and dagger plays and everywhere else where a man is not himself but is seeking himself.

Why does Don Juan always appear as a confidence trickster? He leads a life that no man can afford, namely the life of one who is "only a man," with the result that he inevitably owes a debt to Creation. His economic bankruptcy, as emphasized especially by Molière, stands for a quite different, a total bankruptcy. Without woman, whose demands he is unwilling to recognize, he himself would not be in the world. As a parasite in Creation (Don Juan is always childless) he is sooner or later left with no other alternative than death or capitulation, tragedy or comedy. The Don Juan existence is always an impossible one, even if there is no society worth mentioning for miles around.

Don Juan is not a revolutionary. His adversary is Creation itself.

Don Juan is a Spaniard: an Anarchist.

Don Juan is childless, in my opinion, even if there were 1,003 children! He does not have them, any more than he has a Thou. By becoming a father—by accepting the role of father—he is no longer Don Juan. This is his capitulation, his first movement towards maturity.

Why is there no old Don Juan?

Don Juan, spiritually speaking, is the *hubris* of trying to be a human being alone, a man without a woman. His spirit remains puerile relatively to Creation—therefore the curtain has to fall before Don Juan is thirty-five; otherwise we shall be left merely with an embarrassing fool, precisely in so far as he is a spiritual figure. (Casanova can grow old!)

The Spanish element—we can neglect it, but we can never put Don Juan in some other specific costume, for example German, or Anglo-Saxon or Slavonic; just try it, to see how very much—in spite of our broader interpretation—Don Juan is and remains basically a Spanish creation. The Spaniard (or at least so it seems to me after a brief trip to Spain) knows no perhaps, no both-and, only yes or no. He knows only two wines, red or white; he knows no nuances. There is something magnificent about this that goes right down to everyday life. What is missing is hesitation, adulteration, compromise; but also the wealth of transitions. What is missing is the mental center, sentiment, and to this extent also compassion, great as well as small, one might almost say: human love. When the Spaniard says: I love you! the selfsame words mean: I want you! And his courage, such as Don Juan also possesses, often appears to us as a mere gesture, with which a fatalistic man under the bleak blue of the Spanish sky keeps up his spirits: death or life, what does it matter! Their dances too are filled with this stubborn, arrogant, provocative spirit. Mood is shaken off as something undignified, roughly, positively scornfully trampled on; and however passionate their dance may become, it never ends in intoxication, never in the bliss of release. On the contrary, it ends abruptly in triumph over intoxication, in a pose of total composure. And proudly, of course. And yet this pride always has something empty, something of the substitute about it. Joy in life? The joy in overcoming is greater, more Spanish. The silver-white *torero* facing the black bull, the man who plays out the deadly battle of the spirit, is no other than Don Juan; the *torero* too is not ultimately concerned to preserve his life. That would not be a victory. It is gracefulness that must make him a victor, geometrical accuracy, the element of dance which he opposes to the enormous bull; it is a victory of the playful spirit that fills the arena with jubilation. The black beast to which Don Juan opposes himself is the natural force of sex, but it is a beast which—unlike the *torero*—he cannot kill without killing himself. This is the difference between arena and world, between play and being . . . The best introduction to Don Juan, apart from Kierkegaard, remains a visit to a Spanish bullfight.

A Don Juan who does not kill is inconceivable, even in a comedy. Death is part of him as a child is part of a woman. Astonishingly, we do not hold his murders against him, even less than against a general. And his not inconsiderable crimes, for which any respectable court (and hence also the honoured audience) would normally call him to account, somehow fail to arouse our indignation. Just imagine a Don Juan who ended in prison! His prison is the world. Put differently: Don Juan is of interest to us only in so far as he escapes our disapproval: as a meteor, as a fall which he does not desire, and as a crash whose deadly effect shows how far we are from Paradise.

If he lived in our own day, Don Juan (as I see him) would probably concern himself with atomic physics: in search of ultimate truth. And the conflict with woman, that is with the unconditional will to maintain life, would remain the same. As an atomic physicist too he would sooner or later be faced with the choice: death or capitulation—capitulation of that masculine spirit which obviously, if it remains autocratic, is going to blow up Creation as soon as it possesses the technical ability to do so.

Behind the Don Juan stands boredom, even if it is outplayed with bravura, the boredom that does not yawn but makes faces; the boredom of a spirit that thirsts for the absolute and believes it has learnt that it will never find it; in short, the great boredom of melancholy, the distress of a heart whose desires are dying, so that all it has left is wit. A Don Juan with no wit would hang himself.

Romano Guardini on melancholy:

"The melancholic longs to meet the absolute, but as love and beauty . . . It is the longing for what Plato calls the true goal of Eros, for the highest good that is at the same time the truly real, imperishable and limitless . . . This longing for the absolute is combined in the melancholic with the consciousness that it is in vain . . . Melancholy is the birth pangs of the eternal in man." (Beauty: the clear, pure, transparent, what Don Juan means when he talks about geometry, and naturally he means that geometry which is still imaginable.)

The absolute—a modern playwright will scarcely be expected to make it appear in the guise of a Stone Guest. What are we to do with this horrifying, scarecrow-like apparition? But it is part of the Don Juan story, that collage of all kinds of sagas, of ancient Greek and Breton legends, and this mortgage cannot be paid off by parody alone. Parody presupposes that at the very bottom of his heart the spectator still believes in the thing that is being parodied. Which of our spectators believes that the dead whom we insult will actually appear and sit at our tables? Our parliaments and our conferences, where we bargain over war and other business, would be crowded out with skeletons, and the trapdoor (which would have to be constructed, if we still had any such hope) would be seething with ministers, directors, generals, bankers, diplomats and journalists— No, we no longer believe in all that. What remains to us is poetry, and within its framework the classical legend of Don Juan's descent to Hell can remain. Despairing over the impossibility of his existence, an impossibility that is not manifested as a metaphysical storm, but simply as tedium, it is now Don Juan himself who stages the legend of his descent into Hell—as opera, as fraud, in order to escape, certainly; as art, which only feigns something absolute, as poetry, certainly; but then this legend, with which he is fooling the world, proves to be merely the expressive figuration of his actual, his inner and otherwise invisible, but hopelessly real end.

Naturally it was not these (after) thoughts that moved the author to write the foregoing play—but the wish to write a play.

Translated by Michael Bullock

From ANDORRA

Sacristy, the Priest and Andri.

PRIEST: Andri, we must have a talk together. Your foster-mother wishes it. She is very worried about you . . . Sit down!

ANDRI: *says nothing.*

PRIEST: Do sit down, Andri!

ANDRI: *says nothing.*

PRIEST: You won't sit down?

ANDRI: *says nothing.*

PRIEST: I can understand, this is the first time you've been here. More or less. I remember they once sent you to fetch your football from behind the altar when it came sailing in. *The Priest laughs.*

ANDRI: What are we to talk about, Reverend Father?

PRIEST: Sit down!

ANDRI: *says nothing.*

PRIEST: So you won't sit down?

ANDRI: *says nothing.*

PRIEST: Very well then.

ANDRI: Is it true, Reverend Father, that I am different from everyone else? *Pause.*

PRIEST: Andri, I want to tell you something.

ANDRI: I'm impertinent, I know.

PRIEST: I understand your distress. But you must know that we like you, Andri, just as you are. Hasn't your foster-father done everything he could for you? I hear he sold land so that you could become a carpenter.

ANDRI: But I'm not going to become a carpenter.

PRIEST: Why not?

ANDRI: My sort think of nothing but money all the time, people say, so my place isn't in the workshop, says the carpenter, but in the salesroom. I'm going to be a salesman, Reverend Father.

PRIEST: Very well then.

ANDRI: But I wanted to be a carpenter.

PRIEST: Why don't you sit down?

ANDRI: You're mistaken, Reverend Father, I think. Nobody likes me. The innkeeper says I'm impertinent, and the carpenter thinks so too, I believe. And the doctor says I'm ambitious, and my sort have no guts.

PRIEST: Sit down!

ANDRI: Is it true, Reverend Father, that I have no guts?

PRIEST: It may be that there is something harassed about you, Andri.

ANDRI: And Peider says I'm a coward.

PRIEST: A coward, why?

ANDRI: Because I'm a Jew.

PRIEST: Fancy paying attention to Peider!

ANDRI: *says nothing.*

PRIEST: Andri, I want to tell you something.

ANDRI: One shouldn't keep thinking of oneself all the time, I know. But I can't help it, Reverend Father, that's the way it is. I can't help wondering all the time whether what the others say about me is true: that I'm not like them, not gay, not jolly, just not like them. And you too think there is something harassed about me, Reverend Father. I can quite understand that nobody likes me. I don't like myself when I think about myself. *The Priest stands up.* Can I go now?

PRIEST: Now listen to me!

ANDRI: What do people want from me, Reverend father?

PRIEST: Why are you so suspicious?

ANDRI: They all put their hands on my shoulder.

PRIEST: Do you know what you are, Andri? *The Priest laughs.* You don't know, so I shall tell you. *Andri stares at him.* A splendid fellow! In your own way. A splendid fellow! I have been watching you, Andri, for years?

ANDRI: Watching?

PRIEST: Of course.

ANDRI: Why does everyone watch me?

PRIEST: I like you, Andri, more than all the others, yes, precisely because you are different from all the others. Why do you shake your head? You are cleverer than they are. Indeed you are. I like that about you, Andri, and I'm glad that you have come to see me and that I have had the chance to tell you so.

ANDRI: That isn't true.

PRIEST: What isn't true?

ANDRI: I'm not different. I don't want to be different. And even if he's three times stronger than me, that Peider, I'll beat the daylight out of him in front of everybody in the square; I've sworn that to myself—

PRIEST: As far as I'm concerned you're welcome to.

ANDRI: I've sworn it to myself—

PRIEST: I don't like him either.

ANDRI: I don't want to be popular. I shall stand up for myself. I'm not a coward—and I'm not cleverer than the others, Reverend Father; I don't want you to say that.

PRIEST: Will you listen to me now?

ANDRI: No. *Andri draws away.* I don't like having everyone's hands on my shoulders all the time. *Pause.*

PRIEST: You really don't make it easy for one. *Pause.* To be brief, your foster-mother came to see me. She was here for more than four hours. The good woman is very unhappy. You don't come to meals any more, she says, and you won't talk to anyone. She says you don't believe that people are thinking of your wellbeing.

ANDRI: Everyone is thinking of my wellbeing!

PRIEST: Why do you laugh?

ANDRI: If he's thinking of my wellbeing, Reverend Father, why is he willing to give me everything, but not his own daughter, why?

PRIEST: It is his right as a father—

ANDRI: But why? Why? Because I'm a Jew.

PRIEST: Don't shout!

ANDRI: *says nothing.*

PRIEST: Haven't you any other idea in your head? I have told you, Andri, as a Christian, that I love you—but you have one unfortunate habit, I'm afraid I must say, all of you: whatever difficulties you come up against in life, you attribute absolutely everything to the fact that you are Jews. You really don't make things easy for one with your over-sensitiveness.

ANDRI: *says nothing.*

PRIEST: You're crying.

ANDRI: *sobs, covering his face with his hands.*

PRIEST: What has happened? Answer me. What's the matter? I'm asking you what has happened. Andri! Why don't you speak, Andri? You're shivering. You've lost your senses. How can I help you if you don't speak? Pull yourself together, Andri! Do you hear? Andri! Remember you're a man! Well, I don't know.

ANDRI: My Barblin! *Andri lets his hands fall from his face and stares in front of him.* She can't love me, no one can, I can't love myself . . . *Enter a sacristan with a chasuble.* Can I go now? *The Sacristan unbuttons the Priest.*

PRIEST: You can still stay. *The Sacristan dresses the Priest for Mass.* You've said it yourself: how can other people love us if we don't love ourselves? Our Lord said: Love thy neighbour as thyself. He said: As thyself. We must accept ourselves, and that is what you don't do, Andri. Why do you want to be like the others? You're cleverer than they, believe me, you're more alert. Why won't you admit that? There is a spark in you. Why do you play football like all these boneheads, and rush about the field shouting, simply in order to be an Andorran? They don't like you, I know. And I know why. There's a spark in you. You think. Why shouldn't there also be some among God's creatures who have more intelligence than feeling? I tell you, that is exactly what I admire about you people. Why do you look at me like that? There is a spark in all of you. Think of Einstein! And all the rest of them, whatever their names are. Think of Spinoza!

ANDRI: Can I go now?

PRIEST: No man can change his skin, Andri, no Jew and no Christian. Nobody, God wants us to be as he created us. Do you understand me? And when they say to you: Jews are cowards, then know that you are not a coward if you accept being a Jew. On the contrary. You are different from us. Do you hear me? I say: You are not a coward. Only if you try to be like all Andorrans, then you are a coward . . . *An organ starts to play.*

ANDRI: Can I go now?

PRIEST: Think over what you yourself said, Andri: How can the others accept you, if you don't accept yourself?

ANDRI: Can I go now . . .

PRIEST: Andri, have you understood me?

* * *

Forestage

The Priest kneels.

PRIEST: Thou shalt not make unto thee any graven image of the Lord, thy God, nor of men who are his creatures. I too was guilty at that time. I wanted to meet him with love when I spoke with him. I too made a graven image of him, I too put fetters on him. I too bound him to the stake.

* * *

A room in the Teacher's house. The Señora is seated, Andri standing.

SEÑORA: Since they don't want me to tell you why I came, Andri, I shall now put on my gloves and leave.

ANDRI: Señora, I don't understand a word.

SEÑORA: Soon you will understand everything. *She puts on one glove.* Do you know that you are handsome? *Noise in the street.* They have abused and maltreated you, Andri, but that will stop now. The truth will put them right; and you, Andri, are the only one here who need not fear the truth.

ANDRI: What truth? *Fresh noise in the street.*

SEÑORA: I'm glad to have seen you.

ANDRI: Are you leaving us, Señora?

SEÑORA: I have been asked to go.

ANDRI: If you say no country is worse and no country is better than Andorra, why don't you stay here?

SEÑORA: Would you like me to? *Noise in the street.* I must go. I'm from the other side of the frontier, you can hear how I exasperate them. A Black! That's what they call us here, I know . . . *She puts on the other glove.* There are lots of other things I should like to tell you, and a lot of things I should like to ask. I should like to have a long talk with you. But we shall see each other again, I hope . . . *She is ready.* We shall see each other again. *She looks round once more.* So this is where you grew up?

ANDRI: Yes. *Noise in the street.*

SEÑORA: I ought to go now. *She remains seated.* When I was your age—that goes very quickly, Andri, you're twenty now and can't believe it: people meet, love, part, life is in front of you, and when you look in the mirror, suddenly it is behind you. You don't seem to yourself very different, but suddenly it is other people who are twenty . . . When I was your age—my father, an officer, had been killed in the war. I knew how he thought, and I didn't want to think like him. We wanted a different world. We were young, like you, and what we were taught was murderous, we knew that. And we despised the world as it is, we saw through it and dared to want another one. And we tried to create another one. We wanted not to be afraid of people. Not about anything in the world. We didn't want to lie. When we saw that we were merely keeping silent about our fear, we hated each other. Our new world didn't last long. We crossed the frontiers again, back to where we had come from when we were as young as you . . . *She rises.* Do you understand what I'm saying?

ANDRI: No.

SEÑORA: *goes up to Andri and kisses him.*

ANDRI: Why do you kiss me?

SEÑORA: I must go. *Noise in the street.* Shall we see each other again?

ANDRI: I should like to.

SEÑORA: I always wished I had never known my father and mother. No one, when he sees the world they have left behind for him, can understand his parents. *Enter the Teacher and the Mother.* I'm going, yes, I'm just going. *Silence.* So I'll say goodbye. *Silence.* I'm going, yes, now I'm going . . . *The Señora goes out.*

TEACHER: Go with her! But not across the square, go round the back.

ANDRI: Why round the back?

TEACHER: Go! *Andri goes out.* The Priest will tell him. Don't ask me now! You don't understand me, that's why I never told you. *He sits down.* Now you know.

MOTHER: What will Andri have to say about it?

TEACHER: He doesn't believe me. *Noise in the street.* I hope the mob will leave her alone.

MOTHER: I understand more than you think, Can. You loved *her*, but you married *me*, because I am an Andorran. You have betrayed us all, but Andri more than anyone. Don't curse the Adorrans, you are one yourself. *Enter the Priest.* You have a difficult task in this house, Reverend Father. You explained to Andri what it means to be a Jew and that he should accept it. Now he has accepted it. And now you must tell him what an Adorran is and that he should accept it.

TEACHER: Now leave us alone!

MOTHER: May God stand by you, Father Benedict. *The Mother goes out.*

PRIEST: I tried, but it was no use, it's impossible to talk to them, every reasonable word exasperates them. I told them to go home and mind their own business. Not one of them knows what they really want. *Andri comes back.*

TEACHER: Why are you back so soon?

ANDRI: Andri: She wants to go alone, she says. *He shows his hand.* She gave me this.

TEACHER: Her ring?

ANDRI: Yes.

TEACHER: *says nothing, then stands up.*

ANDRI: Who is this Señora?

TEACHER: Then I'll go with her. *The Teacher goes.*

PRIEST: What are you laughing about?

ANDRI: He's jealous!

PRIEST: Sit down.

ANDRI: What's the matter with all of you?

PRIEST: It's no laughing matter, Andri.

ANDRI: But it's ludicrous. *Andri looks at the ring.* Is that a topaz or what can it be?

PRIEST: Andri, we must have a talk.

ANDRI: Again? *Andri laughs.* Everyone is behaving today like puppets when the strings are tangled, including you, Reverend Father. *Andri takes a cigarette.* Was she once his mistress? I have that feeling, don't you? *Andri smokes.* She's a fantastic woman.

PRIEST: I have something to say to you.

ANDRI: Can't I stand while you say it? *Andri sits down.* I have to be in the shop by two. Isn't she a fantastic woman?

PRIEST: I'm glad you like her.

ANDRI: Everyone is acting so stiffly. *Andri smokes.* You're going to tell me one shouldn't go up to a soldier and knock his cap off when one knows that one is a Jew, one shouldn't do that at all, and yet I'm glad I did it. I learnt something from it, even if it's no use to me. As a matter of fact not a day passes now, since our talk, without my learning something that is no use to me, Reverend Father, no more use to me than your kind words. I believe that you mean well, you are a Christian by profession, but I am a Jew by birth, and that's why I am now going to emigrate.

PRIEST: Andri—

ANDRI: If I can. *Andri puts out his cigarette.* I didn't mean to tell anyone that.

PRIEST: Stay where you are!

ANDRI: This ring will help me. *The Priest says nothing.* To keep quiet now, Reverend Father, not to tell anyone, is the only thing you can do for me. *Andri stands up.* I must go. *Andri laughs.* There's something harassed about me, I know, Reverend Father, you're quite right . . .

PRIEST: Are you doing the talking or am I?

ANDRI: I'm sorry. *Andri sits down.* I'm listening.

PRIEST: Andri—

ANDRI: You're so solemn!

PRIEST: I have come to redeem you.

ANDRI: I'm listening.

PRIEST: I knew nothing about it either, Andri, when we talked together last time. For years the story has always been that he rescued a Jewish child, a Christian deed, so why shouldn't I have believed it? But now, Andri, your mother has come—

ANDRI: Who has come?

PRIEST: The Señora.

ANDRI: *jumps up.*

PRIEST: Andri—you're not a Jew. *Silence.* Don't you believe what I say?

ANDRI: No.

PRIEST: So you think I'm lying?

ANDRI: Reverend Father, one feels a thing like that.

PRIEST: What does one feel?

ANDRI: Whether one is a Jew or not. *The Priest stands up and approaches Andri.* Don't touch me! Keep your hands off me! I want no more of that.

PRIEST: Don't you hear what I say?

ANDRI: *says nothing.*

PRIEST: You're his son.

ANDRI: *laughs.*

PRIEST: Andri, that is the truth.

ANDRI: How many truths have you? *Andri takes a cigarette, which he then forgets.* You can't do that with me any more . . .

PRIEST: Why don't you believe us?

ANDRI: My belief is exhausted.

PRIEST: I swear to you by my soul's salvation, Andri: You are his son, our son, and there can be no question of your being a Jew.

ANDRI: There have been plenty of questions of it up to now . . . *Noise in the street.*

PRIEST: What's going on? *Silence.*

ANDRI: Ever since I have been able to hear, people have told me I'm different, and I watched to see if what they said was true. And it is true, Reverend Father: I am different. People told me how my kind move, like this and like this, and I looked at myself in the mirror almost every evening. They are right: I do move like this and like this. I can't help it. And I watched to see whether it was true that I'm always thinking of money, when the Andorrans watch me and think, now he's thinking of money; and they were right again: I am always thinking of money. It's true. And I have no guts, I've tried, it's no use: I have no guts, only fear. And people told me that my kind are cowards. I watched out for this too. Many of them are cowards, but I know when I'm being a coward. I didn't want to admit what they told me, but it's true. They kicked me with their boots, and it's true what they say: I don't feel like them. And I have no country. You told me, Reverend Father, that one must accept that, and I have accepted it. Now it's up to you, Reverend Father, to accept your Jew.

PRIEST: Andri—

ANDRI: Now, Reverend Father, I'm talking.

PRIEST: —do you want to be a Jew?

ANDRI: I am one. For a long time I didn't know what it meant. Now I know.

PRIEST: *sits down helplessly.*

ANDRI: I don't want to have a father and mother, so that their death shall not come over me with anguish and despair, nor my death over them. And no sister and no sweetheart. Soon everything will be torn to pieces, then neither our promises nor our fidelity will help. I want it to happen soon. I'm old. My trust has fallen out, one piece after the other, like teeth. I have exulted, the sun shone green in the trees, I threw my name in the air like a cap that belonged to nobody but me, and down fell a stone that killed me. I have been wrong, all the time, in a different way from what they thought. I wanted to be right and to rejoice. Those who were my enemies were right, even if they had no right to be, because at the end of all one's understanding one still can't feel that one is right. I don't need enemies any more, the truth is sufficient. I take fright the moment I begin to hope. Hope has never suited me. I take fright when I laugh, and I can't weep. My affliction rises me above everyone, therefore I shall fall. My eyes are big with melancholy, my blood knows everything, and I wish I were dead. But I have a horror of dying. There is no grace—

PRIEST: Now you are committing a sin.

ANDRI: Look at the old teacher, the way he is going downhill, and he was once a young man, he says, with a great will. Look at Barblin. And all of them, all of them, not only me. Look at the soldiers. Damned souls. Look at yourself. You already know now, Reverend Father, what you will do when they take me away in front of your kind eyes, and that's why they stare at me so, your kind, kind eyes. You will pray. For me and for yourself. Your prayers won't even help you, you will become a traitor in spite of them. Grace is an everlasting rumor, the sun will shine green in the trees even when they take me away. *Enter the Teacher, his clothes torn.*

PRIEST: What has happened?

TEACHER: *collapses.*

PRIEST: Speak, in heaven's name! *Two men bring in the dead Señora, lay her down and go.*

ANDRI: The Señora—?

PRIEST: How did that happen?

TEACHER: A stone.

PRIEST: Who threw it?

TEACHER: Andri, they say. The innkeeper saw it with his own eyes.

ANDRI: *tries to run out; the Teacher holds him back.*

TEACHER: He was here, you are his witness.

Forestage

The Somebody enters the witness box.

SOMEBODY: I admit there's no proof as to who threw the stone at the foreign woman that time. I personally wasn't in the square when it happened. I don't want to put the blame on anyone; I'm not the judge of the universe. As to the young lad—of course I remember him. He used to spend all his tips on the juke-box, and when they took him away I felt sorry for him. I don't know what the soldiers did to him after they took him away, we only heard him screaming . . . There must come a time when we are allowed to forget, I think.

Translated by Michael Bullock

From THE FIRE RAISERS

Characters

GOTTLIEB BIEDERMANN
ANNA
SCHMITZ
BABETTE BIEDERMANN
EISENRING
POLICEMAN
WIDOW KNECHTLING
DOCTOR OF PHILOSOPHY
CHIEF FIREMAN
FIREMEN

The Place: Europe
The Time: Today

The stage is dark, then a match flares, revealing the face of Herr Biedermann, who is lighting a cigar. As it grows lighter he looks around him. He is surrounded by firemen in helmets.

BIEDERMANN: One can't even light a cigar nowadays without thinking of fire! . . . It's revolting—*Biedermann hides the smoking cigar and withdraws, whereupon the Fire Brigade steps forward in the manner of a classical Greek chorus. A tower-clock strikes the quarter.*

CHORUS: Good people of our city, see
Us, its guardians,

Looking,
Listening,
Full of good will towards the well-intentioned citizen—
CHORUS LEADER: Who, after all, pays our wages.
CHORUS: Splendidly equipped
  We prowl around your house,
  At once alert and free from suspicion.
CHORUS LEADER: Sometimes, too, we sit down,
  But without sleeping, tirelessly
CHORUS: Looking,
  Listening,
  For that which is concealed
  To be revealed,
  Before it is too late
  To put out
  The first few flickers
  Threatening fire.
  A tower-clock strikes the half.
CHORUS LEADER: Many things may start a fire,
  But not every fire that starts
  Is the work of inexorable
  Fate.
CHORUS: Other things, called Fate to prevent you
  From asking how they happened,
  Monstrous events,
  Even the total destruction of a city,
  Are mischief.
CHORUS LEADER: Human,
CHORUS: All too human
CHORUS LEADER: Mischief that wipes out
  Our mortal fellow citizens.
  A tower-clock strikes the three-quarters.
CHORUS: Much can be avoided
  By common sense.
CHORUS LEADER: In very truth:
CHORUS: It is unworthy of God,
  Unworthy of man,
  To call a stupidity Fate
  Simply because it has happened.

The man who acts so
No longer deserves the name,
No longer deserves God's earth,
Inexhaustible, fruitful and kind,
Nor the air that he breathes,
Nor the sun.
Bestow not the name of Fate
Upon man's mistakes,
Even the worst,
Beyond our power to put out!
The tower-clock strikes the hour.
CHORUS LEADER: Our watch has begun.
The chorus sits down while the clock strikes nine.

Act One

Room.
Gottlieb Biedermann is sitting in his room reading the newspaper and smoking a cigar. Anna, the maid, in a white apron, brings a bottle of wine.

ANNA: Herr Biedermann? *No answer.* Herr Biedermann—*He folds up the newspaper.*
BIEDERMANN: They ought to be strung up. Haven't I always said so? Another fire. And the same old story as I live and breathe: another hawker who settles down in the loft, a harmless hawker . . . *He takes the bottle.* They ought to be strung up! *He takes the corkscrew.*
ANNA: Herr Biedermann—
BIEDERMANN: What is it?
ANNA: He's still there.
BIEDERMANN: Who?
ANNA: The hawker who wants to speak to you.
BIEDERMANN: I'm not at home!
ANNA: That's what I told him, Herr Biedermann, an hour ago. He says he knows you. I can't throw that man out, Herr Biedermann, I simply can't.
BIEDERMANN: Why not?

ANNA: He's far too big and strong . . . *Biedermann draws the cork.*

BIEDERMANN: Tell him to come and see me in my office tomorrow.

ANNA: I have told him, Herr Biedermann, three times, but he isn't interested.

BIEDERMANN: Why not?

ANNA: He doesn't want any hair tonic.

BIEDERMANN: Then what does he want?

ANNA: Humanity . . . *Biedermann sniffs at the cork.*

BIEDERMANN: Tell him I shall come and throw him out with my own hands if he doesn't beat it immediately. *He carefully fills his Burgundy glass.* Humanity! . . . *He tastes the wine.* Tell him to wait out in the hall. I'll be there in a minute. If he's selling something, tracts or razor blades, I'm not hard-hearted, but—I'm not hard-hearted, Anna, you know that!—but I'm not going to have anyone coming into the house. I've told you that a hundred times! Even if we had three beds free I wouldn't consider it. We know what that can lead to—nowadays . . . *Anna turns to go and sees that the stranger has just entered: an athlete, his clothes are reminiscent both of a jail and of a circus, his arms are tattooed, and he wears leather straps round his wrists. Anna creeps out. The stranger waits till Biedermann has sipped his wine and looks around.*

SCHMITZ: Good evening. *Biedermann drops his cigar with astonishment.* Your cigar, Herr Biedermann—*He picks up the cigar and gives it to Biedermann.*

BIEDERMANN: I say—

SCHMITZ: Good evening!

BIEDERMANN: What's the meaning of this? I expressly told the maid you were to wait out in the hall. What possessed you . . . I mean . . . without knocking . . .

SCHMITZ: My name is Schmitz.

BIEDERMANN: Without knocking.

SCHMITZ: Joseph Schmitz. *Silence.* Good evening!

BIEDERMANN: What do you want?

SCHMITZ: There's nothing to worry about, Herr Biedermann: I'm not a hawker!

BIEDERMANN: Then what are you?

SCHMITZ: A wrestler by trade.

BIEDERMANN: A wrestler?

SCHMITZ: A heavy-weight.

BIEDERMAN: I see.

SCHMITZ: That's to say, I was.

BIEDERMANN: And now?

SCHMITZ: I'm out of work. *Pause.* Don't worry, Herr Biedermann, I'm not looking for work. On the contrary. I'm fed up with wrestling . . . I only came in because it's raining so hard outside. *Pause.* It's warmer in here. *Pause.* I hope I'm not disturbing you— *Pause.*

BIEDERMANN: Do you smoke? *He offers cigars.*

SCHMITZ: It's terrible to be as big as I am, Herr Biedermann. Everyone's afraid of me . . . *Biedermann gives him a light.* Thanks. *They stand smoking.*

BIEDERMANN: To come to the point, what do you want?

SCHMITZ: My name is Schmitz.

BIEDERMANN: So you said, well, how do you do?

SCHMITZ: I'm homeless. *He holds the cigar under his nose and savours the aroma.* I'm homeless.

BIEDERMANN: Would you like—a slice of bread?

SCHMITZ: If that's all you've got . . .

BIEDERMANN: Or a glass of wine?

SCHMITZ: Bread and wine . . . But only if I'm not disturbing you, Herr Biedermann, only if I'm not disturbing you! *Biedermann goes to the door.*

BIEDERMANN: Anna! *Biedermann comes back.*

SCHMITZ: The maid told me Herr Biedermann was going to throw me out personally, but I couldn't believe you really meant it, Herr Biedermann . . . *Anna has entered.*

BIEDERMANN: Anna, bring a second glass.

ANNA: Very good.

BIEDERMANN: And some bread—yes.

SCHMITZ: And if you don't mind, Fräulein, some butter. And some cheese or cold meat or something. Only don't put yourself out. A few pickled cucumbers, a tomato or something, a little mustard— whatever you happen to have, Fräulein.

ANNA: Very good.

SCHMITZ: Only don't put yourself out! *Anna goes out.*

BIEDERMANN: You know me, the maid said.

SCHMITZ: Of course, Herr Biedermann, of course.

BIEDERMANN: Where from?

SCHMITZ: Only from your best side, Herr Biedermann, only from your best side. Yesterday evening in the local—I know you didn't notice me in the corner—everyone in there was delighted every time you banged the table with your fist, Herr Biedermann.

BIEDERMANN: What was I saying?

SCHMITZ: Absolutely the right thing. *He smokes his cigar, then:* They ought to be strung up. All of them. The quicker, the better. Strung up. All these fire raisers . . . *Biedermann offers Schmitz a chair.*

BIEDERMANN: Take a seat. *Schmitz sits down.*

SCHMITZ: Men like you, Herr Biedermann, that's what we need!

BIEDERMANN: Yes, no doubt, but—

SCHMITZ: No buts, Herr Biedermann, no buts! You're one of the Old Brigade, you still have a positive outlook. That explains it.

BIEDERMANN: No doubt—

SCHMITZ: You still have civil courage.

BIEDERMANN: No doubt.—

SCHMITZ: That explains it.

BIEDERMANN: Explains what?

SCHMITZ: You still have a conscience, everyone in the local could feel that, a real conscience.

BIEDERMANN: Yes, yes, of course—

SCHMITZ: Herr Biedermann, it's not of course at all. Not nowadays. In the circus where I wrestled, for example—and that's why the whole circus was burnt to the ground afterwards—our manager said to me: Take a running jump at yourself, Joe!—my name is Joseph, you know—take a running jump, he said, why should I have a conscience? Those were his very words. What I need to keep my beasts in order is a whip. Those were his very words. That's the kind of fellow he was. Conscience, he laughed. If anyone has a conscience it's generally a guilty one . . . *He smokes with enjoyment.* God rest his soul.

BIEDERMANN: You mean he's dead?

SCHMITZ: Burnt to death with the whole shoot. *A grandfather clock strikes nine.*

BIEDERMANN: I can't think what's keeping that girl!

SCHMITZ: I'm in no hurry.—*The two men happen suddenly to look into each other's eyes.* And you haven't a bed free in the house, Herr Biedermann, the maid has already told me—

BIEDERMANN: Why do you laugh?

SCHMITZ: Unfortunately there isn't a bed free! That's what they all say the moment they see a homeless person—and I don't even want a bed.

BIEDERMANN: No?

SCHMITZ: I'm used to sleeping on the floor, Herr Biedermann. My father was a charcoal burner. I'm used to it . . . *He smokes.* No buts, Herr Biedermann, no buts, I say! You aren't one of those who talk big in pubs because they're scared stiff. I believe you. Unfortunately there isn't a bed free—that's what they all say—but you I believe, Herr Biedermann . . . Where shall we end up if nobody believes anyone else any more? That's what I always say, where shall we end up? Everybody thinks everybody else is a fire raiser, there's nothing but distrust in the world. Don't you agree? The whole pub could feel that, Herr Biedermann: you still believe in the good in man and in yourself. Don't you agree? You're the first person in this town who hasn't simply treated me like an arsonist—

BIEDERMANN: Here's an ash tray.

SCHMITZ: Don't you agree? *He carefully taps the ash off his cigar.* Most people nowadays believe in the Fire Brigade instead of in God.

BIEDERMANN: What do you mean by that?

SCHMITZ: The truth. *Anna brings a tray.*

ANNA: We haven't any cold meat.

SCHMITZ: That'll do, Fräulein, that'll do—except that you've forgotten the mustard.

ANNA: Sorry! *Anna goes out.*

BIEDERMANN: Tuck in!—*Biedermann fills the glases.*

SCHMITZ: You don't get this kind of reception everywhere, Herr Biedermann. I've had some nasty experiences, I can tell you. No sooner is a fellow like me across the threshold—a man without a tie, homeless and hungry—than they say, sit down, and ring the police behind my back. What do you think of that? I ask for a roof over my head, nothing more, an honest wrestler who has been wrestling all his life; some gentleman who has never wrestled comes along and takes me by the collar—What's the idea? I ask and I merely turn round, just to have a look at him, and already his shoulder's broken. *He takes the glass:* Cheers! *They drink and Schmitz starts eating.*

BIEDERMANN: Well, you know how things are these days. You can't open a newspaper without reading of another case of arson! And it's always the same story: a hawker asks for shelter and next morning the house goes up in flames . . . I simply mean I can understand people being a bit distrustful. *He picks up his newspaper.* Here, look at this! *He puts the open newspaper down beside Schmitz's plate.*

SCHMITZ: I've seen it.

BIEDERMANN: A whole district. *He stands up to show Schmitz.* Here, read this! *Schmitz eats and reads and drinks.*

SCHMITZ: Beaujolais?

BIEDERMANN: Yes.

SCHMITZ: It would have been better with the chill off . . . *He reads across his plate:* "—It seems that the fire was planned and started in the same manner as last time." *They eye one another.*

BIEDERMANN: Isn't it incredible? *Schmitz puts the newspaper away.*

SCHMITZ: That's why I don't read the newspapers any more.

BIEDERMANN: How do you mean?

SCHMITZ: Because it's always the same.

BIEDERMANN: Yes, yes, of course, but—that's no solution, just not reading the newspaper; I mean you have to know what lies in store for you.

SCHMITZ: Why?

BIEDERMANN: Well, you just have to.

SCHMITZ: It will come, Herr Biedermann, it will come. *He sniffs the sausage.* The judgment of God. *He cuts himself a slice of sausage.*

BIEDERMANN: Do you think so? *Anna brings the mustard.*

SCHMITZ: Thank you, Fräulein, thank you.

ANNA: Is there anything else?

SCHMITZ: Not today. *Anna remains by the door.* There's nothing I like better than mustard, you know. *He squeezes mustard out of the tube.*

BIEDERMANN: What do you mean, judgment of God?

SCHMITZ: How should I know? *He eats and glances at the newspaper again.* "—It seems to the experts that the fire was planned and started in the same manner as last time." *He laughs briefly, then fills his glass with wine.*

ANNA: Herr Biedermann?

BIEDERMANN: What is it?

ANNA: Herr Knechtling would like to speak to you.

BIEDERMANN: Knechtling? Now? Knechtling?

ANNA: He says—

BIEDERMANN: I shouldn't dream of it.

ANNA: He says he can't understand you—

BIEDERMANN: Why does he have to understand me?

ANNA: He has a sick wife and three children—

BIEDERMANN: I shouldn't dream of it, I say! *He has jumped to his feet with impatience:* Herr Knechtling! Herr Knechtling! Damn it all, let Herr Knechtling leave me in peace or instruct a solicitor. I'm taking an evening off. It's ridiculous. I won't put up with all this fuss, just because I gave him the sack! And never before in human history have we had such social insurance as we have today ... Yes, let him instruct a solicitor. I'll instruct a solicitor too. A share in his invention! Let him put his head in the gas oven or instruct a solicitor—go ahead—if Herr Knechtling can afford to lose or win a case. Let him try! *He controls himself with a glance at Schmitz.* Tell Herr Knechtling I have a visitor. *Anna goes out.* My apologies!

SCHMITZ: This is your house, Herr Biedermann.

BIEDERMANN: Is the food all right? *He sits down and watches his guest enjoying himself.*

SCHMITZ: Who would have thought such a thing still existed nowadays?

BIEDERMANN: Mustard?

SCHMITZ: Humanity. *He screws the top back on the tube.* I mean who would have believed that you wouldn't grab me by the collar and chuck me out into the street—out into the rain! You see that's what we need, Herr Beidermann: humanity. *He takes the bottle and fills his glass.* God bless you for it. *He drinks with visible enjoyment.*

BIEDERMANN: You mustn't start thinking now that I'm inhuman, Herr Schmitz—

SCHMITZ: Herr Biedermann!

BIEDERMANN: That's what Frau Knechtling says!

SCHMITZ: If you were inhuman, Herr Biedermann, you wouldn't be giving me shelter tonight, that's obvious.

BIEDERMANN: Yes, isn't it?

SCHMITZ: Even if it's only in the attic. *He puts down his glass.* Now our wine is just right. *The front door bell rings.* The police—?

BIEDERMANN: My wife—

SCHMITZ: H'm. *The bell rings again.*

BIEDERMANN: Come this way . . . But on one condition: No noise! My wife has a weak heart—*Women's voices are audible from outside and Biedermann beckons to Schmitz to hurry and help him. Taking the tray, glass and bottle with them they tiptoe out right, where the Chorus is sitting.*

BIEDERMANN: Excuse me. *He steps over the bench.*

SCHMITZ: Excuse me. *He steps over the bench and they disappear, while Frau Biedermann enters the room from the left accompanied by Anna, who takes her things.*

BABETTE: Where's my husband? We're not narrow-minded you know, Anna. I don't mind you having a sweetheart, but I won't have you hiding him in the house.

ANNA: I haven't got a sweetheart, Frau Biedermann.

BABETTE: Then whose is that rusty bicycle by the front door? I got the fright of my life—

Attic.
Biedermann switches on the light, revealing the attic, and signs to Schmitz to come in. They converse in whispers.

BIEDERMANN: Here's the switch . . . If you're cold there's an old sheepskin rug somewhere, I think—but quiet, for God's sake. . . . Take off your shoes! *Schmitz puts down the tray and takes off one shoe.* Herr Schmitz—

SCHMITZ: Herr Biedermann?

BIEDERMANN: Will you promise me that you're really not a fire raiser? *Schmitz can't help laughing.* Sh! *He nods good night, goes out and shuts the door. Schmitz takes off the other shoe.*

Room.
Babette has heard something and listens; she looks horrified, then suddenly relieved; she turns to the audience.

BABETTE: My husband Gottlieb has promised me he will personally go up into the attic every evening to make sure there is no fire raiser there. I'm very grateful to him. If he didn't go I should lie awake half the night . . .

Attic.
Schmitz goes to the switch, now in his socks, and puts out the light.

. . . .

CHORUS: Good people of our city, see
    Us, guardians of innocence,
    Still free from suspicion,
    Filled with good will
    Towards the sleeping city,
    Sitting,
    Standing—
CHORUS LEADER: From time to time filling
    A Pipe to pass the time.
CHORUS: Looking,
    Listening,
    That no fire shall blaze up
    From homely roofs
    To wipe out our well-beloved city.
    A tower-clock strikes three.
CHORUS LEADER: Everyone knows we are there and knows
    That a call will suffice.
    He fills his pipe.
CHORUS: Who puts on the light
    At this hour of the night?
    O woe, I see
    With nerves all on edge,
    Distressed and sleepless,
    The wife.
    Babette appears in a dressing-gown.
BABETTE: There's someone coughing! . . . *The sound of snoring.* Gottlieb! Can't you hear it? *The sound of coughing.* There's somebody there! – *The sound of snoring.* Men! As soon as there's trouble they take a sleeping tablet. *A tower-clock strikes four.*

CHORUS LEADER: Four o'clock.
  Babette puts out the light again.
  But no call has come.
  He puts his pipe back in his pocket; the background lights up.
CHORUS: Beams of the sun,
  Lashes of the eye divine,
  Day is once more breaking
  Above the homely roofs of the city.
    Hail to us!
  No ill has befallen the slumbering city,
  No ill so far today . . .
    Hail to us!
  The chorus sits down.

Translated by Michael Bullock

From BIOGRAPHY

A Game

Part One

When the curtain rises, the working light is on. The whole stage is visible. In the center stands the furniture, representing a modern living-room when the stage is lit for acting: a desk on the right, on the left a sofa, an easy chair, and a floor lamp; a bookcase is suspended in mid-air; no other walls.

A young lady in an evening dress is sitting in the easy chair, waiting; she is wearing horn-rimmed spectacles. Silence. Then a cracked piano is heard from the next room—bars broken off in the middle, repetition as though the player is practicing, then silence again. The young lady goes on waiting. Finally a gentleman enters with a dossier and goes to a lectern in the left foreground that does not form part of the room. He places the dossier on the lectern and switches on a neon lamp.

RECORDER: Right. He has just said, if he could start his life all over again, he knows exactly what he would do different. *The young lady smiles.* You don't mind if we let him make fresh choices? *The young lady nods.* For example, he would like to repeat his first meeting with you. *He leafs through the dossier, then reads out.* "May 26, 1960. I had guests. It got late. When the guests had finally left, she was just sitting there. What can you do with an unknown woman who doesn't leave, who just sits there without speaking at two in the morning? It need not have happened." *He switches off the neon lamp.* Go ahead.

Acting light. Voices outside, laughter, finally silence; soon afterward Kürmann enters whistling to himself until he sees the young lady.

ANTOINETTE: I'm going soon too.

Silence; he stands there at a loss, then begins to clear away bottles and glasses and ash trays; then he is once more at a loss.

KÜRMANN: Don't you feel well?

ANTOINETTE: On the contrary. *She takes a cigarette.* Just one more cigarette. *She waits in vain for a light.* If I'm not in the way. *She lights her cigarette and smokes.* I enjoyed it very much. Some of them were very nice, I thought, very stimulating. . . . *Silence.* Have you anything left to drink?

Kürmann goes to a small liquor cabinet and pours out a whisky; he makes a business of it to emphasize his silence, polite in the manner of a host left with no alternative.

KÜRMANN: Ice? *He hands her the whisky.*

ANTOINETTE: What about you?

KÜRMANN: I have to work tomorrow.

ANTOINETTE: What do you do?

A clock strikes two.

KÜRMANN: It's two o'clock.

ANTOINETTE: Are you expecting someone?

KÜRMANN: On the contrary.

ANTOINETTE: You're tired.

KÜRMANN: I'm ready to drop.

ANTOINETTE: Why don't you sit down? *Kürmann remains standing and says nothing.* I can't drink any quicker. *Silence.* I really only wanted to hear your old musical clock again. Musical clocks fascinate me. The way the figures always go through the same movements as soon as the music starts. It always plays the same waltz, and yet you can't wait to see what happens each time. Don't you feel the same? *She slowly empties her glass.*

KÜRMANN: Another whisky?

She stubs out her cigarette

ANTOINETTE: I'm going now.

KÜRMANN: Have you a car?

ANTOINETTE: No.

KÜRMANN: May I give you a lift?

ANTOINETTE: I thought you were tired.

KÜRMANN: Not in the least.

ANTOINETTE: Nor am I. *She takes another cigarette.* Why are you looking at me like that? Have you a light? Why are you looking at me like that?

Kürmann gives her a light, then goes to the liquor cabinet and pours himself a whisky; he stands with his back to her, his glass in his hand, without drinking.

KÜRMANN: Did you say something?

ANTOINETTE: No.

KÜRMANN: Nor did I. *Silence; she smokes nonchalantly; Kürmann looks at her; then he sits down in an armchair, crosses his legs, and shows that he is waiting. Silence.* What do you think of Wittgenstein?

ANTOINETTE: Wittgenstein? Why Wittgenstein?

KÜRMANN: For example. *He drinks.* We can't just sit here saying nothing until dawn breaks and the birds begin to twitter. *He drinks.* What do you think of the Krolevsky case?

ANTOINETTE: Who is Krolevsky?

KÜRMANN: Professor Krolevsky. He was here this evening. Professor Vladimir Krolevsky. What do you think of Marxism-Leninism? Or I could ask, how old are you?

ANTOINETTE: Twenty-nine.

KÜRMANN: What do you do? Where do you live?

ANTOINETTE: In Paris at the moment.

KÜRMANN: You know, quite frankly it doesn't really interest me, not in the least. I'm simply asking for the sake of something to say, in order to be polite. At two in the morning. You're forcing me to display a curiosity I don't really feel. Quite frankly. And, you know, I only said that so someone should be speaking in this room at two in the morning. *He drinks.* That's all too familiar!

ANTOINETTE: What is?

KÜRMANN: The more silent the lady, the more convinced the man is that he is responsible for their boredom. And the more I drink, the less I can think of to say, and the less I can think of to say, the more frankly, the more personally I shall talk, simply because there are only the two of us. At two in the morning. *He drinks.* That's all too familiar! And yet you're not listening to me at all,

believe me, not at all. You sit there smoking and not saying anything, just waiting until nothing else occurs to me except what you might call the naked fact that we are a man and a woman—
She stubs out her cigarette.
ANTOINETTE: Why don't you ring for a taxi?
KÜRMANN: As soon as you ask me to.
Pause.
ANTOINETTE: I really am listening to you.
Kürmann stands up.
KÜRMANN: Do you play chess?
ANTOINETTE: No.
KÜRMANN: Then you can learn tonight.
ANTOINETTE: Why? *Kürmann goes out.* Why don't you ring for a taxi?
Kürmann comes back with a chess set.
KÜRMANN: Look. These are the pawns. They can't move backwards. This is a knight. And then there are the rooks. Look, these are bishops. One on white, one on black. This is the queen. She can do anything. The king. *Pause, until he has set up all the pieces.* I'm not tired, but we won't speak until dawn starts to break and the birds are twittering outside, not a word. *She picks up her handbag and rises.* You can sleep here, but it would be better if you didn't. To be frank, I'd rather you didn't. *She sits down on the sofa to apply lipstick; Kürmann sits in front of the chessboard and fills his pipe, his eyes on the board.* It's your move.
ANTOINETTE: I have to work tomorrow as well.
KÜRMANN: You're white, because you're the guest. *He lights his pipe.* I'm not drunk, and neither are you; we both know what we don't want. *He strikes a second match.* I'm not in love. *He strikes a third match.* You see, I'm already talking very confidentially, and that's just what I didn't want, and I don't even know your name.
ANTOINETTE: Antoinette.
KÜRMANN: We've only just met for the first time. I hope you won't mind if I don't call you by your Christian name.
ANTOINETTE: Stein.
KÜRMANN: Fräulein Stein—
She closes her tube of lipstick.
ANTOINETTE: I don't play chess. *She takes her powder compact.*

KÜRMANN: I'll explain the moves as we go along. You start with the king's pawn. Good. I cover—also with the king's pawn. Now you bring out your knight. *She powders her face.* Fräulein Stein, I have a high regard for you.

ANTOINETTE: Why?

KÜRMANN: I don't know, but if we don't play chess now, I know what will happen: I shall adore you in a way that will amaze everyone, I shall spoil you. I'm good at that. I shall wait on you hand and foot; you're just the sort for that. I shall imagine I can't live without Antoinette Stein. I shall make a destiny of it. For seven years. I shall wait on you hand and foot until we need two lawyers. *She snaps her powder compact shut.* Let's play chess. *She rises.* What are you looking for?

ANTOINETTE: My jacket.

Kürmann rises and gives her the jacket.

KÜRMANN: We shall be grateful to one another, Antoinette, for seven years, if you now let me ring for a taxi.

ANTOINETTE: Please do.

Kürmann goes to the telephone and rings for a taxi

KÜRMANN: He's coming right away.

ANTOINETTE: Thank you.

KÜRMANN: I thank you. *Pause. They look at each other.* Like two cats. Miaow. You must hiss. Sss. Otherwise I'll hiss. Sss. *She rises and takes a cigarette.* Miaow, miaow, miaow. *She lights the cigarette.* You do it wonderfully, the way you almost close your eyes when you're smoking, the way they narrow to slits, like they are now—wonderful.

ANTOINETTE: Sss.

KÜRMANN: Miaow.

ANTOINETTE: Miaow.

BOTH: Miaow-iaow-iaow. *They laugh.*

ANTOINETTE: Joking apart.

KÜRMANN: Joking apart. *He takes off her jacket.*

ANTOINETTE: What are you doing? *The doorbell rings.* There's my taxi.

KÜRMANN: Joking apart. *He takes off her horn-rimmed spectacles.*

ANTOINETTE: At least put the light out.

KÜRMANN: Can we start again?

Neon lamp on.

RECORDER: Where do you want to start from?

KÜRMANN: The moment when the clock strikes two.

RECORDER: As you like.

Kürmann gives back the horn-rimmed spectacles.

KÜRMANN: Sorry.

ANTOINETTE: That's all right. *She sits down in the easy chair.*

The neon lamp goes out.

RECORDER: Go ahead.

A clock strikes two.

ANTOINETTE: "I really only wanted to hear your old musical clock again. Musical clocks fascinate me. The way the figures always go through the same movements as soon as the music starts. It always plays the same waltz, and yet you can't wait to see what happens each time."

KÜRMANN: I know.

ANTOINETTE: "Don't you feel the same?"

Kürmann goes to the musical clock and winds it up; there is a gay tinkling; he goes on winding until the waltz is over.

KÜRMANN: Is there anything else I can do for you? *He goes to the liquor cabinet.* I'm afraid there's no whisky left.

ANTOINETTE: It doesn't matter. *She takes a cigarette.* What do you think of Wittgenstein?

Kürmann pours himself a whisky.

KÜRMANN: "I have to work tomorrow."

ANTOINETTE: "What do you do?"

Kürmann drinks.

RECORDER: Why don't you tell her?

ANTOINETTE: "What do you do?"

KÜRMANN: Behavior studies. *He drinks.*

RECORDER: Go on!

KÜRMANN: Frau Hubalek comes at eight.

ANTOINETTE: Who is Frau Hubalek?

KÜRMANN: My housekeeper.

RECORDER: Stop!

Neon lamp on.

RECORDER: You can't say that, Herr Kürmann. You no sooner see a young lady in your flat at two in the morning than you're already thinking that your housekeeper comes at eight.

KÜRMANN: Let's start again.

RECORDER: And then you say there's no whisky left, and you've no sooner lied than you take another bottle and pour yourself a whisky.

ANTOINETTE: I didn't even notice that.

KÜRMANN: Let's start again!

RECORDER: From the beginning?

KÜRMANN: Please.

RECORDER: As you like.

KÜRMANN: Why is she suddenly not wearing glasses?

RECORDER: That's up to the lady. You can't tell her what to do, Herr Kürmann. What you can choose is your own behavior. Don't worry about whether she's wearing horn-rimed spectacles or not. And don't keep thinking: that's all too familiar. You come in, whistling to yourself, a man at the pinnacle of his career. You've just been made a professor—

KÜRMANN: I know.

RECORDER: They've just had a surprise party in your honor; you see your wife for the first time. Completely relaxed.

KÜRMANN: That's easily said.

RECORDER: Completely relaxed.

Kurmann goes out.

ANTOINETTE: From the beginning?

RECORDER: If you don't mind.

Neon lamp off.

ANTOINETTE: Shall I wear the glasses or not?

Voices outside, laughter, then silence; soon afterward Kürmann enters whistling to himself until he sees the young lady in the easy chair.

ANTOINETTE: "I'm going soon too."

KÜRMANN: "Don't you feel well?"

ANTOINETTE: "On the contrary." *She takes a cigarette.* "Just one more cigarette." *She waits in vain for a light and lights the cigarette herself.* "If I'm not in the way." *She smokes.* "I enjoyed it very much. Some of them were very nice, I thought, very stimulating. . . ."

Kürmann says nothing.

RECORDER: Go on! *Kürmann goes and pours out whisky.* Don't start thinking about Frau Hubalek.

Kürmann hands a whisky to Antoinette.

ANTOINETTE: "What about you?"

KÜRMANN: "I have to work tomorrow."

ANTOINETTE: "What do you do?"

Pause.

RECORDER: Now you've gone silent again.

Antoinette puts on her horn-rimmed spectacles.

ANTOINETTE: "Why are you looking at me like that?"

RECORDER: The longer you say nothing, the more ambiguous the silence becomes. Don't you feel that? The more intimately you will have to talk afterwards.

ANTOINETTE: "Why are you looking at me like that?"

A clock strikes two.

KÜRMANN: "It's two o'clock."

ANTOINETTE: "I'm going."

KÜRMANN: "Have you a car?"

ANTOINETTE: Yes. *She smokes nonchalantly.*

KÜRMANN: Before she said No, she hadn't a car. Now she says Yes, so that I can't ring for a taxi. I'll never get her out of this flat!

The Recorder steps into the scene.

RECORDER: May I tell you the mistake you are making from the very outset? You no sooner see a young woman in this room, a stranger, than you start thinking of a story you've been through before. Right? That's why you're scared, don't know what to say—

KÜRMANN: I want her to go.

RECORDER: So that she doesn't become your wife.

KÜRMANN: Yes.

RECORDER: You see, your behavior isn't governed by the present, but by a memory. That's the trouble. You think you already know the future because of your past experience. That's why it turns out to be the same story every time.

KÜRMANN: Why doesn't she go?

RECORDER: She can't.

KÜRMANN: Why not?

RECORDER: If she now takes her handbag and stands up, it means she has guessed what you are thinking, and that would be embarrassing for you. Why don't you talk about behavior studies? In a way anyone can understand. Why do you assume that the young

lady wants what you don't want? The ambiguity comes from you.
KÜRMANN: H'm.

RECORDER: You think you know women because every time you meet a woman you repeat the same mistake.

KÜRMANN: Go on!

RECORDER: It's your fault if she doesn't go *The Recorder returns to his desk.* All right.

A clock strikes two.

KÜRMANN: "It's two o'clock."

She stubs out her cigarette.

ANTOINETTE: "Are you expecting someone?"

KÜRMANN: Yes.

RECORDER: Good.

KÜRMANN: But not a woman.

RECORDER: Very good.

KÜRMANN: I'm expecting a boy. *She takes her handbag.* I'm expecting a boy.

RECORDER: But don't say it twice, as though you didn't believe it yourself. And don't say a boy. Only the uninitiated talk like that. Say a student who plays chess. A highly gifted young man. A child prodigy whom you are helping. Talk about his genius. That will do the trick.

KÜRMANN: Was that a knock?

ANTOINETTE: I didn't hear anything.

KÜRMANN: I hope nothing has happened to him.

RECORDER: Good.

KÜRMANN: I get so scared every night—

She crumples up the cigarette pack.

ANTOINETTE: Now I haven't got a single cigarette left!

Kürmann lights his pipe.

KÜRMANN: A student . . . highly gifted. . . . Unfortunately he is pathologically jealous. If he comes along and finds a woman in my flat at two in the morning, he's quite capable of shooting.

RECORDER: Don't exaggerate.

KÜRMANN: A Sicilian . . . but blond, you know, blond with blue eyes. . . . That comes from the Normans. . . . On the other hand, his mouth is Greek. . . . He's a musical prodigy. . . . And he's a great-grandson of Pirandello.

RECORDER: Now you're talking too much.

ANTOINETTE: I hope nothing has happened to him. *Kürmann smokes his pipe hurriedly.* Wouldn't you like to ring up?

KÜRMANN: Where!

ANTOINETTE: Have you a cigarette left?

KÜRMANN: Take my pipe. *He wipes the mouthpiece and gives her the pipe.*

ANTOINETTE: What about you?

KÜRMANN: It's a light tobacco, EARLY MORNING PIPE. *She puts the pipe in her mouth.* You must keep what I've just told you to yourself, Fräulein Stein. The University knows nothing about it. *She coughs.* You have to suck, slowly and regularly. *He takes the pipe and shows her how to smoke.* You see? Like that. *He wipes the pipe and hands it back to her.* Slowly and regularly.

She smokes slowly and regularly.

ANTOINETTE: Can you think at the same time?

KÜRMANN: It mustn't get hot.

She smokes slowly and regularly.

ANTOINETTE: All my friends, I mean all my real friends, live like you. *She puffs out smoke.* Almost all of them. *She puffs out smoke.* The other men are terrible, you know. They almost always misunderstand a woman sooner or later.

KÜRMANN: Is that so?

ANTOINETTE: Yes. *She coughs.*

KÜRMANN: Slowly and regularly.

She smokes slowly and regularly.

ANTOINETTE: If it wasn't for Claude-Philippe!

KÜRMANN: Who is Claude-Philippe?

ANTOINETTE: My friend in Paris. I live with him. A real friend. I can do just as I like. I can come and go, and he always understands.

KÜRMANN: What else does he do?

ANTOINETTE: He's a dancer.

KÜRMANN: Ah.

ANTOINETTE: All other men, almost all, are a bore, even intelligent men. No sooner are there just the two of you than they get confidential or nervous, and suddenly all they can think of is that I'm a young woman. Hardly any of them ever ask what I do for a living, and if I talk about my work, they look at my lips. It's terrible. No sooner are you alone with them in a flat at two in the morning than they start thinking heaven knows what—you can't imagine what it's like! And at the same time they're frightened of it, especially the intellectuals. *She sucks at the pipe.* Now it's gone out. *Kurmann takes the pipe to relight it.* I'm glad I've met you, very glad.

KÜRMANN: Why?

ANTOINETTE: I haven't any brothers. *She stands up.*

KÜRMANN: Are you going already?

ANTOINETTE: I have to work tomorrow too.

KÜRMANN: What do you do?

ANTOINETTE: I'm a translator. I'm from Alsace. Claude-Philippe is a great help to me; he doesn't know any German, but he has such a feeling for it—incredible. . . . *Pause.* I really hope nothing has happened to him.

Kürmann helps her into the jacket of her evening dress.

KÜRMANN: If I can ever help you in any way—

ANTOINETTE: You're very sweet.

Kürmann takes her hands.

RECORDER: Stop! *Switches on neon lamp.* Why do you take hold of her hands now? Instead of standing there like a brother, with your hands in your pockets, such feelings and so on, but with your hands in your pockets like a brother with his sister. *Kürmann tries it.* But relaxed! *The Recorder steps into the scene, takes off the jacket again, and takes Kürmann's place to show him how to do it.* What was your last line?

ANTOINETTE: "I haven't any brothers."

RECORDER: And what do you say then?

KÜRMANN: That wasn't her last line.

ANTOINETTE: "All my friends, I mean my real friends who are friends for life, are homosexuals. Almost all of them. All of them really."

RECORDER: And what do you say then?

KÜRMANN: That's not right.

ANTOINETTE: "If it wasn't for Claude-Philippe."

KÜRMANN: I believe that, but she said that earlier, that she had a real friend in Paris, a dancer. I can't reply to that by saying, "If I can ever help you in any way."

RECORDER: What was his last line?

KÜRMANN: "If I can ever help you in any way."

RECORDER: What do you say now?

ANTOINETTE: "You're very sweet."

> *The Recorder gives her the jacket.*

KÜRMANN: I'm sorry, but that's not right. If I don't give her the jacket till now, how am I to have my hands in my pockets when she starts getting affectionate? You just try it.

> *The Recorder takes back the jacket.*

RECORDER: Right, go on.

ANTOINETTE: "I'm glad I've met you, very glad."

RECORDER: Go on.

ANTOINETTE: "I haven't any brothers."

RECORDER: We've heard that.

KÜRMANN: "What do you do?"

ANTOINETTE: "I'm a translator."

RECORDER: No—

ANTOINETTE: "I'm from Alsace."

RECORDER: —your last line before the jacket!

KÜRMANN: "Claude-Philippe doesn't know any German, but he has such a feeling for it."

ANTOINETTE: "Incredible."

RECORDER: What do you say then?

KÜRMANN: Nothing. I wonder how Frenchmen who don't know German can have a feeling for it. Pause! I admit I could have asked now: what are you translating?

ANTOINETTE: Adorno.

RECORDER: But you didn't say that.

ANTOINETTE: Because he didn't ask.

KÜRMANN: Because I want her to go. I ask myself: why doesn't she stay in Paris? But that's none of my business. Pause. And because I pause, she imagines I'm now thinking of my boy.

ANTOINETTE: "I really hope nothing has happened to him."

RECORDER: Go on!

KÜRMANN: "Are you going already?"

ANTOINETTE: "I have to work tomorrow too."

KÜRMANN: "What do you do?"

ANTOINETTE: "I'm a translator."

RECORDER: Not again!

ANTOINETTE: "I'm from Alsace."

> *The Recorder lets the jacket sink.*

RECORDER: Please let's have the last line before Kürmann gives you your jacket and makes the mistake of taking hold of your hands.

KÜRMANN: Why is that a mistake?

RECORDER: The pressure of your hands will give you away.

ANTOINETTE: "The other men are terrible, you know. They almost always misunderstand a woman sooner or later."

KÜRMANN: "Is that so?"

ANTOINETTE: "Yes."

The Recorder gives her the jacket.

RECORDER: "If I can ever help you in any way—"

ANTOINETTE: "You're very sweet."

The Recorder puts his hands in his pockets; then he steps back out of the part

RECORDER: Got it? Like a brother with his sister. Even if you now give her a kiss, which is possible, don't forget that you're expecting a young Sicilian. Otherwise she wouldn't kiss you. She is relieved that you aren't an ordinary man, Herr Kürmann, not even when you're alone together.

KÜRMANN: I get it.

RECORDER: Give her the jacket again. *Kurmann takes back the jacket.* Right.

She takes a cigarette.

ANTOINETTE: So there were some cigarettes left. *Kürmann gives her a light.* Why didn't I stay in Paris? I should like to start a small publishing firm, my own firm, where I can do what I like. That's why I'm here. And if nothing comes of the publishing firm, I shall do something else. *She smokes.* Something on my own. *She smokes.* Best of all, I should like to run a little gallery—

RECORDER: You hear that?

KÜRMANN: Why didn't she say anything about that?

RECORDER: She wants a life of her own; she isn't looking for a man who thinks she can't live without him and who buys a revolver when he sees one day that she can live without him.

ANTOINETTE: If you want to know, a very much younger man, younger than Kürmann, drove me here, an architect, who wants to go to Brazil with me. *She laughs.* What could I do in Brazil? *She smokes.* That's why I stayed so long—because I was afraid he was waiting for me downstairs.

KÜRMANN: How was I to know that?

ANTOINETTE: That's why I wanted a taxi, in case he was standing by my car waiting. *She smokes.* I don't want any fuss. *She stubs out her cigarette.* Can I have my jacket now?
Kürmann stands motionless.
RECORDER: What are you thinking about?
KÜRMANN: Adorno.
RECORDER: It's too late now. You know now what you could have talked to the young lady about: about Hegel, about Schönberg, about Kierkegaard, about Beckett—
ANTOINETTE: I did my doctorate with Adorno.
RECORDER: Why don't you give her the jacket?
Kürmann gives her the jacket.
KÜRMANN: "If I can ever help you in any way—"
ANTOINETTE: "You're very sweet."
Kürmann puts his hands in his pockets.
KÜRMANN: What kind of car have you got?
RECORDER: Good.
KÜRMANN: Don't forget your handbag.
RECORDER: If you don't make any more mistakes now, in the elevator, you'll have done it: a biography without Antoinette.
Kürmann switches off the ceiling light.
KÜRMANN: I'll take you to the car. *She sits down.* Why is she suddenly so pale?
RECORDER: That's from the pipe.
She lies in the easy chair, eyes closed; her handbag has fallen on the floor.
KÜRMANN: I don't believe her.
The Recorder steps into the scene to feel her pulse, while Kürmann stands to one side filling his pipe.
RECORDER: It's really a minor collapse. You and your EARLY MORNING PIPE! Don't keep saying, It's all too familiar. Her forehead is as cold as ice. *Kürmann lights his pipe.* Do you have to smoke now? Instead of opening a window. You're behaving impossibly, like a brute.
KÜRMANN: Better now than in seven years.
RECORDER: As you like. *She rises.* She can't possibly drive.
ANTOINETTE: I must get home. . . .
RECORDER: Can't you see that?
ANTOINETTE: I must lie down. . . .

RECORDER: You're risking a life. *She takes off the jacket of her evening dress.* Aren't you going to fetch a glass of cold water? The least you can do when a guest is dizzy is to fetch a glass of cold water.

Kürmann goes out.

ANTOINETTE: I'm sorry . . . *She undoes her evening dress; she has to lie down in order not to faint. When Kürmann comes back with the glass of water, she is lying on the sofa.* I'm sorry . . .

KÜRMANN: Drink this.

ANTOINETTE: That has never happened to me before—suddenly—to feel so giddy. . . .

KÜRMANN: Shall I fetch a doctor?

ANTOINETTE: Don't look at me. *Pause.* I feel ashamed.

RECORDER: You'll catch cold.

KÜRMANN: It's all too familiar—

RECORDER: Won't you fetch a rug?

KÜRMANN: —I fetch a rug, then I take my handkerchief and wipe her forehead, her temples, her forehead, her eyelids. I know how I act the Good Samaritan. I shall make coffee, watch over her, in silence, watch over her, take off her shoes so she feels more comfortable, and in the end she'll say, at least put the light out! *Pause.* It's nothing to be ashamed of, Antoinette; it could have happened to anyone, Antoinette; it's nothing to be ashamed of. *He takes off her shoes.*

ANTOINETTE: What are you doing?

KÜRMANN: You'll feel more comfortable like that. *He puts the shoes down on the carpet.*

ANTOINETTE: At least put the light out.

Blackout.

KÜRMANN: Stop! Who put the light out? Stop!

Working light. The whole stage is visible again.

RECORDER: Don't you want to go on?

KÜRMANN: No.

RECORDER: As you like.

Antoinette tidies her evening dress.

ANTOINETTE: Where are my shoes?

KÜRMANN: I beg your pardon?

ANTOINETTE: Where are my shoes?

Kürmann gives her the shoes.

RECORDER: You said, if you could begin your life all over again, you knew exactly what you would do differently—

KÜRMANN: That's right.

RECORDER: Then why do you always do the same thing?

Antoinette puts on her shoes.

ANTOINETTE: He's absolutely right. It didn't have to happen. I wasn't in love either. Not in the least. Not next morning either. *She has put on her shoes and stands up.* What came of it—I too would be glad if it hadn't had to happen. . . .

The Recorder leafs through the dossier.

RECORDER: Where would you like to start again?

KÜRMANN: Earlier.

RECORDER: How much earlier?

KÜRMANN: Before that night. Before I became a professor. Before these people came to have a party in my honor. Before I saw Antoinette for the first time.

RECORDER: All right.

Antoinette takes the jacket of her evening dress.

ANTOINETTE: Good luck. *She leaves.*

KÜRMANN: An idiotic story.

RECORDER: Choose another one.

KÜRMANN: A superfluous story.

RECORDER: You have permission, Herr Professor Kürmann, to start again wherever you like, to choose afresh—*Kürmann takes a bottle of whisky.* Do you hear? *Kürmann pours whisky.* You drink too much.

KÜRMANN: What business is that of yours?

RECORDER: I'm only putting into words what you know youself.

Kürmann stands, drinking.

KÜRMANN: Who are you actually?

RECORDER: I? *Turning the pages.* This here is the life you've led up to now. Till your middle forties. A life that bears looking at. A bit ordinary, I admit. But it seems that as a scientist you're quite eminent. The Kürmann reflex—a concept essential to modern behavior studies, I understand. All you need now is an invitation to Princeton.

KÜRMANN: I asked who you are.

RECORDER: I record. *Kürmann does not understand.* I record what you make of the possibility offered to you here, what you do·

differently in your life. That's all. What reality does not permit, the theatre permits: to change, to begin again, to try out, to try out another biography—

Kürmann looks into his glass.

KÜRMANN: Biography! I refuse to believe that our biography, mine or any other, couldn't look different. Completely different. I only need to act differently one single time—

RECORDER: Go ahead.

KÜRMANN: Not to mention chance! *Pause.* I can't bear the sight of this room.

RECORDER: As you like. *The furniture disappears; so does the bookcase. The stage is empty. Kürmann stands with his glass in his hand, not looking at the transformation.* Go ahead.

KÜRMANN: Just once in my life—when I was seventeen; I was riding a bicycle, I remember it clearly; it was the moment before a storm, but the storm never broke; there were flashes of lightning, dust whirled up to the height of a house; there was a smell of elder bushes and tar—just once I had an insight. For a quarter of an hour. It was a real insight, I know that. But I can't think it over again. I'm too stupid. *He drains his glass.* Too stupid. *He looks at the Recorder.* That's the only thing I want if I can begin again: a different intelligence.

RECORDER: Excuse me—

KÜRMANN: That's all!

RECORDER: —you don't understand the rules of the game. You have permission to choose again, but with the intelligence you have. That is a given fact. You can train it differently. You're free to do that. You can ask it for advice when you have to make decisions, or not. You can use it how you like, to avoid mistakes or to justify mistakes when you have made them. As you wish. You can specialize it so that it draws attention to itself—as an expert intelligence. Or as a political intelligence. Or you can let your intelligence go to wrack and ruin: in a religious faith or in alcohol. Or you can preserve it—by confining yourself to skepticism. As you wish. But you cannot change the scope, or let us say, the basic potential, the atomic structure, of your brain. Do you understand? That is a given fact.

Antoinette appears in an overcoat.

KÜRMANN: What does she want this time?

ANTOINETTE: My handbag. *Kürmann refuses to help.* I left my handbag behind.

KÜRMANN: I said, before I saw my wife for the first time! So she can't have left anything here.

The Recorder indicates to Antoinette with a polite gesture that she is in the way, and Antoinette retires into the background.

RECORDER: Do you want your school days over again?

Change of lighting. A ten-year-old boy appears, dressed in winter clothes.

RECORDER: You remember little Snot?

SNOT: Kürmann, you're a rotten shot.

What a cheesy face you've got.

Hee, hee, hee,

Can't hit me.

KÜRMANN: Shut up.

SNOT: Cheese face, cheese face,

Can't hit me.

RECORDER: They used to tease you because you once told them in grammar school that you would one day be a professor. Does it still annoy you? You became a professor thirty-three years later, in 1960. *Three gentlemen appear in the gown of the university, the Rector carrying a document, which he unrolls.* Just a moment, your Magnificence, just a moment.

KÜRMANN: I know the document.

SNOT: Kürmann, you're a rotten shot.

What a cheesy face you've got.

Hee, hee, hee,

Can't hit me.

RECORDER: You know what happened then.

SNOT: Cheese face, cheese face,

Can't hit me.

ANTOINETTE: What happened? He never told me about that. What did you do to this little fellow?

Snot makes a snowball.

RECORDER. That would be 1927.

KÜRMANN: Yes.

RECORDER: That would mean—

KÜRMANN: Primary school over again

RECORDER: puberty over again

KÜRMANN: final exams over again
RECORDER: your mother's death over again
KÜRMANN: military service over again!
RECORDER: —that too.

Soldiers are heard singing.

CORPORAL: *offstage.* Squad, *halt! Left—face!* Right—*face!*
Order—*arms!* At ease!
KÜRMANN: All that over again?
CORPORAL: Atten—*shun! He appears.* Sir—
RECORDER: Just a moment, Corporal, just a moment.
CORPORAL: At ease!

Snot tries to leave.

RECORDER: Stay here.
SNOT: But my name isn't Snot.
RECORDER: What is it then?
KÜRMANN: His name is Snottler. We called him Snot because he
never had a handkerchief.
RECORDER: Stay here. *He goes to the boy and leads him back to his
place.* Perhaps you won't lose your left eye. Do you hear? Perhaps
you wont' lose your left eye.

The Corporal clicks his heels.

CORPORAL: Atten—*shun!*
RECORDER: Corporal—
CORPORAL: Right shoulder—*arms!*
RECORDER: If I may ask you—
CORPORAL: Forward—*march! The sound of marching footsteps.*
Dress by the right! Eyes—*front!* Left, right, left, right! Dress by
the left! Eyes—*front!* Left, right, left, right! *The Corporal leaves,
following the invisible column. After a time his command is
heard.* Left, right, left, right. . . .

Silence.

RECTOR: May I read out the document now? It represents, I think I
may say, a high point in the life of our esteemed colleague. His
appointment as professor and Director of the Institute for Behavior Studies—
KÜRMANN: Stay where you are.
RECORDER: Perhaps Herr Kürmann doesn't want any high points,
perhaps Herr Kürmann would like to see his mother again.
A Nurse dressed in white appears. She wheels in a white bed and

bends over an old woman who lies in the bed without moving.
NURSE: Frau Kürmann? I can't hear you. What did you say? I can't understand a word, Frau Kürmann—
   A Doctor appears with a hypodermic syringe.
RECORDER: Perhaps all she could have said would have been some trifling thing like, you shouldn't drink, you should marry, you should always wear warm socks.
A young mulatto appears, wearing a bikini and an open blouse over it. She is barefoot; her feet are wet.
HELEN: What's the matter?
KÜRMANN: My mother is dying.
HELEN: What are you going to do?
   The Doctor gives Kürmann's Mother an injection.
DOCTOR: She'll sleep. Her heart is very strong. In three hours give her another injection. I shall be at home. *He leaves.*
NURSE: Frau Kürmann? *The Nurse leaves.*
HELEN: Why don't you go to Europe?
KÜRMANN: Helen—
HELEN: Why don't you go?
A boat appears, of a kind that goes with Helen. She jumps in and takes the oar.
RECORDER: You didn't want to leave Helen. You were afraid you would lose her if you went off to Europe. Besides, according to the dossier, you had no money just then.
KÜRMANN: Give me the dossier!
RECORDER: Here you are. *He gives Kürmann the dossier.* But there's nothing in it you don't know already. Salary for a year, two hundred dollars a month. After your trip with Helen—you bought an old Ford and hired a boat—you have just eighteen dollars left. Too little even for a sea voyage. You might be able to sell the Ford. Your first car, by the way.
KÜRMANN: I know.
RECORDER: Your father was a master baker.
KÜRMANN: I know.
RECORDER: In debt—he drank. *A baker appears with a bicycle. He is drunk and beaming with kindliness.* That would be 1934. It's you seventeenth birthday and you father comes along with a bicycle; it's new and all bright and shiny, the spokes, the handle

bars—all shining; it has a head lamp that also shines, a bell, and four gears. An English bicycle. *The Father rings the bell.* Do you remember? *The Father rings the bell.* According to the dossier, it was the fulfillment of your dearest wish. He probably bought it on the installment plan. That was something you never experienced again: the fulfillment of your dearest wish.

KÜRMANN: No.

RECORDER: Would you like the bicycle again?

FATHER: Hannes!

RECORDER: Just a minute, Herr Kürmann, just a minute.

FATHER: Why doesn't he take it?

RECORDER: Just a minute.

        The Father swears unintelligibly.

KÜRMANN: —then I was seventeen.

RECORDER: Exactly.

KÜRMANN: And the snowball fight?

RECORDER: Was over.

KÜRMANN: And he has still lost his eye.

RECORDER: Yes.

        The Nurse appears with flowers

NURSE: Frau Kürmann, how are you? Better? Look, Frau Kürmann, look. It's a fine day today. I said, it's a fine day outside. Look, Frau Kürmann, look. Flowers from your son in America. *She unwraps the flowers from their tissue paper.* Lovely roses.

MOTHER: Hannes—

NURSE: A loving son!

MOTHER: Hannes—

NURSE: So many roses. *She puts the roses in a vase and leaves.*

RECORDER: You know how it goes on from there. *He takes back the dossier and reads.* "September 1939: Hitler's Germany attacks Poland, declaration of war by Britain and France, You stay in San Francisco. Stalin's Russia also attacks Poland. Spring 1940: Hitler's Germany attacks Holland—"

KÜRMANN: And so on.

RECORDER: "—and Belgium."

KÜRMANN: And so on and so forth.

RECORDER: Why are you losing your nerve? You didn't lose it then. On the contrary, you married. *A Bride in white appears.* Spring

1940: back in Europe to do your military service you meet your first wife, who later commits suicide. *Kurmann does not look around.* Would you like to make a different choice here?

BRIDE: Hannes—

RECORDER: Katrin Guggenbühl, twenty-one, blonde with freckles only child of a pharmacist—you remember? According to the dossier, you knew on the day of the church wedding that the marriage was a mistake. *Wedding bells.* Would you like to make a different choice here?

Kürmann catches sight of the Bride. The Recorder goes over and takes the roses from the vase by the Mother's bed and puts them in the Bride's arms. Kürmann is still holding his empty whisky glass.

BRIDE: Why don't you speak?

KÜRMANN: Katrin.

BRIDE: What's the matter with you? *Kürmann says nothing.* Go on, tell me.

Two Undertaker's Men bring a coffin and leave again.

RECORDER: Perhaps Katrin also knows that this marriage is a mistake, and she is just waiting for you to say so. Why don't you say so? She will break down. Maybe. Of course it would be a shock if you said No now, when the bells are already ringing.

BRIDE: Hannes—

RECORDER: Perhaps you might save her life. *The bells stop ringing.* Herr Kürmann, we're waiting. *To the characters.* Herr Kürmann said, if he could begin his life again, he knew exactly what he would do differently. *To Kurmann.* The boy is waiting to find out whether he loses his left eye or not. Your mother is waiting; it can only be a matter of hours. The Rector is waiting with the document. Helen, who made you a man, is waiting on the coast north of San Francisco. And the bride is waiting with the roses—

KÜRMANN: —for me to become guilty of her death.

RECORDER: Or not. *An organ plays.* Herr Kürmann, you have the choice all over again.

A middle-class gentleman with a top hat and a middle-class lady wearing a hat appear. They stand beside the Bride.

FATHER-IN-LAW: Hannes.

KÜRMANN: Father.

MOTHER-IN-LAW: Hannes.

KÜRMANN: Mother.

RECORDER: Are you afraid of your in-laws?

A Child appears in bridesmaid's dress and hands the Bride a posy of daisies.

CHILD: Oh, dearest bride, we wish to you
Happiness and children too.

The Child curtsies.

MOTHER-IN-LAW: Sweet.

An Evangelical Pastor appears.

RECORDER: Are you afraid of an Evangelical minister? He can't know that he is blessing a mistake. Why don't you speak? You remember: according to the dossier, you are wearing a hired morning suit whose sleeves are unfortunately too long. Every time you pray, you have to pull the sleeves back before you can fold your hands. Out in front of the altar, according to the dossier, what you are chiefly thinking about are the sleeves of the morning coat, and then of the tails, which are also far too long.

KÜRMANN: If she had at least smiled! But she felt ashamed! She was suffering! That was how it started and that was how it went on: she suffered. . . . *Kürmann turns away, not knowing where to put his glass.*

RECORDER: Herr Kürmann.

KÜRMANN: I can hear the organ, oh yes, I can hear it.

RECORDER: Katrin loves you.

KÜRMANN: That's what she thinks.

RECORDER: She's happy.

KÜRMANN: And that's enough for her.

RECORDER: What do you mean by that?

KÜRMANN: Nothing. *The Recorder takes the empty glass from him.* Thanks. *He takes his pipe out of his pocket.* I still dream of you, Katrin, even today, and when I wake up, I always think you know.

RECORDER: What do you dream?

KÜRMANN: That's no one's business.

RECORDER: Why did you marry?

KÜRMANN: To forget Helen.

HELEN: What is he telling you?

KÜRMANN: I misused her to forget Helen, and she misused me to have a child.

RECORDER: Why don't you tell her so? *Kürmann shakes his head.* So it's to stay like that?

KÜRMANN: Yes.

RECORDER: That's final?
KÜRMANN: That's final.
The organ stops.
PASTOR: Amen.
KÜRMANN: If I hadn't married Katrin, it's possible that she wouldn't have committed suicide later.
RECORDER: That's what I mean.
KÜRMANN: And what about our son?
A young boy appears in jeans.
THOMAS: Dad.
KÜRMANN: I'm not a good father, I'm not a bad father; at times I forget him; I'm not a father all the time, but I am his father. When he swims too far out to sea, I'm scared and shout. I learned Latin over again in order to help him, and when he thinks, I'm pleased, and when he wants to know what I think, I try to explain myself. *He takes the pipe out of his mouth.* He exists, can't you see that, he exists!
RECORDER: I understand.
KÜRMANN: —her child.
RECORDER: You love him.
KÜRMANN: That's not the point. You can't think a child out of the world once it's there. *He laughs.* Thomas, tell me—
THOMAS: Dad.
KÜRMANN: —does a son love his father? Does a father love his son?
THOMAS: Dad, I need money.
KÜRMANN: You see?
THOMAS: I've dented the car.
KÜRMANN: Again?
THOMAS: But I had the right of way.
KÜRMANN: How much?
THOMAS: About three hundred bucks.
Kürmann reaches for his wallet.
KÜRMANN: Just a minute, though. That can't be right. Driving license at eighteen, born 1942—then this accident with the car couldn't have happened before 1960 at the earliest; that would mean Antoinette was there again.
RECORDER: Correct.
KÜRMANN: But I don't want that!
The Recorder leads Thomas out again.

RECORDER: His son must be smaller.
   The Doctor comes in with the Nurse.
DOCTOR: Frau Kürmann?
NURSE: She said she didn't want any more injections. *The Doctor feels her pulse.* She said she was lying on a steep mountain; that was why no one could visit her. I gave her another injection at midnight.
   The Doctor closes the dead woman's eyes.
DOCTOR: Inform the son.
HELEN: Now it's too late.
DOCTOR: And bring me her personal effects. *The Doctor leaves the deathbed and walks past Kürmann. They meet as though in a corridor.* Yes, Herr Kürmann . . . her death wasn't particularly difficult, I don't think. Only your mother had a very strong heart. Astonishing for her age.
   They shake hands; the Doctor goes.
HELEN: Now it's too late.
KÜRMANN: Yes.
HELEN: Why didn't you go?
KÜRMANN: Yes.
HELEN: Because of me?
KÜRMANN: Yes.
   Helen takes his arm.
RECORDER: You want to stay with Helen?
KÜRMANN: Yes.
RECORDER: As you like. *Neon lamp on.* So you've made up your mind, Herr Kürmann, to begin again after your mother's death. In 1939 you went to the University of California, where you met a student named Helen. *He reads from the dossier.* "An excursion to Fort Ross. We have a boat, Helen is refused admission to a motel, the night in the boat—"
KÜRMANN: Yes.
RECORDER: So you stay in America. *A husband and wife appear with two children in dirty overcoats, carrying suitcases.* Who are they?
REFUGEE: The young gentleman was very kind; the young gentleman saved our lives.
RECORDER: Is that true?
REFUGEE: In 1940, in the spring.

RECORDER: Do you remember these people?

KÜRMANN: Yes. *Without looking at the group.* It was on the frontier. Midnight. They had been discovered in a freight car. Because the little girl coughed. Now they are standing between the lines. Without papers. Jews. One of the guards wanted to arrest them on the spot. I asked him some question or other. That was all. I kept on asking him until they had vanished behind his back. *The Recorder searches through his dossier.* That was soon after I got back from the USA, pure chance that I just happened to be at that station at that moment, pure chance. *Because the refugee woman starts sobbing.* You won't go to the camp. Don't be afraid. I'm not going to stay in San Francisco.

HELEN: What's the matter?

REFUGEE: The young gentleman is very kind.

KÜRMANN: It cost me very little, but it's possible that this minute saved their lives.

RECORDER: Quite true. *He reads from the dossier.* "4/14/1940. I visited my fiancée and missed the last train, so that I had to spend the night at the station—"

REFUGEE: Spring.

RECORDER: One moment. *He reads from the dossier.* ". . . a married couple with two children and an old man." *He looks at the group of refugees.* The old man is missing.

KÜRMANN: The guard fired. *Pause.* I have to go.

HELEN: Why?

KÜRMANN: I have to.

HELEN: Okay.

KÜRMANN: It's not okay, not at all, but I have to leave you. I really have to.

HELEN: You're a coward.

KÜRMANN: Helen—

HELEN: I always knew you were.

> *Kürmann looks at her helplessly.*

RECORDER: She thinks you're afraid because she's a mulatto. Explain to her that she's wrong.

> *Pause.*

HELEN: Okay.

KÜRMANN: Helen?

HELEN: Good luck. *She exits.*

KÜRMANN: You explain to her!
The refugees take their suitcases.
REFUGEE: The young gentleman is very kind.
The refugees leave.
KÜRMANN: How else could I have chosen? . . .
RECORDER: So that's to stay?
KÜRMANN: Yes.
RECORDER: You don't want to go any further back?
KÜRMANN: No.
*A scream. Little Snot, hit in the eye by a snowball, yells and holds
his hand over his left eye and runs away.*
RECORDER: So that stays.
The dead mother is wheeled off.
KÜRMANN: Yes. . . .
The boat disappears.
FATHER: What about me?
KÜRMANN: I can't change the fact that you're a drunkard, a kindly
drunkard, an affectionate drunkard, but I can't prevent you from
falling downstairs that night or some other night. They found you
in the morning in the bakeshop—you, but no bread.
FATHER: What did he say?
KÜRMANN: Thanks for the bike. *The Father staggers away.* Father!
The bicycle remains.
CORPORAL *offstage*: Squad—*halt!*
RECORDER: Corporal— *The Corporal appears, dripping wet.* What
have you been doing?
CORPORAL: Punishment-swimming.
RECORDER: First Lieutenant Kürmann has just skipped the age of
his military service. He doesn't want to repeat those two years in
uniform.
KÜRMANN: Three years.
RECORDER: Corporal, we don't need you.
CORPORAL: Very good. Squad, atten—*shun!*
RECORDER: All right, Corporal.
CORPORAL: Squad, double time—*march!* Dress by the left! Dress
by the right! Left, right, left, right!
RECORDER: That will do.
KÜRMANN: That's easy to say.
CORPORAL: Squad—*sing!*

A marching song is heard; the Corporal follows the invisible column; the song slowly dies away; silence.

RECORDER: Would you like to hear the document now?

The Rector unrolls the document.

KÜRMANN: Is Katrin still there?

RECORDER: Yes.

KÜRMANN: You go away too.

RECORDER: Do you really want that? *He reads from the dossier.* "This morning in the course of an argument with Katrin, who always wants to forgive, I said: Then go and hang yourself. When I came home from the Institute in the afternoon, she has done it. Now she is lying here in the coffin. My guilt is unbearable. 6/11/1949." *Kürmann says nothing. She is twenty-nine.*

Kürmann looks at her.

KÜRMANN: You go away too.

BRIDE: Hannes—

KÜRMANN: I have gotten used to my guilt.

The Bride steps back; the Parents-in-law and the Pastor, and a few others who join them, form the funeral procession. The coffin is carried by two Undertaker's Men.

RECORDER: Would you like to see her face again?

KÜRMANN: I haven't forgotten it.

The funeral procession leaves.

RECTOR: I understand our colleague completely. The discovery of the Kürmann reflex, a discovery absolutely essential to modern behavior studies, was due to a coincidence. Even if we were to repeat the series of experiments extending over years, who can guarantee that this illuminating coincidence would occur again? I think it would be almost irresponsible for a scientist—

RECORDER: When did this coincidence take place?

KÜRMANN: February '59.

The Recorder leafs through the dossier.

RECTOR: It in no way diminishes your achievement, Professor, if I speak here of coincidence. We know it is not chance that discovers, but the human mind that recognizes the meaning of the chance.

RECORDER: "Sea gull No. 411, experimental series C."

KÜRMANN: Yes.

RECORDER: You don't want to forgo that?

ANTOINETTE: He owes his career to that sea gull.

KÜRMANN: I should like to ask the young lady—for the last time—to grasp the fact that she can't possibly have left anything here.

ANTOINETTE: My handbag.

KÜRMANN: I'm asking for autumn 1959.

RECORDER: Fräulein Stein—

KÜRMANN: Where was she in autumn 1959?

ANTOINETTE: In Paris.

RECORDER: Herr Kürmann wants autumn 1959.

Antoinette leaves.

KÜRMANN: Let someone else worry about her handbag.

The Rector rolls up the document.

RECTOR: Let me know when it's time for me to read out the document.

The three gentlemen in gowns leave.

RECORDER: Well then—

Antoinette comes back again.

ANTOINETTE: Then please tell my husband to see a doctor. Today. The sooner the better. Before it's too late.

RECORDER: Don't you feel well, Herr Kürmann?

KÜRMANN: Rubbish.

ANTOINETTE: When they know what it is, and when it's too late, they always say: a few years ago it would have been curable, quite a minor matter.

KÜRMANN: I'll go to the doctor.

ANTOINETTE: Please see that he does.

The Recorder bows and Antoinette leaves.

RECORDER: And apart from that, what else would you like to do differently in autumn 1959?

KÜRMANN: I'm just thinking it over.

A Stagehand wheels the bicycle away.

RECORDER: You remember autumn 1959. *He leafs through the dossier.* "Tension between Cuba and the USA. / Nigeria becomes independent. / Eisenhower receives Khrushchev. / Somalia becomes independent. / Soviet Moon rocket Lunik II, 160 pounds, crash-lands on the moon."

Kürmann polishes his glasses.

KÜRMANN: Give me the discussion with Krolevsky again. Professor Vladimir Krolevsky, who was later dismissed from his teaching post. That was in December, I think. Our conversation in my flat.

RECORDER: Very well.

Working light. The room is set up again. The cracked piano next door is heard again, always the same bars broken off in the middle and repeated. Since this reconstruction of the set produces a pause, the Recorder takes a cigarette. Finally the bookcase is lowered. The Recorder stubs out his cigarette. Silence.

RECORDER: Herr Kürmann, here's your flat again.

Neon lamp off.

Acting light.

KÜRMANN: What's this thing doing here?

RECORDER: Your old musical clock.

KÜRMANN: Get rid of it!

RECORDER: As you like. *A Stagehand removes the musical clock.* Do you want any other changes? You've only got to say the word. perhaps you would like the desk on the other side?

KÜRMANN: As though that mattered.

RECORDER: You can choose.

Again the cracked piano from next door.

KÜRMANN: Do I have to put up with that?

RECORDER: That's the ballet school. Autumn 1959. You remember, there's a ballet school next door. Unfortunately they always leave the window open.

Repetition of the same bars, accompanied by the Ballet Master's voice; then silence.

KÜRMANN: Did that go on every day?

RECORDER: Apart from Sundays and bank holidays.

KÜRMANN: No one could stick that.

RECORDER: You stuck it.

KÜRMANN: You say I can choose. . . .

RECORDER: But so can the others. You're not alone in the world, Herr Kürmann, and they have rented the house next door, 18 Klettenhof, in order to open their ballet school. These are given facts. If you can't stand it, why don't you choose another flat?

KÜRMANN: What shall I find there?

RECORDER: We shall see.

KÜRMANN: A power saw, perhaps.

RECORDER: Possibly.

KÜRMANN: Or the railway. Or bells chiming. Or the runway of an airport—

An ominous sound is heard.

RECORDER: That was the power saw.

KÜRMANN: Stop.

RECORDER: As you like.

Another sound is heard.

KÜRMANN: What's that?

RECORDER: This is a very beautiful district, but they're building. Because it's a very beautiful district. Construction machinery. But that will only last for a year and a half.

KÜRMANN: And what will happen then?

A third noise is heard.

RECORDER: A kindergarten. *Kürmann shakes his head.* You can choose. *Again the cracked piano next door, the same bars of music broken off, accompanied by the Ballet Master's voice; repetition; then silence.* So you're going to stay in this flat.

Kürmann looks around.

KÜRMANN: So this is what it was like?

RECORDER: You're surprised at your taste?

Frau Hubalek comes in.

FRAU HUBALEK: Herr Professor Krolevsky.

KÜRMANN: Show him in.

Frau Hubalek goes and Krolevsky comes in, a bald-headed man with alert eyes behind rimless spectacles, pale; one imagines incorrectly that he is always smiling. He is wearing a worn overcoat, which he does not take off, and carrying a thin leather briefcase; he holds his hat in his hand. His demeanor is extremely shy. He is short, yet he has a certain air of authority.

KÜRMANN: I think you sat here. *Krolevsky sits down.* I suppose you find this funny, Professor Krolevsky. We've had this conversation once before. You know my reasons for not joining any party, my fundamental doubts. I don't need to repeat myself.

KROLEVSKY: No.

KÜRMANN: Will you have a drink?

KROLEVSKY: I never drink.

Kürmann pours himself a whisky.

KÜRMANN: In short, Professor, I've thought it over. . . . *Pause. Kürmann stands drinking.*

KROLEVSKY: What have you thought over?

KÜRMANN: Our discussion in this room, our private discussion. You there, I here. You need not repeat yourself either, Krolevsky; I know it all. In your eyes I am what is nowadays called a nonconformist, an intellectual who sees through the ruling class, pretty accurately, in any case with horror or at least with disgust; but he leaves it at that. Every now and then I sign an appeal, a declaration for or against—protests for the benefit of my conscience so long as consciences are allowed. Apart from that, the nonconformist works on his career.

KROLEVSKY: Did I say that?

KÜRMANN: You said it differently.

KROLEVSKY: What did I say?

KÜRMANN: You said that work in the Party was the only way to change the world *Frau Hubalek comes in* and in the process, of course, the end has to justify the means. Everyone knows that, and that's precisely why I don't join any party. *He sees Frau Hubalek.* What is it now? *He takes a letter from her.* Thank you, Frau Hubalek, thank you. *Frau Hubalek leaves.* Work in the Party, you say, and this very moment a letter comes from the Senate—would I be willing to take over next spring and so on, in recognition of my scientific achievements and so on, on condition that the Government and so on and so forth.

KROLEVSKY: Congratulations, Dr. Kürmann.

KÜRMANN: Thank you. *He puts the letter down unopened on the desk.* In recollection I always have the impression that you are smiling; yet when I look at you, you really never smile. No more than a chess player. Only you think you know my next move. You already see me as Professor H. Kürmann, Director of the Institute for Behavior Studies. *Again the cracked piano next door but only briefly.* Tell me, Krolevsky, as a cyberneticist, do you think that the biography a man has is binding, the expression of an inevitable progression of events, or do you think that according to chance I might have had a quite different biography, and the biography one actually has, with all the given facts one is sick and tired of, is perhaps not even the most likely? Do you think our actual biography is merely one possible one, one of the many just as possible under the same social and historical conditions and with the same personal disposition? Looked at like that, what can a biography possibly tell us? It's not a question of a better or a worse biography, you understand. I merely refuse to attribute to everything that has happened—because it has happened, because it has become history and therefore irrevocable—a meaning which it doesn't possess.

KROLEVSKY: I understand.

KÜRMANN: You understand?

KROLEVSKY: AB POSSE AD ESSE VALET, AB ESSE AD POSSE NON VALET. *(He lights a cigarette.)* But I believe you had something urgent to tell me—

Again the cracked piano from next door, but this time the exercise seems to be successful, so that it goes on. Five Ballet Pupils dance out from the wings, followed by the Ballet Master; they are not dancing for the audience; it remains a practice.

BALLET MASTER: Stop! What about the points? *He demonstrates without the music.* Got it? *He claps his hands.* Right, children, from the beginning!

Again the cracked piano from next door. They repeat the exercise by dancing out into the wings. One Ballet Pupil remains behind.

Silence.

KÜRMANN: What's that girl doing here?

RECORDER: Do you like her?

KÜRMANN: I'm talking with Krolevsky.

RECORDER: You're talking with Krolevsky. Suddenly you're not listening to yourself; you look out of the window while you're speaking and see the ballet school next door. Suddenly you're rather absent-minded—

KÜRMANN: I don't know this ballet pupil.

RECORDER: But you could get to know her. *The cracked piano is heard from next door, the three bars; the Ballet Pupil performs the appropriate exercises; then silence again.* That's how it was when you were talking with Krolevsky—about biographies.

KÜRMANN. Well?

RECORDER: You have permission to choose again, Herr Kürmann, to choose differently. Perhaps you would like to take her out to dinner—

A Waiter appears with a menu.

WAITER: What would you like, sir?

RECORDER: What is there?

WAITER: CAVIAR RUSSE. SAUMON FUMÉ. FOIE GRAS DE STRASBOURG. ESCARGOTS À LA BOURGUIGNONNE.

RECORDER: You can choose.

WAITER: Or Italian? CANNELLONI. TORTELLINI ALLA PANNA. TORTELLINI CON FUNGHI. LASAGNE VERDI.

RECORDER: H'm.

WAITER: SPECIALITÀ DELLA CASA.

RECORDER: An excellent restaurant, Herr Kürmann, and they don't know you here. *To the Waiter.* What fish have you?

WAITER: I'll show you. *He goes out.*

RECORDER: If you take the girl out to dinner, I can imagine that in four months, when Fräulein Dr. Stein comes from Paris, you will behave entirely differently, Herr Kürmann, with less constraint, more intellectually, more wittily, so that after two o'clock Fräulein Dr. Stein will take her handbag and leave. Biography without Antoinette. . . . *The Waiter comes with a tray full of fish.* Ah.

WAITER: Pike.

RECORDER: Look at this!

WAITER: Caught today.

RECORDER: Very fine.

WAITER: Sole. Whitefish. A very fine tench.

RECORDER: Enough for two?

WAITER: Oh yes.

RECORDER: Trout?

WAITER: We only have them alive.

RECORDER: What's that?

WAITER: SPADA.

RECORDER: SPADA?

WAITER: Swordfish.

RECORDER: Have you ever eaten swordfish?

WAITER: Absolutely fresh lobster.

Kurmann looks at the Ballet Pupil.

RECORDER: Did you see the lobster? *Again the cracked piano next door. The Ballet Pupils dance out of the wings again, followed by the Ballet Master, and the girl who got separated takes her place in the group, which dances out. Silence.* As you like. *The Waiter is still holding the lobster.* Perhaps another time.

WAITER: Thank you, sir. *He leaves.*

RECORDER: You see? You can choose.

KÜRMANN: Go on!

RECORDER: Why do you shout at me?

KÜRMANN: What do you take me for? As though it were a question of choosing a woman! If it's permissible, I'd rather have nothing to do with any woman at all.

RECORDER: As you like.

Krolevsky is still sitting where he was.

KROLEVSKY: AB POSSE AD ESSE VALET, AB ESSE AD POSSE NON VALET. *(He lights a cigarette.)* But I believe you had something urgent to tell me—

Kürmann sits on the edge of the table.

KÜRMANN: To come straight to the point, Krolevsky—you needn't answer me—you are a member of the Communist party, though up to now nobody has found out; at least an important link-man, probably one of the leaders. Your subject, mathematics, doesn't give you away. Your numerous trips, whether to Prague or Paris or Mexico City, are splendidly camouflaged by professional congresses. And you don't drink, so as not to spill the beans late in the night. *He drinks.* Let us suppose that one day it comes out and that on some pretext, at least in the name of the Philosophical Faculty, your continued membership of the teaching body were to be dispensed with, which would naturally rouse us, or some of us, to righteous indignation—suppression of academic freedom and so on. We should have the "Krolevsky Case" on our hands. I myself, as a nonconformist, should draft an appeal: "Dismayed by recent events at our University"—an appeal which would be as concerned as it was thoughtful, which it would be an honor to sign, and beyond that, of course, would not have the slightest effect.

KROLEVSKY. You speak from experience.

KÜRMANN: Certainly.

KROLEVSKY: Dr. Kürmann, what are you trying to tell me?

KÜRMANN: If we could begin again, we all know what we ought to do differently. Signatures for, signatures against, declarations, and the result is the powerlessness of the intelligentsia, of the opposition, force exercised in the name of the constitutional state, terrorization—the cost of never acting. *To the Recorder.* When exactly did this conversation with Vladimir Krolevsky take place? *The Recorder leafs through the dossier.* Soon afterward Professor Krolevsky was arrested, his house was searched, and he was dismissed from his chair.

RECORDER. 12/3/1959.

KÜRMANN: Add it to my dossier.

RECORDER: What?

KÜRMANN: 12/3/1959. Joined the Communist party.

The Recorder writes it down.

KROLEVSKY: I confess, Dr. Kürmann, that you surprise me. The Party will examine your application. According to our inquiries, you have never belonged to any party. I hope you realize what it will mean to your academic career.

KÜRMANN: I realize very clearly what it means, Professor Krolevsky. That's why I'm doing it. *To the Recorder, who comes to Kürmann with the dossier.* What am I to do?

RECORDER: Sign.

Kürmann signs the dossier.

KÜRMANN: Comrade Krolevsky—*Working light.* What's the matter?

RECORDER: The doctor is waiting for you.

A Stagehand brings a white armchair and puts it down in the foreground right; a second Stagehand wheels in an instrument trolley; then they both go. Krolevsky rises.

KROLEVSKY: As far as we are concerned, Dr. Kürmann, our social relations will remain as before. An occasional little chat in the quadrangle of the University. Every now and then. We shall address one another by our official titles. *He shakes hands.* You know, Dr. Kürmann, that henceforth you will be kept under surveillance. *He puts on his hat.* If you give a party here in future, I shall not come to it.

KÜRMANN: Why a party?

KROLEVSKY: When you are made a professor in the very near future.

KÜRMANN: That will never happen!

Acting light in the foreground. A Doctor in a white coat appears and holds a filmstrip up to the light.

DOCTOR: Have you any pain?

KÜRMANN: Where?

DOCTOR: I'm asking you! Your EKG is fine. *He gives Kürmann the filmstrip.* Splendid. *He goes to the instrument trolley.* I'm not quite so happy about your urine.

KÜRMANN: Why?

DOCTOR: We shall see.

RECORDER: You must take off your jacket.

DOCTOR: We need a little blood.

Kürmann takes off his jacket.

RECORDER: You can sit down.

Kürmann sits down and rolls up his sleeve.

DOCTOR: Are you worried about anything? *He inserts needle in Kürmann's arm and extracts blood.* What do you think about the Krolevsky case? *He gives Kürmann a wad of cotton.*

RECORDER: Hold the cotton on it.

Kürmann holds the cotton on it.

KÜRMANN: I had mumps once when I was a child, and once I had measles, but apart from that . . .

The Doctor transfers the blood into a glass vessel.

DOCTOR: Sister Agnes? *He goes out.*

KÜRMANN: What's the date today?

RECORDER: April 12, 1960. Fräulein Stein is still in Paris. She is packing her bag today to leave Paris. You can't alter that.

KÜRMANN: H'm.

RECORDER: She came with the guests who were celebrating your appointment as professor, but you did everything to prevent yourself from becoming a professor. *Acting light in the room also. Two gentlemen in hats and coats appear, accompanied by Frau Hubalek.* It seems to be working!

The gentlemen look around.

FRAU HUBALEK: What can I do for you? Dr. Kürmann is not at home. I'm the housekeeper here. May I ask who you are?

One of them shows a warrant.

RECORDER: Don't get up.

KÜRMANN: They're searching my flat?

RECORDER: You're at the doctor's. *Kürmann sits down again.* Keep the cotton on it. *One of the men opens drawers.* You're under suspicion of wanting to change the world. No one will ever suspect that you merely want to change your biography.

The other man opens books.

POLICEMAN: Frau—?

FRAU HUBALEK: Hubalek.

POLICEMAN: Tell me, Frau Hubalek—

FRAU HUBALEK: I know nothing.

POLICEMAN: Where do you come from?

FRAU HUBALEK: From Czechoslovakia.

POLICEMAN: From Czechoslovakia.

FRAU HUBALEK: What has the Doctor done?

POLICEMAN: You have relatives?

FRAU HUBALEK: In Czechoslovakia?

POLICEMAN: In Czechoslovakia.

FRAU HUBALEK: Why not?

POLICEMAN: Just answer the questions.

FRAU HUBALEK: He doesn't like his books to be touched.

POLICEMAN: How often do you visit your Czech relatives?

FRAU HUBALEK: Never.

POLICEMAN: That's not very often.

FRAU HUBALEK: It's enough for me.

The Nurse appears in the foreground.

NURSE: Doctor will be here in a minute. *She takes something and goes away.*

POLICEMAN: Tell me, Frau—

FRAU HUBALEK: Hubalek.

POLICEMAN: Are there any other rooms?

The Policemen and Fau Hubalek go out.

RECORDER: They won't find anything, but don't worry: suspicion remains suspicion, and suspicion is enough.

Room in darkness. In the foreground the Doctor comes back.

DOCTOR: It's nothing serious. All the same, you must look after yourself. There's no joking with the liver. . . . Mind you, NO FOIE GRAS, NO ESCARGOTS À LA BOURGUIGNONNE, nothing spiced. No pepper, mustard, curry. No seafood on any account—

Neon lamp on.

RECORDER: I'm making a note. *He makes notes.*

DOCTOR: No stone fruit: apricots, cherries, plums, peaches. No garlic. Nothing that causes flatulence. Cottage cheese whenever you like, as much cottage cheese as possible—

RECORDER: Vegetables?

DOCTOR: Yes, but without salt. Apart from cabbage. No French beans, in fact no beans at all, no onions—

RECORDER: Nothing that causes flatulence.

DOCTOR: Nothing cold. No beer. No whisky and vodka and so on, no gin, kirsch, pear brandy, and so on, Steinhäger, grappa, marc, and so on, cognac, calvados and so on. Under no circumstances.

RECORDER: Wine?

DOCTOR: You say your father used to drink?

KÜRMANN: So it seems.

DOCTOR: Above all, no white wine.

RECORDER: How about red wine?

DOCTOR: No alcohol at all.

RECORDER: What can he drink then?

DOCTOR: Milk.

RECORDER: Mineral water?

DOCTOR: But not carbonated. Tea. But no strong tea, of course. And then camomile, linden blossom, peppermint, rosehip, and so on. Absolutely no coffee. Do you like yogurt?

RECORDER: Do you like yogurt?

DOCTOR: Yogurt whenever you like. As much cottage cheese as possible. Vegetables whenever you like, but without salt. No seafood on any account—

RECORDER: We've had that.

DOCTOR: I'll tell you one thing you can eat: blue trout.

RECORDER: That's somthing.

DOCTOR: Without butter.

RECORDER: Lobster?

DOCTOR: For heaven's sake!

RECORDER: You've been lucky. Herr Kürmann very nearly had a lobster the other day.

DOCTOR: For heaven's sake! ˙

RECORDER: Meat?

DOCTOR: Boiled. That's perfectly all right. Without fat. Nothing stewed. Boiled or grilled. Without salt. Without spices, as I said. No sausages and so on—

RECORDER: Bread?

DOCTOR: Crispbread.

RECORDER: Nothing that causes flatulence.
DOCTOR: As much cottage cheese as possible. *The Nurse enters.* I'm
  coming.
 The Nurse wheels the instrument trolley away.
RECORDER: Anything else?
DOCTOR: Sweat. Sweat as much as you can.
RECORDER: How?
DOCTOR: Sport, walking, sauna. *He puts his hand on Kürmann's
  shoulder.* It's nothing serious, a slight enlargement of the liver;
  apart from that, I found absolutely nothing. The most important
  thing of all, my dear sir, is no excitement, no excitement of any
  kind. . . .
*Working light. The whole stage is visible again; a number of people
are gathered in the background, gentlemen in dinner jackets, ladies
in evening dress, all with champagne glasses in their hands. The
 Doctor has gone.*
KÜRMANN: Not a word about cancer.
RECORDER: No.
KÜRMANN: Apart from that, he didn't find anything.
RECORDER: You can put your jacket on again.
KÜRMANN: As much cottage cheese as possible. . . .
RECORDER: What are you thinking about?
 Kürmann rises and takes his jacket.
KÜRMANN: Who are these people?
RECORDER: Friends.
KÜRMANN: What do they want?
RECORDER: They've come to celebrate with you.
KÜRMANN: What for?
RECORDER: You've been made a professor.
*Acting light in the room. The room is full of Guests; they are
standing in groups, chatting; it is impossible to make out a word.*
KÜRMANN: Professor?
RECORDER: Quite frankly, I'm surprised.
KÜRMANN: A member of the Communist party doesn't get made a
  professor in this country in 1960. That's impossible.
RECORDER: Unlikely.
 Kürmann shakes his head.
HENRIK: Hannes!
RECORDER: They're calling you.

HENRIK: Where has he got to?

Kürmann shakes his head.

RECORDER: The guests want to go. It's late. *He helps Kürmann into his jacket.* That's something I don't have to explain to you, Professor Kürmann; no system guarantees that the probable will happen in every case.

Kürmann is discovered.

HENRIK: There you are.

SCHNEIDER: It's two o'clock.

HENRIK: We're leaving you now, Professor.

Kürmann disappears among the Guests; a buzz of voices; Guests leave the room in groups, until only the young lady in the evening dress is left exactly as in the beginning; she is sitting in the easy chair, waiting; she is wearing the horn-rimmed spectacles. Voices of the departing Guests outside; soon afterward Kürmann comes back—without whistling.

ANTOINETTE: "I'm going soon too."

Pause.

KÜRMANN: "Don't you feel well?"

ANTOINETTE: "On the contrary." *She takes a cigarette.* "Just one more cigarette." *She waits in vain for a light and lights up for herself.* "If I'm not in the way." *She smokes.* "I enjoyed it very much. Some of them were very nice, I thought, very stimulating. . . ." *Pause.* "Have you anything left to drink?" *Kürmann does not move.* "Why are you looking at me like that?"

Silence.

Translated by Michael Bullock

From TRIPTYCH

Three Scenic Panels

Third Panel

A marble bench in a public place, nothing else visible. Night. Francine and Roger are sitting on the bench in the radius of light of an overhanging street lamp.

ROGER: Say something, Francine! *She is silent.*

ROGER: There, right in front of us, the black Renaissance, the park railings. I haven't forgotten those, with their gilded, pointed spikes. Yet I would have sworn the bench was cast iron and wood. And those traffic lights in the distance: silence on red, a sudden roar on green—*He takes a cigarette and lights it.*

ROGER: Yes, Francine, it was here.

The sound of traffic in the distance, then silence. The traffic lights, which cannot be seen, change every fifty seconds. It is obviously a crossing where a big street meets a smaller one; in one direction the volume of traffic is large, and the sound of a great many cars can be heard when the light turns green, occasionally the harsh roar of a bus; in the other direction the cars are isolated, and the noise is not always the same every fifty seconds; the first phase lasts some time (up to seven seconds), the second phase, following after fifty seconds, lasts only a short while.

FRANCINE: You don't have to accompany me, Roger.

ROGER: That's what you said.

FRANCINE: There are times, Roger, when I hate you, but I shall never forget, Roger, that I once loved you very much.

ROGER: That's what you said.

FRANCINE: We should never have lived together.

Pause.

FRANCINE: At this time of night there are no trains. What is the point of going to the station so early? I can't see why you shouldn't come back to the hotel and rest until it's time for your train.

ROGER: That's what you said—

He smokes:

ROGER: —and I decided it would be better to go, not to the hotel with you, but to the station. And after that we never saw each other again.

He stamps out his cigarette.

ROGER: Your family looks on me more or less as your murderer. At any rate, that's what I hear indirectly. Others don't go quite that far. But they felt, our friends did, the need to take sides. The ones who adored Francine had to condemn me. When I mentioned your name, their silence was sometimes quite comical. I never found out how much they really knew about our relationship. They're tactful people, most of them. But at the time I lost several friends. I was told you wouldn't allow my name to be mentioned in your presence—

She takes a cigarette.

ROGER: This morning, just after I arrived, I met Madame Tailleur, or whatever she calls herself, that friend of yours. I wouldn't have recognized her, a ghost from the past. She wanted to know what I was doing in Paris. And the look she gave me! As if Paris were banned to me for all eternity.

He gives her a light; she smokes.

ROGER: My father—in all his eighty years I never found out what he really believed—he was no mystic, heaven knows, but he always knew what my dead mother was thinking. When he sold the house, never a doubt that his late wife approved. No need for her to know that he had messed things up with an inept bit of speculation, she was an understanding woman, and she always took his side. A convenient ghost. When we, his sons, didn't agree with him, it was always she who thought him right. He was an alcoholic. And he never doubted that she read the newspaper, too—his newspaper, of course. The long-haired youngsters: she hadn't lived to see those, but she found them as dreadful as he did. When he changed his political views, because they were proving too costly, and when he left the party, his dead wife left it, too. No doubt about it. I despised him, found all his communing with the dead repulsive. . . .

She sits silent, smoking.

ROGER: It was this bench, I'm certain of it. The only one under a street lamp. We didn't feel like sitting in the dark. . . . A year later I got married. You've never seen Ann. I got to know her in Texas, and we have a son, as perhaps you've heard. He's a schoolboy now.

She sits silent, smoking.

ROGER: Say something, Francine, about yourself.

She smokes, her eyes straight ahead. He looks at her.

ROGER: We probably reacted exactly the same way after we parted: you decided you were right, I decided I was right, and all we had left was bitterness. Which is easier on the memory than remorse. Your affair with Roger, mine with Francine, maybe they differ in the degree of their significance, but the dates are the same. . . .

Silence, the heavy traffic is heard, then stillness, then the lighter traffic.

ROGER: If Ann were to walk down this avenue now, she wouldn't be surprised to see me talking to you. She was jealous in the beginning, because I was always justifying myself to Francine, sometimes for hours on end. And she felt it was not her I was contradicting, but you. Poor Ann, it wasn't easy for her. I realized that later. But though I never mentioned your name again, she could still feel your presence, inevitably. . . . Ann's a photographer. . . . She's four years younger than you—that is to say, she was. Now Ann is already somewhat older than you. It's all very strange.

Pause.

ROGER: Incidentally, I did see you again—just once. Almost as close as we are now. I don't think I was mistaken. You were standing on the opposite escalator—it was in Berlin, at the Zoo underground station, in the morning. Can that be right? I was going down, you up, your hand on the railing, alone, and you were looking straight ahead, not exactly radiating cheerfulness, but not unhappy, either.

You were deep in the thought. Afterwards I felt I'd been quite right not to call out: Francine.

She extinguishes her cigarette against the marble.

ROGER: Or did you recognize me, too?

Pause.

ROGER: I never visited your grave.

A news vendor appears.

NEWS VENDOR: LE MONDE!—

Francine buys a newspaper; it takes some time, since she has to search for change, and obviously has difficulty with the unfamiliar coins without her glasses. At last she finds the right coin, and the news vendor goes off.

ROGER: You bought a newspaper—yes—to have something to read after we'd parted, when you were alone in the hotel bedroom.

She puts on her spectacles.

ROGER: Why did we part?

She glances at the title page.

ROGER: Vietnam . . . You knew how it would end before I did, though you didn't live to see it. But history proved you right. When I read about Chile today, I know exactly what Francine thinks about it.

She turns a page.

ROGER: Ernst Bloch is dead now, too—

She puts the newspaper down on the bench.

ROGER: The future holds nothing but fear.

Pause.

FRANCINE: Shall we go?

He does not move.

ROGER: Later I heard, from other people—and they couldn't have made it up, it can only have come out of your head—I heard I'd been blackmailing Francine for three whole years with threats of suicide.

He puts another cigarette between his lips.

ROGER: Did I do that, Francine?

He flips his lighter and takes the cigarette from his lips before he has lit it.

ROGER: Maybe you went through my drawers, I don't know, but you didn't find a revolver there. I didn't have one. I could always have jumped from the balcony. But I never threatened you with such nonsense. I did go to the Dolomites, that's true, but it wasn't meant as a threat—surely? What else, then? After a party where we'd all been drinking I did once try my hand at being a cat burglar—

He tries to laugh.

ROGER: Was that blackmail?

He throws his cigarette away.

ROGER: I think it's wretched of you, Francine, if that's the way you told our story: saying I blackmailed you for three years with threats of suicide.

She takes a cigarette and at the same time brings out her lighter, so that he can only look on as she lights her cigarette.

ROGER: That's how you smoked. And soon we shall start to feel cold. Later the gendarme will pass by and wonder why we are not in bed. I've never forgotten how you said: NOUS ATTENDONS LE MATIN, MONSIEUR! and how he gave a salute. Later still, when the traffic has stopped, we shall hear an ambulance siren in the distance. . . .

The traffic noises are still audible every fifty seconds: though becoming, not weaker, but shorter, so that the stillness gradually increases; sometimes only a single bus can be heard.

ROGER: Say something, Francine!

She smokes, looking straight ahead.

ROGER: For a time—after your death—I toyed with feelings of guilt. I set you up as my judge, in order to make you speak. But you didn't listen when I made my confession, and you looked at me as if it were impossible that I should ever understand. You said nothing—or you just repeated what you said then, here on this bench. . . . Francine, next year I shall be fifty, but you are always thirty-three.

He rises to his feet, without really knowing why he has done so; she continues to sit, unchanged; he stands with his hands in the pockets of his coat.

ROGER: WE SHOULD NEVER HAVE LIVED TOGETHER.

He looks at her:

ROGER: Do you know what I have often thought? That Francine is in love with her love. And that has nothing whatever to do with the man she may have met. Francine belongs in the ranks of the Great

Lovers. She loves her bliss, she loves her fear and her longing and her bitterness, the exaltation of her yielding, and if the man thinks it has anything to do with him, he has only himself to blame. Francine is not in love with herself, I don't mean that. She just loves—like the Portuguese nun. She loves her love.

He sees that she is not listening to him.

FRANCINE: I shall work.

ROGER: So you said.

FRANCINE: Immerse myself in work. *She extinguishes her cigarette against the marble.*

ROGER: That's what you said, and I understood that our parting was decreed, whatever else we would say that night.

She takes her lipstick from her handbag.

ROGER: Why didn't you want to have our child?

She makes up her lips without looking in her pocket mirror; he sits down again on the bench.

ROGER: And you never did have a child. So far as I know. Later I began to suspect that the people in Geneva might have made a mess of things that time.

He looks at her:

ROGER: Francine, was that it? *She puts her lipstick back into her handbag.*

FRANCINE: It's two o'clock, Roger, and last night we hardly slept at all. Let's be sensible.

ROGER: That's what you said.

FRANCINE: What is the point of going to the station so early? I can't see why you shouldn't come back to the hotel and rest until it's time for your train.

He is silent.

FRANCINE: What's to happen now with the flat?

He is silent.

FRANCINE: It was you who decided we should part, Roger, last night. For once you showed more courage than I, and for that I am grateful.

ROGER: That's what you said.

FRANCINE: When you've been drinking you can never remember what you said.

ROGER: We had both been drinking.

Pause.

ROGER: What did I say, Francine?
Pause.
FRANCINE: Roger, I'm making no demands.
ROGER: That's what you said.
Pause.
FRANCINE: I can go to live with Marieluise. Anytime. But how do you imagine I can work in her attic?
He is silent.
FRANCINE: Roger, you have never helped me.
He is silent.
FRANCINE: You talk like a landlord. A mere transaction. You say: I'll make you a present of the flat, all it needs is fifteen minutes with a lawyer and the flat is yours, furniture included.
ROGER: That's what I said.
FRANCINE: That's your first thought: lawyers.
He is silent.
FRANCINE: Roger, I have only one request—
ROGER: And I stuck to that: I made no attempt to find out your new address, I didn't appear one day on your doorstep, I didn't ring your bell.
Pause.
FRANCINE: What can I do with six rooms by myself?
He is silent.
FRANCINE: How can you ask what work I shall do? When for a whole year I've been talking about qualifying as a lecturer. You don't take my work seriously.
He is silent.
FRANCINE: Don't worry about me. That's not what I need, your concern. I can read timetables for myself.
He is silent.
FRANCINE: All I need from our flat is my books. Nothing else. The dictionaries in particular. And my clothes.
ROGER: You sent for those.
FRANCINE: If any letters come for me—
ROGER: I always sent them on to Marieluise. As arranged. Some bills as well, perhaps—I don't know. And in the first weeks there were also some telephone calls. I didn't have any number to pass on.
Pause.

FRANCINE: Stop looking at me like a sheepdog.
> *He is silent.*

FRANCINE: You'll go off to Austin, and we'll be relieved, both of us, not to have to prove anything to each other any more.

ROGER: I did go to Austin.
> *Pause.*

FRANCINE: It would be better not to write to each other, Roger, ever. Let's promise that, Roger. Never.
> *He is silent.*

FRANCINE: Roger, you don't need me.
> *He is silent.*

FRANCINE: Who was it who whitewashed the whole flat when you were away in Trieste, all six rooms, standing by myself on the ladder?
> *He is silent.*

FRANCINE: What could I find to do in Austin?
> *He is silent.*

FRANCINE: When we went househunting together, you wanted a large old building with high ceilings, and I agreed with you. Yes, I felt positive that we were not just any old couple.

ROGER: We were Francine and Roger.

FRANCINE: Yes.

ROGER: And so we are.
> *Pause.*

FRANCINE: Roger, I'm getting cold.
> *He is silent.*

FRANCINE: You want me to need you, that's what love means to you. When you're feeling sure of yourself I'm a burden on you. It's when you're feeling unsure that you cling to me, and that's not what I'm here for, Roger.
> *He is silent.*

FRANCINE: There are times when I hate you—

ROGER: That's what you said. *A gendarme comes in and stops before them.*

FRANCINE: NOUS ATTENDONS LE MATIN, MONSIEUR. *The gendarme salutes and goes off.*

ROGER: Today, out in Orly—yesterday I didn't even know I'd be flying to Paris, and this morning, when I had the ticket in my hand and heard them announce the flight, I was still unable to tell myself why—it was only in Orly, after arriving there with no luggage, and when I was sitting in the taxi, that I felt this mad hope that it might all never have happened, and that we should meet you and I, in this avenue. . . . Incidentally, nobody knows I am in Paris. Except Madame Tailleur. WHAT ARE YOU DOING IN PARIS. This is what I'm doing: talking to the dead. *The traffic noise has subsided; now nothing is heard except an occasional bus, then silence again.*

FRANCINE: Have you another cigarette? *He offers a pack of cigarettes, but no lighter.*

ROGER: There are times when I forget you. I'm still wearing the watch Francine gave me. But it doesn't remind me of you. And there are places we visited together, Strasbourg, for instance—the cathedral there reminds me of other cathedrals, not of Francine. That's how it is sometimes. I wouldn't confuse your handwriting with anybody else's, were I to see it, no, but I can't recall what it was like. And your body, your naked body . . . Oh, that can be agony—in the street, among the crowds at the traffic lights, I see hair that is your hair exactly. I know it's not possible, but I don't start walking when all the others do, I wait until I have forgotten you again.

FRANCINE: Have you a light? *He gives her a light.*

ROGER: Sometimes I dream of Francine. You are always different from the person I know, and usually in the company of strangers. I try to show you that by stretching out my arms, I can fly above the roofs. Which is not allowed, of course. Sometimes you are tender towards me, Francine, in my dreams. I know that tells me nothing about you, Francine, none of it is news of you. *Pause.* Perhaps we parted to show ourselves we could live without each other, and so we could, as long as you were alive.

She looks straight ahead, smoking.

ROGER: Did you go to Hanoi?

She looks straight ahead, smoking.

ROGER: You're tired, Francine.

FRANCINE: Desperately.

ROGER: That's what you said.

She looks straight ahead, smoking.

ROGER: Do you recognize this piece of paper?

He takes a piece of paper from his wallet.

ROGER: How that got into my wallet I've no idea. Like something drawn by a child. Railings. But nothing behind them. Could it be yours? I never saw you drawing.

She extinguishes her cigarette against the marble and again takes her lipstick from her handbag to paint her lips, this time looking into the small pocket mirror; a single bus is heard, then silence.

ROGER: I suppose you heard that I met her once, your Marieluise. At a party. We were standing at a cold buffet, and I probably asked her how Francine was getting on—otherwise I shouldn't have heard the words I did: YOU HAVE NEVER LOVED ANYBODY, ROGER, AND YOU NEVER WILL LOVE ANYBODY. I assumed this judgment came from you, and I left.

She moves her lips to settle her makeup.

ROGER: Would you still say that today?

She puts her lipstick back in her handbag.

ROGER: I know next to nothing about your life after we parted that night. You stayed in Paris. I kept my promise, I never went in search of you, as long as you were alive—

A single car is heard.

FRANCINE: Perhaps that was a taxi.

She has risen to her feet.

FRANCINE: It's two o'clock, Roger, and last night we hardly slept at all. Let's be sensible.

She looks at her watch:

FRANCINE: Half past two. *He remains seated and looks at her.*

ROGER: Is that the suit you were wearing?

Again a single bus, then silence.

ROGER: When I heard about your operation, the first one—the people didn't know I knew Francine Coray, so they spared no details—I wrote you a letter, but I didn't send it. I didn't dare to, Francine. Then, six months later, there was talk of X-ray treatment. . . . That time I did fly to Paris, but out there in Orly I knew some white nun would come and tell me my presence was not desired.

He puts a cigarette between his lips.

ROGER: I knew Francine was going to die.

He takes the cigarette from his lips.

ROGER: Say something, Francine.

Silence.

ROGER: Incidentally, I'm not alone again. My boy is allowed to visit me once a month, and for a fortnight each year. Ann is living with another man. It may even have been from me that she learned what was once said of me over a cold buffet: YOU HAVE NEVER LOVED ANYBODY. . . . A statement like that sticks like the mark of Cain.

He lights his lighter, then extinguishes it.

ROGER: I imagine you burned all my letters. I hope so—that they're not lying around in that woman's house, Madame Tailleur. . . . I haven't burned yours, Francine, though I haven't reread them, either. I should be afraid to. Phrases like in the Song of Solomon, but now they no longer apply. I've put them in a cardboard box, your letters, and sealed them in the approved way: with a candle and sealing wax, a drop of wax on the string, then a thumb on the hot wax, my fingerprint as seal.

He lights a cigarette.

ROGER: You were no longer a student when you decided against having our child, and I'd just passed my fortieth birthday. I didn't insist on it, no, I certainly didn't. On the journey to Geneva I asked you again, two or three times. You never realized how shocked I was by your determination. No, I didn't let you see that—on the contrary, in fact. I professed to understand you completely. Maybe my masculine understanding hurt you, I don't know. We were alone in the compartment, you pulled your coat over your face. But we were still in love for some time after that—

The siren of an ambulance is heard in the distance; it comes closer, though not very close, then fades again.

ROGER: What had really come between us, long before that, we didn't talk about at all that night. Not a word. At any time. Just like any other couple.

She sits down again on the bench, her handbag under her arm, ready to leave.

ROGER: What did we talk about until three in the morning?

Again a single bus, then silence.

ROGER: Once, in one of my dreams, I saw you drawing or painting. one sheet of paper after another. What you were drawing so intently I couldn't see. All I saw was one piece of paper after another, and you, a grown woman, looking happy, as absorbed as a child, earnest but happy. My presence didn't upset you. Then I asked you to give me one of your drawings, you didn't say I could, but you left it to me to take one or not—and then I woke up. When I turned on the light, I felt pleased, quite convinced I possessed a drawing of yours. A sign. I looked for it on the floor, on the table, in the pockets of my jacket—of course I didn't find anything.

He takes the piece of paper from his coat pocket.

ROGER: I suppose I must have scribbled this myself.

Slowly he crumples the piece of paper.

ROGER: Your silence, Francine—I understood your silence, as long as you were still alive. *The gendarme comes in exactly as before.*

FRANCINE: NOUS ATTENDONS LE MATIN, MONSIEUR. *The gendarme salutes and goes off.*

ROGER: One shouldn't talk with the dead. *She puts the newspaper into her handbag.*

FRANCINE: You don't have to accompany me, Roger. Straight on, turn right through the gate, then straight ahead and through the other gate and straight on across the bridge—I know, I can find the way. *He stamps out his cigarette.*

ROGER: When I got the news, a printed card, incidentally, with a text chosen by your family—before then it had always seemed possible that we might meet again. Quite by chance. You never sought a meeting, I know that, Francine, and I didn't dare to, and then suddenly the thought that we might see each other again had vanished.

He rises to his feet.

ROGER: But I did accompany you. *She remains seated.*

FRANCINE: We did once have a good time together, Roger, a great one. I thought the two of us, you and I, would rethink the whole world. Everything. And there must be something like that: a couple that sees itself as the first couple ever, as the inventor of the idea of couples. Us! The world may be shocked by our arrogance, but it can't hurt us. We have known grace. That's what I believed. And we knew the idea of possession didn't enter into it. Otherwise we should have got married. Once, at the very beginning, you said: There is nothing on this earth that cannot be rethought. And that was the bond between us, Roger. We mustn't let anyone know that we, Roger and Francine, were rethinking the world including all its dead. The orgies of argument we enjoyed, Roger! And I felt certain we loved more than just each other. You me and I you—all that is interchangeable. So you said! But what brought us together was not interchangeable. Other couples were just man and woman, we decided, and we were that, too, but on top of everything else: as a sort of extra bonus. And you know, Roger, our desperation at that time was never petty—wrong-headed perhaps, but never petty, and we could say terrible things to each other— things we could no longer say now. . . . That's when we bought the big flat. We talked a lot of rubbish, Roger, sometimes I and sometimes you, and sometimes both of us together, but at that time I really did believe I could rethink things, you could rethink things. We weren't dead, Roger, never dead—as we are now.

He looks at her the way one looks at a person who cannot know what he has been saying, and keeps silent.

FRANCINE: And we were proud of each other, you know. We didn't treat each other with kindness or compassion, or expect it, either. We saw each other as two people who had been singled out—yes, I mean that: singled out—me by you and you by me. We moved no mountains, and you often laughed at my optimism. You know, Roger, even in our mistakes we became bolder. We didn't misuse our feelings of tenderness, using them to hide from each other, or to comfort ourselves. . . . Yes, Roger, that's how it was. For a time.

He sits down again.

ROGER: Go on!

FRANCINE: Roger, I'm getting cold.

ROGER: I'm listening.

She is silent.

ROGER: When a memory suddenly finds itself alone in the world, it becomes another story, Francine, a very different one. My need to feel I was in the right—that has vanished since you died, and memory suddenly starts to release other things, now I see you in front of me.

He gazes at her tenderly:

ROGER: You with your narrow forehead and your big teeth, a blond horse with spectacles!

She removes her glasses and puts them into her handbag.

ROGER: And with your eyes like water.

Pause.

ROGER: Incidentally, our flat no longer exists. The house has been torn down—

Pause.

ROGER: A short while ago I had a conversation with a girl. I hardly know her, an ambitious youngster in search of a scholarship—that's why she came to see me. She had been having an abortion, she said: she felt I ought to know, so I wouldn't think she was always late for appointments. Maybe her frankness embarrassed me, she said, but she was anxious that I should understand her. It was, as she told me: BECAUSE I DON'T KNOW WHO THE FATHER IS. . . . Up till then it had never occurred to me that our case might have been the same. *Pause.*

FRANCINE: There are times, Roger, when you would like to slap my face. You don't do it because you know it would mean you would never see me again.

ROGER: That's what you said, Francine; then you took your hand-bag—I could have sworn it was a blue one—

She picks up her white handbag.

ROGER: —and got up.

She rises to her feet.

ROGER: And off we went with scarcely a word: straight on, turning right through the gate, then straight ahead and through the other gate, and straight on across the bridge to our white hotel.

She is standing, he remains seated, in the manner of a person sitting alone, hands in pockets, not knowing what to do next, staring straight ahead into the darkness.

ROGER: Suddenly—have you ever had this experience?—suddenly I realize it isn't true, something I had always maintained, which I had once believed. Suddenly it might all be quite different. It can seem like an awakening, in the middle of the day. A sentence I once heard, maybe years ago, comes into my mind, and suddenly it means something quite different. That is happening more and more frequently to me now. Without any reason I can see. I wake up, realizing that a joke I made yesterday isn't a joke at all. Or I remember some sentence which for years had aroused my indig-nation, and to which I reacted indignantly at the time. But now: I can't really see why that particular remark upset me so. I don't understand why I reacted as I did. . . . I don't know if you've ever had that experience, Francine.

Pause.

ROGER: Do you know, there isn't a single photograph of Francine that reminds me of you? Except a childhood photograph: young

Francine, looking as I've never seen you look, together with a large sheepdog.

Pause.

ROGER: Say something!

Pause.

ROGER: Once, after you'd been to Moscow, you spoke about Lenin—how the sight of him in that mausoleum made you feel sick, his wise head empty of thought for the past fifty years. . . . That's the trouble: we live with the dead, and they don't rethink.

Pause.

ROGER: I'm looking forward to a holiday in Iceland with my youngster. I've been telling him how volcanoes and glaciers originate, and now I have to show him that there are such things. He's too old for fairy tales. We're going to Iceland this coming summer. For a fortnight. With a tent and sleeping bags.

Pause.

ROGER: Francine, say something.

FRANCINE: You don't have to accompany me.

ROGER: No, Francine—say something you didn't say then. Something you thought later. Something you would say now—that would set us free of our history, Francine.

Again the siren of an ambulance is heard in the distance; the sound comes nearer, then fades in the opposite direction.

FRANCINE: Roger, I really am cold.

ROGER: Once, months ago, I had the idea that I ought to shoot myself through the head, so that I could hear Francine again.

FRANCINE: And you're cold, too. *He remains seated.*

ROGER: Francine, say something. *He suddenly shouts:* Say something! *Pause.*

FRANCINE: Roger, we've said it all.

ROGER: Have we?

FRANCINE: I told you I would work. Or go to Hanoi, if that were possible, to report on things from the other side.

Pause.

FRANCINE: It was you who decided we should part, Roger. For once you showed more courage than I, and for that I am grateful. *Pause.* We should never have lived together. *Pause.* How can you ask what work I shall do? When for a whole year I've been talking about qualifying as a lecturer. You don't take my work seriously.

Pause. Stop looking at me like a sheepdog. *Pause.* You'll go off to Austin, Roger, and we'll be relieved, both of us, not to have to prove anything to each other any more. *Pause.* Roger, you have never helped me. *Pause.* What can I do with six rooms by myself? *Pause.* Roger, you don't need me. *Pause.* Don't worry about me. That's not what I need, your concern. I can read timetables for myself. *Pause.* It would be better not to write to each other, Roger, ever. Let's promise that, Roger. Never. *Pause.* We did once have a good time together, Roger—

ROGER: Go on! *Pause.*

FRANCINE: All I need from our flat is my books. Nothing else. The dictionaries in particular. And my clothes. *Pause.* Roger, I'm making no demands. *Pause.* When we went househunting together, you wanted a large old building with high ceilings, and I agreed with you. Yes, I felt positive that we were not just any old couple. *Pause.* That's your first thought: lawyers. *Pause.* Roger, I have only one request: that you never try to find out my new address. Do you promise that? I don't want you appearing one day on my doorstep, ringing my bell. *Pause.* Roger, I'm cold. *Pause.* You want me to need you, that's what love means to you. When you're feeling sure of yourself, I'm a burden on you. It's when you're feeling unsure that you cling to me, and that's not what I'm here for, Roger. *Pause.* What could I find to do in Austin? *Pause.* There are times when I hate you, Roger, but I shall never forget that I once loved you very much.

ROGER: Go on!

FRANCINE: There are times when I hate you—

ROGER: Go on!

FRANCINE: There are times when I hate you—

She stands and looks on as, without haste, he reaches into his coat pocket, as if he were searching for his lighter, and, still without haste, releases the safety catch of a revolver. He does it, not in the manner of a man who is used to it, but as if it had been explained to him.

ROGER: Go on!

FRANCINE: You never loved anybody, Roger, you are not capable of that, and you never will love anybody. *Pause.*

ROGER: So that remains.

She looks on as, without haste, he puts the revolver to his temple, as if he were alone; no report, but sudden darkness, then daylight: the bench is empty, the traffic sounds, now loud, are heard again every fifty seconds, the silence between each change very short.

Translated by Geoffrey Skelton

PART III

ESSAYS AND SPEECHES

EMIGRANTS*

Reference to Georg Büchner, Hesse's great son, are on display everywhere in Zurich. On the hill above my hometown, at the so-called Rigiblick, is his second grave, which as a dutiful boy, football tucked under my arm, I viewed with impatient reverence. And below in the old quarter of Zurich, when we are inspecting the midnight house fronts after being kicked out of the pubs at closing time by the amiable police, we come upon the legend (earlier a plaque, now unfortunately an inscription in the mortar): Georg Büchner, writer and natural scientist, lived here in the winter of 1836/37 and died, aged 23.

By the way, in the same row of houses, next door on the left, is another plaque, legible from afar: Lenin, leader of the Russian Revolution, lived here from February 21 to April 2, 1917.

Emigrants. Revolutionaries. With differences, to be sure. One leaves behind *Woyzeck;* the other, the Soviet Union. There are few emigrants who realize the hope of all emigrants: not only to return to the country they had to flee, but by returning to revolutionize it. One of these few is Lenin. Büchner dies in exile, as the inscription states—as writer and natural scientist. He is a natural scientist not by accident, nor just on the side. He studies the nature (not the morality) of fish and amphibians, likewise the nature of men when they are fed peas, for example; and he has a dreadful, if not surprising foreboding that a revolution that delivers heads and a few

*Speech on the occasion of the awarding of the Georg Büchner Prize, 1958.

liberties but no bread for the starving masses must fail. He is a realist who probably had no match among the Young Germans; not a *Sturm und Drang* writer whose passionate disposition strays into politics now and then, but a political genius in his own right. Herwegh is right when he laments the loss of not merely a writer but a political leader: "He surely should have been a lodestar for us in these half-baked times gone mad." For as far as the writer is concerned, this particular writer, the political is not mere illustration but his very experience of suffering. He is a political being—in the agitation, in the capitulation, in the vision of the *Woyzeck* fragment. Because for him, at a time when Germany is still procrastinating over its bourgeois revolution, the next revolution is already brewing, the proletarian one whose leader will later live next door, exactly 80 years later, Spiegelgasse 12 and Spiegelgasse 14, separated by a so-called fire wall. It could just as well be about Büchner, though in fact it is about his friend Becker, that the German examining judge notes already in 1839: "It was inevitable that he succumbed in Switzerland, where anything goes, even excesses, to a communism that unfortunately had already laid extensive claim to his soul."

In fact 1848 does come!

But then again we read: "Today in rather deplorable weather the Büchner commemoration took place. Approximately 150 participants—mostly students of all nations—followed the black, red, and gold flag of the German students out from the politechnic. Professors were also strongly represented; less so the Zurich Germans, who may feel less sympathetic toward a republican of Büchner's ilk in view of the political changes in Germany."

That was 1875.

The list of German emigrants who waited in Switzerland hoping for a different Germany is impressive, even if we confine ourselves in this context just to writers. Not far from Zurich, out there on the little island of Ufenau, Ulrich von Hutten, fighter with sword and pen, has found repose in exile. Not all who died here with us were persecuted: Rainer Maria Rilke, for example. Also Stefan George, whose spirit has nothing at all in common with Switzerland's, wasn't yet persecuted in 1933; on the contrary, he fled from official approval. In Thomas Mann's case, there are two different parts: a first sojourn because the fatherland expels him, and a final one because a German-speaking country suffices as homeland. And don't forget Nietzsche, who banishes himself of his own accord to the heights of the Engadine. Richard Wagner is among those who are waiting out a short thunderstorm, leaving behind a marble tablet here and there. Hermann Hesse, on the other hand, settles here for good already after the First World War and becomes a citizen, thus assisting Switzerland to its second Nobel Prize in literature.

But then—after an emigration of the avant-garde (a bloodless but not insignificant one), after Wedekind, after Hugo Ball and Tristan Tzara and others who sit in the Café Odeon and launch Dadaism—after that come once again the classical refugees who, like Georg Büchner, are fleeing a sentence of death. Dachau or Switzerland! I do not speak of the nameless ones, but I so speak of the fact—which perhaps can be understood or at least rationalized, but not covered up by self-praise—that many nameless people at that time were turned back to certain death. Georg Kaiser goes into hiding; Zuckmayer still has his premiere in Zurich, takes a bow, and disappears. Thomas Mann speaks publicly against Hitler; Musil wanders like a ghost through the country, unrecognized. Many of them have to stay in the mousetrap (not "loge" but mousetrap) that Switzerland is at that time—Jews above all, bound to us for better or for worse. Out of this situation emerges the Zurich Schauspielhaus (just as the University of Zurich, founded a few years before Büchner's first lecture, cannot be imagined without the participation of German emigrants).

Then, after 1945, as the emigrants of the Hitler period in part are staying on because they have entered into a symbiosis with us (something neither side foresaw) and in part are setting out with meager luggage and great hope to return to their homeland, we are visited by writers whom I should not wish to count as part of the emigration. Granted, these are refugees from the bitter cold and dreary hunger of those years, but they are arrogant, bringing little with them except the notion of having suffered more than everyone else and taking in nothing at all except our standard of living (for which they despise us as philistines). This goes on until the German monetary reform—thank God for that!—wipes out such fraternization.

But the emigration, the real one, remains unforgettable. One day—and let him be the last on this sketchy list—Bert Brecht is simply sitting there, having arrived from Germany via Denmark, Finland, Moscow, China, and Hollywood, shyly inquiring how things look now over in Germany.

> The city of my fathers, how can I find it?
> Following the swarms of bombers
> I come home.
> Where does it lie? Yonder where huge
> Mountains of smoke arise,
> There in the flames
> It stands.
>
> The city of my fathers, how shall it receive me?
> The bombers arrive before me. Deadly swarms
> Announce my approach. Conflagrations
> Precede the son's return.

I remember how he opens and reads the letter, which we have carried from Berlin, hand-delivering it to him like ancient messengers: an invitation to Germany, signed by a Russian officer. And I recall how Brecht makes a trial crossing over the German border at the customhouse in Constance for the first time in fifteen years. Inhibited by his determination to avoid ceremony, he is mute for awhile; then, relighting his cigar (which poor B. B. has, after all, let go out) and poking his neck about his shirtless coat collar (his involuntary gesture of embarrassment), he comments on the weather in Germany in order to distract us, while surreptitiously inspecting the homeland that in his great pain he has lamented as "pale mother."

But getting back to Büchner. "For the last six months I've been utterly convinced," writes Büchner from Strassburg, "that nothing is to be done and that anyone who sacrifices himself right now is foolishly risking his neck."

Let's address ourselves to this sentence. Büchner was a writer of political commitment, even if he didn't write his *Danton* to teach revolution but "to make money," as his brother quotes him. To which one would have to add that he also wrote out of delight in his genius and out of distress, that is, the distress of a political being. Disgust at taking action, the deadly boredom that besets his Danton, this powerful orator who would just as soon not talk any more and in fact doesn't bother to defend himself; the boredom that

Leonce plays away by blowing linguistic soap bubbles, while in Lenz's case it freezes into madness—this is the same Büchner who a moment ago still wanted to change the world (that is, the grand duchy of Hesse) and who writes in a love letter: "I felt as if I were crushed under the terrible fatalism of history." And in the same letter: "What is it within us that lies, murders, steals? I no longer care to pursue the thought. If only I could lay this cold and martyred heart on your breast!" In my opinion, Büchner, when he writes, does not take a leave of absence from politics. On the contrary.

"I find in human nature a horrifying sameness, in the human condition an inescapable force, granted to all and to no one. The individual is merely foam on the waves," we read in the same letter to his bride.

"... a ludicrous struggle against an iron law. To recognize it is our utmost achievement, to control it is impossible." To which one would like to add: to portray it is the only way to recover from our impotence. Neither *Danton* nor *Woyzeck* are propaganda plays. Nonetheless we would like to know where Büchner stands, even without the *Hessische Landbote,* and we sense his commitment exactly at the point where he liberates himself from it through the act of creation—even in the comedy *Leonce and Lena,* where the laughter (at least that's how I hear it) emerges from the inversion of commitment.

"Peace to the huts! War to the palaces!" That's the sound of the activist. "Oh, if only a person could see the top of his head for once! That's one of my ideals. That would do me good." That's Leonce. "What people won't do out of boredom! They study out of boredom, they fall in love, marry, and reproduce out of boredom and finally die out of boredom, and—that's the humor of it—they do everything with the most serious faces, without realizing why and God knows what they mean by it."

This strikes a more familiar note today, the note of anticommitment, humor out of disgust, *End Game* notes, clownerie-cum-nothingness, currently playing in every German city as Ionesco farce—"... and—that's the humor of it—they do everything with the most serious faces, without realizing why and God knows what they mean by it." One wonders what Georg Büchner might have to say to our present-day society.

"Peace to the huts! War to the palaces!" Well, huts are few and far between, let's face it (at least in the West); and what he would perhaps take for palaces don't belong to princes but to multinational corporations; and Büchner would be astounded, as he was then: "Friendly villages everywhere, and then, the closer you come to Zurich and along the lake, widespread prosperity . . . The streets aren't full of soldiers, job applicants, and lazy bureaucrats; you don't risk being run over by a nobleman's coach."

We have to report to Georg Büchner: the republic, still a dangerous word in his time, is proclaimed on either side of the border. A widespread prosperity exists not only the closer you get to Zurich. Getting run over by a nobleman's coach is the least of our worries, and besides, everyone is insured. Capitalism can afford to be more social than its opponents, and oppression is without arbitrariness. No right-thinking person goes to jail these days, and inquisition is out of the question, or at least it doesn't go beyond boycott wherever possible. At any rate no one persecutes us when we talk about our freedom; on the contrary, we are supposed to talk about our freedom, the louder the better, and if we don't talk about freedom, it's only because the governments themselves talk so much about it. In fact, all things considered, we are free to express our own opinions, at least about God, if not about nuclear weapons. Georg Büchner would be astounded! And truth to tell—again just between you and me—we feel scarcely more comfortable than his captain: "I can feel it, there's something rapid out there." One feels the razor at the throat.

"So say something, Woyzeck! What's the weather like today?"

"It's bad, Cap'n, bad. Wind." We feel uneasy.

"Hollow—you hear that? It's all hollow down there!"

"I'm scared."

"It's so strangely quiet. You feel like holding your breath. Andres!"

"What?"

"Say something!"

Stage direction: *(Stares off into the landscape.)*

Let's take a look at the landscape, where it's so strangely quiet (at least in the realm of literature)—not with a view to aesthetic questions, but to the questioning of our commitment as writers today. At first glance it appears that the younger (post-Brechtian) literature rather leans toward anticommitment, to farce à la *Leonce* under the label of French avant-garde. I don't know how long the spectator's adventure of being fooled while waiting for meaning survives as adventure, for man has a strange penchant for meaning, for making sense. I only know this: what lies behind the *Leonce* farce is not a penchant for nonsense as fashion, but rather Georg Büchner, and that means (permit me a word that has long since become fashionable), despair, as we know it from his letters. "Why should a thing like this [meaning society] walk around between heaven and earth? Its whole life consists only of attempts to dissipate its most dreadful boredom. Let it die out, that is the only new thing it can still experience."

This is more than playing with antiplay.

"And the masses themselves? For them there are only two levers: material poverty and religious fanaticism. Any party that knows how to operate these levers will conquer. Our times demand iron and bread—and then a cross or something like that." I quote this well-known passage from a letter to Gutzkow because it shows where Büchner, rapidly instructed by experience, cancelled his commitment to activism. "And then a cross or something like that." This is not blasphemous but anti-ideological, as said before in *Danton* in one of the prison scenes: "Try following your rhetoric to the point where it becomes flesh and blood. Look around you: all this you have spoken."

That is still discovery.

"And then a cross or something like that."

This already represents experience—with a sweep of the hand that casts aside all emblems, not the cross in particular but everything that may be used to label crusades.

Doesn't this Büchner speak like a contemporary?

Faced with the choice of making a political commitment to Eastern or Western dogma, most of us (judging from our works) choose art-for-art's sake, which for the most part is a camouflage. What other alternative do we have for remaining truthful? We can't write the arsenal of weapons of our existence, but we can upset the arsenal of phrases used by both sides for warfare the clearer we become as writers (that is, the more concrete), the more unintentional in that unconditional honesty vis-à-vis the living that distinguishes the artist from the mere talent.

Everything living contains its own contradiction, which subverts ideology, and so we needn't be ashamed if our writing is accused of being subversive. We needn't shout it from the rooftops, but that's what our political commitment is all about! What the newspapers, on behalf of the vested powers, publish daily in battle-ready columns we subvert with each true portrayal of a creature. By not taking a position (isn't that the way it is put?) on alternatives that are not real ones, we make a definite impact. Never fear on that score. For what is more detestable to either camp than a portrayal of the human being, which renders both camps obsolete.

That's one thing.

The other thing that defines our anticommitment is touchier to discuss. George Büchner fleeing across the border, and all the German emigrants who gathered around Solothurn, where our police arrested them lest they go running back to feudatory Germany with the torch of the republic—they all still believed in the Fatherland. A single wish burned in their gallant hearts: back to the Fatherland! Or better yet: Forward to a new Fatherland!

They waited and hoped, whereas we, I think, no longer wait and hope. Do you believe in a new Germany? I'm just asking. Do I believe in a new Switzerland? I am Swiss and desire to be nothing else, but my commitment as a writer is not to Switzerland, nor to any other country.

"At heart one is always something of a nationalist," I read in my own *Sketchbook 1946–1949*.

> . . . when I see my compatriots [in Milan] plundering the Italian shops with their Swiss currency, I turn pale with anger. Why exactly? My obvious disappointment betrays the secret assumption we all have, that the nation to which we belong must be a model nation, simply because we ourselves happen to belong to it—which gives one every reason to feel angry, rather, with oneself!

This is the other point, the question whether we are turning the national element into a goal just because it can't be eradicated, or else (as is more usual today) into annoyance at ourselves. I am thinking of German friends in Italy or Greece who scarcely finish shaking hands before announcing their indignation over how many Germans there are in Italy or Greece. Is that cosmopolitan servility or is there more to it? The question urges itself whether and to what extent the German intelligentsia are willing and able to love their own people. Not to glorify nor vilify, but to love them—that is, to accept them. And what is meant by "people" is not, of course, "the nation of writers and thinkers," but the German nation. Are the German writers fond of it? Nor are we talking about folklore with old customs and traditions, but about the actual Volkswagen-folk. What is disquieting is the common need among writers to start right out talking about the elite (whereby those who happen to be present rank for all time among the elite); for then the race as a whole gets disavowed—by despisers of the common man, who, granted, aren't princes, but as Büchner observes, ". . . they speak their own language, while the people lie before them like manure on the field." Büchner loved his people and suffered: ". . . because one really has to say, with the best will in the world, that they have come to have a certain lowmindedness and, sadly enough, are no longer accessible on virtually any level save directly through the pocketbook."

Börne, in contrast, already speaks in a different way about the people: "I had to laugh," he writes from Paris, "when I came to Darmstadt and remembered that a fearsome revolution was supposed to have taken place here a few days ago. . . . There is a stillness in the streets similar to what we have around here [in Paris] at night, and the few people who pass by tread no louder than snails . . . So much for the grumbling of the German people."

This, I think, is the tune of the average elitist today, the cosmopolitan's scorn of the German philistine, that ill will with which Nietzsche still had the dimension of a curse and today is part of the vocabulary of tourists ingratiating themselves with one another: disavowal of one's own people the moment one appears part of the crowd. Now we come to our question, which is definitely a literary one.

If writers in fact can't stand their own people, how are they supposed to describe human beings without becoming mere satirists or else drifting off into a portrayal of universal man, with the risk that man himself gets lost? Take Proust, for example. It goes without saying that his characters altogether, whether noble or base, are French. He doesn't extol France if someone he is portraying achieves greatness, nor does he revile France if most of them prove loathsome. With Musil as well (and, of course, things are different in Austria) the Austrians he dissects are always Austrian people, that is, people who happen to be Austrian. Or García Lorca! How strange he would seem to us had he not accepted his people once and for all. Isn't it precisely because their Spanishness doesn't become an issue for them that his people seem like people? It's an old insight, hence bears no further elaboration: world literature is never created by running away from but portraying one's own kind. One can portray people only if one has experienced them. But does experience suffice? One would also have to accept them—and that includes the economic miracle boys too, I'm afraid. For mere satire doesn't accomplish much. It doesn't make us great writers. And above all, satire still doesn't rid us of Fatherland. In other words, if being free of Fatherland is considered a goal of our commitment, in no way do I mean by that disavowal of one's own people; on the contrary, I mean freedom vis-à-vis one's own people by accepting them in their reality once and for all.

I'm almost finished.

Georg Büchner as writer with political commitment and Büchner as emigrant—from there we set out in search of our own position as writers. I'm sorely tempted to mention (but I won't) names of contemporary German writers, not necessarily personal acquaintances, with whom I feel connected in this search—connected, whether in commitment or anticommitment, not least through the emigrant element. It's no accident that I have concerned myself with emigrants. The emigrant element that forms a bond between us expresses itself in our not being able, nor even wanting, to speak in the name of our Fatherlands. It expresses itself in our feeling that our place of residence in any corner of the modern world, whether we change it or not, is temporary. We could live in Munich or Männedorf or Rome. Places of residence are according to choice; they are often according to whim and accident of convenience, determined above all by personal connections. We make one condition: our place of residence shall allow us the unspoken feeling of not belonging. Or as Friedrich Dürrenmatt, when asked by a Swiss critic how he deals with Switzerland as a problem, answered quite simply: "You are mistaken, Herr Doktor. Switzerland is no problem for me. Sorry. It's just a pleasant place to work, that's all."

What I mean, then, when I speak of the emigrant element (and this could be demonstrated with many biographies, not just German ones: think of the American writers who go to the States only to visit or to maintain their passports but otherwise live in Spain—if possible with a beard—or in Rome or at the very least in Paris; yes, even the French themselves, who up to now have considered Paris a synonym for world, are moving to the country, settling at the lake of Geneva or on Capri) what I mean, then, is not the oft-invoked homelessness of the Left, but the feeling in general of alienation anywhere and everywhere. This is not melancholy, by the way; it is a clear-and-dry feeling:

> Home is an indispensable need, but it has nothing to do with countries [*Sketchbook 1946–1949*]. Home means human beings whose nature we can perceive and grasp. To that extent it does perhaps have something to do with language, but it certainly does not lie in language alone. Words form bonds only when we find ourselves on the same wavelength.

Thus being free of Fatherland doesn't mean being homeless. Nor does it mean (at least not in the primary sense) the growing awareness of modern man that radioactivity is no respecter of national borders. That's in addition. That awareness, which editorials can't talk us out of any more, makes us view with irony the various things that still go under the banner of nationalistic policy, appearing to us like specters at the embrasures of a medieval fortress—that is, useless and insane. But our feeling of alienation is more deeply rooted. We have become emigrants without leaving our Fatherlands; all we have to do is admit it to ourselves. The first stop for Büchner was Strassburg. Our first stop is irony. The second stop for Büchner was Zurich, where he worked as precisely as possible while his friend back in the Fatherland perished; where he lectured, using his own slide specimens, on the comparative anatomy of fish and amphibians. Our second stop is also work, whether in Zurich or elsewhere, as precisely as possible, as truthfully as possible, as subversively as possible. There is for us also (even without typhoid) no return to the Fatherland.

"Canons constantly rattle by under my window, troops drill on the open squares, and artillery is being mounted on the city walls . . . The whole thing is only a comedy," writes Büchner from Strassburg, "The king and the legislature rule, and the people applaud and pay." Are not we who write, then, fighters simply through our awareness that so much is comedy? It's only a question, again and again, of how to fight. Is silence itself a weapon? The king and his legislature are waiting for our oath of allegiance—in vain, I hope, unless they extract it once more by torture. We don't want to promise to be martyrs, rather we want to be writers as long as we possibly can. Are not we who try to get through life by writing, then, pledged to another authority, loyal in another sense, witnesses to another freedom that is unconditional and independent of the succession of kings and legislatures? Are we not joined across national borders, across language borders, across racial borders in our affirmation of the individual (we ourselves being nothing else but individuals), united in the rejection, implicit in our productivity, of Fatherlands in general? I put the question. And I should not wish to be misunderstood; we are not idealists. It's not as though there were no history that stamps us as individuals. We are dependent on our origins. We don't want to be internationalists, nor dreamers. "Be embraced, millions!" is not our battle hymn. What is, then?

We are searching for it. We only know we have to come to terms with the national element without either denying or making a goal of it. To this end I am not advocating abolishing the frontier between the Federal Republic of Germany and little Switzerland, for example, or the frontier between little Switzerland and France (ever in the van and on the verge of again becoming *la grande nation*). Nor do we mean the kind of European integration that most certainly will come; for the fact that the same jeeps and jet bombers are standing by now in Greece, Spain, Germany, France, Turkey, and neutral Switzerland by no means extinguishes chauvinism. Such alliance, in response to an East–West confrontation, are only for the standardization of weapons—which, too, would not be unwelcome in the event of these weapons being used once more against one another. To each the same épée—that's only fair! But we mean something else by European integration. What unites us is the spiritual ordeal of the individual in the face of such confrontations, the awareness of our impotence, and the question of what to do.

"For the last six months I've been utterly convinced that nothing is to be done and that anyone who sacrifices himself right now is foolishly risking his neck."

George Büchner, who was not lacking in courage, wrote that on his way into exile, and it sounds like resignation. But what a feat this selfsame George Büchner has wrought by portraying a single creature, Woyzeck by name, in such a way that no present or future ideology could ever make us forget him!

We don't have his genius.

We have talent.

Even that is a charge. The truthfulness of the portrayal—and it matters not whether what gets portrayed is merely a conventional or eccentric marriage or the monstrous deformation of the human being who has to kill for the state (a soldier)—the truthfulness, whenever it is achieved, always isolates us. But it is the only thing we have to pit against our impotence: images, nothing but images, images, and more images; desperate ones and those that are not; images of the creature so long as it lives.

"In all, I demand life," we read in *Lenz*, "the possibility of existence, and then all is well; we must not ask whether it is beautiful or ugly, the feeling that the work of art has life stands above these two qualities and is the sole criterion of art."

It is resignation, but a combative resignation that joins us; an individual commitment to truthfulness; the attempt to make art that is neither national nor international but something more, namely, a ban against abstraction that must be continually enacted, a ban against ideology and its fatal front lines. These cannot be fought with conspicuous bravery of the individual on the field of battle; they can only be subverted through the work of each individual on his own ground.

Translated by Alice Carey

FOREIGNIZATION I*

A small *Herrenvolk*† imagines itself imperiled; it calls for man-power and human beings arrive. They don't feed on our prosperity; on the contrary, they are indispensable for it. But they are here. Guest workers or foreign workers? I opt for the latter. They are not guests whom we serve in order to turn a profit. They are working, and what's more, away from home because right now they can't make it in their own country. You can't blame them for that. They speak another language. Even for that you can't blame them, especially since the language they speak is one of our four national languages. But it makes everything more difficult.

They complain about living quarters unfit for human habitation at exhorbitant rents, and are not at all enthusiastic. One isn't used to that. Still, one needs them. Were the small *Herrenvolk* not so renowned among themselves for their humanity, tolerance, and so on, it would be easier knowing how to deal with the foreign work-ers. They could be accommodated in regular camps, where they could even be allowed to sing, and then they wouldn't foreignize the street scene. But you can't do that. They aren't prisoners, nor even refugees. So they are hanging around our shops making purchases, and if they have an accident on the job or get sick, they are lying

---

*Foreword to *Siamo Italiani,* a collection of interviews with Italian workers, by Alexander Seiler.
†"master race."

around our hospitals to boot. One feels foreignized. Little by little one does start to take offense.

Exploitation is a worn-out word, except when the employer himself feels exploited. It's said they are saving a billion francs per year and sending the money home. That wasn't part of the plan. They are thrifty. Strictly speaking, they can't be blamed even for that. But the fact is they are here, human beings foreignizing us, when in fact, as noted, all that was ever wanted was manpower. And not only are they human beings, they are different: Italian. They line up at the border. It's frightening. Try to see it from the viewpoint of a small *Herrenvolk*. If Italy were suddenly to close its border, that too would be frightening. What to do? The stringent measures you'd have to impose would not overjoy those affected by them, not even the affected employers. There's a boom going on but no joy in the country. The foreigners are singing. Four together in a sleeping space. The federal government won't tolerate any interference by an Italian labor minister. After all, there's such a thing as independence, even if one is dependent on foreign dishwashers and bricklayers and hod carriers and waiters and so on—independence from the Hapsburgs just as from the European Common Market.

The plain facts: 500,000 Italians. That's a big chunk—as big as the black chunk in the United States. That's indeed a problem. Unfortunately, our own. It seems they do good work, even excellent; otherwise it wouldn't be profitable, and they'd have to leave, and the danger of foreignization would be averted. They have to behave quite impeccably, better than tourists, or else the host country will forgo its boom. Admittedly this threat isn't spoken aloud, except by a few hotheads who don't know the first thing about economics. In general the mood keeps to a tolerant nervousness.

There are just too many of them—not at the construction sites and not in the factories and not in the stable and not in the kitchen, but during after-hours. Especially on Sunday there are suddenly too many of them. They are conspicuous. They are different. They have an eye for the girls and women (as long as they are not permitted to take their own abroad).

It's not that one is a racist. After all, not being racists is a tradition, and the tradition has been sanctioned in the condemnation of French or American or Russian conduct, not to mention that of the

Germans, who coined the concept of *Hilfsvölker*.* Still, they're just different. They endanger the individuality of the small *Herrenvolk*, though what that is no one likes to define, except in terms of self-praise, which is of no interest to the others. However, in the interviews following this introduction, it is the others who define us.

Do we want to read about such things?

A book of this kind, which presents material rather than a thesis, can be read along various lines. Perhaps the most productive way, if I were not Swiss, would be to read it only as literature, for instance. How does it sound when simple people talk about themselves? There are sections in almost every conversation that recall the Bible, sections so lapidary and concrete in the circumstantiality of the account that I sit up and listen, even if the facts are known to me. What do they experience? The human being as manpower in a free enterprise society, to be sure. But their experience remains completely apolitical, a feeling that identifies itself as homesickness. Not a single revolutionary is speaking out here. There is something touching about that. All of them speak of their families. That is their ethos, a Christian ethos, also a very Mediterranean one. Separation from their family, saving up for their family, living with their family, the hope of a little house, not abroad but in Sardinia or Romagna or Sicily—these are the things they keep talking about. Sometimes it sounds almost antique. Culture appears not as education but as a practical heritage; humanity not as theory. Here speaks a kind of people who are courteous even in complaint. No educators of the world, they. And money as money is not the measure, not even for the more simple-minded ones. Even if they are scarcely aware what standard they have, they still have it and are not prepared for others not knowing what it is. A peculiar breed of people: quite humble, actually; naïve; not servile and not obsequious, but not arrogant either, just not prepared for humiliation; not very nationalistic, incidentally, even during the Diaspora; not power-seeking; trusting in life. Like children, many are frightened of the snow in a strange country, and it takes them a long time to realize what kind of coldness it is that frightens them.

* "inferior races."

The other side we know: the myth, which Switzerland confers upon itself, and the fact that the myth solves no problems; consequently, the hysteria of helplessness. Every problem that we ourselves have to deal with means sending the concept of Switzerland out for repair. Let's hope it works.

Translated by Alice Carey

SWITZERLAND AS *HEIMAT?**

M r. President, Ladies and Gentlemen.
Since it is the Swiss Schiller Foundation that convenes us,
one could talk about Friedrich Schiller (who as a Swabian poet was
not obliged to celebrate the historical-real Switzerland) and thus
about William Tell. It could be demonstrated why this father with
crossbow and son (for Hodler without son, but never without
crossbow) has to be debunked from time to time—not because he
never existed (you can't blame him for that) but because alive as
figure of the legend (which actually is a Scandinavian one) and
endowed, as he is, by Friedrich Schiller with German idealism, he
rather gets in the way nowadays of our Swiss self-image.

However, I would like to talk about something else.

An honor from one's *Heimat* (and that's how I view this occasion,
and I am touched) raises above all the question, what do we really
mean by *Heimat?*

According to Duden:

"*Heimat, die* (plural rare): where someone is at home; country,
region or town in which one is (born and) raised or has maintained
permanent residence and feels safe, or felt safe." What Duden says
also goes for our dialect: "Often used to express or arouse a particularly emotional mood." Recently, however, we have developed a
distaste for the word. One bites on quotation marks—"Heimat-
style," "bells of Heimat," etc.—and is reminded of the wartime
maxim, *Loose lips harm the Heimat.* And so Heimat smacks less of
country or city (where, according to Duden, one is at home) than of

*Speech on the occasion of the awarding of the Grand Schiller Prize.

a safe and sound world, and thus of the falsifications of history as the Heimat-lore taught in school.

Dear Countrymen:

I was born on Helios-Strasse. neighborhood as Heimat. The first schoolhouse (still standing) belongs to it, as well as a butcher's shop where I am allowed to catch flies for my frog. Further on, between Hegibach and Hornbach, is a sewerage tunnel. Here I stand bent over, a little kid barefoot in the stinking sewage, already frightened by the echo of my own voice. And then that other echo, when the gang up above, testing my courage, whistle down through a shaft into the hollow silence that terrifying silence between individual drops of moisture. In the distance, much too small, the hole with daylight. So anxiety is also part of it; overcoming the anxiety for the sake of belonging. Better to wade through shitwater than to be an outsider in the neighborhood.

What else is part of Heimat? What Duden means by it is not that easy to translate. *My country* enlarges and limits Heimat at the very outset to a national territory. *Homeland* presupposes colonies. *Motherland* sounds more affectionate than *Fatherland* which has a tendency to demand something and less protects than wants protecting with life and limb. With *la patrie*, right away a flag gets hoisted—and I cannot say that at the sight of a Swiss cross I will immediately and under all circumstances feel in a Heimat mood. Indeed, the opposite can happen. Never, if I remember correctly, have I experienced such acute homesickness as when I was a soldier in the army, which calls itself "Our Army."

What about the Pfannenstiel? Landscape as Heimat. I know the names of the fields there that are not recorded, or, if after decades I have forgotten them, at least I remember having known them. Heimat has to do with remembrance—not with remembrance of a one-time event (Akro-Corinth when the sun rose did not become Heimat, nor Monte Alban in Mexico); Heimat arises from a wealth of recollections that can scarcely be dated anymore. It's almost as if to say, this landscape, this gravel pit, this logging trail know you (perhaps more than you would like). In this sense of landscape as the scenery of years lived, there would be a lot to list, of course—not just the Pfannenstiel and the Lindenhof and the Greifensee, but also a dune at the North Sea, a few Roman lanes, a rotten pier on the Hudson.

Our dialect is part of my Heimat. Our dialect offers many words, above all, words denoting that which is material. Often I won't know high German synonyms for them. Merely giving it a dialectal name wherever possible makes the environment, at least the material things, seem more familiar. By the way, as a writer dependent on the written language, I am grateful for our dialect. It keeps alive our awareness that language, when we write, is always an art material. Naturally, there are also people speaking our dialect with whom one would not shake hands, unless forced by social circumstances. If we don't know each other at all, the dialect we have in common can even alienate us. For example, in the dining car of a Trans-European Express train from Paris to Zurich, the gentleman opposite, who speaks the better French with the waiter, is just now urbane and congenial. But soon enough our very dialect leads us astray. Suddenly we are no longer talking how we think but rather how Swiss among Swiss are expected to talk in order to confirm to each other that they are Swiss and among themselves. What does belonging mean? There are people who do not speak our dialect and are still part of my Heimat, insofar as Heimat means "here I know I belong."

Can ideology be a Heimat?

(Then one could choose it.)

And how does it work with love of Heimat? Does one have a Heimat only if one loves her? I'm just asking. And if she does not love us, does one then have no Heimat? What must I do to have a Heimat, and above all what must I not do? She appears to be sensitive, our Heimat; she doesn't like it if one keeps an occasional sharp eye on the people who own the most Heimat in acres or in a safe deposit box. For who else, if not these people and their paid spokesmen, would have the simple right to deny us our love of Heimat?

Neighborhood, landscape, dialect . . . There must be something else that produces a sense of Heimat, a feeling of belonging, an awareness of belonging. I am thinking, for example, of a construction site in Zurich, a place of professional activity. A desk is also such a place and yet not comparable; my desk can also be in Berlin. It really does, as Duden says, have to do with place. For me it was primarily the Zurich *Schauspielhaus*. A public place, part of Zurich, and antifascist. Rehearsals out there in the foyer, rehearsals here on the stage (whatever the results)—and all within a political consensus that did not stop with the executive committee of the administrative board, a competent committee in its majority. Even when I had no play of my own in pocket or in mind, it meant belonging also at the rehearsal, of others, in those days at Friedrich Dürrenmatt's as well. It happened every time. Scarcely had I dropped my suitcase at the hotel than I was off to my first destination in Zurich, the *Schauspielhaus,* and only afterwards to this or that pub. Bodega Gorgot, for example. That one still exists, filled by later generations, so that one feels like Rip van Winkle in the folktale: past (perfect) as Heimat in the present.

But something is still missing. The literature that strives after a feeling of Heimat by reconciling itself *a priori* to our country's history and its present, is considerable. But I feel more in the Heimat mood with Robert Walser: exile as pseudo-idyll, the diminutive as expression of hidden despair. A great compatriot who took refuge in grace. Gottfried Keller, certainly; but his letters and journals provide me with more of a Heimat than the Seldwyla of his stories, that insidious model of conciliation. Jeremias Gotthelf turns me into a marveling guest in the Emmental, not into a native. Heinrich Pestalozzi gives me more of a Heimat in his revolutionary ethos than in our environment—but then I am thinking now also of Georg Büchner, of Tolstoy . . .

Or do one's friends quite simply suffice?

By the way, let's not forget native dishes, fancy as well as simple ones; and wines, which after the second sip (at the very latest) promote the good feeling that one knows one's way around in the world—at least here. And I've forgotten the main railroad station in one's hometown, different from all others in the world: here one did not arrive for the first time; here one left for the first time.

Heimat. Where this concept becomes more critical is in Berlin. Week after week I see the wall (from both sides) zigzagging through the city, barbed wire and concrete, topped by the cement tube whose roundness offers no grip to a fugitive (ace sportsmen have attested that this barrier is virtually insurmountable, even if there were no shooting); the watchtowers and searchlights on sand, where every forbidden footstep shows; the watchdogs. On either side the same weather and very nearly the same language. The Heimat that remains (the difficult Heimat) and the other Heimat that can no longer become one . . .

With friends it is like this: one was a parachutist in the German *Wehrmacht,* another a war prisoner in Russia, still another a war prisoner in America, one a bazooka-toting schoolboy in the *Volks-sturm;* another was raised in Mecklenburg and can't forget it; an American friend was in Korea and never speaks of it; yet another, a Jew, was in prison for ten years under Stalin. And one gets along with them no less than with friends in Biel or Basel or Solothurn or Zurich. No less, but differently; the former are friends, the latter are friends and compatriots. Our experiences are more similar, our biographies comparable; and for all the differences in temperament, we have, after all, the same federal government, the same national history.

So, Switzerland as Heimat after all? Without doubt there is a need for Heimat, and although I cannot readily define what I feel to be Heimat, I may say without hesitation: I have a Heimat, I am not without a Heimat, I am glad to have a Heimat. But can I say it is Switzerland?

Switzerland as territory. If one comes after a period of years from Rome, for example, then Ticino is comparatively Helvetian—around the lakes to an alarming degree even. When the locals here say *"il nostro paese,"* I am touched, provided they don't mean by that the lakefront properties but rather Switzerland, that is, the same federal railroad caps and the same defense tax . . . *il nostro paese* (although we should keep in mind that the locals in these valleys of fading Italianism are not entirely persuaded by the distinction we make between Swiss Germans and Germans). I myself, resident in the Ticino, would never say the Ticino is my Heimat, although I feel comfortable there.

Is one obliged to feel comfortable in one's Heimat?

There is no doubt, moreover, that Heimat stamps us—which in the case of a writer shows up perhaps especially clearly, that is, readably. If I convene the figures of my fiction—Bin on his journey to Peking; Stiller, who would like to escape from himself in Zurich; Homo Faber, who loses himself because he belongs nowhere; the snug and smug Mr. Biedermann, and so on—then it's not necessary for me to show my Swiss passport. Andorra is not Switzerland, only the model of a fear that it could just as well be Switzerland—a Swiss's fear, obviously. Gantenbein plays the blind man in order to attune himself with the environment. Count Öderland, figure of a supposed legend and according to his name likelier Scandinavian, seizes an ax because he can no longer physically stand the drained and rigidified society he represents as public prosecutor. And although a revolt of this kind took place not here but in Paris in 1968, the French press called it *un rêve helvétique*. To that extent are we stamped.

One doesn't select one's Heimat.

Nonetheless I hesitate to say my Heimat is Switzerland. Others say Switzerland and mean something different. Our constitution does not stipulate who exactly gets to determine what is Swiss or un-Swiss. The federal prosecutor's office? The Friday-night regulars at the local pub? The university council? The financiers and their sterling press? The Swiss Officers Association?

Heimat. If Heimat is the particular locality where we as children and pupils have our first experiences with the environment (both the natural and the social one); if consequently Heimat is the district where, through unconscious conformity (often to the point of loss of self in early years), we arrive at the illusion that the world is not foreign here, then Heimat is a problem of identity—that is, a dilemma between foreignness in the district to which we belong by birth or self-alienation through conformity. The latter (it applies to the vast majority) requires compensation. The less often I arrive at an experience of who I am on account of conforming to the district, the more often I will say "I as a Swiss . . ." or "We as Swiss . . ." and the more in need I am of being considered a proper Swiss in the mind of the majority. Identification with a majority composed of conformists as compensation for the person's self-identity, which has been neglected or stunted through social pressure—this forms the basis of all chauvinism. Thus chauvinism as the opposite of self-confidence. The primitive expression of the fear of becoming the foreigner in one's own nest is xenophobia, which gets confused so easily with patriotism. That's another bankrupt term that by now can only be used in quotation marks—which is wrong. A patriot (without quotation marks) would be one who has found or never lost his identity as a person and hence recognizes a people as his own: a Pablo Neruda, a rebel (in the fortunate case a great one) and poet who recites to his people another language than the language of accommodation and thereby gives back, or bestows on them for the first time, their identity—which inevitably, in either case, is revolutionary. For the masses of conformists have no Heimat; they only have an Establishment, complete with flag, masquerading as Heimat—and owning the military to boot. Not only in Chile.

Concerning our country; it seems that our younger compatriots are much more relaxed—not uncritical, but more relaxed. The Switzerland they experience is the Switzerland after the Second World War—that is, they feel less thrown back upon this country than we did for many years. Where we grow agitated over a recollection, they shrug their shoulders. What provides them with Heimat? Even when they remain in the country, they live with the awareness that terms like *federalism, neutrality,* and *independence* represent an illusion in an age of the rule of multinational corporations. They see that not much emanates from their country. The armchair heroes of the cold war have made their careers, whether in banking or cultural politics or both together. That which could give our younger compatriots a political Heimat, namely, a constructive contribution to a Europe policy, is scarcely in evidence. What they see instead: Law and Order. And toward the outside, a Switzerland that remains silent in the interests of private economic relations, that is more than sparing (compared to other small states like Sweden and Denmark) of any official declaration of intention. Which admittedly might not alter world affairs. Still, it could serve to nationalize our moral participation in world affairs, and that already would be something. We would then be able to declare solidarity with Switzerland.

Unbehagen im Kleinstaat.* It is probably not "malaise in the mini-state," my dear Professor Karl Schmid, that is troubling some Swiss. Not the fact of being a small state. *Besoin de grandeur*† does not aim at big-statehood. The nostalgia is of another kind. Agreeable as it may be, the thesis that only psychopaths can suffer from malaise in today's Switzerland still doesn't prove the social health of Switzerland. How much of a Heimat the state is—and that means how worthy of defense—will always depend on the extent to which

---

*Title of a book by the historian Karl Schmid, Zurich 1963.
†Title of an essay by the Swiss French writer Ferdinand Ramuz.

we can identify with the state institutions and, what is more, with their present administration. In many cases we succeed. And then again not. A democrat has difficulty identifying with Swiss military justice, where the army sits as judge in its own case.

Should I nevertheless dare to combine my naïve desire for Heimat with my citizenship, that is, to declare that I am Swiss—not just the bearer of a Swiss passport, born on Swiss territory, and so forth, but Swiss by confession—then I may no longer say Heimat and content myself with the Pfannenstiel and Greifensee and Lindenhof and our dialect, not even with Gottfried Keller. In that case disgrace is also part of my Heimat—for example, the Swiss refugee policy in the Second World War, and other things in our time that are happening, or not happening.

This is not, I know, the dress-pattern notion of Heimat according to the department *Heer und Haus.** It is my own conception.

Heimat is not defined by comfortableness. He who says *Heimat* takes more upon himself. If I read, for example, that during critical hours and days our embassy in Santiago, Chile (a villa, one can picture it—not grandiose but still a villa), has no beds for adherents of a legitimate government who are looking not for beds but for protection against barbaric lawlessness, torture, and execution (with assault rifles of Swiss origin), then I see myself as Swiss through and through, bound to this my Heimat—once again—in anger and shame.

Now come my thanks. I thank the Swiss Schiller Foundation for this high honor from the Heimat—not without knowing of the earnest embarrassment of one or another of the board members; all the more earnest my thanks. I thank Adolf Muschg for his speech. I thank all of you for coming.

Translated by Alice Carey

---

*Swiss government office for wartime public relations.

QUESTIONNAIRE 1987*

QUESTION 1: Are you sure you are really interested in the preservation of the human race, once you and all the people you know are no longer living?

QUESTION 2: And, if yes: Why don't you act differently than you have so far?

QUESTION 3: What has changed human society more: the French Revolution, or a technical invention such as electronics, for instance?

QUESTION 4: Considering everything we owe today to technological super-mobilization—take for example the sector of kitchen hardware, etc.—do you think one really has to be grateful to the technologists and therefore also to the defense ministers who put our tax money at their disposal?

QUESTION 5: As a layman, what would you like to see invented in the near future? Briefly state why.

QUESTION 6: Could you still imagine a human existence (that is: in the First World) without the computer?

QUESTION 7: If so: does the mere thought of it seize you as cold terror, or rather as nostalgia, or as nothing, since nothing cannot be seized by the computer.

---

*Words of thanks on the occasion of the bestowal of an Honorary Doctorate by the Politechnical Institute of Berlin, June 29, 1987.

QUESTION 8: Which products (for which there has been no need whatsoever since the dawn of mankind) have arrived on the market in the short time span since you have been alive (name the products without mentioning the manufacturer) and why do you buy these products:
(a) to help economic growth?
(b) because you believe in commercials?

QUESTION 9: The dinosaurs survived for 250 million years; how do you picture economic growth extending over 250 million years? (State briefly)

QUESTION 10: If a technologist considers himself apolitical because he does not give a damn about which power-brokers make use of his technological inventions: What do you think of him?

QUESTION 11: Assuming you accept the existing society, since no better one has been realized anywhere else: Do you think governments are still necessary at all—in an age of decisions by data that always serve as an excuse for the decision-making of all those governing?

QUESTION 12: If a contemporary has heard of laser beams, and yet has no idea what a laser beam really is, honestly: Can you as a scientist in good faith take the opinions and the political demonstrations of such laymen seriously?

QUESTION 13: Do you believe in a republic of scientists?

QUESTION 14: At what point did technology begin not to bring relief to our human existence (which was the original purpose of gadgets), but to establish instead an extra-human regime over us, and to steal from us the nature it has subjugated?

QUESTION 15: Do you consider technomania to be irreversible?— assuming that the Catastrophe could be avoided.

QUESTION 16: Can you picture a society in which scientists are made responsible for crimes that have become possible only through their inventions, a theocracy, for example?

QUESTION 17: Assuming you not only accept the existing society, but respond with tear gas to anyone questioning it: Are you not afraid that man will inevitably be stultified by the removal of a great utopia, or is this precisely the reason why you feel so postmodern-comfy?

QUESTION 18: Now that the Apocalypse can be technically realized, how do you relate to the biblical metaphor of the forbidden apple from the tree of knowledge?
(a) do you believe in the freedom of research?
(b) do you agree with the pope who forbade Galilei to have the earth turn around the sun?

QUESTION 19: If you seek to invent a product that makes lying in public impossible: Who do you think would sponsor your bold invention?

QUESTION 20: What would you have rather not invented?

QUESTION 21: Does it happen that a technological invention, once realized, refuses to be applied in a way not intended by its inventor?

QUESTION 22: Can you imagine that the human spirit we have trained is programmed for self-destruction of the species?

QUESTION 23: What, except for wishful thinking, speaks against it?

QUESTION 24: Do you know what motivates you to do research?

QUESTION 25: Do you, as scientists, believe in an emancipated technology, i.e., in technological research within the framework of a *universitas humanitatis*, or, in other words: do you believe in a Polytechnical Institute in Berlin?

Translated by Rolf Kieser

ACKNOWLEDGMENTS

Every reasonable effort has been made to locate the owners of rights to previously published works and the translations printed here. We gratefully acknowledge permission to reprint the following material:

From *Homo Faber* by Max Frisch, English translation copyright © 1959 by Michael Bullock. Reprinted by permission of Harcourt Brace Jovanovich, Inc., and Methuen, London.

From *Montauk* by Max Frisch, copyright © 1975 by Suhrkamp Verlag Frankfurt am Main, English translation copyright © 1976 by Max Frisch and Geoffrey Skelton. Reprinted by permission of Harcourt Brace Jovanovich, Inc.

From *Sketchbook 1946–1949* by Max Frisch, copyright 1950 by Suhrkamp Verlag Frankfurt am Main, English translation copyright © 1977 by Max Frisch and Geoffrey Skelton. Reprinted by permission of Harcourt Brace Jovanovich, Inc.

From *Man in the Holocene* by Max Frisch, copyright © 1979 by Suhrkamp Verlag, English translation copyright © 1980 by Max Frisch and Geoffrey Skelton. Reprinted by permission of Harcourt Brace Jovanovich, Inc.

From *Sketchbook 1966–1971,* English translation copyright © 1974 by Max Frisch and Geoffrey Skelton. Reprinted by permission of Harcourt Brace Jovanovich, Inc.

From *Triptych* by Max Frisch, copyright © 1980, 1978 by Suhrkamp Verlag Frankfurt am Main, English translation copyright © 1981 by Max Frisch and Geoffrey Skelton. Reprinted by permission of Harcourt Brace Jovanovich, Inc.

From "Überfremdung 1" (pp. 374–76) and "Die Schweiz als Heimat? Rede zur Verleihung des Grossen Schiller-Preises" (pp. 509–18) from *Gesammelte Werke in zeitlicher Folge,* volume 6 © Suhrkamp Verlag Frankfurt am Main, 1976.

From "Emigranten. Rede zur Verleihung des Georg Büchner Preises 1958," volume 4, from *Gesammelte Werke in zeitlicher Folge* © Suhrkamp Verlag Frankfurt am Main, 1976.

"Fragebogen 1987" by permission of Max Frisch.